PROBLEMS OF THE MODERN ECONOMY

The United States and the Developing Economies

PROBLEMS OF THE MODERN ECONOMY

General Editor: EDMUND S. PHELPS, *Columbia University*

Each volume in this series presents
prominent positions in the debate of
an important issue of economic policy

THE BATTLE AGAINST UNEMPLOYMENT

CHANGING PATTERNS IN FOREIGN TRADE
AND PAYMENTS

THE GOAL OF ECONOMIC GROWTH

MONOPOLY POWER AND ECONOMIC PERFORMANCE

PRIVATE WANTS AND PUBLIC NEEDS

THE UNITED STATES AND THE DEVELOPING ECONOMIES

LABOR AND THE NATIONAL ECONOMY

INEQUALITY AND POVERTY

DEFENSE, SCIENCE, AND PUBLIC POLICY

AGRICULTURAL POLICY IN AN AFFLUENT SOCIETY

THE CRISIS OF THE REGULATORY COMMISSIONS

The United States and the Developing Economies

Edited with an introduction by
GUSTAV RANIS
YALE UNIVERSITY

REVISED EDITION

NEW YORK
W·W·NORTON & COMPANY·INC·

Copyright © 1973, 1964 by W. W. Norton & Company, Inc.
All rights reserved. Published simultaneously in Canada by George J. McLeod
Limited, Toronto. Printed in the United States of America.

Library of Congress Cataloging in Publication Data
Ranis, Gustav, ed.
  The United States and the developing economies.
  Bibliography: p.
  1. Economic assistance, American—Addresses, essays,
lectures. 2. Underdeveloped areas—Addresses, essays,
lectures. I. Title.
HC60.R2   1973   338.91′73   72–141594
ISBN 0–393–05461–6
ISBN 0–393–09999–7 (pbk)

1 2 3 4 5 6 7 8 9 0

The Poor Nations, reprinted from *The Rich Nations and the Poor Nations* by Barbara Ward by permission of W. W. Norton & Company, Inc. Copyright © 1962 by Barbara Ward.

The Engineering of Development, from *The Great Ascent* by Robert L. Heilbroner. Copyright © by Robert L. Heilbroner. By permission of Harper & Row Publishers, Inc., and A. D. Peters and Company.

Post-war Growth in Historical Perspective, from *Economic Progress and Policy in Developing Countries* by Angus Maddison by permission of W. W. Norton & Company, Inc. Copyright © 1970 by George Allen & Unwin, Ltd.

Two Decades of Development: The Pearson Report, from *Partners in Development* by Lester B. Pearson. Copyright © 1969 by Praeger Publishers, Inc. Reprinted by permission of Praeger Publishers, Inc., New York, and The Pall Mall Press, Ltd., London.

The Agricultural Revolution in Asia, by Lester R. Brown. From *Foreign Affairs*, Vol. 6, No. 4. Copyright © by The Council on Foreign Relations, Inc., New York. Reprinted by permission from *Foreign Affairs*, July 1968.

The Green Revolution: Cornucopia or Pandora's Box? by Clifton R. Wharton, Jr. From *Foreign Affairs*, Vol. 47, No. 3. Copyright © 1969 by The Council on Foreign Relations, Inc., New York. Reprinted by permission from *Foreign Affairs*, April 1969.

Foreign Assistance as Capital Inflow. From *International Economics* by Thomas C. Schelling. Copyright 1958 by Allyn and Bacon, Inc. Reprinted by permission of the publisher.

The Role of External "Aid." From *The Development of the Indian Economy* by W. B. Reddaway. Copyright © 1962 by Massachusetts Institute of Technology. Reprinted by permission of Massachusetts Institute of Technology and Richard D. Irwin, Inc.

The Food Problem of Developing Countries, by Thorkil Kristensen for the Organization for Economic Cooperation and Development. Copyright © 1968 by OECD, Paris.

Technical Assistance, from *Economic Development, Theory, History, Policy* by Gerald M. Meier and Robert E. Baldwin. Copyright 1957 by John Wiley & Sons, Inc. Reprinted with permission of the publisher.

Loans, Grants, and the Tying of Aid, from *Foreign Aid Policies Reconsidered* by Goran Ohlin. Copyright © 1966 by OECD, Paris.

Foreign Aid—A Critique, from *Essays in International Finance* by Albert O. Hirschman and Richard M. Bird. Copyright 1969. Reprinted by permission of the International Finance Section of Princeton University.

External Aid: For Plans or Projects? by Hans W. Singer, from *Economic Journal*, September 1965. Copyright © 1965 by the Royal Economic Society, Cambridge, Eng. Reprinted by permission of the Royal Economic Society.

Project *versus* Program Aid: From the Donor's Viewpoint, by Alan Carlin, from *Economic Journal*, March 1967. Copyright © 1967 by the Royal Economic Society, Cambridge, Eng. Reprinted by permission of the Royal Economic Society.

Economic Dualism—At Home and Abroad, by Gustav Ranis, reprinted from *Public Policy*, Fall 1969. Reprinted by permission.

Private Foreign Investment, from *Partners in Development* by Lester B. Pearson. Copyright © 1969 by Praeger Publishers, Inc. Reprinted by permission of Praeger Publishers, Inc., New York and The Pall Mall Press, Ltd., London.

How to Divest in Latin America, and Why, from *Essays in International Finance* by Albert O. Hirschman. Copyright 1969. Reprinted by permission of the International Finance Section of Princeton University.

World Economic Adjustment, by Harald B. Malmgren. Reprinted from *Trade for Development*, Overseas Development Council, Washington, D.C., 1971, pp. 65–77.

Rationale for Development Assistance, reprinted by permission from *Development Assistance in the Seventies: Alternatives for the U.S.* by Robert E. Asher, © 1970 by The Brookings Institution.

Foreign Economic Aid: Means and Objectives, by Milton Friedman. From *The Yale Review*, Summer 1958. Copyright 1958 by Yale University Press. Reprinted with permission.

Economic Aid Reconsidered, by Charles Wolf, Jr. From *The Yale Review*, Summer 1961. Copyright 1961 by Yale University Press. Reprinted by permission of Charles Wolf, Jr., and *The Yale Review*.

Using Aid to Promote Long-Run Political Development. Reprinted with permission of The Macmillan Company from *Aid, Influence and Foreign Policy* by John M. Nelson. Copyright © 1968 by Joan M. Nelson.

The United States and Latin America, by J. P. Morray from *Latin America: Reform or Revolution?* edited by James Petras and Maurice Zeitlin. Fawcett Publications, New York, 1968, by permission.

Aid Relationship for the Seventies—A Comment on the Report of the Commission on

International Development, by I. G. Patel, from *The Widening Gap* by Barbara Ward *et al.,* Columbia University Press, 1971, pp. 295–311. Reprinted by permission of the publisher.

Toward Public Confidence in Foreign Aid, by Edward K. Hamilton, from *World Affairs,* Vol. 132, No. 4, March 1970, pp. 287–304, The American Peace Society.

Contents

Introduction ix

PROLOGUE
BARBARA WARD · The Poor Nations 1

PART ONE: The Developing Economies: A New Commitment
ROBERT L. HEILBRONER · The Engineering of Development 11
ANGUS MADDISON · Post-war Growth in Historical Perspective 22
LESTER B. PEARSON · Two Decades of Development: The Pearson Report 33
LESTER R. BROWN · The Agricultural Revolution in Asia 55
CLIFTON R. WHARTON, JR. · The Green Revolution: Cornucopia or Pandora's Box? 67
GUSTAV RANIS · LDC Employment and Income Distribution 80

PART TWO: Aid Instruments and Allocation Criteria
THOMAS C. SCHELLING · Foreign Assistance as Capital Inflow 99
W. B. REDDAWAY · The Role of External "Aid" 104
OECD · The Food Problem of Developing Countries 110
GERALD M. MEIER AND ROBERT E. BALDWIN · Technical Assistance 116
GORAN OHLIN · Loans, Grants, and the Tying of Aid 121
ALBERT O. HIRSCHMAN AND RICHARD M. BIRD · Foreign Aid—A Critique 136
HANS W. SINGER · External Aid: For Plans or Projects? 149
ALAN CARLIN · Project versus Program Aid: From the Donor's Viewpoint 158

GUSTAV RANIS · Economic Dualism—At Home and
Abroad   172
LESTER B. PEARSON · Private Foreign Investment   184
ALBERT O. HIRSCHMAN · How to Divest in Latin
America, and Why   209
HARALD B. MALMGREN · World Economic Adjustment   218

PART THREE: The Economics of Foreign Assistance

ROBERT E. ASHER · Rationale for Development Assistance   231
MILTON FRIEDMAN · Foreign Economic Aid: Means and
Objectives   250
CHARLES WOLF, JR. · Economic Aid Reconsidered   264
JOAN NELSON · Using Aid to Promote Long-Run Political
Development   279
J. P. MORRAY · The United States and Latin America   295
I. G. PATEL · Aid Relationship for the Seventies—
A Comment on the Report of the Commission on
International Development   307
EDWARD K. HAMILTON · Toward Public Confidence in
Foreign Aid   326

Suggested Further Readings   349

Introduction

POVERTY ABROAD expresses itself in per capita incomes below $100 a year, in savings rates near 5 percent, in an overwhelming scarcity of capital, inadequate educational structures, and Malthusian pressures on the land. Accidents of nature or climatic conditions have here and there endowed some regions with exportable natural resources—oil, mineral ore deposits, or particular tropical foods and other primary commodities. But even such prosperous enclaves have usually had a severely limited impact on the general well-being of the societies in which they are located.

The problems faced by developing countries are not everywhere the same. The pressure of population against natural resources, for example, is much lower in Africa and Latin America than in Asia. But in most developing countries, the only dependable resource found in abundant supply is people. Moreover, in spite of spreading efforts to have birth control keep pace with public health advances, in only a very few places have fertility rates begun to fall along with mortality, so that, in most of the underdeveloped world, population growth continues unabated. The result is the well known vicious cycle of high total consumption, low saving, static per capita income, and, more and more recognized in recent years, rising unemployment. Lagging fifteen years behind the population explosion, the expansion of the labor force is not being matched by expansion in efficient employment opportunities. Concern with unemployment and underemployment, as well as with the distribution of income, is now reaching the same level of importance in the developing world as the straight per capita income growth problem did a decade ago.

Thus, the demands placed on the leadership of the developing countries are larger than ever. Not only must there be progress, broadly defined, but also it is no longer reasonable to expect people with annual incomes limited to $60 or $70 per capita to postpone substantial rises in their consumption levels while savings rates are increased, or to follow the economists' advice of investing in the most advanced regions while the rest of the population waits until "some future date" when redistribution becomes possible. Clearly the pressures for a more equal distribution of income, both personal and regional, are making themselves increasingly felt. Although the record of development, in terms of per capita income growth, in the '50s and '60s has not been as bad as most people seem to think, new questions are being asked and new answers must be found.

Of course, the less developed countries (LDC's) might be expected to solve their problems on their own, but it is also clear that the contemporary coexistence of poor and rich nations has to make a substantial difference, given the low level of savings, of entrepreneurial capacity, of educational structure that Barbara Ward points to in the Prologue to this volume, as the heritage of long centuries of colonialism. Regardless of the positive or negative contribution of the rich to the poor in the past, the presence of the industrial countries on the same globe has to affect the problem of poverty in the developing world, through the contribution of foreign savings, via the flow of aid and private capital, and through the movements of trade and technology across frontiers.

In the period immediately following World War II, alleviation of the resource constraints of the poor nations mainly through providing foreign assistance had the highest priority. More recently, other aspects of economic interconnectedness on a shrinking globe have come to the fore. Such interconnectedness must be analyzed not only in terms of how goods are exchanged in trade, but also in terms of the movement of science and technology as it affects the quality of the total effort. Inevitably, we are thus involved in the central question of why all this should be of concern to the developed countries—in particular the U.S.—when admittedly the costs are substantial, the risks large, and the returns unclear.

Part One summarizes the record of development in the developing world over the past two decades, both the considerable accomplishments as well as some of the failures, which affects the prospects for the '70s. Part Two deals largely with the economics of interconnectedness between rich and poor, and especially the instrument of foreign assistance. Part Three examines the current shared crisis of the will to help as well as to be helped.

THE RECORD OF DEVELOPMENT

In spite of general skepticism by politicians and on Main Street, the fact is that very substantial progress has been made in the less developed world over the past two decades. The productive capacity of two-thirds of the globe's inhabitants, taken together, has increased significantly; what is more, much has been learned by both the rich and the poor nations about the process of development and about the nature of the interconnectedness between them. In short, the record of the last two decades of development by no means justifies a sense of despair over the insolubility of the problem. Per capita growth rates of more than 2 percent for the developing world as a whole of course mask substantial country-by-country variations, with some exceptionally good performers (like Mexico, Ivory Coast, Korea, and Taiwan) raising the averages. Nor can we claim that any such, even partial, picture of accomplishment is traceable in any direct fashion to relationships with the rich countries. Still, the overall record stands in stark contrast to the common view that development is hopeless, the task endless, the methods of aiding it obsolete and unrealistic, the whole enterprise a "give-away."

The major burden of success in development must clearly rest on the shoulders of the countries themselves. Robert L. Heilbroner lists increased agricultural productivity and the reallocation to more efficient employment of disguised unemployed agricultural labor as the major ingredients of such "self-help" efforts. As he points out, the potential is there; what is required is a set of policies which permits the activation of large numbers of peasants in overwhelmingly agrarian societies to be mobilized for the building of capital infrastructure and industry. This cannot be done by simple concentration on industrialization. The agricultural sector must be marshalled as a source of saving and of human energies if the economy is to spurt ahead of population pressures.

Angus Maddison analyzes the development problem of the contemporary poor countries in historical perspective. These countries are latecomers trying to telescope the stages of growth traversed earlier by their now rich neighbors. The coexistence of rich and poor nations during the colonial period probably contributed to the present backwardness of the poor, if only in terms of a "relative" siphoning off of talents, initiative, resources, and the imposition of policies favoring the region's role in a wider scheme of international specialization, rather than a narrower scheme of national development. Whatever the consequences of interdependence in the past, however, such interdependence clearly presents an opportunity for today's developing countries pursuing their own national objectives. The choice is not slow growth under autarky *vs.* rapid growth under neocolonialism; as has been demonstrated, interdependence can serve as an instrument of national growth.

The selection from the Pearson Commission underscores this point. The performance of the less developed world during the past 20 years is carefully examined, not only at the aggregate level but sector by sector, and in terms of human as well as physical infrastructure. Foreign assistance has financed no more than ten percent of developing countries' investment and no more than twenty percent of their imports. Nevertheless, aid and trade have been very important in alleviating the ever present resources tightness of the developing world. Moreover, they have had a major catalytic impact on the performance of the entire system through their influence on the efficiency of total resource use.

Part of the overall good performance record of the less developed world, especially Asian countries such as India which recently have emerged from relative stagnation to fairly substantial growth, has been attributed to the so-called Green Revolution. Coming on top of a change in domestic policies toward a relatively greater role for the market, this major agricultural breakthrough related to new seed/fertilizer combinations has been thought by some to signal the beginning of the end of the hitherto endless cycle of poverty and of the development struggle itself. Lester R. Brown, for example, believes that more than productivity change is involved in the Green Revolution, and that "as farmers learn to control their own destiny they may become more susceptible to family planning and other departures" as well.

There are others, however, who are much more skeptical about this technological breakthrough as a really fundamental departure. As Clifton Wharton points out, the substantial increases in productivity in the Subcontinent have thus far been concentrated in irrigated land, among the relatively larger, well-off farmers. Moreover, even if the new technology were to spread farther, the increased susceptibility to pestilence, problems of inadequate marketing, of regional inequality, and of difficulties in maintaining this kind of quantum jump, all suggest trouble ahead. Certainly it is simplistic to view the Green Revolution as the panacea for the development problem.

This is not the first time that "the" key ingredient in the development package was thought to have been found. Just as capital assistance under the Marshall Plan rescued postwar Europe, technical assistance under President Truman's Point Four Program was expected to solve the problem of development in Asia, Africa, and Latin America. Later on, the developing world saw a return to emphasis on capital, then on judicious combinations of both. Similar temporal "fads" have been in evidence with respect to the allocation by sector, from concentration on infrastructural development, to industry, to education, most recently to population control. No wonder we encounter a certain skepticism when "miracle" seeds are put forward as yet another "answer," instead of as a major contribution to the answer.

Unfortunately, the key to progress remains complicated—especially when we realize the subtle recent changes in the objectives of developing countries. The truly "balanced" growth that is required can be achieved only with a change in the overall policy mix. Luckily we do have evidence, if in a small number of countries to date, *e.g.* Korea and Taiwan, that a shift from the import substitution syndrome of the '60s to a policy package favoring export substitution in the '70s can yield sustained growth, along with, not at the expense of, better performance in employment and distribution. This is the subject of the editor's contribution to this section.

FOREIGN AID AND DEVELOPMENT:
ANALYSIS AND INSTRUMENTS

We are now in a position to probe a little more deeply into the economics of the relationship between rich and poor, in particular, the potential significance of foreign assistance in the development process. Regardless of the method of financing or of its physical form, *i.e.* whether food, machinery, or tanks are actually sent abroad, the essential significance of foreign aid is that it provides the developing economy with additional real resources. The flow of dollars enables the recipient nation to import more than it exports and thus enables it to do "more things" than would otherwise be feasible. These "things" may be "more investment" serving economic growth objectives, or "more consumption" serving distributional objectives, but could equally well be "more wars" or "more luxury housing." It is difficult to predict what particular sector or activity in the recipient country will, in fact, be ultimately strengthened by a particular type of assistance. Aid, for example, may enter in the form of food, thus releasing domestic resources from food production and freeing them for defense. Conversely, the arrival of tanks under a military assistance program may, in fact, ultimately represent an addition to industrial capacity by freeing funds for industrial investment that otherwise would have been used for the purchase. In short, as long as funds and resources are shiftable or "fungible" between uses, we cannot be sure what the final effects will be. Even after all the dust has settled, we can determine the consequences of a given conglomerate aid package (*e.g.* did it increase employment, strengthen military capacities, increase the capital stock, or increase consumption?) only if we know, or can estimate, what the developing economy would have done in the absence of aid.

This is not a counsel of despair; it merely reminds us that aid represents but a marginal addition to the total resources at the recipient economy's disposal. Clearly, aid packages must be negotiated on an overall basis in the light of agreed-upon objectives and levels of domestic effort in the recipient country.

In the first contributions of Part Two, Thomas C. Schelling concentrates on exposing the often misunderstood dual role of aid—providing the financial flow of additional savings, on the one hand, and the commodity flow of additional real resources, on the other. He rigorously traces, step by step, what happens once aid has been given, regardless of its form and initial recipient. This permits him to demonstrate that the ultimate beneficiary must always be the government of the developing economy, whose tight overall resources situation has been somewhat alleviated as a consequence.

It is, of course, true that additional domestic savings and additional foreign savings are not completely substitutable, precisely because the real resources on the other sides of these coins are not fully substitutable. A particular type of machine, for example, cannot simply be obtained by increasing domestic savings, but must be imported, either by translating the new domestic savings into exports or by calling on foreign savings directly. Foreign aid thus has the additional value of providing specific bottleneck goods to the developing economy. The contribution by W. B. Reddaway serves two purposes: it further clarifies the aforementioned dual role of aid by application to the particular (and intrinsically interesting) case of India, and it underlines the importance of specific import requirement bottlenecks, *i.e.* the balance-of-payments constraint.

Foreign aid can, of course, take a number of financial forms, *e.g.* grants, debt relief, soft and hard loans, as well as a number of commodity contents, *e.g.* raw materials, food, people, capital equipment. With respect to aid tied to a particular commodity, the article by the OECD points out the dual purposes of food aid both in supporting the exports of donor countries in politically sensitive areas and in helping the less developed countries.[1] While it may be important to maintain a world food reserve for cases of crop failure and famine, food aid, if not handled carefully, may hurt incentives and retard agricultural production in the recipient countries. Foreign assistance not tied either by country or by commodity is, of course, more attractive. Realistically, however, this choice may not be available; the less developed countries have had to trade off the tied nature of aid against the quantity legislatures are willing to vote.

Gerald Meier and Robert Baldwin examine some of the issues involved in providing people and know-how through technical assistance. While technical assistance constitutes a minor component of the total foreign assistance package in terms of dollars, it can be of very great importance since it has the power to affect the efficiency of the use of the total resources available to the recipient, including its own. Though there can be no doubt of the mediocrity of many of the technical advisors running about the developing world, carefully chosen technical assistance and

---

1. The same general argument could be made for any aid tied to the country of origin, at least at times of less than full employment.

advisory personnel can make (and have made, on occasion) a major catalytic contribution.

The mix of instruments which make up the total U.S. aid package has changed considerably over the years. In the immediate postwar years, while Western Europe was receiving capital assistance under the Marshall Plan (which was all Europe needed for purposes of "reconstruction"), aid to the developing countries consisted almost entirely of technical assistance. The Korean War shifted emphasis towards military assistance and to a lesser extent, to the economic aid necessary to support military efforts. In 1946–52, military assistance was 9 percent of the total; in 1953–57, it was up to 52 percent; in the late '60s, with the abatement of the Cold War (and the moving of military assistance destined for the "hot war" in Indo-China to the Defense budget), it dropped to less than 20 percent. What it will be under the Nixon Doctrine, which calls for relatively larger volumes of military assistance, is as yet unclear.

Within the economic assistance category, dominated by capital flows, the shift has been increasingly from soft loans, payable in local currency, to soft dollar repayable loans, to hard (near-commercial) dollar repayable loans. The contribution by Goran Ohlin discusses these different forms of financial aid. Although some advocate commercial or hard loans as preferable to grants, for political and efficiency reasons, *i.e.* they appeal to legislatures as more "businesslike" and may lead recipients to more careful allocation, Ohlin points out that such loans often lead to the accumulation of overwhelming debt burdens by developing countries. He also expands on the practice of tying aid to the country of origin, a habit which serves the balance of payments of the donors very little, but does have the effect of reducing substantially the quality and effectiveness of aid. Thanks largely to efforts by the Nixon Administration, there seems to be a better than even chance that multilateral aid untying by the major donors may become a reality in the not-too-distant future.

The selections by Albert Hirschman and Richard Bird, Hans W. Singer, and Alan Carlin revolve around the question of the choice of program versus project aid as a form of capital assistance and the related extent of intervention at the micro or macro levels which is likely to be both feasible and effective.

Hirschman and Bird lay out the general issues attending the

choice between project and program aid. The authors then emphasize the dangers of donors getting too deeply involved in a recipient's domestic affairs. Their main contention is that arm-twisting with respect to the obtaining of policy commitments from developing countries in return for general budget or balance of payments support is likely to have overwhelmingly negative effects on other relations between the countries concerned. Singer indicates his reasons for preferring program aid, which is more flexible, has a shorter gestation period, and is therefore favored by recipients. He believes that there are fewer frictions inherent in this type of relationship than in the large number of detailed stipulations and commitments attending project assistance. Carlin takes the opposite view, pointing out that the admittedly few conditions attached to program aid are usually much more sensitive, *i.e.* they go to the heart of the recipient's domestic policy. Thus, unless program aid is simply turned over without any strings, the amount of friction can be expected to be larger in this case. Moreover, in terms of the efficiency of the program, he feels that a bundle of projects permits the same exercise of influence on either the macro or micro levels, depending on what suits the purpose of the donor. He contends that the problem of the shiftability of resources, which Singer points to, can be solved easily by selecting projects at the margin, thus influencing the allocation of the total scarce foreign exchange resources.

The process of aid giving is inherently friction laden, whether project or program aid is chosen. But the essential question is whether or not supporting recipients with annual checks in the mail is an adequate response to the needs of taxpayers and citizens in either the rich or the poor countries. Nonintervention in a country's fiscal or exchange rate policies is, after all, really intervention on behalf of the *status quo*. The analogy between program and project assistance in application to problems of economic dualism within a rich country, the U.S., is drawn in the editor's contribution to this section.

In addition to government capital, developing countries, especially the successful ones, can of course expect to attract increasing volumes of foreign private investment—much of it government-guaranteed. For example, in 1969, out of a total of $13.5 billion capital flow, $7.3 billion was in the form of official aid, the rest private. The question of the merits and demerits of private investment has been a subject of even greater sensitivity as between the rich and the poor; in fact, this is one subject on which the Pearson Report, from which the next selection was taken, could not avoid dissent. That the potential benefits of foreign investment are substantially larger now than during the so-called colonial period cannot be doubted, but how often it fails to do much less than it is capable of is another question. Automatic flows of management and technology, along with scarce capital, plus market access, must be pitted against monopolistic practices and the possible inhibition of domestic entrepreneurship, technology, even saving.

Just as the Pearson Commission accentuates the positive, Albert Hirschman sees foreign investment as a very mixed blessing. He holds that a policy of selective withdrawal of foreign private investment after some period of time may be in the best interests of both the recipient and donor countries. Otherwise, he maintains, superior foreign techniques and management will displace local industry and entrepreneurship. Moreover, if emerging investment opportunities are seized by foreign firms, any development achieved may be at an unacceptable cost in political autonomy. There is clearly merit on both sides of this rather emotion-laden argument. But what is often lost sight of is that the case against the excessive profits of foreign investors is often really as much a case against the kind of policy environment which admits unacceptably large windfalls by foreign and domestic entrepreneurs alike.

The selection by Harald Malmgren continues the discussion of the role of foreign investment via the increasingly important multinational corporation, but in the broader context of trade and other aspects of rich/poor interconnectedness on a shrinking globe. Increasing protectionism among the rich countries in response to the growth of labor-intensive production and exports from the best performing developing countries represents a major, if somewhat ironic, obstacle to development. The economic cost must be borne by rich and poor alike, in terms of reducing world efficiency, but it is especially felt by countries just beginning to move forward in a sustained fashion. Politically, it undoubtedly represents the major cause of friction on the development scene.

Present trends toward the internationalization of production, through the multinational corporation or otherwise, present difficult policy options not only for the developing countries, who must weigh the economic benefits of foreign investment against their political costs, but also for the rich countries who must decide whether or not to fight long rear guard actions on behalf of their own labor intensive industries. Perhaps the best way, politically, for the rich countries to maintain a decent-sized aid effort, while at the same time allocating funds effectively from the point of view of the economies of the poor, would be a major rechanneling of funds toward a program of adjustment assistance within the domestic economies of the rich. This would permit the international division of labor to operate more smoothly and with a smaller time lag. Malmgren points out that unless the import policies of the rich are somehow rationalized, we can look forward to even more serious conflict for some time to come. In fact, the more successful the developing countries, with the help of our assistance and advice, the greater the likely conflict. For example, it is the more successful developing countries, *i.e.* those which have begun vigorously to export industrial goods, which were hurt the most by the temporary 10 percent U.S. import surtax of 1971.

THE CRISIS IN FOREIGN ASSISTANCE:
RATIONALE AND METHODS

When all is said and done, the basic question before us remains: why should the U.S. continue to be concerned about the developing countries? For one thing, the Cold War logic is no longer relevant. East and West do not confront each other today in the same way as before—certainly not in the sense of a competition for the "hearts and minds" of people in the third world. From the commercial self-interest point of view, do we still "need" the developing countries, in terms of markets and raw material sources, as we once did? Today the developing countries' share in world trade is down to 18 percent from more than 30 percent in 1950; synthetics and substitutes can be expected to continue to replace any raw material (even oil) whose steady supply at reasonable prices is threatened; the bulk of markets in a growing world economy is with other members of the developed world. In short, if the less developed countries disappeared from view entirely, would this affect our existence materially?

Even if we answered this question affirmatively, and even if the fate of two-thirds of humanity were not a matter of indifference to us (for old-fashioned humanitarian reasons as well), can we afford such concern any longer? Charity begins at home, and we have become increasingly aware in recent years of our own domestic problems of poverty, pollution, race, all of which lay heavy claim to both our energies and budgetary resources. Our apparently chronic inflationary problem, loss of competitive position, vanishing export surpluses and mounting balance of payments deficits—all culminating in the Nixon policy package of 1971—are well known and surely further constrain what otherwise might be a generous impulse to help. Moreover, as we have seen, if the less developed countries are successful and begin to export vigorously, as in the cases of Korea and Taiwan, they present a serious problem for some of our sick industries, exacerbating difficult political and economic problems of adjustment at home. In a very practical sense, the cost-benefit ratios of any special involvement with the less developed countries seem most unattractive.

But that is not all; there is yet another argument made for disengagement, just as persuasive, but this time coming from the "liberal" side of the aisle. And that is, following Senator Fulbright's version of the domino theory, that "one thing leads to another," until, as in Vietnam, concern and aid pull us gradually into military adventures for which this country has lost its tolerance. We are, after all, neither the world's policeman nor the world's Santa Claus—especially if Santa Claus inevitably ends up wearing a badge.

It is in this atmosphere of creeping neo-isolationism and mounting difficulties at home that the skeptical attitude in the White House and in Congress toward developing countries and foreign assistance must be seen. Little wonder that foreign aid allocations have been declining steadily during the past few years, both in absolute amount and in terms of any appropriate measure of the real burden, as, for example, a percentage of our gross national product (GNP). While the U.S. has the highest per capita income in the world, in 1969 it ranked twelfth among the sixteen OECD countries in terms of the proportion of its

GNP devoted to foreign assistance—behind such countries as France, Portugal, Australia, Belgium, Netherlands, Japan, Sweden, Canada, Denmark, Norway, and the U.K., most of which were increasing their absolute and relative contributions largely in response to the urgings of U.S. policy makers. (If a progressive sharing principle were adopted, the United States would, of course, look even worse.) While Congress has been the major wielder of the ax, it is also significant that Presidential requests have come down considerably as well, in keeping with the previous year's appropriations rather than previous year's requests—not to speak of base line needs. The U.S., once the leader in concern and action on behalf of the developing countries, has been dragging its feet increasingly, since 1965, with serious effects for the total aid effort.

On the trade side as well, the less developed countries received little benefit from the Kennedy Round—perhaps the last gasp of liberal trade for some time. They are bound to be hurt badly by the current trend toward "voluntary" and involuntary restrictions on many of their major exports as well as by the "fall-out" from unmet international monetary problems. There is increasing skepticism that meaningful trade preferences for developing countries to which the U.S. is officially committed can be negotiated in the present atmosphere.

Such serious deterioration of concern on the rich countries' side, influenced heavily, but not exclusively, by U.S. fatigue, has been accompanied by growing weariness and suspicion on the part of the world's poor. As expectations go unrealized, often because promised aid did not materialize, and as the strength of nationalistic and anti-imperialist forces abroad increase, a mutually reinforcing downward spiral has set in which threatens to undermine all facets of relations between the rich and the poor countries—trade, aid, and at times even the niceties of diplomatic intercourse.

Whatever our attitudes toward the developing countries, however, they are with us and not likely to disappear. Moreover, to ignore them is hardly feasible and to let them drift on their own not very practicable. That our globe is shrinking and interdependence intensifying is a commonplace that is, nevertheless, true, whether we are discussing nuclear proliferation, environmental pollution, or the simple implications for our comfort of one-third of humanity increasingly opulent and two-thirds increasingly desperate.

This, in general, has been the verdict of a spate of recent national and international reviews and appraisals. The most important and prestigious of these was the Pearson Commission Report in 1969. At the same time, a U.N. Committee for Development Planning under the chairmanship of Professor Jan Tinbergen came out with working guidelines for the second United Nations Development Decade in the '70s. The U.N. family itself as an instrument of development aid was treated in a report by Sir Robert Jackson. Finally, at the national level, President Nixon commissioned the Rockefeller Report with emphasis on the Western Hemisphere and a Presidential Task Force on International Development under the chairmanship of Rudolph Peterson to develop "a new U.S. approach to aid for the 1970's."

While these appraisals vary considerably in emphasis, they have a number of features in common. First, they all emphasize the amount of unfinished business in the less developed world. Much progress, they agree, has, in fact, been made. Much has been learned and much still can and needs to be accomplished. Second, with the exception of the Rockefeller Report, they argue for a clearer separation of the various categories of aid in relation to the multitude of motives governing the total funds voted by parliaments. The current "mixed bag" approach, throwing long-term development, short-term political, and short-term strategic *cum* military objectives together in the effort to "sell" an assistance package, helps form coalitions in Congress but also muddies the waters and gives rise to unrealistic expectations. Third, they favor channeling future U.S. foreign assistance increasingly through multilateral as opposed to bilateral hands. This is believed to be both in the interest of greater efficiency, the separation of aid from politics, and the reduction of the inevitable frictions inherent in the aid process.

Most of the reports recognize that whether or not a combination of long-term self-interest, humanitarianism, and past accomplishments is sufficient to overcome politicians' disinterest, weariness, and skepticism is mainly a question of will, in the U.S., mostly on the part of the executive branch of government. Dominated by staffs of experts who believe in and commission such reports as those cited above, they invariably call for quantitatively larger efforts, qualitatively extending beyond growth targets to the emerging problems of employment, income distribution, and urbanization. None address themselves to the problem of how to convince politicians and their constituents in the rich countries.

Specifically, with respect to the U.S. effort, the Peterson Task Force found the humanitarian motive most persuasive and recommended that the downward trend in development assistance in evidence since 1965 be reversed, without, however, suggesting the United States commit itself to any particular amount, such as the 1 percent of GNP target previously endorsed by the United States and organizations such as the OECD. The Peterson group also pointed out that only $2.7 billion, or about 40 percent of the approximately $6 billion total allotted for foreign assistance in fiscal year 1969 was addressed to development; the rest, in one form or another, was for security purposes. It recommended separating out the various functions of foreign assistance, placing those concerned with short-term political objectives, *e.g.* the shoring up of particular governments, with the State Department, military assistance with the Defense Department, and relatively "clean" development assistance in two new institutions—an International Development Corporation for capital assistance and an International Development Institute for technical assistance "to seek new breakthroughs in the application of science and technology to resources and processes critical to the developing nations."

The Nixon Administration, after proposing to the Congress what it called "a major transformation" of the foreign assistance effort, has failed to follow up vigorously on these recommendations. At this stage no one seems very interested in reform, in killing the aid program outright, or even in putting old wines into new bottles (as has been done frequently in the past—witness the continuous relabelling of the agency responsible for foreign aid: from FCA, FOA, MSA, ICA-DLF, to AID). In the short run, Congressional indifference may keep things more or less as they are. The increased separation of the military and security components from the economic seems to have a chance, though complicated by the as yet unclear implications of the Nixon Doctrine for future (presumably higher) levels of military assistance. So does the trend toward an increased multilateralization of aid, through the World Bank and the regional banks. If this trend continues, "true" multilateral flows will be raised from their present 10 percent of the total, and aid channeled under multilateral "umbrellas" raised from the present 60 percent of the total. For the longer run, any attempt to forecast the U.S. role in the less developed world, quantitatively or qualitatively, is bound to be heroic—certainly before the scars of Vietnam have had a chance to heal.

The selection in Part Three by Robert Asher argues that the search for a rationale goes on, now that many of the original premises in favor of foreign aid no longer hold true. Among the remaining powerful motives he discusses is, first, the threat to peace from excessive poverty, a new type of security motive; second, the fact that development yields jobs and markets and material benefits on both sides; third, the general need for political stability in a world which is trying to maintain some sort of order; and finally, the humanitarian objective which holds that the responsibility for mitigating poverty and misery does not end at the national boundary (which he also finds the most convincing of all). As President Kennedy stated in his Inaugural, "to those new states . . . of half the globe struggling to break the bounds of mass misery, we pledge our best efforts to help them help themselves for whatever period is required . . . If the free society cannot help the many who are poor, it can never save the few who are rich." Aid is increasingly viewed less as a weapon in the Cold War arsenal or as a means of buying votes in the U.N. and more as an act of very long-run enlightened humanitarianism. *Pari passu*, its volume is declining.

Milton Friedman approves these admittedly general objectives of foreign aid but believes that "the means are inappropriate to the objectives." A staunch believer in the beneficial workings of the free-market system, he contends that government-to-government loans and grants must inevitably lead to a centrally coordinated and controlled economy which is inefficient and in which foreign capital displaces, rather than supplements, domestic saving. By forcing resources exclusively into the hands of government planners who are asked to make all the detailed allocative decisions, foreign aid stifles the developing economy's forward progress and plays into the hands of our adversaries. Citing the example of the United States in the nineteenth century, Friedman would much rather leave the job to the international flow of private capital.

This position is vigorously challenged by Charles Wolf, Jr., who denies that U.S. aid must necessarily strengthen the developing country's public sector; on the contrary, he argues that the tighter the overall resources constraint, the more likely that the developing economy's private sector will be starved of foreign exchange. Wolf starts with the basic assumption of an activist government consciously engaged in an overall (domestic and foreign) resources calculation and planning effort, while Friedman disputes the need for any but the most limited role for the public sector. Wolf points out that only the government can be counted on, in the typical case, to weld a conglomeration of people and physical resources into one nation and one economic system, and to create the requisite economic and social overheads (roads, schools, utilities) without which growth in the private sector cannot get started. Granted that the nineteenth century United States would probably not have qualified for foreign aid today, but that does not necessarily condemn today's criteria. Rather, it serves to underline the sharp contrast between the growth pattern of an "empty" land, rich in resources and able to draw on the entrepreneurial capital and skill resources of Europe in an era of remarkable international factor mobility—and that of the poor contemporary labor surplus country trying to achieve the same goals over a shorter period of time in a world of autarky and protectionism.

Joan Nelson proposes that foreign assistance be clearly linked to long-term political development objectives as an integral part of the development process. She points out that frequently political and economic development must go hand in hand as when peace, law and order, and administrative efficiency serve economic growth; but they may also act antithetically as when rapid economic development leads to temporary instability. She urges that aid relationships include assessments of the manner in which developing countries' political evolutions are affected and that both donor and recipient consider the important political by-products of economic programs. In formulating aid programs, political development goals should be studied and assigned priorities; otherwise, political maturation and economic growth may suffer in the long run.

J. P. Morray, dealing with U.S.-Latin American relations, especially with Brazil, criticizes the basic motives of U.S. assistance as too closely linked to the protection of private investment and argues that the U.S. is practicing economic colonialism at its worst. Similar attacks on foreign assistance motives and accomplishments are currently on the rise, particularly from the radical left.

I. G. Patel, on the other hand, a spokesman for the less developed countries, though very critical of foreign aid as it has been practiced, wants to improve, not scuttle it. He emphasizes that aid should be given on a non-interventionist low key basis, with the volume not determined exclusively by development performance. Instead, developing countries should be assured of definite long term commitments on a "trust basis." Patel's argument is that the people of the developing nations will demand performance of their own leaders and it is neither necessary nor becoming for the rich countries to act like school masters of the poor. He objects to the double standard of aid negotiations at which the donors' parliaments and public opinion dominate and must be placated, while the recipients' parliaments and public opinion must be manipulated in order to support mutually agreed upon public policies.

There can be no doubt that there is a basic dilemma here. On the one hand there is an obligation which countries' governments incur relative to their own taxpayers—to ensure a minimum effectiveness of the use of resources committed to foreign aid. On the other hand, if the means of surveillance are so clumsy that they erode the basic relationship of trust and confidence then, of course, the mutually agreed-upon purposes of development cannot be served. Perhaps multilateralization of both the aid allocation and of the related review of performance are the only answer in the long run. But this probably does require being willing to make do with somewhat lower available levels of assistance, at least in the short run.

The final selection by Edward K. Hamilton makes this point. The U.S. aid structure in the sixties appears no longer feasible politically in the seventies. Aid has no effective lobby. While Hamilton supports most of the reforms suggested by the Peterson Task Force as incorporated in Nixon's proposals to the Congress, he takes a further step in proposing the creation of an International Development Council composed of representatives of the donors, bilateral and multilateral, as well as the recipients. Such a Council would have advisory authority to coordinate foreign aid, especially of the multilateral variety, while reducing duplication and some of the irritations and political suspicions which attend the current negotiation and implementation process. But, ultimately, even the most efficient aid program, administered by multilateral angels and urged by a convinced executive branch, cannot gather the necessary support in the parliaments of the rich countries without understanding and confidence on Main Street.

PROBLEMS OF THE MODERN ECONOMY

The United States and the Developing Economies

Prologue

The Poor Nations

BARBARA WARD

Barbara Ward, Albert Schweitzer Professor of International Economic Development at Columbia University, has written and lectured widely on problems of the newly emerging countries. This paper is an extract from her book The Rich Nations and the Poor Nations, *published in 1962.*

How ARE we to define the 'poor' nations? The phrase 'under-developed' is not very satisfactory for it groups together very different types of under-development. India and Pakistan, for instance, are heirs of a great and ancient civilization and have many of the other attributes—in art, literature, and administration—of developed states, even though they are also very poor. Other areas—one thinks of the Congo—are developed in virtually no sense at all. I think, therefore, that perhaps the most satisfactory method of defining poverty at this stage is to discuss the question simply in terms of per-capita income—the average income available to citizens in the various countries. If you fix the level of wealth of 'wealthy' communities at a per-capita income of about $500 a year, then eighty per cent of mankind lives below it. It is chiefly among the privileged nations living round the North Atlantic that we find levels of annual income above the 500-dollar mark. Indeed, in the United States or Canada, it is three and four times above the minimum. Australia and New Zealand also belong to this group. In the Communist bloc, Czechoslovakia is moving up into it, and so is Russia. In fact, it is a marginal question whether they should not now be included among the rich. But what is certain is that the mass of mankind live well below the income level of $500 per head a year; and in some countries—one thinks particularly of India—per-capita income may be as low as $60. Yet between 400 and 500 million people live in India—something like two-fifths of all the poor people in the uncommitted world. So the gap between rich and poor is tremendous and, as we have already noticed, it is tending to widen further.

What is the cause of this? Why is there this great blanket of poverty stretched across the face of the globe? Before we attempt an answer, we should, I think, remember that ours is the first century in which such a question can even be put. Poverty has been the universal lot of man until our own day. No one asked fundamental questions about a state of affairs which everyone took for granted. The idea that the majority could have access to a little modest affluence is wholly new, the break-through of whole communities to national wealth totally unprecedented.

To return to our question: the contrast between the wealth of the West and the poverty of nearly everybody else does have some puzzling features. For centuries, for millennia, the East had been the region of known and admired wealth. It was to the Orient that men looked when they spoke of traditional forms of riches: gold and diamonds, precious ointments, rare spices, extravagant brocades and silks. In fact, for over a thousand years, one of the great drives in the Western economy was to open trade with the wealthier East. And one of the problems facing that trade—as far in the past as in the days of imperial Rome—was the West's inability to provide very much in return. It is hard to sell bear rugs to merchants at Madras, especially during the monsoon. Nor is the contrast between the East's endowment and the relative poverty of the West simply a matter of history. Today, for instance, Indonesia seems obviously better endowed in a whole range of ways than are some European countries—one might perhaps pick Norway.

In spite of these puzzles, there are some underlying physical causes which explain why some countries have been left behind in the world's present thrust towards greater wealth. Many of the tropical soils have been submitted to millennia of leaching under the downpour of heavy rains and are precarious soils for agriculture. Nor is the climate of tropical regions precisely designed for work. When the temperature rises to ninety degrees and the humidity to ninety per cent, you do not feel like rushing out and solving one of the first problems in Euclid. Even less do you want to cut a tree—favourite occupation of Victorian gentlemen—or dig a ditch.

Wherever the monsoon is the rain-bringing force, there is an underlying element of instability in farming. The concentration of rain in a few months creates expensive problems of control and storage. Rivers vary from raging torrents to dry beds. And if the monsoons fail in India or South-east Asia, then there is quite simply no agriculture because there is no water.

Another fact making for poverty is that the great tropical belt stretching round the world has only limited sources of energy: no coal and not too much oil outside the Middle East, Venezuela, and Indonesia. One must conclude, therefore, that certain original differences exist in the actual endowment of resources in the advancing Northern Hemisphere and the relatively stagnant South. Nonetheless, I think the profound reason for the contrast of wealth and poverty lies in the fact that the various revolutions which have swept over the face of the Western world in the last hundred years exist at only a chaotic or embryonic stage among the poorer states.

The biological revolution of more rapid growth in population is on the way in these areas. But the other vast changes—an intellectual revolution of materialism and this-worldliness, the political revolution of equality, and above all the scientific and technological revolution which comes from the application of savings and the sciences to the whole business of daily life—are only beginning the process of transforming every idea and institution in the emergent lands. The revolution of modernization has not yet driven these states into the contemporary world. The greatest drama of our time is that they will be swept onwards. But we are still uncertain over the form these revolutions will finally take. Everywhere they have started; nowhere are they yet complete; but the trend cannot be reversed. The modernizing of the whole world is under way.

Millennia ago, hunting and food-gathering began to give way before the advance of settled agriculture. So today the transformation of society by the application of reason, science, and technology is thrusting the old static subsistence economies to the backwaters of the world. In the wealthier lands, the first stage of this transformation has been completed in the emergence of the modern, wealthy, reasonably stable, technologically adept capitalist state. In the poorer lands, the first stage only has opened. The contrast between world wealth and world poverty largely turns upon this lag in time.

Now we must examine the impact of change upon emergent

lands—and we should remember again the distinction between poorer lands such as India which are at the same time rich in culture, history, and tradition, and tribal lands, whether in Africa, Australia, or Latin America, which lack even the rudiments of a developed tradition. The biological revolution brought about by a sudden acceleration of the birth-rate could not take place in these countries until colonial rule abolished local wars and until modern medical science and modern sanitation began to save babies and lengthen life. That these changes were introduced *before* the establishment of a modern economy is one of the most fateful differences between East and West, and one to which we will return. But until the second half of the nineteenth century most of these lands still followed the old millennial pattern of a population rising to the limits of production and then falling back into violence, struggle, and death where the limits were surpassed.

Now let us turn to a second force: the new revolutionary emphasis on work and effort devoted to the things of *this* world, the drive of interest devoted to changing and bettering man's physical environment. In traditional or tribal societies, this force is, in the main, lacking. Very largely, the material organization of life and, above all, the natural sequence of birth and death, of the seasons, of planetary change, have been taken as given: they were not the subject of speculative activity. In primitive tribal society one can say that nature is very largely accepted as impenetrable by reason. It can be propitiated. It can be worked on by human will through magic. A flood may be diverted by drowning a male child. But no one connects the precipitation of rain at the head of the watershed with the expected annual flow and devises earthworks to avert disaster. Life is lived in the midst of mystery which cannot be manipulated, beyond very narrow limits, in answer to human needs.

The chief aims of these societies were not this-worldly in our modern sense. Take, for instance, the significant Victorian phrase 'making good.' We understand it in terms of making money, of achieving material success in the broadest sense. In pre-modern society no such meaning could possibly have been attached to any activity thought of as being 'good.' In tribal society, approved behaviour implies strict observance of tribal laws and customs. In archaic civilization, the good man, the man of wisdom, is the man who observes the rules and duties of his way of life: the rich man, in magnificence, affability, and alms-giving; the poor man, in work and respect. No group, except the despised merchant, devotes his life to accumulation. And even the merchant tends, as he did in China, to turn his wealth into land and leave the life of capital-formation behind as soon as his fortune permits the change. Such societies incline of their very nature to be backward-looking, to preserve rather than to create, and to see the highest wisdom in the effort to keep things as they are. Under these conditions no underlying psychological drive impels people to work and accumulate for the future. Wisdom is to wait on Providence and follow in the ways of your forefathers, ways of life compatible with great serenity, great dignity, profound religious experience, and great art, but not with the accumulation of material wealth for society as a whole.

The lack of a third revolution—equality—has worked in the same sense. There was no concept of equality in traditional society. As one knows from still-existing tribal societies, leadership lies with the old men of the tribe. There is no way for the 'young men' to claim equality. They simply have to wait for the years to pass. Seniority (as in the American Senate) also ensures that the leaders are men who respect the backward-looking traditions of the group and have a vested interest in the unequal prestige conferred by advancing years. It is the inescapable recipe for extreme conservatism.

When tribal society is left behind, the values supported by the leaders are still conservative. They are fixed by an inviolate upper order. Save in times of immense upheaval, the peasant does not reach the throne. King, warrior, landlord form a closed order to which recruitment is in the main by birth.

Another facet of equality—a vital facet for economic growth—was lacking: since there was no national community as we understand it, competitive drives based on national equality were also absent. The tribe is a sort of tiny nation, a nation in embryo, but it cannot exercise the same economic influence as the modern nation because it is too small to be a significant market. In any case, tribal agriculture is devoted to subsistence, not to exchange.

The larger post-tribal political units were, in the main, dynastic or imperial units—one thinks of such loose structures as the India of the Guptas or of China's gigantic bureaucracy—in which there was little interconnection between the scattered cities and the great mass of people living their isolated, subsistence village lives. Certainly there was not enough economic and social coherence to define a market in such terms that a merchant would feel himself in competition with other vigorous national markets and could operate with driving energy to defend national interests against the rival national interests of others. The competitive 'equality' of Western Europe's commerce was wholly absent. As one sees again and again in human history—or in daily life—people do not begin to act in new ways until they have formulated the idea of such ways in their minds. The idea of the nation was immensely reinforced—but also in part created—by the rivalry of commercial interests in Western Europe.

Now we turn to the last and most pervasive of the revolutions, the crucial revolution of science and saving. There is virtually no science in tribal society. There is a good deal of practical experience, skilled work, and early technique. It seems possible, for instance, that primitive farming developed as a result of close observation of nature's cycle of seed and harvest and its imitation in fertility rites and religious festivals. But the idea of controlling material things by grasping the inner law of their construction is absent.

In great traditional civilizations such as India and China, there certainly was enough intellectual ferment for a vast scientific break-through to be theoretically possible. Many of the most acute minds in those societies devoted themselves to systematic thought for generations. In the Eastern Mediterranean, among the Chaldeans and the Egyptians, some of the basic mathematical tools of science had been forged long before the Christian era. Yet the break-through never came.

Primitive and archaic societies match their lack of scientific *élan* by an equal lack of sustained saving. Every society saves something. Saving is, after all, not consuming. If everything were consumed, men would be reduced to hunting and fishing—and even these occupations require rods and spears. But in settled agricultural societies, seed-corn is set aside for the next harvest and men do the hedging and ditching and field-levelling needed to carry production forward year by year. Probably such saving for maintenance and repair—and more occasionally by land-clearing and irrigation, for expansion—does not surpass four or five per cent of national income in any year.

The savings which make possible a general change in the techniques of productivity—more roads, more ports, more power, more education, more output on the farms, new machines in the factories—must rise dramatically above the five-per-cent level. Economists fix a level of about twelve to fifteen per cent of national income as the range needed to cover all possible increases in population, some increase in consumption, and a high, expanding level of investment. And no traditional society ever reached this level.

One reason for this fact takes us back to the revolution of equality. The merchant in the Orient never achieved decisive political influence. There were no city corporations, no charters based on autonomous rights. As a result, the merchant never achieved full security either. The government of kings and emperors was a government above the law, depending upon the monarch's whim. There is a brilliant phrase used by one of the young gentlemen of the East India Company to describe the uncertainties of the commercial calling in India. He describes the monarch and his tax-gatherers as bird's-nesters who leave a merchant to accumulate a nestful of eggs and then come to raid them all. One can well understand that under such conditions the stimulus to sustained capital accumulation is fairly marginal. On the contrary, the tendency is to put money that is earned from trade—and a great deal of money was earned—either into hoards of currency that can be hidden or else into jewels which are easily transportable and easily hid. But neither of these reserves makes for the expansion of productive enterprise.

In short, the chief point that distinguishes tribal and traditional society is that all the internal impulses to modernization have been largely lacking. And yet today these societies are everywhere in a ferment of change. How has this come about? Where did the external stimulus come from? There is only one answer. It came, largely uninvited, from the restless, changing, rampaging West. In the last 300 years, the world's ancient societies, the great traditional civilizations of the East, together with the pre-Iberian civilizations of Latin America and the tribal societies of Africa, have all, in one way or another, been stirred up from outside by the new, bounding, uncontrollable energies of the Western powers which, during those same years, were undergoing concurrently all the revolutions—of equality, of nationalism, of rising population, and of scientific change—which make up the mutation of modernization.

Towards the close of the nineteenth century a spurt of population began throughout India and the Far East. But this spurt had a different consequence from the comparable increase in the West. Western lands were relatively under-populated—North America absolutely so—when the processes of modernization began. The growth in numbers was a positive spur to economic growth; it brought labourers into the market and widened the market. At the same time the new machines, the new developing economy based on rising productivity, expanded the possibilities of creating wealth in a way that more than outstripped the growth in population. But in the Far East, in India, where population was already dense, the effect of the colonial impact was to increase the rate of the population's growth without launching a total transformation of the economy. More births, longer lives, sent population far beyond the capabilities of a stumbling economy. Today the grim dilemma has appeared that population is so far ahead of the means of satisfying it that each new wave of births threatens in each generation to wipe out the margin of savings necessary to sustain added numbers. The West, where growth in population acted as a spur to further expansion, has not faced this dilemma, and in the East it is not yet clear how so grave a dilemma *can* be faced.

Colonial rule brought in the sense of a this-worldly concern for the advantages of material advance by the simplest and most direct route—the 'demonstration effect.' The new merchants, the new administrators, lived better, lived longer, had demonstrably more materially satisfying lives. The local people saw that this was so and they began to wonder why and whether others might not live so too. Above all, the local leaders saw vividly that the new scientific, industrial, and technological society enjoyed almost irresistible power. This, too, they naturally coveted.

At the same time, the colonial system did set in motion some definite beginnings in the processes of technical change and economic growth. There was some education of local people in the new techniques of Western life. Some merchants in the old societies, the Compradors in China, for instance, or the Gujaratis in India, began to exercise their talents as entrepreneurs in a new, settled, commercial society. Some of the preliminaries of industrialization—railways, ports, roads, some power—the preliminaries we call 'infrastructure'—were introduced to the benefit of the new colonial economy. Some export industries expanded to provide raw materials for the West. Virtually nothing was done about basic agriculture; but plantation systems did develop agricultural products—tea, pepper, ground-nuts, jute—for the growing markets of Europe.

Above all, the new political ideas streamed in. Western education gave an *élite* a first look at Magna Charta. In their schoolbooks in India the sons of Indians could read Edmund Burke denouncing the depradations of Englishmen in India. The new sense of equality, inculcated by Western education, was reinforced by the daily contrast between the local inhabitants and the colonial representatives who claimed to rule them. Personal equality fused with the idea of national equality, with the revolt educated men increasingly felt at being run by another nation. The whole national movement of anti-colonialism was stirred up by Western ideas of national rights and national independence, and by the perpetual evidence that the rights were being denied.

The important point to remember, however, if one wishes to grasp the present contrast between the rich nations and the poor, is that all these changes, introduced pell-mell by colonialism, did not really produce a new and coherent form of society, as they had done in the West. There was no 'take-off,' to use Professor Rostow's phrase, into a new kind of society. The colonial impact introduced problems that seemed too large to be solved, or, at least, problems that offered immense difficulty to any solution. Take, for instance, the problem of population. You could not deny medicine; you could not resist sanitation; yet all the time life lengthened, the birth-rate went on going up, and you could almost watch population beginning to outstrip resources that were not growing in proportion because saving and capital formation were still inadequate. Yet the rising population continuously made saving more difficult.

This small level of saving meant that all economic developments under colonialism—or semi-colonialism—were on too small a scale to lead to a general momentum. China is a good example. After the Opium Wars the British compelled the crumbling Manchu Empire to open its ports to Western trade. In the so-called treaty ports, quite a rapid rate of economic and industrial expansion took place. Europeans brought in capital. Some Chinese entrepreneurs joined them. International trade soared. The customs, also under European control, grew to be an important source of revenue. Plans for building railways were prepared. Meanwhile, however, the desperate, over-crowded countryside where the bulk of the people lived slipped steadily down into deeper ruin. Little economic activity could spread beyond the Westernized areas; for there were no markets, no savings, no initiative—only the dead weight of rural bankruptcy.

The same patchiness affected social life and education. All over Asia the educational system began to produce an *élite* who believed in Western ideas of law, Western ideas of liberty, of constitutional government. But behind them there was little general change among the people at large and, above all, no trace of change in the vast number—eighty or more per cent of the population—who lived on the land where the old, unchanged, subsistence agriculture went on as before. And so there came about what one can only call a kind of dual society, in which the scattered growing-points of a modern way of life were restrained almost to the pitch of immobility by enormous forces of inertia inherent in the old framework of society.

Throughout the uncommitted world, in the traditional societies of China and India, in large parts of Latin America, and in the primitive emergent countries of Africa, old and new remained locked in a kind of battle, stuck fast in an apparently unbreakable deadlock. And how to break out of it; how to get the forces of modernization flowing through all of society; how to change leadership; how to get the new cadres in education; how to stimulate massive saving; how to get agriculture transformed: all these urgent and irresistible problems of the new society still wait to be answered.

This is a fact which the West cannot ignore. Most of the dilemmas of the under-developed areas have been stirred up by Western impact. Yet I think it is not entirely untrue to say that the Western powers are not looking very hard to find answers to these dilemmas. And this, I think, is for a very good reason. They have largely forgotten about their own transition. They are not conscious of the fact that a hundred years ago, even fifty years ago, many of them were struggling with just these problems of changing leadership, of developing new social groups, giving rights to new classes, finding methods of achieving greater saving, and securing a technological break-through on a massive scale. We take our development so much for granted that we hardly understand the dilemmas of those who have not yet travelled so far.

PART ONE The Developing Economies: A New Commitment

The Engineering of Development

ROBERT L. HEILBRONER

Robert L. Heilbroner of the New School for Social Research has written many books and articles, both scholarly and popular, in the areas of the history of ideas and development. This selection is taken from his 1963 volume entitled The Great Ascent.

WE MUST set ourselves two questions to answer. First, is economic development possible? That is, given the starting point, the deficient productivity, the lack of capital, the population pressures —in short, all the *economic* variables in the development equation—is it possible to arrive at a sanguine economic forecast for output and incomes in the developing nations?

And second, whether development is possible or not, how does a nation try to mount its economic offensive? What are the economic forces which can be brought to bear, what are the needed shifts in and additions to the collective national effort? In a word, how does a nation pull itself up by its bootstraps?

THE HIDDEN POTENTIAL

From what we have learned about the strictly economic aspect of underdevelopment we know what the core process of economic expansion must be. It must consist of raising the low level of productivity which in every underdeveloped area constitutes the immediate economic cause of poverty. This low level of productivity, as we have seen, is largely traceable to the pervasive lack of capital in a backward nation. Hence if such a nation is to grow—if it is to increase its output of food, to expand its scale and variety of manufacturing—clearly its first economic task is to build up capital. The meager productive capacities of bare hands and bent backs must be supplemented by the enormous leverage of machines, power, transport, industrial equipment of every kind.

But how does a backward nation begin to accumulate the capital it so desperately needs? The answer is no different for a backward nation than for an advanced one. In every society, capital comes into being by saving. This does not necessarily mean putting money in a bank. It means saving in the "real" sense of the word, as the economist uses it. It means that a society must refrain from using all of its current energies and materials to satisfy its current wants, no matter how urgent these may be. Saving is the act by which a society releases some portion of its labor and material resources from the tasks of providing for the present so that both can be applied to building for the future. Again, as the economist would put it, saving means the freeing of labor and resources from consumption-goods production so that they may be applied to capital-goods production.

This release of productive effort directed to present consumption wants, in order to make room for effort directed at the future, does not present an overwhelming problem to a rich nation. But the problem is different in a poverty-stricken one. How can a country which is starving restrict its current life-sustaining activities? How can a nation, 80 percent of which is scrabbling on the land to feed itself, redirect its energies to building dams and roads, ditches and houses, railroad embankments and factories, which, however indispensable for the future, cannot be eaten today? The peasant painfully tilling his infinitesimal plot may be the living symbol of backwardness, but at least he brings forth the roots and rice to keep himself alive. If he were to build capital—to work on a dam or to dig a canal—who would feed him? Who could spare the surplus when there is no surplus?

In capsule this is the basic problem which most underdeveloped lands face, and on the surface it seems a hopeless one. Yet when we look more deeply into it, we find that the situation is not quite so self-defeating as it seems. For a large number of the peasants who till the soil are not just feeding themselves. Rather, in so doing, they are also robbing their neighbors. In the majority of the underdeveloped areas, the crowding of peasants on the land has resulted in a diminution of agricultural productivity far below that of the advanced countries. In India, a hectare of land produces only about one-third of the crop raised on a hectare in the United States. Hence the abundance of peasants working in the fields obscures the fact that *a smaller number of peasants, working the same fields, could raise a total output just as large—and maybe even larger.* One observer has written: "An experiment carried out near Cairo by the American College seems to suggest that the present output, or something closely approaching it, could be produced by about half the present rural population of Egypt."[1] Here is an extreme case, but it can be found to apply, to some degree, to nearly every underdeveloped land. It is widely estimated that between 15 and 30 percent of the agricultural population of most underdeveloped economies produce zero net output.[2] Whatever little crop they eke out is only won at the expense of someone else.

THE PEASANT PROBLEM

Now we begin to see an answer to the dilemma of the underdeveloped societies. There does exist, in nearly all of these societies, a disguised and hidden surplus of labor which, if it were taken off the land, could be used to build capital. It is, to be sure, capital of a special and rather humble sort, capital characterized in the main by large projects which can be built by labor with very little equipment—roads, dams, railway embankments, simple types of buildings, irrigation ditches, sewers. However humble, these underpinnings of "social capital" are essential if a further structure of complex *industrial* capital—machines, materials-handling equipment, and the like—is to be securely anchored. Thus, peasant labor released from uneconomic field work makes possible a crucially important first assault on the capital-shortage problem.

This does not mean, of course, that the rural population should be literally moved, en masse, to the cities where there is already a hideous lump of undigestible unemployment. It means, rather,

1. Charles Issawi, in Ragnar Nurkse, *Problems of Capital Formation in Underdeveloped Countries* (Oxford, Basil Blackwell, 1953), p. 35, footnote 2.
2. *Ibid.*, p. 35.

that the inefficient scale of agriculture conceals a reservoir of both labor and the food to feed that labor. By reducing the number of tillers of the soil, a backward society can create a work force available to build roads and dams, while at the same time this transfer to capital building will not result in a diminution of agricultural output.[3]

This extraordinary feat of legerdemain lies at the heart of the economic side of development. It is not, however, only an *economic* feat. It is also intimately connected with another process which lies at the social core of development. This is land reform. For one cannot, after all, just go and "move people" in a living society. Deep-rooted legal and social institutions of landowning, of tenant-landlord and tenant-moneylender relationships must first be broken. Vested privileges in the old order must be overcome, often over the determined opposition of the landowning classes. Thus, the mechanics of economic development immediately plunges us into the social and political problems of development.

But we can now also see something else of great importance. We can see that land reform is not just a matter of justice, of rescuing the peasant from the domination of a feudal landlord or a rapacious moneylender. It must also be a functional step, a step toward the formation of land units large enough to be farmed scientifically for high output. Land reform which merely breaks up large estates in order to parcel out tiny plots of soil is at best only a political palliative for the underdeveloped nation. Economically, it may even be a step backward toward fragmentation and inefficient subdivision.

However, let us revert to the immediate economic problem. An underdeveloped society can increase its agricultural output and simultaneously "find" the labor resources it needs for development tasks. But where is the saving—the release of consumption goods—we talked about? This brings us to a second necessary step in our process of capital creation. When agricultural produc-

---

3. In sparsely settled lands we cannot apply the same strategy because there is no surplus population on the farm. Here we must *create* a surplus farming population by first raising agricultural productivity through better seeds, better technology, etc. This "created" surplus labor force can then be set to work building capital. The basic concept of this great transfer of resources is elegantly set forth in Ragnar Nurkse's classic *Problems of Capital Formation in Underdeveloped Countries.*

tivity has been enhanced by the creation of larger farms (or by improved techniques on existing farms), *part of the ensuing crop must be saved.*

In other words, whereas the peasant who remains on the soil will now be more productive, he cannot enjoy his enhanced productivity by eating up all his larger crop. Instead, the gain in individual output must be siphoned off the farm. The extra crop raised by the fortunate peasant must be saved by him, and shared with his formerly unproductive cousins, nephews, sons, and daughters who are now at work on capital-building projects.

We do not expect a hungry peasant to do this voluntarily. Rather, by taxation of various sorts, or by forced transfer, the government of an underdeveloped land must arrange for this essential redistribution of food.[4] *Thus in the early stages of a successful development program there is apt to be no visible rise in the peasant's food consumption, although there must be a rise in his food production.* Instead, what is apt to be visible is a more or less efficient, and sometimes harsh, mechanism for assuring that some portion of this newly added productivity is "saved"—that is, not consumed on the farm, but made available to support the capital-building worker. That is why we must be very careful, in appraising a development program, not to measure the success of the program by individual peasant living standards. For a long time, these may have to remain static—possibly until the new capital projects begin to pay off.

What we have just outlined is not, let us repeat, a formula for immediate action. In many underdeveloped lands the countryside already crawls with unemployment and to create a large and efficient farming operation overnight would lead to an intolerable social situation. Nor should we believe that the creation of such a modern agricultural sector can, in fact, be achieved overnight. Peasants, no matter how impoverished their condition, do not acquiesce gladly in radical rearrangements of traditional ways, nor do they relinquish without protest their tiny properties or their traditional connection with the soil. In the communist countries the collectivization of peasant holdings has everywhere

---

4. Nurkse makes a sage comment in this regard. Speaking of the use of collective farms in Russia he writes: "The word 'collective' has here a double meaning. The collective farm is not only a form of collective organization; it is above all an *instrument of collection." Op. cit.*, p. 43 (italics added).

been bitterly opposed. In nations as different as Cuba, China, Poland and Yugoslavia, zealous attempts to "reform" peasant attitudes and institutions have met with determined resistance, even to the point of sabotage. Even milder methods, such as the formation of cooperatives in India, have not met with much success in the face of inadequate educational backgrounds and technical experience.

Therefore, the social changes required to bring about a substantially improved condition of agriculture are likely to present severe problems to development-minded governments, whether authoritarian or democratic. Yet from the logic of the process there is no escape. In nearly every backward land, agricultural productivity *must* be enhanced if development is to take place, not merely to provide growing populations with food, but to create a labor supply for the formation of capital. Hence, an amalgamation of small farming units into large ones and a displacement of a considerable portion of the peasantry from the land are necessities for almost every developing country, no matter how painful the procedure.[5] The rate at which this can be accomplished, however, is apt to be slow. At best, we can envisage the process as a long-term transformation which extends over many years. It shows us, nonetheless, that a basic mechanism of development is the enforcement of a huge internal migration from agricultural pursuits, where labor is wasted, to industrial and other pursuits, where it can yield a net contribution to the nation's progress.

INDUSTRIALIZATION

We have seen how a backward society has the hidden potential to build social capital. But capital-building is not just a matter of freeing men and food. Peasant labor may construct roads, but it cannot with its bare hands build the trucks to run over them. It may throw up dams, but it cannot fashion the gen-

5. In the West, the absence of the extreme population pressure characteristic of the underdeveloped lands made this rationalization of agriculture a less pressing precondition of development. Nonetheless, a rationalization process took place in many parts of Europe, especially in Northern Germany and England. England's early economic impetus was much facilitated by the enclosures which, by the mid-nineteenth century, had transferred half the arable land from smallholders to large commercial estates.

erators and power lines that are needed if a dam is to produce energy. In other words, what is required to engineer the Great Ascent is not just a pool of labor. It is also a vast array of *industrial* equipment, which is the integral core of growth for all modern economies.

Sooner or later every developing region, if it is to carry its material advancement beyond the level of a fairly efficient agricultural economy, must build such a structure of industrial equipment—a structure of machine tools and lathes, of specialized machinery of all sorts.[6] But there is a new difficulty here. For unlike dams and irrigation ditches and basic housing, this new industrial capital itself requires prior capital. Roads and dams may be built, at least up to a point, by the sheer application of human labor working with the most primitive equipment, but lathes and looms, power shovels, and machine shops cannot. The machines and equipment needed must themselves be made by other machines and equipment. There is a kind of endless circle here into which an underdeveloped country cannot break.

In fact, of course, it is not a circle but a spiral, for in the dim past the first machines were fashioned by primitive hand methods. If the underdeveloped countries had time, they could build an industrial capital sector much as the West originally did, by the slow process of accretion from handicraft. But time is most needed in the race for development. Hence, if industrial capital is to be added to the huge "public works" of social capital, the underdeveloped lands must find a way of bringing it into being in very rapid order.

What is that way? In part, this critical equipment can be built within the developing country from its own manufacturing facilities, for only the most primitive regions have *no* machine shops or industrial capacity. But this is, at best, only a small part of the total industrial equipment required. Many kinds of tools and apparatus are simply beyond the technical abilities of even the most advanced underdeveloped regions. And no underdeveloped country has even remotely the capacity to produce the

6. This is not to say that every small nation-state of the moment, from Upper Volta to Vietnam, can legitimately aspire to become a Switzerland or a West Germany. The point rather is that massive industrial centers must be built up within the great geographic regions of Asia, South America, and Africa if these entire areas are to escape from their present agricultural servitude.

overall volume of industrial capital needed to sustain a rapid upward climb.

Hence, the general answer to the problem cannot lie within the underdeveloped economies themselves. Instead, in the first stages of industrialization, before the nucleus of a machine-building sector has been laid down, the necessary germinal core of industrial capital must be obtained from abroad. Some may be purchased by the underdeveloped country in exchange for that part of its output which it has saved—i.e., not consumed—and shipped abroad as exports of raw materials or handicrafts. Some may be received as the result of private investment by Western corporations or individuals. And some may be had as "foreign aid" —that is, as gifts or loans from the advanced nations.

Now, for the first time, we touch on the vital problem of the relationship of an underdeveloped nation to its more developed world neighbors, a matter to which we shall shortly return. But it is worth a moment's thought to place this relationship in proper perspective. Clearly, the pace of *industrialization* will depend heavily (although not exclusively) on capital goods obtained from abroad, whether by trade, investment, or aid. Yet it is also important to see that industrialization is itself only a stage in the overall process of development. An industrial sector built before there is a supporting base of social capital, or before there has taken place a degree of agricultural reform, or before there has become visible some change in social attitudes, is likely to result only in an industrial enclave coexisting with a nondeveloped peasant society. This very circumstance exists, in fact, in the Damodar Valleys of India and the Union Minières of Katanga. For an industrial sector to take root, for it to exert a widespread economic and social influence throughout society, it will not suffice merely to bring in the machinery and equipment of industrialization. These must rather be planted in soil which has been at least partially prepared to receive them. Industrialization then appears as the capstone of a successful development effort. And by the same token, the sheer growth of industrial output, without reference to agricultural output or to much less easily measurable skills and attitudes, is an inadequate index of the progress of the Great Ascent itself.

AN OVERALL VIEW: THE TAKE-OFF

Perhaps it is time to bring our investigations into focus. Let us assume, for the moment, that an underdeveloped economy has begun to change its agriculture, begun the slow metamorphosis of social habitudes, and succeeded in obtaining a flow of industrial capital from its own exports, from private investments, and from international aid. Can we then predict whether such a nation can start on a steady economic expansion which in time will bring it out of poverty and into the first stages of a modest well-being? Can we determine if it will generate capital at a fast enough rate to bring it, in W. W. Rostow's well-known phrase, to the point of "take-off"—that is, to the point at which its additions to capital make possible a *self-sustaining* increase in production?

An economist cannot answer this question for any particular country in the abstract. But he can isolate the main terms in the development formula which allow us to see how the different variables in the economic development process interact. They are three:

1. *The rate of investment which an underdeveloped nation can generate.*

This depends on the proportion of its current effort that can be devoted to capital-creating activity, at first largely of a social, later of an industrial, kind. Clearly, the higher the saving—provided, of course, that it goes into capital products and is not merely hoarded—the more feasible the "take-off" becomes. In addition, foreign aid, although not "generated" from within, can be counted as part of the investment of a developing nation.

2. *The productivity of the new capital.*

The saving which goes into new capital eventually results in higher output. But not all capital boosts output equally. A million-dollar steel mill, for example, may have a very different effect on output from a million-dollar housing project. We can see that the higher the productivity of capital, the sooner will take-off be possible. On the other hand, some "low pay-out" investment, such as schooling, is necessary in order to move ahead with "high pay-out" capital, such as a modern factory.

3. *Population growth.*

This is the negative factor in the equation. If growth is to become self-sustaining, the rise in output must proceed faster than the diluting effects of population expansion. Otherwise *per capita* output may be static or falling, despite a seemingly high rate of growth.

Here is what might be called the "iron law" of economic growth.[7] So long as the amount of savings coupled with the fruitfulness of that savings result in a rise in output which is faster than the rise of population, cumulative economic growth will take place.[8] Each year an increment of output will be won over the year before, and this increment in turn will yield *its* increment in successive years. Even seemingly small annual gains can in this way pyramid in time to impressive amounts, just as a small sum left to compound at a low rate of interest will, over the years, grow to large size.

On the other hand, if the amount of savings is so low, or the productivity of the capital projects in which it is invested is so small, that increased output fails to match increased population, the result must be stagnation or even retrogression. And this absence of economic growth will continue until one or more of the variables in the equation is changed—until savings rise, or the productivity of investment increases, or the rate of population expansion falls.

Thus economic theory begins to clarify for us the logistics of the Great Ascent—or, for that matter, of growth in an advanced nation. It shows us the principal economic variables which determine the great equation of economic progress. It allows us to think about a problem of enormous complexity within a fairly clear-cut framework of relationships. And to revert to the two questions with which we introduced our excursion into the theory of development, our analysis shows us not only that economic growth, starting from underdevelopment, is *possible,* but also the mechanics by which it becomes possible.

Nonetheless, caveats are called for. As we have been at some

---

7. The term is that of Dr. H. W. Singer.
8. If, e.g., savings are 10 percent of income and if productivity ratios are one-third—that is, if each dollar of investment yields 33 cents of additional output—then over-all growth will take place at 3.3 percent a year (10 percent times one-third). As long as the rate of population increase is less than 3.3 percent a year, per capita incomes will rise.

pains to indicate, development does not consist solely of, nor can it be solely measured by, quantitative output. At best, a sheerly economic analysis of growth points to a necessary, but not a sufficient, condition of the Great Ascent, and in singling out the criterion of output, it tends to divert attention from the critical factors of social and political change.

In addition, an emphasis on the economic variables tends to make of growth itself a purely mechanical process. It assumes, rather than demonstrates, that such a thing as "sustained" growth in fact occurs once the magical point of "take-off" is reached on the development curve. Yet a number of economies—such as those of Argentina or Turkey—have "taken off," only to make forced landings; others—one thinks of France before the war—did become airborne but never flew very high; still others, presumably in orbit, crashed—as did the United States in 1929. The variables, in other words, cannot be pushed to the critical threshold and then left to themselves; on the contrary, it may take nearly as much effort to keep growth going as to get it going.

Hence it is well to keep the iron law of economic growth in perspective. It is a useful tool of analysis, not a magic formula for success. But if we use it cautiously, it can help us appraise the chances for economic growth of the underdeveloped areas.

Post-war Growth in Historical Perspective

ANGUS MADDISON

Angus Maddison, previously Director of the Development Department of the OECD, also with the Harvard Development Advisory Service, Ghana Project, is presently back with the OECD as a Consultant on Education. This selection is taken from his book, Economic Progress and Policy in Developing Countries, *published in 1970.*

THE CENTRAL ISSUE of our times is the unequal income of nations. Its importance outweighs most of the domestic problems in rich countries, and the division of the world into rich and poor has become more significant than the ideological cleavage between communism and capitalism. There are twenty-five rich countries where real income is between $1,300 and $3,200 a year, but more than 100 countries where income ranges from $150 to $1,300 a year. Two-thirds of the world's population live in the latter group. Their poverty cannot be cured simply by transfers of income. The rich would have to give away more than half their income to achieve a levelling in consumption standards. Poverty can be abolished only by increasing output in the poor countries, and the limited aid which they receive must be used for this purpose.

The raising of income levels is generally called economic growth in rich countries, and in poor ones it is called economic "development." There are good reasons for differentiating the two processes. Economic "growth" is less urgent. In rich countries, most people can now expect to live out their natural life spans medicated against preventable disease, with more than enough to eat, fairly adequate housing, reasonable working conditions, access to leisure, education, and entertainment. In the post-war period they have been reasonably free of unemployment and major economic insecurity. There are still squalid cities and ugly pockets of poverty, and the desire for increased material comfort is far from satiated. But further progress is largely a matter of providing new frills. Improvement in the quality of life is a more pressing concern than the growth of output. In the rest of the world, problems are different. In Asia the average person dies fifteen years earlier than in Europe. Debilitating disease is still widespread. Famines have disappeared, but diets are inadequate. Housing standards are miserable. Underemployment and unemployment are widely prevalent. Education is poor in quality and not available to many who could benefit from it. Disparities between the income of different groups and regions are much greater than in the developed world. In these countries, a 3 percent increase in income means only $10 a year, in the rich countries an extra $60, but the $10 is more important than the $60 because the needs are greater.

The distinction between growth and development is also important because the problem of increasing incomes is more complicated in poor countries. In rich countries, resources are mobile, technical and managerial skills abound, organized scientific research has institutionalized technical progress, knowledge is easily diffused, there is a well articulated institutional and financial structure, and the fortune of the economy is not tied to a few commodities. In poor countries, problems of structural adjustment are much greater, skills are poor, resources are not as flexible, and the economies are more unstable. The modern sector is often a highly specialized enclave. Poor countries have a much more rapid population growth than most rich countries have ever experienced. Economic policy must not merely manage and modify growth forces which are already present; it must also break the obstacles to growth and create the dynamism itself.

On the other hand, the very backwardness of poor countries presents opportunities which the developed world did not have when it operated at similar income levels. There is a much wider range of technological choice. Foreign aid can add substantially to growth potential. Government policy can play a bigger and more active role. The sequence of development will be different from that of the rich countries, and the post-war experience of several countries—Greece, Israel, Spain, Taiwan and Yugoslavia—has shown that the income gap between rich and poor can be reduced.

The treatment of "developing" countries as a distinctive group occurred first in studies by international organizations which are the main providers of standardized economic statistics. The grouping was consolidated politically by the creation of the United Nations Conference on Trade and Development (UNCTAD), in which eighty-six politically independent countries constituted themselves a pressure group, claiming special privileges in trade and aid on the grounds that they are underdeveloped.

But the group is heterogeneous. Some countries which claim membership, such as Argentina, Chile, Israel, Spain, and Venezuela, are closer to the rich than to most of the poor, and it is questionable whether current definitions of the "developing world" are rational.

The distinction between rich and poor countries can only be made by reference to output or income per head. But the figures of national accounts statisticians are misleading when converted at official rates. Exchange rates reflect the purchasing power of currencies in terms of items entering international trade, whereas we need to measure differences in the price level for all goods and services. We have attempted to provide estimates of the type required, and the results are summarized in Table 1. Real product per head in 1965 varied from about 5 percent of the US level in Pakistan to over 40 percent in Israel, i.e. the dispersion *within* the developing world is almost 1 to 9.[1] This is much wider than in the developed countries, where the income spread is less than 1 to 3.

It is interesting to see how the income gap between countries has changed over time. In 1870, Indian income was about a fifth of that in the USA and about half of that in Japan. In 1965 it was a seventeenth of the US level and an eighth of the Japanese level. India and Pakistan have always been very poor and their

1. The table shows levels of *domestic* product (GDP). The domestic product is usually produced with the help of foreign capital and the owners of this capital receive payments of interest and dividends. The amount remaining when foreigners have received interest and dividends is the *national* product (GNP). In developing countries this is usually smaller than GDP. However, developing countries normally use more resources than their GNP because they are net recipients of foreign capital and aid. Israel is a case where external resources are very large, so that real resources available per head were $1,538 in 1965 as compared with GDP per head of $1,340. Venezuela in another extreme case, where payments of profits to foreign investors were much larger than capital receipts, so that resources available per head were only $1,143 as compared with GDP per head of $1,264. All of these figures are at factor cost, i.e. they exclude indirect taxes and subsidies. They would all be higher at market prices.

income level has less than doubled in the past century, whereas in Japan income per head increased more than sevenfold.

Near the top end of the scale, Argentina has also had very slow growth. In 1870, Argentina was more prosperous than some European countries, and not far behind the United States. Its natural resources were so great in relation to population that it could pay wages high enough to attract seasonal immigrants from as far away as Italy. It is now relatively poor because of retarded growth. It is a dropout from the developed world.

Most of the other countries have experienced fairly substantial long-run gains in income. In all cases, growth has been slower than in Japan or the United States, but they have not been stagnant economies, and some of them, such as Brazil, Colombia, Ghana, Malaya, Mexico, Taiwan and Yugoslavia have been fairly dynamic.

The countries we are dealing with are therefore very different, both in their present level of development and in their economic history.

In most respects, the circumstances in which these economies have operated in the post-war period are very different from those in the past. The leverage of their own policies is much greater and foreign aid has played a significant new role. They are not repeating "stages" of growth already experienced by the developed world. It is not, therefore, necessary to analyze their economic history in any detail. However, it is useful to survey briefly the major historical reasons for their backwardness.

Most of them were late starters. When their modern growth started in the 1870s, the UK, USA and France had already had a century of rising per capita income. Their development was not due to spontaneous internal forces but was induced by the rapid development of cheap transportation facilities for bulky cargoes. Steam shipping, refrigeration, the opening of the Suez Canal, and the introduction of cable communications were a necessary complement to railways for exploiting the benefits of international trade. Once they entered the world market, their trade expanded rapidly. There were few tariff and no quantitative restrictions on trade. Foreign demand for primary products like cotton, coffee, rubber, and cocoa expanded rapidly. Trade raised productivity by enabling them to specialize. In important cases it provided a profitable use for land and labor which had been idle before the

TABLE 1. *Level of Real Gross Domestic Product at Factor Cost Per Head of Population*
Dollars at 1965 US Relative Prices

	1965	1950	1938	1913	1870
Argentina	1,272	1,036	865	788	412
Brazil	482	351	231	—	—
Ceylon	271	241	208	—	—
Chile	863	678	595	545	—
Colombia	375	305	263	182	—
Egypt	295	191	178	176	—
Ghana	230	184	—	117	—
Greece	676	301	432	315	—
India	182	149	156	138	103
Israel	1,340	572	—	—	—
Malaya	528	490	—	221	—
Mexico	423	283	205	178*	120†
Pakistan	152	126	133	117	88
Peru	397	255	—	147	—
Philippines	269	207	218‡	201	—
South Korea	255	158	—	—	—
Spain	975	374	520‡	419	—
Taiwan	573	267	348	206	—
Thailand	254	159	—	—	—
Turkey	289	203	201	—	—
Venezuela	1,264	828	493	—	—
Yugoslavia	736	312	279	217§	—
France	1,990	1,159	954	774	426
Germany	2,109	934	1,072	811	404
Italy	1,345	663	676	521	379
Japan	1,466	438	703	366	209‖
UK	1,985	1,394	1,236	1,037	658
USA	3,179	2,356	1,513	1,239	503
USSR	1,495	734	548	339	226

* 1910; † 1877; ‡ 1929; § 1909–12; ‖ 1879.

transportation revolution. The forces of expansion continued until 1929, and were not seriously interrupted by the 1914–18 war.

The fortunes of different countries depended a good deal on the size of trade in relation to income, the natural resource endowment, and the amount of foreign capital they received. In Ghana, a highly specialized cocoa industry was built up by peasant farmers, who were able to raise their income substantially without a great deal of investment. Malaya, specializing in rubber and tin, enjoyed rapid growth from the 1880s onward, and attracted nearly six million Chinese immigrants and a limited amount of foreign capital. Ceylon, with a similar type of economy, attracted Indian immigrants to rubber and tea plantations. The highly commercial export economies of Malaya and Ceylon needed to import food and this provided an opportunity for Thailand and Burma to use previously idle resources of land and labor to expand rice production and exports. Taiwan experienced rapid growth as a Japanese colony, with major increases in productivity of rice and sugar for export. In India, by contrast, there were no significant natural resources to exploit, and the expansion of trade had only a marginal influence in raising income levels.

In most of the developing countries, the rate of investment generally remained low, and modern techniques of production did not spread throughout the economy. In no case were there deliberate policies of industrialization until the 1930s. They remained heavily dependent on imports for industrial goods, although in some cases they did develop a textile industry. Growth was, therefore, different in character from that in the developed world. It was diffused from outside rather than autonomous. And it was generally slower. Trade rather than investment was the engine of growth.

The only late starter which made enough progress to become a "developed" country was Japan. Initially, Japan was subject to the same colonial-type commercial treaty as the rest of Asia, so that the government could not impose protective tariffs. But the Japanese carried out a major institutional revolution in 1867 and created a tax structure, banking system, and legal framework that were highly conducive to growth. They introduced a modern system of compulsory education, created a heavy armaments and shipping industry, carried out land reform, promoted agricultural research, started government enterprises, and subsidized private industry. In the late nineteenth century, the government carried out half the investment in the economy and by the 1920s Japan was investing 20 percent of its GNP. Japan had certain peculiar features which helped such a development to take place. It had had a very large economic surplus in its old system of feudal rice levies which was converted into government revenue by the Meiji reforms. Its lack of natural resources left it no alternative to industrial development. Finally, it had a large, well-educated class of *samurai* who were politically willing to make basic institutional changes and to provide the bureaucratic expertise, technical capacity, and business leadership required.

The Japanese model had no counterpart elsewhere until the 1930s, when the world crisis forced some of the countries into more vigorous development policies.

Until the 1930s, none of these countries made a positive attempt to stimulate local banking, shipping, insurance, export credit, technical education, or to create government enterprise in fields where the initial risks were large. Agricultural research, where it did take place, was confined to export crops and not extended to the subsistence sector.

The failure to follow the Japanese model characterized both independent countries and colonies. In Latin America, the institutional structure created by the Spanish and Portuguese was much less favorable to growth than that implanted in North America, and was not changed by political independence. Most of the Spanish speaking countries retained a system of serf labor. Nearly all land was divided into large scale properties (*latifundia*), and the masses had no access to land ownership. This system was eliminated in Western Europe between 1780 and 1810, and in Russia in 1860, but did not begin to change in Latin America until the Mexican revolution of 1910. The Brazilian economy was based on Negro slavery until 1888. These societies benefited from international trade, but were slow to modernize their institutional structure and promote industrialization. Latin America was dominated by semifeudal oligarchies and foreign commercial interests until the 1930s, when the world crisis brought about a collapse of the old regimes in Argentina and Brazil, and Cardenas consolidated the Mexican revolution.

In Asia and Africa, colonial regimes broke open traditional societies to international trade. By introducing law and order to countries which would otherwise have been in violent civil commotion (as in a good deal of Latin America), and by building railways, they opened up local markets. In places where there was surplus labor or land, *laissez-faire* and railways were enough to secure substantial growth. It is interesting to note that Marx, writing in the *New York Daily Tribune* in the middle of the nineteenth century, saw colonization in a dual role "at once destructive and regenerative."[2] In particular, he expected it to spark the development of a modern capitalist economy in India. It is not by any means clear that local nationalist regimes would have followed a much more energetic development policy than that of colonial regimes. Indian nationalist economists like Romesh Dutt and Dadhabhai Naraoji were liberals who would probably have raised tariffs but otherwise followed a largely *laissez-faire* policy. Mohandas Gandhi had no great liking for modern economic development.

A good deal of the backwardness of poor countries is, therefore, due to the fact that (*a*) their development started when several of the developed countries had already a century of economic growth and (*b*) growth, once started, was due mainly to the productivity gains of international specialization—and not to high investment, industrialization, and technical change, as in the developed world. However, there is a third reason for their backwardness. Many of these economies were dominated politically by the developed countries. Effectively, most of them were colonies until the 1930s, and for this reason they suffered from various forms of foreign exploitation. Some kinds of exploitation did not necessarily hinder their growth. The control of the economy by a colonial bureaucratic elite was not necessarily worse for development than control by a local semifeudal oligarchy. The displaced local elite in colonies naturally had strong grievances at their loss of power and income, and the presence of a foreign ruling class may have helped destroy a few native industries producing luxury goods, such as the textile industry of Dacca. But the growth-impeding impact of foreign economic domination was due mainly to certain characteristics which allowed the developed world to draw resources away from these economies.

In the first place, the nationals of developed countries who were engaged in commerce and investment usually enjoyed special privileges. They often had extraterritorial legal status and tax privileges, and could nearly always count on the metropolitan country to use military pressure or gunboat diplomacy to enforce their claims. They usually had access to land and mineral rights on extremely favorable terms, and enjoyed a monopoly position

2. See the discussion of Marx's views on India in J. Strachey, *The End of Empire*, London, 1959.

in banking and shipping. In India, the managing agency system perpetuated the foreign commercial dominance originally introduced by the East India Company. The capital and enterprise of the developed world therefore creamed off a monopolistic surplus. This was a serious loss to countries in the first stage of capitalist development when the savings rate was still very low. These characteristics of foreign enterprise applied in Latin America as well as in the colonial economies. Under Porfirio Diaz, the privileges of foreign investors in Mexico were at least as great as in British India. However, the massive Latin American defaults on foreign debt in the 1930s did something to offset the earlier element of monopoly profit.

At various times in the past, colonial powers have levied direct tribute on subject nations, i.e. they remitted part of the local tax revenues to the metropolitan country. Thus, when Mexico was a Spanish colony, half the public revenue was remitted to Madrid. This practice on the part of colonial governments had generally disappeared by the second half of the nineteenth century, though the UK did accept "gifts" from India of $750 million during the first world war. Nevertheless, there was a steady outflow of funds from India because of the presence of a foreign government. This went to pay Indian army and civil service pensions and to finance home education for children of British parents in India. It included remittances of savings by British servants in India. We must include interest on nonrailway public debt, in view of the fact that the debt was incurred to finance colonial wars. We must also add a rough estimate of the element of monopoly profit in private dividend remittances. There has been a good deal of argument about the size of this burden on the Indian economy, but the latest evidence suggests that it amounted to about 1.7 percent of GNP a year from 1921 to 1938.[3]

We know that colonial regimes inhibited the development of human resources. In 1911, there were 66,000 British in the Indian army and police and 4,000 in the civil government. At that

3. See A. K. Banerji, *India's Balance of Payments*, Asia Publishing House, London, 1963, pp. 80, 115, and 137. We have included private remittances for education, savings remitted by public servants, government pension payments, interest on nonrailway public debt, and a third of private dividend remittances. National income figures were taken from S. Sivasubramonian, *National Income of India*, Delhi School of Economics, Delhi, 1965. They were adjusted upward by 12.5 percent to approximate GNP.

time, there were only sixty Indians in the top rank of the civil service and even fewer Indian officers in the army. Foreign investors were also reluctant to develop local technical and managerial competence. Privileged employment opportunities were reserved for nationals of the metropolitan country. Thus, they blocked Indian access to managerial skills in large-scale commerce, shipping, railway, banking, and jute. A quarter of the managerial personnel in the Indian textile industry in the 1920s were foreigners supplied by the managing agencies.[4] In Egypt, the Suez Canal Company did not use Egyptian pilots; in Ceylon and Malaya, most of the supervisory personnel in plantation agriculture were expatriates until relatively recently. The opportunities for local people were even worse in Belgian, Dutch, and French colonies than they were in these British controlled countries. All of this is in striking contrast to the intensive Japanese pursuit of Western skills, knowledge, and education.

In general, colonial governments followed conservative fiscal, monetary, and exchange rate policies. They tended to have balanced budgets, to maintain excessive foreign exchange reserves, and did not set up national monetary authorities until a late stage. They did not impose exchange controls, or allow debt moratoria or devaluation, unless it suited their own interest. In this respect, India suffered by comparison with Latin American countries, which followed much more expansionist policies in the 1920s and 1930s when India was trying to adjust to an overvalued currency by deflationary methods.

Finally, the commercial policy of colonialism allowed no scope for tariff protection as a way of building up domestic industry. This was a weapon which had been used by all of the industrial powers at some stage in their own development, particularly by the USA and Russia, but it was not permitted in British colonies until the 1920s, and low tariffs were also imposed on nominally independent countries like Egypt, China, Iran, Thailand, and Turkey, whose tariff powers were restricted by commercial treaties. In this respect, the situation in Latin America was different. Brazil escaped from British dictation of its commercial policy in

---

4. Details on India in this paragraph are from *Census of India 1911*, Vol. I, Pt. II, pp. 374–6, Calcutta, 1913; P. Woodruff, *The Men Who Ruled India, The Guardians*, Cape, London, 1963, p. 363; D. H. Buchanan, *The Development of Capitalistic Enterprise in India*, Cass, London, 1966.

1844 and imposed high and rising duties on textiles for revenue purposes, which had a substantial protective effect. This was also true in Argentina and Mexico. India was able to develop a textile industry without tariff protection, and to build up exports to the unprotected markets of China and Japan. But it was only in the crudest products such as cotton yarn that the Indian industry was able to withstand competition from Manchester, and from the 1890s onward it started to lose ground steadily to Japan.

Two Decades of Development: The Pearson Report

LESTER B. PEARSON

Lester B. Pearson, former Prime Minister of Canada, was appointed Chairman of the Commission on International Development in 1968. This selection was taken from Partners in Development, 1969, *the Report of the Commission on International Development.*

THE EMERGING NATIONS

THE PHASE OF ECONOMIC HISTORY in which we live began some two hundred years ago when industrial growth began to accelerate in England. In the nineteenth century it spread to Europe and North America. Between 1850 and 1950, income per head rose by an average of 2 percent a year in these countries—a rate which multiplied incomes by seven in the course of that century and produced dramatic changes in standards of living. Throughout the nineteenth century, technological and economic change was largely confined to Europe, the United States, and later Canada and Australia. The only notable Asian participant was Japan, which began its rapid modernization around 1870. Some other Asian, Latin American, and African countries made significant economic progress between 1880 and 1913, caused primarily by the rapid expansion of world trade and free capital movement during that period. But basic change in their economic and social structure was limited. The relative stagnation in world trade after 1913, the dislocations caused by the two world wars, and the effects of the Great Depression of 1929–31 slowed the progress that had begun.

After World War II, over sixty new countries gained formal independence within fifteen years. Emancipation from alien rule was accompanied by a growing political consciousness within these countries and by demands for modernization and progress. They entered political independence with a backlog of deep poverty, with little accumulated capital or experience of industrialization, and with only a vague understanding of the complexities of rapid change in their societies and economies. Many considered political independence and economic development synonymous, unaware of the long and slow process by which the power and affluence of the industrialized countries had been reached.

Rarely, if ever, has the world faced and absorbed political change on so large a scale in so short a time. As European and other countries had done earlier, the new African and Asian countries faced conflicting political, sectional, and cultural pressures in trying to build viable nations. Some countries were torn by internal disruption. In others the political framework proved unequal to the stress. But, compared with what history might have led the world to expect, the turmoil has been limited.

On the economic side, the emerging nations and low income countries everywhere faced a problem of immense magnitude. The existence of a vast fund of technological and scientific knowledge in the industrialized countries was a great asset, but it also proved to be a mixed blessing for countries who were starting late on the road to development. Technological advance greatly increased the rate of obsolescence of machinery and equipment for which developing countries were dependent on imports. At the same time, the export markets for primary products were narrowed by advances in technology which led to cheaper synthetic substitutes. Imitation of labor saving production processes prevalent in the industrialized countries limited the impact of investment on employment. There was also a sharp upswing in the rate of population growth in the developing countries at a time when possibilities of employment or emigration were much more limited than in the case of Europe during the Industrial Revolution.

For these and other reasons, doubt was widespread twenty years ago whether rapid progress could be achieved. Underdevelopment—low levels of technology, high illiteracy rates, low savings ratios, high birth rates, inefficient public administration, political instability—seemed to be a vicious circle from which only a fortunate few might hope to escape. These fears, however, proved to be exaggerated. The record of the past twenty years proves that economic development is feasible, given adequate effort and sound policies. It gives more ground for encouragement than is generally realized, but it also shows that growth is neither easy nor automatic.

ECONOMIC GROWTH

Between 1950 and 1967, the less developed countries as a group increased their total production of goods and services (Gross Domestic Product) by an annual average rate of 4.8 percent. This is considerably faster than the growth rates estimated for the presently industrialized countries in the early stages of their development: 2 percent in the United Kingdom between 1790 and 1820, 2.7 percent in Germany between 1850 and 1880, about 4 percent in the United States between 1820 and 1850, and some 4 percent in Japan between 1876 and 1900. However, the accelerating rate of population growth in the developing countries held down the rate of growth of incomes per head to an average of 2.0–2.5 percent a year. But even this per capita income growth also compares favorably with the early experience of the industrialized countries. The spectacular rate of increase which the industrialized countries have achieved in the post-war period is a new experience even to them.

The most encouraging feature of the progress in the poorer countries is the wide dispersion of good development experience. It is not confined to countries of any particular geographical area, topography, race, religion, or population size. This is clear from the following list of forty-one countries which have achieved a minimum increase of 2 percent per head for ten years or more since 1955:

Africa: Gabon, Guinea, Ivory Coast, Liberia, Libya, Malawi, Mauritania, Nigeria, Sierra Leone, Tunisia, U.A.R., Zambia

America: Barbados, Bolivia, Chile, El Salvador, Guatemala, Jamaica, Mexico, Nicaragua, Panama, Peru, Trinidad & Tobago, Venezuela

Asia: Iran, Iraq, Israel, Jordan, Korea (South), Lebanon, Malaysia, Pakistan, Saudi Arabia, Syria, China (Taiwan), Thailand

Southern Europe: Cyprus, Greece, Spain, Turkey, Yugoslavia

There have, however, been other countries, equally dispersed, whose growth has been considerably slower. In the 1960s, such countries as Indonesia, Argentina, Algeria, Ghana, and Uruguay have had very little increase in income per head, and in some countries, there has been a decline.

Despite these exceptions, the growth record has been good. This is also confirmed by the experience of the first Development Decade launched by a 1961 Resolution of the U.N. General Assembly. The average total growth rate for seventy low income countries since 1960 has been in line with the 5 percent annual target established for the Decade and some twenty countries have maintained a growth rate of over 6 percent per annum in the 1960s.

If the present rate of growth in developing countries is maintained, it will quadruple income per person in sixty to seventy years. For countries that now have per capita incomes of $400 a year or more (Mexico, Chile, Venezuela, Gabon, Greece, Cyprus), this would mean reaching levels of income currently enjoyed in Western Europe; for countries with present per capita incomes of less than $100 (India, Pakistan, Indonesia, Mali, Nigeria), it would mean great improvement but neither affluence nor the capacity to assure a wide range of choice to their citizens.

The present rate of growth is not the best that can be achieved. Much of the effort in the past twenty years has gone into basic facilities which have taken a long time to complete and are not yet fully reflected in the growth figures for the past two decades. They have, however, made it possible to accelerate economic modernization, and have increased the capacity for growth. The pace of economic change in countries which are latecomers to industrialization has often accelerated after the groundwork has been completed.

Of the population in the less developed world (excluding mainland China), 22 percent live in countries where per capita income has grown at less than 1 percent a year, 48 percent live in countries where it grew between 1 and 2 percent, and 30 percent in countries where per capita income grew by more than 2 percent a year. Apart from the consequences of natural disasters, the fall of prices in world markets, or other uncontrollable factors, the reasons for the poor performance in the slow growing countries have included lack of commitment to economic development, limited capacity for economic management, and unwillingness to face the political and social implications of basic structural change. These countries have failed to establish efficient administrations, to insulate economic policy from arbitrary political influences, to establish incentives to farmers, and to undertake tax and other reforms necessary to mobilize adequate resources for development.

However, the problems of the past two decades have not been limited to the slowest growing countries. Even in those countries where overall growth has been good, there have been many deficiencies—both in general economic policy and in specific sectors. The many achievements are discussed by sector in the following sections, but these global averages, of course, mask shortcomings within individual countries.

In a number of developing countries, economic plans have been formulated but often poorly implemented, and national priorities are either ill-defined or badly adhered to. Also, in most cases, these countries have ignored—until very recently—the importance of agricultural development, or, if they have recognized this sector as important to rapid economic growth, they have been unwilling to use market incentives to influence production levels. They have only recently begun to recognize that measures to make income distribution more equitable not only serve a social objective, but also are necessary for a sustained development effort. In addition they too often suffer from significantly overvalued exchange rates, and many have at times been guided more by political predilections about the function of the public sector than by a realistic assessment of its managerial and administrative capacity.

Many of these problems are the inevitable components of the development process, since the technological and administrative capacity of these countries is inadequate. Yet, as noted above, the developing countries have grown despite these deficiencies, and, more important, they have increased considerably their capacity for future growth. Furthermore, the development which has occurred has not been merely a matter of income growth. It has aimed, in the broadest sense, to improve the quality of life in order to create a better and healthier community.

SAVINGS AND INVESTMENT

Despite a common impression that poor countries are too poor to save anything, they have in fact mobilized the bulk of their investment capital. In the 1960s, domestic savings financed 85 percent of total investment. This is a dramatic achievement, since a high savings rate accomplished at low levels of income means a heavy sacrifice. For an individual, it may mean putting aside income, usually through taxes, which could otherwise be spent on food or shelter. For governments, it means foregoing expenditures for welfare and other pressing current needs. Where there are large regional and cultural disparities, political or even national survival may hinge on a delicate balance of these choices.

In the past twenty years, in spite of all obstacles, impressive efforts have been made to raise savings. Some countries achieved very high rates of capital formation by any standard—over 20 percent of GNP. Indeed, the average savings and investment rates in low income countries during the 1960s compared favorably with the historical investment rates of about 10 percent in Europe and the United States in the last century, although they were lower than the current rates in industrial countries.

This encouraging performance is attributable partly to the growing ability of governments to collect revenues, partly to the growth of banking and other financial institutions, and partly to increasing opportunities for profitable reinvestment. In 1960-65, at least seventeen developing countries were collecting over 20 percent of their national income in tax revenues, another twenty countries between 15 and 20 percent, and twenty-nine countries between 10 and 15 percent. The ability of governments to tax is important because it reflects a growing sense of national community and raises funds necessary for investment or for increased social services.

There has also been impressive progress in some countries in setting up commercial banks, investment corporations, savings and loan associations, cooperative financing institutions, and stock exchanges. Many countries have established successful development banks to promote industrial projects, finance agriculture, and promote low cost housing and house ownership.

The growth of savings in low income countries also reflects the great improvements in opportunities for profitable investment created by growing consumer income and by replacement of imports. These opportunities have often been assisted by government policy, by the growth of entrepreneurial groups, by the adoption of modern management techniques, by the introduction of modern technology, and by external factors, particularly the availability of foreign exchange for investment.

Savings and investment rates vary widely among countries. Some, like Brazil, Ghana, Iraq, Ivory Coast, Malaysia, and Thailand, save and invest a much larger proportion of their income than the average. In some others, the proportions remain disappointingly low and there have been cases where the ratio of savings to income has actually declined over time. However, in a large number of countries the proportion of each *additional* unit of income which is saved is higher today than ever before. This means that these countries are choosing to invest more and more of the fruits of growth in further expansion, instead of spending them on consumption. This increasing ability and willingness to save is profoundly important for development, for progress toward self-sustaining growth largely depends on adequate savings performance.

AGRICULTURE

Until quite recently it seemed that the hopes for rapid economic progress in many of the poorest countries were doomed by very slow growth of the huge agricultural sector. Agricultural production barely kept pace with population growth, and in many areas it fell behind. The less developed countries, which had been net *exporters* of 14 million tons of cereal grains each year in the 1930s, became net *importers* of 10 million tons per year in the 1960s. Imports rose even further in 1966 and 1967 after the monsoon rains in South Asia had failed two years in succession. There was widespread prediction of imminent famine.

These dire forecasts could not take into account the progress that has now been made in seed research, in irrigation practices, in extension work, and in agricultural education. They also ignored the impact price incentives could have on agricultural practices and production. As controls over production were relaxed and prices for farm products were made remunerative, farmers proved willing to adopt a new technology with amazing rapidity.

The situation today is radically different from earlier pessimistic forecasts. A good part of the developing world is now experiencing a major breakthrough in food production, widely characterized as the Green Revolution. In 1968–69, India's food output was about 8 million tons larger than the previous record of 89 million tons in 1964–65. Pakistan increased its wheat production by 50 percent in two years. Ceylon's rice production has gone up by 34 percent between 1966 and 1968, and in the Philippines two bumper rice harvests seem to have ended half a century of dependence on imported rice. The most dramatic advances have been concentrated in Asia.

These dramatic increases are well illustrated by experience in India and Pakistan. Indian agriculture employs 70 percent of the population and contributes 46 percent of the national product. Yet, before the mid-1960s, agriculture received only about 15 percent of the Indian public development expenditures and was not regarded as a potential growth sector. Little attention was paid to price incentives for farmers, to the provision of such agricultural inputs as fertilizer, improved seeds, and farm machinery, or to problems of farm credit. The droughts which struck large parts of India in 1965 and 1966 made it necessary to raise the level of food imports to 10 million tons a year. This highlighted the necessity of a drastic revision of agricultural policy.

Almost simultaneously, new high yield varieties of wheat and rice became available. These "dwarf" varieties had been developed in Mexico and the Philippines under the sponsorship of the Ford and Rockefeller Foundations. They permit profitable application of up to three or four times as much fertilizer as traditional varieties, which, combined with irrigation and pesticides, makes possible a doubling or tripling of yields. These improved strains were quickly adopted in India, investment in agriculture was expanded, and support prices were raised. Together, these steps represented substantial new incentives which led to improved yields.

In West Pakistan, lack of drainage had by the 1950s raised the groundwater level, which put large areas of farmland out of production by increasing salinity in the soil. However, the threat of disaster was turned into a blessing. The solution to the salinization problem was the sinking of deep tubewells to lower the water level by intensive pumping, which permitted the saline soil to be reclaimed. The tubewells also produced large supplies of irrigation water. Originally, it was assumed that massive public programs would be required, but individual farmers adopted this innovation spontaneously because of the tremendous rise in yields made possible by the increased groundwater supply. The surge in private tubewell development became one of the most spectacular elements of agricultural modernization in West Pakistan. In 1959–60, about 1,300 of these wells were installed by private farmers. By 1963–64, the annual rate of installation had accelerated to 6,600, and by 1967–68, to about 9,500. Although, from a technical point of view, these wells were not very efficient, they were extremely profitable. Private and public tubewell irrigation accounted for nearly half of the expanded agricultural output during the period 1959–60 to 1965–66.

As in India, the introduction of the new varieties was swift. The acreage under the new wheat seeds rose from 200,000 acres in 1966–67 to 2.3 million acres the following year. The new rice variety called IR-8 was planted on 9,000 acres in 1967, which produced the seed for almost 900,000 acres in 1968. Fertilizer supplies, largely financed by foreign credits, were rapidly expanded, and dramatic increases in grain production did in fact occur.

The Green Revolution has been a matter of both new technology and new policy. Although it is too early to say how deep and how rapid the impact will be and whether similar breakthroughs will be repeated in other parts of the world, the prospects for growth obviously look very much brighter. Above all, it has been demonstrated that the peasant farmer, contrary to many expectations, is not hopelessly fettered by custom and tradition and that he is not insensitive to costs and prices. Given the reasonably secure expectation of large returns, he is likely to respond. The lessons of this experience for development policy extend beyond the sphere of agriculture.

In the fertilizer field, which, as we have seen, is essential to the new agricultural technology, progress has been striking. There have been substantial cost reductions in the post-war period and further improvement is in prospect. The capital cost of new nitrogen plants is almost 50 percent lower than for "old" (pre-1963) plants. Consumption has risen rapidly. In India, fertilizer supplies were increased by almost 80 percent in 1966–67 over the previous year, and by another 50 percent the following year. Domestic fertilizer production more than doubled between 1965 and 1968; imports of fertilizer and fertilizer raw materials now equal over one-fifth of India's total export earnings. In Pakistan, fertilizer use has doubled every two years since 1960. Increases in other developing countries have been equally dramatic. Compared to the average for the five years ending in 1956–57, total consumption of nitrogenous and phosphatic fertilizer in 1967–68 was five times as great, and potash use had increased sixfold.

The growth of several nonfood crops, though not as dramatic as that in wheat and rice, has also been substantial. Between 1953 and 1967, cotton production in Asia and Africa rose by 40 percent, and this has been the basis for rapid growth of the textile industry in these areas. Coffee production in Africa has almost tripled from 393,000 tons to 1,145,000 tons in the same period, so that Africa now produces about 30 percent of the world's coffee. This rapid growth of coffee exports from Africa has created marketing problems, but it does illustrate the potential of tropical agriculture for diversification and higher productivity.

INDUSTRY

Between 1950 and 1967, the average growth of manufacturing in less developed countries was over 7 percent a year, compared to almost 6 percent for the world as a whole (excluding Communist countries). This was achieved despite their shortages of foreign exchange and domestic skills, the small size of domestic markets, and the barriers against exports. Progress was shared by all regions and brought about a significant change in the structure of many economies.

All varieties of industrial policy have been tried by different countries. Development strategies in Latin America, as well as in South Asia, have often emphasized the building of domestic industries to produce goods previously imported. Industrialization in Africa is still in its infancy but has also been oriented toward the replacement of imports of consumer goods. In East Asia, on the other hand, intensive efforts have been made in such countries as South Korea, Taiwan, and Singapore to build up exports of manufactures. At the same time, such countries as Burma, Cambodia, and Indonesia (before 1966) have pursued a more inward looking course.

In Latin America, the manufacturing sector now contributes between 15 and 30 percent of total national income. In Asia, the share of manufacturing has doubled to a range of 15–20 percent.

In Africa, manufacturing activity still accounts for less than 10 percent of total income, but in the U.A.R. it reaches 20 percent and in countries such as Tunisia, Kenya, and Morocco it is already 12 percent or more. Low income countries as a whole now produce about two-thirds of all the consumer goods they need, about 40–50 percent of the intermediate goods, and 20–30 percent of the capital goods.

Much of the industrialization has been fostered through policies involving very large subsidies in the form of tax rebates and high tariff protection. In many such cases, new industries have been so extensively supported that they have become a burden rather than a benefit to the economy. On the other hand, where favorable conditions have existed for competitive and export oriented industrialization, growth has been both rapid and beneficial to the economy as a whole. Today, however, even outward looking countries like Thailand and Malaysia consider it unsafe, in view of the great uncertainties of their access to the markets of the developed countries, to do more than substitute for imports in their industrialization.

Not all the advance in this field has been quantitative. A great deal has been learned about industrialization and about the links between industrial progress and growth in other sectors. Experience has shown that industrialization, unless it is integrated with parallel development in agriculture and other sectors of the economy, can generate serious foreign exchange shortages, inflation, and other economic imbalances. There is now better analysis of overall priorities, economic feasibility, and international comparative advantage. There has been a large increase in the supply of skilled labor and in most developing countries there is now a growing nucleus of people capable of managing modern technology. There also is a clearer understanding of the respective roles of the public and private sectors and increasing recognition of the importance of price incentives and market discipline for both public and private producers.

TRANSPORT, POWER, AND STEEL

Much of the effort and money invested in development has been directed to the immense need in all developing countries for those general facilities necessary for advance on any economic front—for roads, railroads, power plants, and rapid communications which are the foundations of all modern economies. As a result, this infrastructure has improved beyond recognition, particularly in Asia and Africa. It has already contributed to the increases in agricultural and industrial production, but the full benefits are by no means yet reflected in increases in trade and personal mobility. Road networks have grown in size to accommodate the rapid growth of commercial truck and bus fleets, as has railway traffic.

The production of electric power has increased rapidly between 1951 and 1967. Although in many parts of the developing world demand still runs ahead of supply, power production has met the needs of rapidly growing industries, provided irrigation for agriculture, vastly improved service for urban consumers, and made a small start on rural electrification. The production of electric energy multiplied by seven in Asia, five in Africa, and four in Latin America in the last twenty years.

These categories of infrastructure have been particularly favored by some aid givers and lenders, among them the World Bank, and the premise that these investments are basic to the attack on economic and technological underdevelopment has been vividly confirmed.

Steel consumption, along with power and transportation, is also one of the basic indicators of industrialization. India, now the thirteenth largest producer of steel in the world, consumes over 7 million tons a year while Argentina, Brazil, and Mexico consume between 2 and 4 million tons. In most of the developing areas, steel consumption has risen rapidly.

PUBLIC HEALTH

There is probably no other area where social improvement has been realized which is of such direct benefit to individuals in developing countries as that of public health. Life expectancy at birth has been raised faster than was thought possible. In a decade or two, most of the developing world has recorded gains in life expectancy which took a century to achieve in the industrialized countries. Today that expectancy stands at about fifty years, a level attained in Western Europe and North America at the beginning of this century. There are, of course, wide variations among developing areas. In Africa, mortality is higher and life expectancy shorter. In Latin America, on the other hand, life expectancy approximates that of the industrialized world in the inter-war period.

This remarkable catching up is the underlying cause of the grave problem of population growth, to which we shall return. This does not detract from its value. In human terms, it has been the most convincing demonstration of the power of applied science. It has lifted people's spirits and raised their sights in planning for the future. It has increased the capacity to work, and it has opened up territories for new cultivation where disease had previously been rampant.

By and large, this improvement is due to sweeping measures to prevent communicable disease. Malaria has been virtually eliminated by a world-wide campaign under the leadership of the World Health Organization (WHO), although there appears to be some resurgence of DDT-resistant strains. The number of deaths attributed by WHO to other epidemic diseases has also declined sharply in the developing world. Therapeutic health services remain sparse but have been very considerably enlarged in almost all developing countries.

EDUCATION

In this area of strategic importance to the process of development there has been spectacular change.

Free and universal education has, in principle, been accepted as a basic human right and in the new nations primary school education was also offered as a constitutional right. The initial reluctance of parents in rural communities to forego the earnings of child labor has yielded to the social prestige and economic value of education. Total enrollment in schools and universities almost tripled between 1950 and 1965. This investment will begin to bear fruit in the next two decades.

There was initially a rapid growth of enrollment in primary schools, from 57 million to 137 million between 1950 and 1965. As these children completed the first cycle of their schooling, the pressure mounted for expanded facilities at the secondary level. Thus, secondary school enrollment grew at an even faster pace than primary school enrollment, from 1.5 million students in 1950 to 5.8 million in 1965. Students in post-secondary schools and universities increased from 1 million to 3.5 million in the same period.

The share of education in national budgets has increased proportionately to enrollment, and now amounts, on the average, to 16 percent. More than ten countries devote some 25 percent of their public resources to education. The annual rate of growth of educational expenditures between 1960 and 1965 has been 13 percent in Asia, 16 percent in Africa, and over 20 percent in Latin America.

When private and local government expenditures are added to central government outlay, it becomes clear that developing countries are devoting about 5 percent of their national income to education. This represents a serious strain on the limited national expenses, but nonetheless is still less than the 7 percent the developed countries spend for the same purpose.

Serious doubts can be raised about the efficiency of educational systems in certain developing countries. There is no doubt, however, that the growth of educational opportunities has been dramatic and has broadened the horizons of millions of people. Children, whose parents at their birth would not have dreamed of being able to offer them such opportunities, are now in school, with potential access to a new world. As a result of higher education and special training programs, there is today a substantial body of competent administrators, scientists, and engineers in Asia, Latin America, North Africa, and the Middle East. There is also a growing number of teachers in all developing countries. The absolute numbers of educated people are growing. Their presence immeasurably influences the organization of their societies and contributes to the growing awareness of the promise of development.

ECONOMIC MANAGEMENT

The achievements so far described would not have been possible without significant improvements in the capacity of the less developed countries to manage their economies and administer their development programs.

To begin with, the last two decades have seen the development of statistical services, which are essential for sound social and economic policy. The data often remain poor or incomplete, but they are much better than they were, and decision making can now be based on more informed judgment. The monetary and financial system has been brought under the control of central banks and finance ministries where economic managers are learning which tools are appropriate to their unique problems.

The capacity to plan and implement development programs has also improved, though planning remains ahead of implementation in most countries. The capacity to prepare development plans depends on a relatively small group of well-trained individuals. These can be trained quickly abroad and they can be supplemented readily by small numbers of foreign advisers. The implementation of such plans, however, involves the whole administrative structure of the government together with the private sector. Because administrative structures are still weak, effective implementation is still too rare. Yet implementation is the test of a plan's realism as an instrument of development, of the accuracy of project analysis, and of the capacity of the country to invest and to operate better public services.

India was the first of the low income countries to accord detailed planning a central role in its development effort. But many countries have learned from India's experience. Aid givers have pressed for more systematic planning, which has become more widespread and provided advisers and helped in the training of local planners and technicians. In Latin America, although some countries had begun planning activities earlier, the acceptance of the principle of planning at Punta del Este in 1961 stimulated some governments to set up planning commissions for the first time.

The whole concept of planning has gradually changed in the direction of indicative prescription rather than detailed quantitative production targets. It involves systematic analysis of resources required and available, establishment of priorities, and a careful assessment of projects. It is recognized that planning has an indispensable function whatever the system of ownership, that not only the public sector but also the market mechanism and the private sector can and should be used to achieve national objectives.

None of this is easy. The first Latin American plans, for instance, were in the nature of very general investment budgets without specific provisions for implementation and did not have much impact on policy decisions. There, as elsewhere, frictions have arisen between the planning commissions and ministries of finance and other branches of public administration. In most countries, this conflict has been resolved by bringing planning commissions closer to policy making and giving them a more prominent role. Planners have also come to shift their interest more toward administrative coordination and economic policy and away from the drafting of abstract schemes. This is all to the good.

By and large, then, there has been marked improvement in many countries, which has often been reflected in their second and third plans. Priorities are more realistically assessed, and implementation has improved. The seeds of dynamic change have been planted.

INTERNATIONAL TRADE

Not all of the conditions necessary for growth and development are in the control of the poorer nations themselves. By far the most important of the external conditions for growth is the opportunity to expand participation in world trade. The greatest contribution which the industrialized countries have made to international development in the post-war period has been the steady growth in their own economies which generated the rapid and steady growth in world markets.

In the last period of rapid expansion of world trade, from 1880 to 1913, even many less developed areas enjoyed quite rapid economic growth. Stagnation from 1913 to 1950 was due primarily to the throttling of international trade by two world wars and the Great Depression of the 1930s.

In the post-war period, their exports have again increased quite fast under the influence of the unprecedented upsurge of world trade. The growth rates of individual developing countries since 1950 correlate better with their export performance than with any other single economic indicator. If the expansion of world trade were to flag, the development effort would undoubtedly be retarded.

The total volume of exports from low income countries grew at an average of 4.7 percent a year between 1953 and 1968, although adverse price trends were aggravated by the simultaneous increase in the prices of goods and services imported from advanced countries. In the 1960s, export earnings rose by more than 6 percent a year. Moreover, twenty countries increased export volume by more than 8 percent a year, and another twenty-five countries by more than 6 percent a year, the increase in volume being partly offset by price declines.

This record is good, but the fact remains that the value of exports from most developing countries grew significantly less rapidly than world trade as a whole, which increased by an average of 6.9 percent a year. The share of low income countries, therefore, steadily declined from 27 percent in 1953 to 19 percent in 1967. Even their share in world trade of primary products, which comprise the bulk of their exports, fell from 54 percent to 42 percent. One reason was the slow increase in demand for their traditional exports. Furthermore, trade liberalization in the post-war period has been aimed chiefly at expanding trade among the industrial countries. The effect of such adverse external factors was compounded by the economic policies of some of the developing countries themselves, which, in effect, amounted to systematic discouragement of exports as compared with other productive activities in the economy. Neglect of agricultural development transformed others from major exporters of cereals into large importers. Many failed to profit from booming export markets because they were not able to move resources into new lines of production. In some countries, especially in Latin America, chronic inflation, together with exchange rates which failed to keep up with rising price levels, have penalized exporters and increased their financial risks.

There has also been significant change in the structure of exports from developing countries. The share of foodstuffs and agricultural raw materials declined from three-fifths of total exports to less than half during 1953–67. The share of manufactures, fuels, and minerals rose correspondingly. Thanks to the discovery of new oil fields, earnings from fuel exports increased at a rate of 7–8 percent annually. Earnings from metals rose by 6–7 percent per annum, in large part due to a sharp rise in prices in the 1960s. But perhaps the most interesting development was the expansion of manufactured exports, rising from an annual growth of 7.5 percent in 1953–55 to 11.5 percent in 1963–65.

The weakest sector was agricultural exports, where earnings increased by only 2–3 percent per annum. Despite a considerable increase in volume, earnings from tropical beverages actually declined and those from agricultural raw materials were sluggish. For beverages such as coffee, tea, and cocoa, growth is of course narrowly limited by the slow expansion of demand in industrial countries. Demand for agricultural raw materials has been held in check by the competition from synthetics and also by technological progress which has reduced the requirement for raw materials per unit of output. These forces will continue to limit the growth potential of many traditional exports from developing countries and pose particularly difficult problems for countries heavily dependent on them.

The promotion of exports has taken many forms. Favorable exchange rates and fiscal and credit incentives to exporters and to producers of exportable goods and services, including tourism, and support of foreign marketing have, in many countries, yielded expanding foreign exchange earnings. New manufactured exports have been generated on a substantial scale in such countries as Korea, Mexico, Pakistan, the Philippines, Taiwan, and Brazil. These exports sometimes include processed agricultural products originating in a rural sector which itself has become diversified as a result of public policy. Other countries such as Turkey, Peru, and several Central American and African countries have succeeded in expanding traditional exports of primary products by combining encouragement of domestic production with aggressive external marketing.

THE CONTRIBUTION OF FOREIGN AID

Throughout the last twenty years, the developing countries have received large amounts of assistance from the industrialized world. Official development assistance, as distinct from private investment and government loans on commercial terms, amounted to almost $6.5 billion in 1968. Foreign aid of this magnitude has represented a major international effort. Ever since 1950, the number of countries and international agencies providing assistance has expanded. It is clearly a central question to any assessment of international development whether or not this has been a significant contribution to progress.

Measured against the total income of the developing countries, aid resources have been a small fraction, amounting to only about 2 percent. However, by many other measures, aid has been of great importance. It has financed about 10 percent of investment in the developing countries. This has increased the rate of growth in total production and consequently the amount available for consumption and for investment. A difference of 10 percent in the investment level can mean the difference between staying comfortably ahead of population growth while steadily improving public services, or barely keeping pace. Moreover, the overall figure for developing countries hides much diversity. For several countries, such as Jordan, Korea, Pakistan, Tunisia, and India, foreign aid accounted for between 20 and 50 percent of total investment, and others were even more dependent on aid.

The importance of foreign aid is also demonstrated by the proportion of imports in developing countries which are financed by it. On the average, some 20 percent of imports from developed to developing countries has been aid financed, and in many countries the percentage has been even higher. In 1967, official aid disbursements equalled about 30 percent of imports in Pakistan, 35 percent in India, and 30 percent in Indonesia. In most such countries, imports of consumer goods, with the exception of food, medicine, and the like, are strictly limited. Imports consist essentially of new machinery and equipment, raw materials to operate industry, and fertilizer, pesticides, and other requirements of agriculture. Of course, aid financing has been of great importance in some consumer areas, providing, for example, large amounts of food to the developing countries ($1.6 billion in 1967) while they were incapable of self-sufficiency in foodgrains. In many cases, this has warded off starvation, while in others it has supplemented a substandard diet.

However, the development value of aid has been most evident in providing the machinery and equipment for industry, for the building of roads and railways, and for the creation of new ports and the telecommunication facilities. In agriculture, it has helped considerably to finance the Green Revolution by making available rapid increases in fertilizer supplies, pumps for irrigation, and pesticides for plant protection.

Yet, despite these aid contributions, the correlation between the amounts of aid received in the past decades and the growth performance is very weak. First, aid was only one component in the flow of external resources. Many developing countries, especially the relatively advanced, also received large amounts of private capital. Moreover, growth has been deeply affected by the amount of foreign exchange needed for debt servicing, by the growth of exports, and by general domestic policies which determine the rate and composition of investment. Thus, Taiwan achieved a rate of growth of 9 percent a year between 1957 and 1967, with foreign resources, including substantial private investment, financing 25 percent of imports, while Pakistan achieved a growth rate of 5.2 percent a year in the same decade with foreign financing of 42 percent of imports.

What was universally true was that there was a close link between growth and import capacity. Except in the few cases where export opportunities were exceptional—notably in oil countries such as Iran, Iraq, Libya, and Venezuela—all the fast growers in the developing world received substantial amounts of foreign financing of all kinds, including foreign investment.

The low correlation between aid and growth is also explained by the fact that much aid was given in ways which did not make it as efficient a contribution to development as it could have been. For one thing, a considerable portion was allocated on essentially political criteria without regard to whether the recipient made effective use of it or not and without regard to general economic performance. For another, even aid which was extended with the objective of promoting economic growth was given with little or no previous experience. Finally, aid has often been directed at the promotion of financing of exports from developed countries with little relevance to development objectives in the receiving countries. In recent years, however, aid has increasingly been given for purposes of long term development and with greater concern for economic performance on the recipient side. Aid agencies, both bilateral and multilateral, have acquired a greater familiarity with the problems of developing countries and recipients have learned much about how to use the help given.

The impact of aid becomes clear in country or sectoral contexts. The growth of transport and communications which has revolutionized the developing world and which forms the basis for industrial and agricultural growth has been financed largely by development assistance. The 5 percent annual growth in railway traffic in South Asia, for example, has been supported by loans of $894 million to India's railway system and $390 million to Pakistan's. The 18 percent annual increase in power generation in Turkey and surrounding countries was supported by $259 million in loans. In Africa, the growth of cotton, palm oil, peanut, and foodgrain production depended heavily on aid financing.

But the contribution of aid cannot be expressed in purely financial terms. Aid has financed the work of large numbers of personnel and very extensive training programs in the developing countries. It has thus contributed to the transfer of technology and ideas. In 1965 alone, there were over 100,000 experts and volunteers working in the developing countries, financed under official programs, and over 80,000 students and trainees were studying in the industrialized countries. To these must be added the consultants, engineers, and analysts engaged in preparing and implementing capital projects as well as those experts and trainees supported by private organizations; these are nearly equal in numbers to officially financed personnel.

This two way flow of people has powerfully stimulated change, introduced new management skills, raised educational standards, and helped to create much infrastructure and expanded industry. For instance, achievements in Africa have been made possible by large transfusions of operational personnel, foreign advisers, and educational experts. In health, foreign assistance has helped to eradicate malaria and smallpox and other dread diseases. In India, agricultural universities have grown rapidly, many of them supported by teams of foreign experts. Indeed, the concept of relating agricultural education to the requirements of the rural sector was introduced from abroad.

The process of preparing and examining development plans, to which aid has helped give rise, has fostered the growth of systematic allocation of resources, the careful analysis of projects and programs, and the increasingly professional assessment of policies. Aid financed experts have assisted in institution building on all levels: public administration, staff colleges, domestic consulting firms, schools of business administration, savings and loan associations.

The role of foreign aid, then, has not been merely to supplement domestic resources. It is the essence of the dilemma of the developing countries that even when they possess considerable potential economic resources, such as unmined minerals or an abundance of unskilled labor, they are often not in a position to mobilize them, combine them, and transform them into the goods and services which they themselves, or the world market, require. In this area, aid has to a large extent been a catalyst.

Though it has played a relatively minor quantitative role, foreign aid has had a part in all the achievements enumerated here. In addition, it has been of first importance in the psychology of development. Economic policy aimed at growth requires a certain boldness, a willingness to experiment. The growth process is still mysterious, and no decision maker can be absolutely certain that any of the effects of any particular change in policy such as devaluation, import liberalization, export subsidy, land reform, or labor intensive rural programs will produce precisely the effects planned, nor can any expert or adviser so guarantee. Results will depend on many variables. Moreover, developing countries live so close to the margin of subsistence that even minor economic reverses have major political and economic consequences. A cushion of foreign resources makes it possible to pursue bolder policies and take steps to accelerate development that might otherwise not be possible. The provision of aid, and the mutual examination of problems which this entails, has made possible basic reforms in most of the major developing countries which otherwise would not have occurred.

The provision of aid, and the new relationships it has created between sovereign states, has not been without problems. There have been problems in the way aid has been provided and there have been mistakes in the way aid has been utilized. Nonetheless, it is clear that aid, increasingly focused on the imperatives of long term development, has helped to make possible a good record of development in the past two decades.

In addition to its more tangible contributions, in many countries aid has made a critical difference simply by directing new attention and energy and resources to the specific task of promoting economic and social development. Although still inadequate to the need, increasingly circumscribed with regulations, and not always directed at development objectives, this massive transfer of resources has helped the transformation of the developing countries. Aid has been a novel enterprise, and it has been carried out on a basis of trial and error. But never before have so many concerned themselves with the task of improving the lot of mankind. It is abundantly clear that it has been a labor well worthwhile.

The Agricultural Revolution in Asia
LESTER R. BROWN

Lester R. Brown is a Senior Fellow with the Overseas Development Council. He has written extensively on world food needs and problems of agricultural development. This paper was taken from Foreign Affairs, *July 1968.*

FOR THOSE whose thinking of Asia is conditioned by the food crises of 1965 and 1966, the news of an agricultural revolution may come as a surprise. But the change and ferment now evident in the Asian countryside stretching from Turkey to the Philippines, and including the pivotal countries of India and Pakistan, cannot be described as anything less. This rural revolution, largely obscured in its early years by the two consecutive failures of the monsoon, is further advanced in some countries—Pakistan, the Philippines, and India—than in others, but there is little prospect that it will abort, so powerful and pervasive are the forces behind it.

That the agricultural revolution of the less developed world began in Asia is fortunate, since it is densely populated and has a rapid rate of population growth. In this respect, Asia is unique among the world's major geographic regions. Western Europe is heavily populated but its population grows slowly; Latin America's population is expanding rapidly but as yet most of the region is sparsely populated. Of the world's 3.3 billion people, 56 percent live in Asia; one-third of the world's population, an estimated 1.1 billion, live in Asia outside China. It is this part of the world and this third of mankind that this article deals with.

Historically, as Asia's population increased, it was supported by traditional agriculture on an ever expanding area of cropland. As the post-war population explosion gained momentum in the late 1950s and early 1960s, the supply of new land was used up, but the productivity of land under cultivation increased little. The result was a slowdown in the rate of gain in food production and a growing concern that population growth and food production were on a collision course.

The gravity of the situation came into focus as the monsoon on the Indian subcontinent failed two years running, in 1965 and 1966. The United States responded by shipping the equivalent of nearly one-fifth of its wheat harvest, feeding 60 million Indians for nearly two years. This record shipment, the largest ever between two countries, was sufficient to stave off famine.

As of mid-1968, both the food situation and food production prospects in Asia have changed almost beyond belief. The Philippines is self-sufficient in its staple food, rice, for the first time since 1903. Iran, with a substantial expansion in wheat acreage, is actually a net exporter of wheat this year. Ceylon's rice harvest climbed 13 percent above the previous record, as it both expanded the area under cultivation and raised yields.

Pakistan's wheat crop, harvested in April and May, is estimated to be 30 percent above the previous record. So is India's. The total Indian foodgrain crop, officially estimated at 100 million tons, is up 32 percent from last year's drought depressed levels and, more important, up 12 percent from the previous record. Good weather has helped boost the harvest on the Indian subcontinent this year, but increases above the previous record are largely the results of solid technological progress—more efficient varieties, more fertilizer, and better farm practices.

What has caused this remarkable turnabout? One factor is new political commitments at the top in several countries. Short-changing agriculture is no longer either feasible or fashionable. This new political climate has led to firm allocations of budgetary and foreign exchange resources. India, for example, increased its budget for agricultural development by one-third in 1966–67; it is now using the equivalent of nearly one-fifth of its foreign exchange earnings to import fertilizer and raw materials for manufacturing fertilizer. Turkey's imports of fertilizer may make up the largest single item in overall imports this year, exceeding for the first time petroleum and petroleum products. The availability of fertilizer in Pakistan is twice that of two years ago and several times that of 1960; it is expected at least to double again by 1970.

Many governments which heretofore neglected agriculture have been encouraged to give agriculture a higher priority by the "short tether" policy of the United States, whereby food aid agreements are of short duration and renewal depends on local effort and performance. The overall scarcity of foodgrains, particularly rice, in many Asian countries increased prices to the point where it suddenly became very profitable for large numbers of farmers to use fertilizer and other modern inputs.

While some factories contributing to the takeoff in agriculture are of recent origin, others have been long in the making. The agricultural infrastructure is capable of supporting current advances because of several years of AID investment in farm-to-market roads, in irrigation projects, and in agricultural research and training. Investment in irrigation systems over the years provides a vast acreage of well watered land, much of it well suited to the intensive use of modern farm technology. Adequate supplies of water and fertilizer are needed to attain high yields. The training of some 4,000 Asian agriculturists over the past decade, sponsored jointly by AID, the U.S. Department of Agriculture and the Land Grant Universities, contributes to a corps of trained professionals capable of adapting and disseminating new technology.

The availability of fertilizer has increased severalfold over the past decade, partly as a result of expanding indigenous production and partly because of steadily rising imports. The financing of fertilizer imports is now a major AID activity, requiring a sizable portion of the agency's budget. Investment by fertilizer manufacturers and other supporting industries has helped to fuel the takeoff in agricultural production. Countries in which U.S. firms have built or are building fertilizer plants include South Korea, the Philippines, Taiwan, India, Iran, and Malaysia. Fertilizer produced in these plants could increase the region's annual food producing capability by an estimated 25 million tons of grain. Other agrobusiness activities such as the manufacture of pesticides and farm equipment are also contributing to the rapid growth in food production.

Perhaps the most exciting development is the rapid spread of new, high yielding varieties of cereals. The Mexican wheats now proving so adaptable throughout Asia are the product of more than twenty years of work by the Rockefeller Foundation. Efficient new rice varieties are coming principally from the International Rice Research Institute in the Philippines, an institution founded jointly by the Rockefeller and Ford Foundations in 1962 and devoted solely to the improvement of rice production in the tropics and subtropics. Work on high yielding varieties of corn, sorghum, and millet is concentrated in India, where the Rockefeller Foundation is providing leadership for the program. Areas planted to the new varieties went from a few hundred acres in 1964-65 to about 23,000 acres in 1965-66, nearly 4 million acres in 1966-67, and over 20 million acres during 1967-68, the crop year just ended. Plans and expectations indicate a further expansion of up to 40 million acres in the coming year.

Several factors are responsible for this rapid gain in acreage. The new varieties often double yields of traditional varieties; their superiority is so obvious that farmers are quickly persuaded of their merits. This contrasts sharply with improved varieties made available in the past, which were only marginally superior to varieties being used. Another reason is the degree to which the high yields attained on the experimental plots are transferable to field conditions. There are reports of instances in which farmers actually attained higher yields under field conditions with large acreages than researchers did on experimental plots.

The availability of these new seeds has enabled many Asian countries to shorten materially the agricultural development process. The importing of numerous varieties in small quantities for testing purposes was in itself an effort to achieve a shortcut; food deficit countries availed themselves of the results of plant breeding work undertaken elsewhere. But they did not stop there. Once it was demonstrated that a given high yielding variety was adapted to local growing conditions, large tonnages of seed were imported, thus eliminating the several years required to multiply and accumulate sufficient supplies of seed locally.

Pakistan imported 42,000 tons of seed wheat from Mexico during 1967, enough to plant 1.5 million acres. As a result, Pakistan now has enough seed to plant its entire wheat acreage to Mexican wheats. India imported 18,000 tons of Mexican wheats in 1966. This, coupled with indigenous multiplication of seed from the initial introduction of the same varieties, enabled Indian farmers to plant 8 million acres this year—the target acreage for 1970-71, and more than double the target of 3.5 million acres for 1967-68. Turkey, starting later than India or Pakistan but determined to catch up, imported 21,000 tons of high yielding wheat, including some U.S. varieties, for use on a much smaller acreage. Both the import of samples of the new varieties initially, and the larger shipments later, represent a massive infusion of a new technology at a nominal cost, with potentially widespread application. They constitute a windfall gain in food production for many of the less developed countries.

The new varieties possess several distinctive characteristics. They are almost all short stemmed, so they can absorb large quantities of fertilizer without lodging (becoming topheavy and falling down); they are much more responsive to fertilizer at all levels of application. A given amount of fertilizer produces a much greater increase in yield than with the older varieties of grain. And unlike high yielding varieties of cereals developed in the United States or Japan for rather specific growing conditions, these varieties are adapted to a much broader range of latitudes.

The new varieties of rice are early maturing, ripening in 120 to 125 days compared with 150 to 180 days for the older varieties. They are also rather insensitive to the length of daylight and thus can be planted at any time of the year if the prevailing temperature and water supply permit. With adequate water, some farmers in the Philippines and India are harvesting two or even three crops each year. Where water supplies are not sufficient to grow rice during the dry season, farmers grow high yielding hybrid grain sorghums or hybrid corn. Triple cropping of rice, or rice in combination with sorghum or corn, is resulting in yields under field conditions as high as 8 tons of grain an acre each calendar year. This contrasts with average yearly rice yields in Japan of just over 2 tons an acre and wheat yields in Europe of less than 2 tons an acre. The introduction of the early maturing Mexican wheats in northern India and Pakistan is permitting the double cropping of wheat and corn, with wheat grown during the *rabi* (winter) season and corn during the *kharif* (summer) season.

Introduction of the new varieties is changing not only the technology of production but also the economics. The potentially far reaching economic implications of the agricultural revolution are only now becoming clear. Projected demand for agricultural inputs such as fertilizer, pesticides, water, and irrigation equipment must be recalculated. Many of the assumptions underlying current strategies of agricultural development must also be reexamined. For example, in the short run, the profitability of using fertilizer will increase demand above what it would otherwise have been. Over the longer run, however, the demand for fertilizer may be lower than would otherwise be the case since a smaller amount of fertilizer will be required on the more responsive varieties to reach a given level of production.

High rates of return on investments in production inputs, reflecting a more favorable economic climate due to better prices for farm products and more efficient new technologies, are mobilizing rural savings not previously available for production purposes. Investment is on the rise not only in those things which increase output in the short run, such as fertilizer, but also in those which boost food producing capability over the long run, such as tubewells and irrigation pumps. Over the course of five years, Pakistani farmers in the cotton and rice growing areas of the former Punjab, where the water table is quite near the surface, have installed some 32,000 private tubewells, costing from $1,100 to $2,500 each. The value of the supplementary irrigation made possible by these wells is such that farmers characteristically have paid for them in two years. A large proportion was installed without government assistance or subsidy of any kind. The number of low-lift pumps installed in East Pakistan, totaling 2,200 in 1965, is expected to increase to 14,000 by 1969, greatly increasing the potential for double cropping rice during the dry season. Similar high rates of return on small scale irrigation investments are reported in India, where the number of wells is also climbing at an astronomical rate.

Early maturing varieties of rice which ripen during the monsoon require mechanical drying before storage, since the time-honored method of spreading rice in the roadside to dry is not feasible. The demand for grain drying equipment, now climbing rapidly, was not anticipated. Similarly, the use of pesticides, often uneconomical when average rice yields were 1,000 to 1,500 pounds of milled rice an acre, is suddenly very profitable on the new varieties, averaging 3,000 to 4,000 pounds. Growth in demand for both pesticides and application equipment such as knapsack sprayers and dusters will be closely associated with the spread of the improved seed.

The new varieties, with their potential for multiple cropping, place a premium on fast preparation of the seedbed. Farmers planning to double crop or triple crop their land may no longer have several weeks to prepare the ground with bullocks or water buffalo; they may have to use power driven farm equipment to prepare the seedbed quickly and plant the next crop. Even in some countries where new varieties are not yet widely spread, the profitability and feasibility of farm mechanization are being increasingly recognized. In Thailand, where the movement of goods from farm to market is largely by canal or river, rice fields are prepared principally by water buffalo. Under these circumstances, farmers are discovering it is more economical to hire someone with a tractor to plow the rice fields for a few dollars an acre than to feed and care for a team of water buffalo all year just to use them for a few weeks at plowing time. Some 20,000 to 25,000 imported tractors plowed an estimated one-fourth of the rice acreage this past year, mostly on a custom-hire basis—not unlike the way in which wheat is harvested in the Great Plains of the United States.

The more intensive farming methods associated with the new technology require more farm labor. The new varieties will not respond to the traditional practice of planting the crop and then virtually forgetting it until harvest time. Substantial amounts of additional labor must be invested in applying fertilizer, weeding, and the like. Expansion of the area that can be multiple cropped is also resulting in a more effective use of the rural labor supply, particularly during the dry season. In Asia, where underemployed labor constitutes one of the world's largest underutilized resources, this promises a major economic gain. For the first time, there is the possibility of significant labor scarcities in localized rural areas.

Changes associated with the new farm technology have a social as well as an economic impact. The exciting new cereal varieties are so superior to the traditional varieties and so dramatic in their impact that they are becoming "engines of change" wherever used. They may be to the agricultural revolution in Asia what the steam engine was to the industrial revolution in Europe.

Successful adoption of the new seed requires the simultaneous adoption of new cultural practices and the use of modern inputs. The seasonal rhythm of rural activity, once determined largely by the monsoon, is changing as farmers begin to double crop and to introduce new combinations of crops. Farmers taking advantage of the new technology must enter the market; they cannot remain subsistence farmers. Rural Asians will change and innovate—when it is to their advantage to do so. Significantly, there may be some spinoff from this breakthrough in agriculture, this initial break with tradition. Family planners should take heart. As farmers learn that they can indeed influence their destiny, they may become much more susceptible to family planning and other equally "radical" departures.

Not all changes wrought by the new technology are desirable. In some areas, tenants are being reduced to farm laborers as landowners discover the profitability of the new technology in the current economic setting. Even though income to the landless may rise, the socioeconomic gap between the landowners and the landless may widen. Dissidents among the landless group in some states in India now form the nucleus of the opposition parties. Among those who own land, the income gap between those owning fertile, well watered land and those with marginal land is also likely to widen. While many of the former may easily triple or quadruple output, the latter may not be able to employ the new technology at all. Those who can, and are thus permitted to enter the market, are likely to become more vocal and more interested in influencing the economic policies affecting their fortunes in the marketplace. Political activization of rural populations is an expected concomitant of the agricultural revolution now under way.

The leadership in most Asian countries is not unaware of the political implications of recent changes in rural areas. Prime Minister Demirel of Turkey feels strongly enough about the crash program in wheat production, initiated at his behest less than two years ago, to have it directed and monitored from his office. Some observers think President Marcos of the Philippines, who has brought his country to self-sufficiency in rice by emphasizing rural development, may be the first President of the Philippines ever to be reelected to office. Former Prime Minister Maiwandwal of Afghanistan was so impressed with the production potential of the Mexican wheats and with the urgent need to arrest Afghanistan's growing dependence on imported wheat that he assessed each of the Ministries 2.5 percent of its current year's development budget to create a fund to launch an accelerated wheat production program. Two years later, the Afghans appear to be progressing toward their goal of self-sufficiency in wheat. President Ayub of Pakistan shows a deep personal interest in the agricultural programs under way in his country and follows their progress on an almost daily basis. India's progressive C. Subramaniam, former Food and Agriculture Minister, took advantage of the food crisis to mobilize support for and launch the accelerated food production effort responsible for much of India's gain.

Recent agricultural progress should not induce complacency. Many difficult problems lie ahead, especially in the fields of farm credit, water development, plant disease, foreign exchange availability, marketing, and price incentives.

Purchases of farm inputs are often concentrated initially among the larger farmers who are able to finance their own purchases. The rate at which small farmers adopt new technologies is frequently determined by the availability of farm credit on reasonable terms. If, like the great majority of Asian farmers, they are dependent on the local moneylender for credit, often at interest rates ranging from 20 to 100 percent a year, they may not find it profitable to use modern inputs such as fertilizer. Available evidence indicates that fertilizer distribution in some parts of India and West Pakistan is beginning to slow because of a lack of credit.

Intensive cultivation of the new high yielding varieties requires, in addition to an adequate supply of water, a far more sophisticated system of water control and management. At present, not more than one-third of Asia's rice land is considered suitable for the new short stemmed rice varieties. Excessive and erratic flooding during the monsoon or rainy season is not conducive to the intensive cultivation of rice, which requires hand-weeding and the use of fertilizer and pesticides. Either too little or too much water can be damaging.

Associated with the massive introduction of exogenous varieties is the risk that some local insect or disease could suddenly wipe out the entire acreage, thus creating possible famine not unlike that occurring in Ireland more than a century ago. The worst of this threat may have passed, however, for the number of new varieties has already reduced dependence on any single one. Each year that passes should make the threat less dangerous.

Rice production during the dry season, once limited by the lack of varieties adapted to the off season, is now limited by a lack of water. This can be remedied either by developing underground water resources, which are quite abundant in some areas, or by using pumps to lift water from the numerous rivers and canals that flow through many of the rice growing areas during the dry season. The exploitation of unused water resources will expand the acreage suitable for planting the high yielding rices. Few, if any, developing countries are endowed with all the raw materials needed for manufacture of chemical fertilizers—phosphate rock, potash, sulfur, and natural gas or naphtha. As the use of fertilizer expands, many countries, chronically faced with a scarcity of foreign exchange, are hard pressed to find enough hard currency for the required imports. For some individual countries, such as India, this scarcity of foreign exchange could effectively reduce the rate of agricultural progress.

Frustrating though these problems may be, the dominant constraint on agricultural growth is likely to be inadequate marketing systems and an overall lack of markets. The recent emphasis on agricultural development has been concentrated on the expansion of production; marketing has been largely neglected, with the result that some of the promising gains made in production may be negated. Over the past decade many of Asia's large coastal cities—Karachi, Bombay, Madras, Calcutta, Colombo and Djakarta—have become increasingly dependent on imported foodgrains. To become self-sufficient requires not only producing a surplus in the countryside sufficient to feed these cities, but also having a marketing system capable of moving rural surpluses to the cities, when needed. This means farm-to-market roads, storage facilities, and a marketing-intelligence system to rationalize the movement of commodities.

Several Asian countries, such as Pakistan, the Philippines and Turkey, could produce exportable surpluses of grain within the next few years, joining Thailand and Burma. If they do, they must develop the transport and storage facilities needed to move potentially large surpluses of grain from often remote rural areas into world markets. If exportable surpluses develop, there will be mounting pressure on Japan and the EEC countries—where cereal production is often subsidized at prices double the world market price—to reduce subsidies and permit imports.

Problem areas notwithstanding, an agricultural revolution is under way in Asia. The new cereal varieties provide a means for tapping some of the vast, but as yet largely unrealized, food producing potential of the tropics and subtropics, putting them on a more competitive footing with the temperate zone cereal producers. The agricultural breakthrough occurring in several major Asian countries can be repeated in Latin America and Africa. Mexico, which once depended on imports for nearly half its wheat needs, is now exporting small quantities of both wheat and corn. Kenya, until recently a food aid recipient, has produced an exportable surplus of corn, its food staple. Tunisia and Morocco are introducing the Mexican wheats. Much of the technology now being applied in Asia will also be applied in both Latin America and Africa, if the necessary top level political support and proper combination of economic policies are forthcoming.

The farm sector now constitutes from one-third to one-half of most Asian economies. It is conceivable that the 2 percent rate of increase in food production prevailing during the early and mid-1960s could accelerate to 4 or 5 percent yearly over the next few years, provided markets can absorb the additional output. The additional purchasing power thus generated for both production and consumer goods will stimulate a more rapid rate of growth in the nonfarm sector. The net effect should be a much more rapid rate of overall economic growth than would otherwise have prevailed. If the Asian agricultural revolution continues, it could well become the most significant world economic development since the economic rebirth of Europe following World War II.

This agricultural revolution is not the ultimate solution to the food-population problem, but it does buy some much needed additional time in which to mount effective family planning programs. If food scarcity lessens as anticipated in some of the major food deficit countries, governments recently preoccupied with real or impending food crises can again turn their attention to the business of development. Although the need for food aid is likely to lessen sharply within the next few years, capital needs for investment in the agricultural infrastructure are certain to increase. The need for technical assistance seems likely to rise as the problems generated by dynamic movement in agriculture increase. The need for foreign private investment in agrobusiness will also rise sharply as farmers clamor for the inputs they need to take full advantage of the new genetic potentials available to them.

The positive economic effects of an agricultural takeoff in Asian countries are quite evident. What is not so readily realized is that it will bolster the confidence of national leaders in their ability to handle other seemingly insoluble problems. It may also strengthen their faith in modern technology and its potential for improving the well-being of their people.

The Green Revolution: Cornucopia or Pandora's Box?

CLIFTON R. WHARTON, JR.

Clifton R. Wharton, Jr. is an agricultural economist, previously Executive Director of the Agricultural Development Council, now President, Michigan State University. This article was taken from Foreign Affairs, *April 1969.*

THE APPLICATION OF SCIENCE and technology to traditional agriculture has begun to produce dramatic results, above all in Asia. The rapid application of certain food grains in the developing world is being particularly widely heralded, and justly so, as the Green Revolution. The discussion of the phenomenon tends to cluster around two views. On the one hand, some observers now believe that the race between food and population is over, that the new agricultural technology constitutes a cornucopia for the developing world, and that victory is in sight in the "War on Hunger." Others see this development as opening a Pandora's box; its very success will produce a number of new problems which are far more subtle and difficult than those faced during the development of the new technology. It is important to give careful attention and critical analysis to both interpretations in order to be optimistic about the promise of the Green Revolution where justified, and at the same time to prepare for the problems that are now emerging. The Green Revolution offers an unparalleled opportunity to break the chains of rural poverty in important parts of the world. Success will depend upon how well the opportunity is handled and upon how alert we are to the inherent consequences.

It is now generally believed that major technological breakthroughs in food production have lifted the spectre of famine in the immediate future and postponed the prospect of Malthusian population disaster. Startling developments have been accomplished in wheat, rice, and corn—major food staples in much of the developing world. The possibilities for doubling or even tripling production are based upon new high-yield varieties coupled with adequate supplies of water, fertilizer, pesticides, and modern equipment. Overnight, the image of agriculture in the developing countries has changed from that of an economic backwater to that of a major potential contributor to overall development. The new varieties are rapidly spreading both within countries and across national boundaries. A recent estimate of the International Agricultural Development Service of the U.S. Department of Agriculture reveals that in Asia alone the estimated acreage planted with these new high yield varieties rose from 200 acres in 1964–65 to 20 million in 1967–68. Traditional food importing nations like the Philippines and Pakistan are becoming self-sufficient and have the prospect of becoming net food exporters.

It will be no easy task to achieve the potential increased production offered by the new technology, particularly when it involves millions upon millions of diverse farms and farmers scattered over the countryside. If the increased production is in fact obtained, this will automatically produce a whole new set of second generation problems which must be faced if development is to be sustained and accelerated. Therefore, two considerations need to be borne in mind. First, there is reason to believe that the further spread of new varieties will not be as fast as early successes might suggest. Second, the new problems arising from the spread of the new technology, whatever its speed, need to be foreseen and acted upon now. The probable developments in each case have the greatest significance for economic growth and for the conduct of international relations.

The reasons for believing that the new technology will not in fact spread nearly as widely or as rapidly as supposed and predicted include, first, the fact that the availability of irrigated land imposes at least a short run limit to the spread of the new high yield varieties. Most of these require irrigation and careful water control throughout the growing cycle. In most Asian countries about one-fourth to one-half of the rice lands are irrigated; the remainder are dependent upon monsoons and seasonal rains. The speed with which additional land can be converted to the new technology depends on the rapidity with which new irrigation facilities can be constructed; and here the high capital costs are likely to be a retarding factor.

Large scale irrigation projects can seriously strain the investment capacity of developing nations. For example, the massive Mekong River development scheme, involving Laos, Cambodia, Vietnam, and Thailand, has been estimated to require a capital investment over the next 20 years of about $2 billion, roughly 35 percent of the annual national income of the four countries involved and exceeding the annual net new investment of all the countries of Southeast Asia combined. Further, significant additional costs are involved in converting existing irrigation systems to the requirements of modern agriculture. Many of the old gravity irrigation systems were not designed to provide the sophisticated water controls demanded by the new varieties. (For example, each plot must be controlled separately throughout the growing season.)

Second, there are doubts about the ability of existing markets to handle the increased product. Storage facilities and transport are inadequate and crop grading often deficient. Not only must the marketing system be expanded to handle a larger output, there also is an increased need for farm supplies and equipment. Fertilizers, pesticides, and insecticides must be available in the right quantities, at the right times, and in the right places. Given the inadequacy of the agricultural infrastructure, the need to expand and modernize marketing systems is likely to reduce the pace of the Revolution.

Because many of the new varieties, especially of rice, do not appeal to the tastes of most consumers, it is difficult to calculate the size of the market. Some argue that until newer varieties which are closer to popular tastes are developed, the market will be limited.

Third, the adoption of the new technology is likely to be much slower where the crop is a basic food staple, grown by a farmer for family consumption. Such farmers are understandably reluctant to experiment with the very survival of their families. Peasant producers are obviously far more numerous in the developing world than are commercial farmers, and the task of converting them to a more modern technology is considerably more difficult. So far, spectacular results have been achieved primarily among the relatively large commercial farmers. Some semisubsistence farmers have begun to grow the new varieties, but the rate at which they adopt them may be slower.

Fourth, farmers must learn new farming skills and develop

expertise of a higher order than was needed in traditional methods of cultivation. The new agronomic requirements are quite different as regards planting dates and planting depths; fertilizer rates and timing; insecticide, pesticide and fungicide applications; watering; and many others. Unless appropriate extension measures are taken to educate farmers with respect to these new farming complexities, the higher yields will not be obtained.

Fifth, many of the new varieties are nonphotosensitive and the shorter term will allow two or three crops a year instead of one. Multiple cropping is good, but there may be difficulties if the new harvest comes during the wet season without provision having been made for mechanical drying of the crop to replace the traditional sun drying. In addition, there may be resistance if the new harvest pattern conflicts with religious or traditional holidays which have grown up around the customary agricultural cycles.

Sixth, failure to make significant institutional reforms may well be a handicap. There is evidence in several Latin American countries that a failure to make needed changes in policies now detrimental to agriculture, or a reluctance to effectuate the institutional reforms required to give real economic incentives to small farmers and tenants, has been primarily responsible for the very slow spread of Mexico's success with new varieties of wheat and corn to its neighbors to the south.

From all this one may deduce that the "first" or "early" adopters of the new technology will be in regions which are already more advanced, literate, responsive, and progressive, and which have better soil, better water management, closer access to roads and markets—in sum, the wealthier, more modern farmers. For them, it is easier to adopt the new higher yield varieties since the financial risk is less and they already have better managerial skills. When they do adopt them, the doubling and trebling of yields mean a corresponding rise in their incomes. One indication of this is the large number of new private farm management consultant firms, in the Philippines, which are advising large landlords on the use of the new seed varieties and making handsome profits out of their share of the increased output.

As a result of different rates in the diffusion of the new technology, the richer farmers will become richer. In fact, it may be possible that the more progressive farmers will capture food markets previously served by the smaller semisubsistence producer. In India, only 20 percent of the total area planted to wheat in 1967–68 consisted of the new dwarf wheats, but they contributed 34 percent of the total production. Such a development could well lead to a net reduction in the income of the smaller, poorer, and less venturesome farmers. This raises massive problems of welfare and equity. If only a small fraction of the rural population moves into the modern century while the bulk remains behind, or perhaps even goes backward, the situation will be highly explosive. For example, Tanjore district in Madras, India, has been one of the prize areas where the new high yield varieties have been successfully promoted. Yet one day last December, 43 persons were killed in a clash there between the landlords and their landless workers, who felt that they were not receiving their proper share of the increased prosperity brought by the Green Revolution.

Other experts argue that the new technology's stimulus to production and income cannot be stemmed. It is true that the rapidity with which the new seed varieties have spread in country after country belies the customary view of an inert, unresponsive peasantry. In 1965, India began a program of high yield varieties which set a goal of 32.5 million acres by 1970–71; last year's crop season saw 18 million acres already planted, which contributed to the most successful year in recent Indian agricultural history (some 100 million tons of food grains, 11 million over the previous record year of 1964–65). Self-sufficiency in food grains is predicted in three or four years. Other countries are experiencing similar situations where the demand for the new seeds is outstripping the available supplies and black markets are even developing in seeds and fertilizer.

Nevertheless, if we assume that the new varieties will continue to live up to expectations and spread rapidly and widely, the increased production will in turn lead to a new set of difficulties. First, large tracts planted in one of the new varieties may be susceptible to disease and infestation which could cause massive losses. Heretofore, reliance upon seed selected by individual farmers meant that neighboring farms growing the same crop usually planted two or more different varieties or strains. This heterogeneity provided a built-in protection against widespread plant diseases, since not all varieties are equally susceptible. But where a single variety is introduced, covering large contiguous areas, the dangers of pathologic susceptibility are multiplied. For example, the new wheat introduced from Mexico into the Indo-Gangetic belt in India and Pakistan has involved a small range of genotypes—and the same has been true in Iran, Turkey, and certain Middle Eastern countries. Any change in the spectrum of races of wheat rust in any of these countries could threaten the wheat crop on a massive scale, since it would involve the entire area.

Two steps are necessary to avoid these dangers: first, a diversified breeding program which can continually produce new varieties; second, an able and well-organized plant protection service which can quickly identify dangerous outbreaks and initiate prompt steps to combat them. Both activities must rely primarily upon national organizations rather than the regional or international ones. Both demand a skilled, well-trained staff. Some nations have recognized these dangers and are taking steps to meet them, but others still have not been made sufficiently aware. Aid givers—public and private—who are responsible for promoting the new varieties bear an equal responsibility to promote indigenous research and plant protection services. The outbreak of any major disease which wipes out the harvest of thousands of farmers is far more likely to be blamed on the producers and spreaders of the miracle seed than on Fate. Agricultural development could be set back several decades.

Next, it is vitally important to expand the entire complex of services and industries required to achieve the higher production. Any government or foreign aid agency which distributes the "miracle" seed but fails to provide the insecticide and fertilizer in the appropriate quantities when and where needed is courting political disaster; unless these inputs are available and used, some local, traditional varieties will outyield the new ones. A seed industry, agricultural chemical plants, processing and storage firms, factories producing hand sprayers, dusters, water pumps and engines—these are just a few of the agriculturally related industries which must develop if the Green Revolution is to take hold.

The skills and the capital needed cannot be provided solely by the public sector. Private capital must also be utilized. In a few countries the spread of the new technologies has already forced an abrupt departure from the previous practice of having government agencies serve as the major or sole distributor of the required inputs. Private industry, especially American, has stepped in to provide a new, more dynamic pattern of distribution. In the Philippines, for example, ESSO has become a major distributor of fertilizer and agricultural chemicals. Frequently, such ventures have involved links with local firms. In India, the International Minerals and Chemicals Corporation, with the Standard Oil Company of California, built a fertilizer plant with a yearly capacity of 365,000 tons; the U.S. firms provide the management but control is held by an Indian firm. Storage silos, seed multiplication firms, and even integrated farm-to-retail firms are just a few of the activities for which private U.S. resources are being harnessed to serve the Green Revolution.

Equally important are the increased farm services which are required, particularly agricultural credit. For example, from studies conducted at the International Rice Research Institute, it is estimated that whereas the total cash costs of production for the average Filipino rice farmer using traditional methods and varieties is about $20 a hectare, the cost rises to $220 when the new, high yielding IR-8 is grown. Although the yield may increase threefold, leading to a net return four times greater than with traditional varieties, the farmer must have access to substantially greater credit to finance his operations. Especially for the poorer farmers with low cash reserves who may want to adopt the new varieties, the village moneylender and merchant will not be adequate unless they in turn have access to additional funds. Indeed, the Green Revolution must be accompanied both by an increase in the amount of credit available and by the expansion and modernization of credit institutions and mechanisms. Tapping the capital markets in the modern urban sector must be encouraged, and ways must be found at the village level to mobilize local capital, especially the increased savings which are possible from higher farm incomes. The Green Revolution will generate increased cash which, if properly marshalled, can contribute to capital formation and agricultural progress.

Third, much more attention must be devoted to marketing the increased output. Where there has been semisubsistence agriculture, the impact of the new technology upon the *marketed* product is even greater than on total production. If the crop is a food staple and if the peasant farm family traditionally consumes some 70 to 80 percent of its total product each year, a doubling of output does not lead to a doubling in the amount retained for family consumption. Some modest increase in consumption is likely, but the bulk of the increased production will enter the market. Thus a doubling in yields in a semisubsistence agriculture usually leads to much more than a doubling of the amount sold.

The impact of this explosive increase upon the traditional marketing network and storage capacity can be calamitous. The case of India is illustrative. During the past crop year, India experienced a marvelous increase in food grain production, but the marketing network and storage facilities were not prepared to cope with it. The result can be seen in the mountains of food grain stored in schools and in the open air under conditions which are apt to reduce if not negate the gains. The food deficit psychology which underlies the failure of planners and policymakers to anticipate these results is not limited to the developing nations. Aid givers were equally surprised. Strangely, the lessons of the Indian experience did not yet seem to have affected the thinking and planning of other nations which are promoting the new technology.

Fourth, the slowness with which the food deficit psychology dies also has an important consequence in terms of government pricing policies. The fact that agriculture, even semisubsistence agriculture, does respond to price, is only gradually becoming accepted. But the shock which quantum jumps in food production may have on domestic prices has not been sufficiently appreciated. The downward pressure on prices, especially where transport is deficient and storage is inadequate, may in fact be so severe as to have a disincentive effect upon producers. Unless adequate attention is given to developing a sound pricing policy to prevent excessive dampening of incentives, the spread of the new technology may in fact be cut short before any takeoff has occurred. Premature discouragement could produce a reversion leading to a slowing up in food production or even a rejection of the new technology.

It has been amply demonstrated throughout the world that peasant and subsistence farmers are responsive to favorable prices, provided the return is real and they receive the benefit. For example, from 1951–53 through 1961–63, the farmers of Thailand in response to favorable prices increased their exports of corn at an average annual compounded rate of 35.8 percent; casava, 25.0 percent; and kenaf, 43.8 percent. Filipino farmers responded to a governmental price support program for tobacco by changing from native to Virginia tobacco and then booming production from 3 million kilos in 1954 to over 30 million kilos in 1962. The list of crops where peasant farmers have responded to favorable prices is large—rubber, oil palm, coffee, jute, wheat, barley, sorghum, millet, gram, cotton. Thus, if the full potential offered by the new technology is to be realized, every effort must be made to insure that there is in fact a significant return to the producer and that the rapid rise in output does not lead to a counterproductive slump in prices.

Fifth, the goals of increased food production are frequently couched in terms of some desirable, minimal standards of nutrition. Such nutritional goals are commendable, but they can be attained only by individuals who have the income with which to purchase the better diet. Effective demand for food depends upon both the income of the demanders and the price of the food. If the increased production leads to lower costs and prices, then consumers will be able to increase their food purchases and hopefully to raise their levels of nutrition. Equally important is the need to increase incomes so that the greater production entering the market can be purchased. The food problem in a developing world is both a problem of production and supply and a problem of demand and income. Unless the higher levels of effective demand materialize, the prospect will be market gluts, price depression, and in certain cases, shifts by the farmers away from the higher yielding varieties. Hence, every effort must be made both to reduce the unit costs of the increased food output and to augment the incomes of consumers who purchase food; otherwise, the second bowl of rice will not be bought—despite the technical feasibility of producing it.

Sixth, one of the major avowed aims of most nations which are eagerly promoting the Green Revolution is to achieve self-sufficiency in food production. In Southeast Asia, for example, the Philippines already claims to have become self-sufficient. Malaysia predicts that she will be self-sufficient by 1971; Indonesia by

1973. Some believe that these target dates are overly optimistic. But if the rice deficit nations of the region such as Malaysia, Indonesia, and the Philippines eventually become self-sufficient by successfully adopting the new technology, what will happen to the rice surplus nations like Burma and Thailand whose economies are heavily dependent upon rice export? To whom will they sell their rice? Self-sufficiency of presently rice deficit nations will not only be detrimental to the rice exporting nations, but will reduce one of the few areas of economic interdependence in the region. Unless action is taken in advance to offset the predictable impact of the new technology, hopes of promoting regional economic integration will be substantially reduced. Whether or not one agrees with the goal of self-sufficiency for these nations, the policies have been adopted and will be pursued. Many developing nations spend some 30 percent of their foreign exchange on food imports and wish to eliminate this drain as well as the irritation of chronic deficits in domestic production. We should anticipate the predictable consequences of these policies—in this case major economic dislocations in trade—so that we can be equally ready with developmental efforts or foreign assistance to reduce the dimensions of the problem. Unless the exporting nations take immediate stock of their prospects and seek to diversify their agriculture, the impact of such trade distortions could have major consequences for their economies and pace of development.

Seventh, a critical question is whether these technological developments are a "once-and-for-all" phenomenon. How likely is it that new technological improvements will continue to be made? The application of science to agriculture over the last 300 years has resulted in a tenfold increase in yield per acre on the best farmed lands in the temperate zone. This expansion is what led to the production controls introduced by the surplus nations, such as the United States, to keep demand and supply in reasonable balance. Today's Green Revolution is the result of a similar application of science to agriculture in the developing world. But it should be noted that the institutionalized application of science is largely concentrated at present in food crops. Before World War II, primary attention in agricultural research in the developing world was devoted to the major crops—rubber in Malaysia, sugar in the Philippines, coffee in Kenya, palm oil in

Nigeria, coffee in Brazil, bananas in Honduras. Staple food crops were either ignored or received scant attention. Thus the successes of the recent application of science to peasant agriculture could be interpreted as an exploitation of a "technical gap" in food crops left by years of neglect. If current developments merely represent a "catching-up," then as soon as population overtakes current developments, we are back to "square one."

Much will depend upon whether or not the necessary manpower is trained in each country to provide a continuing human resource which can produce a constant stream of new technology. The manpower trained in the Rockefeller Foundation's Mexican program has always been a greater contribution, in my view, than the new varieties. Successful adoption should not deflect attention from the importance and role of continuous agricultural research. The development of indigenous competence to engage in agricultural research is critical and becomes even more critical as the new varieties are adopted. The target should be not *a* new technology but ever-new technology, and this requires skilled manpower.

These are only a few of the possible consequences of the successful spread of the new technology. There are several broader consequences and issues which can be raised only as questions in this brief presentation:

To what extent will the diffusion of the new technology accentuate the displacement of rural people and heighten the pace of migration to the cities? If higher yields per acre as a result of multiple cropping plus mechanization force surplus manpower out of agriculture, what are the prospects for increased employment in industry and services to absorb this manpower?

For the average developing nation the Green Revolution means that instead of devoting two-thirds to three-fourths of its agricultural resources to food production, these resources may now be shifted to other higher paying crops. The question then becomes, what crops and for what markets?

If agriculture becomes more modern, dynamic, and wealthy, will the nonagricultural sector allow agriculture to retain a significant share of this increased income or merely follow the previous patterns of taxing agriculture for nonagricultural development?

What will be the political significance of these changes if successful adoption of the new technology leads to an economically invigorated and strengthened rural population—almost invariably a large majority in developing nations? Will rural based political parties and movements emerge to alter the recent dominance of urban centers?

What will be the global effect of a food explosion in the tropical and subtropical world? Will such developments lead to an improved reallocation of productive specialization among the developed and developing world, or will nationalistic trade barriers continue to flout natural comparative advantages?

One final danger lies in assuming that there is no longer an urgent need for measures to reduce rates of population growth. While the new developments provide a splendid gift of time to allow a holding operation, effective population measures continue to be essential. Whether one assumes a growth rate of 2.5 or 3 percent, the inexorable fact is that, give or take a few years, the population of the developing world will double in about 25 years.

The significance of the food-population problem is more than humanitarian and developmental; it also has critical implications for the conduct of international relations. Relations between nations are often profoundly affected by long run forces over which men can exercise only limited control in the short run. The food-population race is an excellent example of such a set of forces. Predictions regarding both population and food, as well as their interaction over varying lengths of time, must be taken into account in the conduct of developmental assistance, not only by aid giving nations and international organizations, but by the governments of the developing nations themselves. Policies and programs designed to win the race between food and population may have unintended, though often predictable, consequences which could have a very broad impact.

Charles Malik once said, "one of the principal causes of both international conflict and internal strife is unfounded expectations. These are based ultimately either on deception or on a belief in magic." [1] What we have in hand seems to many people to approach magic; let us hope that it does not become the source of deception.

1. Charles H. Malik, "What Shall It Profit A Man?", *Columbia Journal of World Business,* Summer 1966.

To speak of the possible consequences and problems associated with the next phase of the Green Revolution should not be misinterpreted as a plea for the suppression of the Revolution because, like Pandora's box, it will lead to even greater problems than those it was designed to eliminate. On the contrary, I would strongly argue that the list of second-generation problems is a measure of what great opportunities exist for breaking the centuries-old chains of peasant poverty. They also demonstrate how closely interrelated are the various factors which impel or retard agricultural development. This complex interrelationship makes interdisciplinary research and cooperation vital if the current problems are to be solved and future ones anticipated. The most realistic prediction is that each country is likely to experience a different set of these problems and that there will be variations among countries between the two extremes of optimistic and pessimistic prognoses.

The quiet, passive peasant is already aware of the modern world—far more than we realize—and he is impatient to gain his share. The Green Revolution offers him the dramatic possibility of achieving his goal through peaceful means. It has burst with such suddenness that it has caught many unawares. Now is the time to place it in its long range perspective and to engage in contingency planning so that we may respond flexibly and quickly as the Revolution proceeds. Perhaps in this way we can insure that what we are providing becomes a cornucopia, not a Pandora's box.

LDC Employment and Income Distribution
GUSTAV RANIS

This selection by the editor was prepared for the World Bank and will appear in the Bank's Economic Studies Series.

THIS PAPER is in three parts. The first section presents a brief survey of the few known facts on LDC employment and income distribution. Section II summarizes the state of our present understanding of the problem. Section III deals briefly with the possible role of foreign assistance in this context.

I

With respect to the nature and size of the problem, there is general agreement that the LDCs have not performed too badly during the '60s, in terms of overall or even per capita income growth. There is also general agreement that such "good" aggregate performance has concealed increasing disparities in regional rates of growth, income inequalities, and other distributional malfunctionings—with rising unemployment and underemployment rates as a major feature. Even where countries have been growing at 5 or 6 percent annually in real terms and industrial sectors at 10 to 15 percent, the rate of growth of labor efficiently absorbed by the modern commercialized sectors has been on the order of only 2 or 3 percent at maximum. If we deal with manufacturing only, all LDCs taken together experienced growth of manufacturing output in excess of 7 percent from 1955 to 1965 while the rate of labor absorption was just above 4 percent. The latter especially differs greatly by region; for example, industrial labor absorption rates relative to rates of industrial output growth have been higher in Asia than in Latin America (2.5 percent); moreover, these employment elasticities of industrial output have been not only low, but falling everywhere during the past two decades.

With respect to agriculture, Asia stands out as the main labor surplus area suffering intensively from rural underemployment and poverty. Africa and most of Latin America are more favorably endowed with land and natural resources generally. However, recent evidence seems to indicate that rural Africa is beginning to shorten its fallow period and increase the use of fertilizer, while Latin America similarly is beginning to run up against land shortage problems which can be solved only by the heavy application of capital. Moreover, even where efficient jobs still exist in agriculture, the existence of urban-rural wage gaps seems to lead to problems of urban drift. In other words, the problems of unemployment-underemployment and of associated income maldistribution are relevant to a vast preponderance of the LDCs, certainly to more than 90 percent of their populations. Thus, when the low absorptive capacity of manufacturing is coupled with increasing population growth and the existing backlog of underemployment in the agricultural sector, a review of the '50s and '60s leaves us with the unmistakable impression that we have a rather serious sociopolitical as well as an economic problem on our hands.

If we translate this performance of the past into some sort of estimate of the size and magnitude of the problem in the future, we can only become even more concerned. Even if we should be completely "successful" starting tomorrow in reducing population growth to zero as a result of family planning efforts, we must anticipate a serious labor force explosion based on the already existing population over the next 15 years. No matter what happens on the population front, the labor force in most of the developing countries can be expected to grow at rates of 3.5 to 4 percent annually over that period. Contrast that with 2 to 3 percent absorption rates. Clearly, if LDCs stay more or less on present tracks there is little hope of avoiding increases in the backlog of unemployment—never mind mopping it up.

And how large is that backlog? There is a good deal of discussion on the difficulty of measuring the extent of either open or disguised unemployment. Clearly the rates of open unemployment which are obtained through employment exchanges or even sample surveys in the urban centers of the developing world are low estimates, mainly because there is an interaction between the supply of jobs and participation rates. People who despair of finding full-time jobs are unlikely to consider themselves openly unemployed, in our sense of the concept. The case is similar for the underemployed, both urban and rural. In the absence of official unemployment insurance, people are much more likely to consider themselves "employed" whether they are selling a couple of cups of tea a day in the distributive trades and service sectors of the urban centers or performing some small tasks around the rural household. The very meaning of being employed, i.e., the intensity of work, the productivity of work, the hours of work, needs to be redefined in terms of non-Western concepts. Open unemployment is largely irrelevant, even in the cities. Essentially there are only two states, efficient (income equals marginal product) employment and disguised (income exceeds marginal product) unemployment.

We see little point in arguing whether total LDC underemployment and unemployment in existence today [1] is typically 20 percent or 30 percent of the total labor force. We start with the assumption that wherever there are sizable pools of people who are being supported, through informal social security arrangements of one kind or another, so that their income exceeds their contribution to output, there exists a serious economic and social problem which we may call unemployment. The overwhelming question is bound to be if and how enough efficient employment can be generated to accommodate the projected increases in the labor force, not to speak of coping with the already existing backlog of the unemployed.

With respect to income distribution, data are even more difficult to come by. We know that personal income is distributed more unequally in LDCs, taken as a whole, than in DCs, taken as a whole, and that this is true in both the agricultural and the nonagricultural sectors. The reason is mainly a more unequal distribution of assets plus less redistribution through tax and expenditure policies. Moreover, it is not clear whether or not intra-LDC income distribution has markedly worsened over time, while it is obvious that the sensitivity to disparities, in either the interpersonal or interregional dimension, has risen sharply. The safest over time statement on the factual side is that intra-LDC distribution of income has probably worsened somewhat. One source of this increasing income inequality seems to be the in-

1. Somehow added together, either as the full-time unemployment equivalent or, more reasonably, as the total "dead weight" difference between marginal products and wages (or income shares) in both sectors.

creasing size of the wage gap between the subsistence (mainly agricultural) and the commercialized (mainly nonagricultural) sectors. As the nonagricultural sector increases in relative size and since that sector has within itself greater income inequality, the overall distribution of income within LDCs has probably tended to worsen for both these reasons—with some clustering toward the middle ranges.

It should be noted that when there exists a good deal of unemployment in a developing country, combined with a relatively narrow and personalized social security system, with very little tax-cum-expenditures-induced redistribution, unemployment, high income variance, and unequal income distribution all tend to be closely related. Moreover, in addition to this obvious relationship at the lower end of the poverty spectrum, they are likely to be related through the effects of income distribution on output mixes. The more unequal the distribution of income, so the argument runs, the more capital and import intensive the demand of consumers beyond the subsistence level. If there are good empirical reasons to believe that goods and services enjoying a high marginal income elasticity of demand by the rich tend to be characterized by more capital intensive technology, policies ensuring a more equal distribution of income will affect employment favorably by permitting a more labor intensive output mix. Thus, while mortality and illiteracy rates have fallen across the board, income distribution has probably not improved for a number of reasons, and regional income distribution has undoubtedly worsened. There is hardly an LDC which does not exhibit at least a pale version of the North-East Brazil, East Pakistan regional disparity problems.

II

Before we can discuss the nature and scope of possible solutions to the above set of problems it is necessary to summarize the present state of our understanding as derived from research and experience to date. We know that unemployment in the LDCs is by and large caused not by Keynesian deficiencies in effective demand but by supply conditions, i.e., shortages of factors complementary to unskilled labor, such as capital, skilled and managerial labor, and entrepreneurial capacity. A second general point which is emerging more and more clearly is that growth and employment must be viewed as of one piece and that the common (at least implicit) assumption that they must be competitive regardless of the policy setting is likely to be wrong. Finally, we have increasingly come to recognize that our analysis—and therefore the policies which follow from the analysis—must be sensitive to the type of developing economy we are talking about. India, a large domestically oriented economy, must be analyzed differently from Taiwan, a small, open economy. A country's current phase of development must be viewed in historical perspective; Taiwan in the fifties differs from Taiwan in the sixties.

The garden variety of LDCs may be characterized as open and labor surplus in which the main problem is to reallocate underemployed labor and savings from the large agricultural hinterland to the small, fully employed, nonagricultural sector with the help of trade. The time phasing is relevant with respect to both changes in the underlying resource endowment conditions and the changing appropriateness of alternative policy packages.

The first or import substitution phase is normally fuelled by raw material and other agricultural and land-based exports, plus foreign aid. Here the typical policy package consists of exchange controls, import licensing, budget deficits, overvalued exchange rates, and low interest rates, usually resulting in a substantial spurt in industrial growth accompanied by the discouragement of agriculture and exports, relatively low domestic savings, low rates of technology change, and low rates of efficient industrial labor absorption. Unemployment and income distribution, regional or personal, are neglected. The main objective is to force resources into infrastructure and the large scale industrial sector, while buying time for industrial entrepreneurial maturation.

The well-known severe distortion of relative factor and output prices during this period yields unnecessarily capital intensive techniques and output mixes. On the issue of industrial employment, for example, maximum utilization of the factor endowments—specifically maximum use of surplus labor—has to take a back seat as long as capital and imports are undervalued and receipt of an import license or a bank loan bestows large windfall profits and becomes the major objective of entrepreneurial activity. The tools employed in the pursuit of industrialization during this phase *ipso facto* create barriers between the endowment and prices so that LDCs obtain larger industrial outputs at the expense not only of lower industrial employment but also of lower output and employment in the economy as a whole.

To the extent that import substitution is a necessary historical phase one should, of course, distinguish between good and bad forms of it, e.g., tariffs are better than quotas, and cases of flexible, i.e., downward trending, protective regimes are better than inflexible or rigid regimes. The main point here, however, is that the record of the last two decades is a poor basis for judging the inevitability of a conflict between employment and output objectives; it may be seriously misleading with respect to the future, given the policy package which obtained in most of the developing world during the '50s and '60s and, in fact, continues to dominate in most. Especially in the labor surplus economy context, it is easy to document the possibility of increasing both total employment and output and moving towards a more equitable distribution of income at the same time. But this is likely to occur only as the country moves into a second, export substituting phase with the help of a new policy package.

The latter phase is characterized by the shift from a raw material to an unskilled labor based pattern of development, mainly through the exportation of labor intensive, nontraditional industrial products. To permit the economy to be thus responsive to a changing endowment picture, a different policy package is required, entailing substantial readjustments in the previously distorted relative prices (exchange rates, interest rates, internal terms of trade). Deficits are reduced, inflation is curbed, and more people become involved as markets are rediscovered. Exports and agriculture are no longer discriminated against. Technology change and employment come to the fore.

The empirical record of countries like Korea and Taiwan over the past decade (and that of Japan historically) indicates that once direct controls in various markets are replaced by a more market oriented allocation (e.g., tariffs plus close to equilibrium exchange rates for quantitative restrictions), the whole structure of the economy and its performance in relation to output and employment generation can change rather dramatically. The agricultural sector can begin to play its proper historical role of generating productivity increases and surpluses which, when successfully channeled into the commercialized nonagricultural sector, can provide employment opportunities for the surplus unskilled labor force. A more broadly based industrial development pattern, with indigenous labor using technology and output mixes assuming a much greater importance, begins to take over. In consequence of the new policy package, the reallocation of agricultural workers in both Taiwan and Korea (as well as historical Japan) proceeded at a much more rapid clip, leading to a decline from 56 percent of the labor force in Taiwan's agriculture in 1953 to 40 percent in 1968, and from 65.9 to 52.5 percent in Korea over the same period.[2] Meanwhile, the increase of manufacturing employment rose from 4.3 percent annually in 1955–65 (import substitution) to 8.2 percent annually in 1966–68 (export substitution) in Taiwan. In Korea, the rate of annual labor absorption by the industrial sector reached 13.3 percent during the middle sixties.

At the aggregative performance level, Korea's overall growth up to the early '60s was just about enough to keep up with population growth, while savings rates were negligible or even negative. As a consequence of substantial devaluation in 1964, import liberalization, and in the following year, a major interest rate reform (i.e., a doubling of rates), a major transformation took place. Not only were domestic savings allocated more efficiently, as the huge gap between low official rates and astronomical curb rates was closed, but the total volume of savings increased dramatically, to the 15 percent range in recent years. Exports which had grown at annual rates of less than 15 percent have been growing at 30 to 40 percent ever since. Per capita incomes, rising at 1.6 percent annually in 1955–66, are now growing at rates of 8 to 10 percent. A similar story can be told for Taiwan. Thus, all the current talk, based largely on a review of performance in the import substituting '60s, of having to "dethrone the GNP" in favor of employment may be quite premature; it is much more sensible to consider building a "better," more labor intensive throne for the GNP.

2. In these cases this meant absolute reductions in the size of the agricultural labor force. Few other LDCs did as well—most continued to exhibit import substitution symptoms. All LDCs taken together reduced their agricultural working populations from 73.3 percent to 70.7 percent of the total during the '50s and at approximately the same rate in the '60s—with agriculture having to absorb most of the increase in the labor force.

This central point can perhaps be best illustrated in terms of the conflict usually cited between industrial labor productivity, which is assumed to be a good thing, and employment, also a good thing. If one wants higher labor productivity, one must permit employment to fall; if one wants full employment, one can only get it at the price of lower labor productivity. That statement is not only unexceptionable, but also tautologically true. As output per worker goes up, the number of workers per unit of output always falls, and it looks as if the conflict we often hear about is established. However, it is important to recall that we are usually talking about an economy in which we have a relatively small commercialized nonagricultural sector, engaging perhaps 10 or 20 percent of the labor force, surrounded by a large ocean of subsistence agriculture, and "soft" portions of the nonagricultural sector, e.g., services and distributive trades, characterized by underemployment. The question then arises as to whether the level or rate of increase of labor productivity on that small island is really a meaningful criterion in terms of any possible objective of the economy. If, for the sake of illustration, we choose the most advanced modern technology cooperating with a few hundred workers for our industrial island, this would of course guarantee tremendous labor productivity. Alternatively, if we spread the same capital over several thousand workers in the form of much less glamorous, labor intensive types of capital structures, labor productivity (or per capita income) of workers on the island would be much lower, but there would now be many more of them, as more of the underemployed could be put to productive work. As a consequence, the *total* output and employment generated in cooperation with the scarce capital stock in the economy as a whole, i.e., overall per capita income, is much higher, even though the productivity *of those who are employed* is much lower. This remains true, as long as the labor surplus condition persists. Once the reallocation of workers from the noncommercialized to the commercialized sectors has proceeded at a sufficiently rapid clip to outpace population growth and ultimately to dry up the reserve army of the underemployed, labor is no longer a surplus commodity but is competitively bid for like any other factor of production, with the major social problems now approaching those of the mature economy.

The unnecessarily low responsiveness to the factor endowment of both technology and output mix during the import substitution phase makes itself felt in a number of ways. In spite of the overhang of an underemployed reserve army, we know that international real wages, for example, are often several hundred percent above the reservation price of unskilled labor in agriculture. We note that this wage gap phenomenon is mainly caused by a combination of government and union pressure for redistribution and is most marked when the large scale industrial sector, in particular, makes substantial profits on the basis of raw material exploitation, especially if foreign ownership is involved. The larger the wage gap, of course, the more likely the premature inflow into the urban areas, with people becoming disguisedly unemployed in the cities while waiting for the few well-paying jobs. With the commercialized nonagricultural sector often amounting to as little as 10 percent of the total economy by size, if the total labor force grows at close to 3 percent, labor absorption by this sector has to be at the rate of at least 30 percent; if unemployment is not to rise with high, exogenously pulled wages, it is not surprising that, even where the organized industrial sector has been growing rapidly, the rate of labor absorbed has been much below this rate, and falling, in most of the LDCs.

Some theoretical work seems to indicate that industrial job creation may be counterproductive if it induces even more people to drift into the cities ahead of employment, as the expectation of getting a job is raised. But we should keep in mind that this model makes more sense in Africa where productive employment opportunities in agriculture may still be relatively more abundant—and that it unequivocally sees a rising wage gap, not compensated for by changes in labor quality (e.g., as turnover rates decline), as the major culprit.

The same holds with respect to the effects of overvalued exchange rates and artificially low interest rates which bias production towards import and capital intensity. Especially in a small LDC for which trade is necessarily important, the continuation of an administered price policy makes it difficult for the factor endowment to be reflected along the economy's production functions in terms of either technology choice or output mix. Only the lifting of the veil, at least partially, between factor endowments and relative prices will permit an economy to take advantage of its resources at any point in time, as well as ease its movement from one phase to another, i.e., from a raw material to an unskilled labor fuelled phase and, ultimately, to a skill and technology based phase of development.

Thus, critical to the unemployment problem as viewed in the context of a two sector developing economy are 1) the initial extent of discrepancy between factor endowment and factor use, i.e., the extent of unemployment; 2) the relative pressure of population growth over time; 3) productivity increases in agriculture which are possible in the short term, even in an economy poor in natural resources; and 4) the extent of factor price distortions, including the size of the wage gap between the two sectors. Let us proceed now to summarize relevant research results, at a somewhat less aggregative level.

In the industrial sector, first of all, we know that there exists tremendous variance in capital productivity by industry across countries and, even more relevant, across different scales within the same industry in a given country. It seems clear that substantial substitution possibilities exist for a given quality output and given quality factor inputs, contrary to the opinion of many policy makers, engineers, and technicians. Taking the static case first, in a study of Karachi industry in the '50s, medium sized firms stood out as the most efficient in terms of their ability to utilize or "stretch" scarce capital most effectively, even though at lower levels of labor productivity. Similar studies have been made in Colombia and India, all indicating that firms of medium size, relatively labor intensive in response to the lower wage levels faced, turn out to be among the best static allocators of capital. Recent evidence, for example, in the production of light engineering goods, including pumps in the West Punjab during the middle '60s—not to speak of Granick's evidence on metal working in the Soviet Union—indicates that even the manufacture of light capital goods is subject to a substantial amount of flexibility with respect to the use of labor. Except in continuous process industries, or in industries near the crude raw material processing end of the production spectrum, there has been a persistent underestimation of the technology choice available and persistent overestimation of the dominance of capital intensive choices, where a range exists.

Construction, both in highways and housing, is well known as the sector with the greatest technical flexibility and most opportunity for labor intensive techniques to be employed, often as part of a machine paced production process. It should also be noted that construction is characterized by the predominance of unorganized labor with relatively little bargaining power, few tenure rights, and relatively low wages. The substantial flexibilities encountered in this sector, once relative prices are less distorted, should be viewed as more generally instructive.

The service sector which, of course, includes both modern capital intensive banking and transportation, as well as traditional labor intensive personal services, and distributive trades, has been growing exceedingly fast in most LDCs. As is well known, most of this growth is in the "soft" or supply-of-labor-pushed (rather than the "hard" or elasticity-of-demand-pulled) areas, leading to the displacement of rural by urban disguised unemployment.

With respect to the agricultural sector, there is increasing evidence in work on India by Mazumdar, Colombia by Berry, Brazil by Cline, and West Pakistan by Falcon and Gottsch, that small and medium scale farms are characterized by superior efficiency in the use of land. In virtually all of these studies, it seems clear that the larger farm size, the lower the output per unit of scarce resource, i.e., the less intensively the land is being utilized. Economies of scale arguments which are sometimes summoned to support large scale units in industry have less force here.

We next turn to dynamic arguments. There is a substantial school of thought, led by Galenson and Leibenstein (and again with a good deal of support among engineers and policy makers), to the effect that, even though there may exist static flexibility, in both technical choice and output mixes, the resulting labor intensive production yields larger wage bills relative to profits and consequently lower rates of saving and capital formation. While the evidence is by no means unequivocal on this subject, it can be said that the Galenson-Liebenstein hypothesis has not stood up well to empirical tests. This is because the large output per unit of capital generated in the medium and small scale firms is likely to swamp the unquestioned tendency for given profits to yield higher saving than given wages. Unless you make some rather unusual assumptions about the elasticities of substitution, total profits will increase more as a consequence of substitution in a labor-using direction. In a study of Karachi industry as well as in studies conducted by the U.N. Industrialization Program, the relative effects, in terms of the final impact on saving within the firm, of allocating capital to the more labor intensive medium and small scale enterprises, were found to be not only positive but substantial.

There is another even more important sense in which dynamic considerations enter in a central fashion, and that is through the adoption of labor saving as opposed to capital saving innovations, especially as a country moves into the export substitution phase and market prices begin to approximate their equilibrium levels more closely. If, for example, in spite of the overhang in underemployed and unemployed labor, the real industrial wage is high and rising, producing a widening wage gap, the incentive for adopting labor saving innovations from the shelf of technology is enhanced. On the other hand, if wage restraint is exercised so that the expectation is for real wages not to drift upward very much, the incentive to innovate in indigenous labor using directions, on top of the imported technology, is substantially strengthened.

Many officials and scholars share the view that most technological change, especially in the nonagricultural sector, must take place abroad, and that it has to be labor saving. If LDCs, in fact, had only a narrow set of initial technological choices open to them and only a limited capacity to do anything major in the way of local adaptations, this would mean, in the extreme, that a recipient is always forced to import the latest model from the most advanced of the mature countries—a most unrealistic case —and unable to make any capital stretching changes "on top of" the import in response to a substantially different factor endowment—equally unrealistic. As the history of Japanese development and the contemporary records of Korea and Taiwan indicate, indigenous capital stretching capacity can be of the greatest importance once the policy setting has turned more favorable and permitted the economy to try to absorb—and export by incorporation in labor-intensive commodities—its relatively abundant resource.

With respect to the industrial sector in particular, indigenous capital stretching may be of three kinds: 1) relating to the machine proper; 2) relating to the production process as a whole but emphasizing the importance of activities within the plant and peripheral to the machine; and 3) relating to the production process as a whole but emphasizing plant size and differential processing arrangements at various stages.

With respect to the machine proper, the simplest, most important example of capital stretching seems to be one which relates to the utilization of machinery in place, mainly by adjusting shifts and speeds of operation relative to the country of origin. For example, triple shifting plus a speed-up does not "wear out" machines more than three times as fast as normal operations, and, when accompanied by more attention to repair and maintenance, can be very important in quantitative terms. The average work week per machine in the textile industry of historical Japan amounted to at least two or three times that encountered in the U.K. and the U.S. at the time. Sometimes, along with the higher speeds, cheaper raw materials can be used and compensated for by additional unskilled labor in handling the extra quality controls and repairs necessitated. As late as 1932, weekly man hours per 1,000 homogeneous spindles ranged from 330 in Japan to 165 for the U.K. and 143 for the U.S.

With respect to machine-peripheral operations, the handling, transporting and packaging within the plant by human instead of mechanical conveyor belts can also be very important. Activities which may look inefficient and wasteful to the untrained eye often constitute highly efficient, sometimes machine-paced, capital saving adaptations. For example, in the production of Korean plywood, what at first appears as a production process very similar to that carried out in the U.S., on inspection turns out to be full of important variations on the basic theme. In the U.S., machinery is used to detect defective pieces of lumber and the entire side is then discarded. In Japan, defective pieces of lumber are located and cut out by hand. In Korea, the defective area (knothole) is located and patched up by hand.

The same is true for marked international differences in the same electronics process, especially in assembly operations. For example, in Korean subsidiaries, the same process, with wage rates ten times lower than their equivalent in the U.S., shows 20 percent greater utilization of the capital stock. Feeding and packaging on the assembly line are done by hand instead of automatically and, with the greater speeds of operation due to faster operator pacing, additional labor is deployed in testing, inspection, and repair.

The third type of capital stretching innovation, i.e., of the plant saving variety, is often characterized by the coexistence of different historical stages of production in the same industry or even firm. For example, in textiles, spinning may be done at the large scale factory level, with purchasing and marketing similarly enjoying economies of scale, while weaving is performed in extensions of the rural household, courtesy of the putting-out system. Even in the most modern industries subcontracts are common for specific preparatory and finishing processes. Since plant amounts to close to 60 percent of total investment in plant and equipment in most of the developing countries, the deployment of labor intensive machinery, e.g., looms, over a large number of scattered miniplants can be substantially plant saving while additional substantial amounts of labor can be harnessed in satisfying demands for the additional transportation and handling requirements.

The point is sometimes raised that any two dimensional discussion of industrial capital-labor substitution possibilities may be misleading since it does not take into account shortages of supervisory, skilled, or managerial labor which, if included, would tend to yield greater capital intensity. No doubt, such information, if available, should be included in any analysis. But it is not clear why this should necessarily affect results in any particular direction, and the OECD finds "little empirical evidence one way or the other."

With respect to technological change in agriculture, the Green Revolution, where it has occurred, is likely to be land saving and labor using in nature, even though all of the returns are by no means in. Demands for 50 percent more workers in rice and 33 percent more in wheat have been recorded after technology change which shortens growing seasons and increases the possibilities for double and triple cropping. In Taiwan, for each 1 percent increase in the double cropping index a 1 percent increase in labor inputs demanded has been reported. Under such circumstances, the mechanization of agricultural operations as a wholesale solution is not likely to be a sensible course of action. But selective mechanization, even though it increases the capital-labor ratio in one process, e.g., land preparation, may well permit double cropping on the same land, thereby yielding a reduction in the overall capital-labor ratio, and thus constitute an example of a land saving innovation. Most of the evidence collected by experts like Ruttan and Johnston indicates that the largest potential for technological change in LDC agriculture is of the chemical-fertilizer variety and at the intensive margin rather than of the mechanical-machinery variety at the extensive margin.

III

Given the problem as defined here, and given the analytical framework and findings which have been uncovered to date, the solutions are by no means easy. Nevertheless, one can cite a number of policy conclusions and simultaneously refer to the possible role of foreign assistance in that context.

At the most general level, but nevertheless the most important, it is clear that there exists a unique and useful role for administered pricing in the early import substitution phase, if, in fact, this phase can be kept in bounds both in terms of the type of tools used and the time span over which it is permitted to dominate the scene. We all know the formidable obstacles in the way of a gradual termination of hothouse conditions once the bona fide objectives of such policies, i.e., infant industry protection and infrastructural construction, have been satisfied. Such obstacles emanate in part from the industrialists who have become accustomed to windfall profits and partly from civil servants who have become accustomed to power—and to the rewards for power which facilitate decision making during this phase of development.

Governments and those who aid governments have an obligation, at this level of generality, to insure that policy changes do occur in spite of these formidable obstacles, and not only in response to LDC economies' scraping bottom in terms of an increasingly dismal performance on both the output and employment fronts. In brief, persuasion, gentle pressure, and aid ballooning to ease the transition towards a more market determined regime, both in terms of output mixes and in terms of technology choices, cannot be avoided.

There can be little doubt that the program loan and related discussions explicitly on the transition from one policy package to another is required. Enriching cost-benefit analyses on projects to take the employment dimension into account cannot do the job in isolation. In fact, it should be candidly admitted that donor concentration on projects, specifically the foreign exchange component of projects, often works in just the opposite direction, i.e., induces import and capital intensity. A liberal interpretation of local cost project financing at a minimum and, even better, the liberal use of program lending represent important ways in which the foreign exchange made available to a country can be spread more widely. At the same time, it is infinitely easier for donors to argue policies which permit changing endowments to be reflected more clearly in productive activities when their own contribution is clearly nondistorting.

On the specifics of changing from administered to a more market oriented pricing structure, we need not reiterate what is fast becoming the conventional wisdom, i.e., a preference for tariffs over quotas; uniform tariffs over individually negotiated ones; downward trending tariffs over fixed tariffs; exchange rates which are adjustable over fixed pegs; import liberalization permitting access to new and small importers and industrialists over rigid licensing; and at least partial allocation of credit through high interest rates over discretionary lending to only the established signatures by the banking system.

On the wage front, no one in his right mind expects reducing real wages to be a politically feasible act; nevertheless, it is clear that wage restraint is of the essence if the underemployed who are outside the presently employed and unionized pool—and thus disenfranchised—are to have any voice in the matter. A de-emphasis on ILO type minimum wage legislation, overtime for night work, and other social welfare regulations, encouragement of permanency of workers (converting them into fixed costs), can be viable, even today, once properly understood—for example, in the case of the Tri-partite Agreement in Kenya.

The so-called rural-urban wage gap is especially important and subject to policy advice, particularly in Latin America and Africa. If a high profit, possibly foreign owned, natural resource based industry constitutes a political embarrassment to an LDC government, this embarrassment should not be met by government pressure to increase wages—which wage increases usually spread to other sectors not exploiting natural monopolies (like the civil service)—but by sharing in what are considered socially undesirable profits, through taxation, or the renegotiation of royalty arrangements.

Specific policies which are common practice in the commercialized or industrial sector and should be opposed by aid giving agencies include accelerated depreciation in place of tax holidays, labor legislation discriminating against night work and double-shifting, labor laws making it difficult for employers to fire workers—all leading to increased capital intensity.

Moreover, there should be encouragement, including temporary subsidies, of subcontracting, especially into the rural areas, in order to take maximum advantage of the local labor supply as well as dispersed entrepreneurial and saving capacity. More attention has to be directed to the "connectivity" of the agricultural and nonagricultural sectors in most LDC's. Such "connectivity," both physical and institutional, is very much in evidence in all of the relatively few "success" cases. It is important from the standpoint of minimizing output and employment conflicts by economizing on both private and social (urban) capital requirements, and it has significant, additional, incentive-related advantages with respect to agricultural productivity change.

In the agricultural sector, aid agencies should lean against subsidies for tractors and other heavy equipment via overvalued exchange rates, low duties, and low excises on domestic production, all threatening uneconomic and wholesale mechanization in the wake of the Green Revolution. Moreover, land reform may well be necessary where latifundia and other large holdings prevent the intensive use of land and other scarce inputs.

At the individual project level, anywhere, we of course agree in principle that the Little-Mirlees guide to cost-benefit analysis, or any other less sophisticated method of arriving at partial equilibrium decisions, can benefit from greater sensitivity to the employment problem. This can be done through more thoroughgoing shadow price adjustments for both capital and unskilled labor as well as possibly for skilled managerial and technical personnel. But since in the kind of mixed economy we are likely to be talking about, most "projects" are really carried out by thousands of medium and small scale entrepreneurs in either the industrial or the agricultural sectors, maintaining the proper mix of macro policies is much more to the point.

One other obvious area is in the potential for trade in labor intensive industrial goods, as LDCs *en masse* move towards export substitution. This means not only support for temporary preferences but, perhaps more importantly, the need for a more sensible and thoroughgoing adjustment assistance policy in the developed countries. If all the LDCs, in fact, began to take the policy advice offered, and accelerated their growth, exports, and employment on a broad front, rear guard actions by the politically powerful labor intensive "sick" industries in the advanced countries can be expected to become more and more bitter. In fact, it could be argued with some conviction that, from the point of view of efficiency as well as political feasibility, the best aid program might be one spent in large part in the domestic economies of the advanced countries, in return for a lowering of quota and tariff barriers on the relevant commodities.

Related, and equally obvious, is the need for donors to encourage LDCs to turn their attention from traditional markets among advanced country trading partners and towards potential new markets in other LDCs. Clearly, the U.S. is not going to be willing, or able, to absorb much of the potential increase in labor intensive products which could be generated by a really vigorously growing LDC world. But we need only recall the constantly changing structure of comparative advantages, production and trade in the 19th century to realize that the understandable fascination—even obsession—with the traditional country trading partners may be as serious a mistake as the reluctance to move to export substitutes. Intra-LDC trade accounts for only 3 to 4 percent of world trade. Market as well as product diversification is called for.

Finally, aid givers might consider what contribution can be made to greater rationality in the process of technology transfer and adaptation. In addition to the donor's influence in terms of overall science and technology policy, which is directly related to the increased market orientation of the economy referred to earlier—permitting indigenous talent to come forward and be tested—there may be room for international institutes to help devise labor using adaptations and modifications. There is a frequently heard complaint that modern labor using technology just does not exist and does not therefore constitute a viable option. Moreover, there is a good deal of resentment of the notion of second-hand obsolete machinery being forced on LDCs. What should be emphasized is the need for devising new but labor using production functions. The LDCs account for only 2 percent of the world's expenditure on Research and Development, but that is perhaps as it should be if late comer advantages are to be realized. However, much of what is spent is on the basic instead of the applied side. Perhaps in selected areas, for example shoes, it might be possible to support international research institutes for the express purpose of stimulating local laborsaving adaptations. In this fashion, it may well be possible to achieve economies of scale and avoid duplication of effort with every LDC attempting to devise a capital stretching shoe technology.

In summary, I do not believe it makes sense to talk in simple terms of having to increase the growth rate in order to take care of the employment and income distribution problem. Nor is it possible, as has been shown over the last two decades, to carry on business as usual and to have a "supplementary" strategy, either rural public works or labor intensive industrial work projects, to pick up as much of the backlog of unemployment left in the wake of the "primary" strategy of development. What is instead required is a strategy which permits substantial gains in output by means of a much more factor endowment sensitive strategy. Before we rush into public works projects or even the administratively difficult subsidization of labor intensive technology we should endeavor to do away with existing discrimination in favor of capital intensity. If we took that first step in simply clearing the boards and making the allocative game a fair one, we would be going a long way in the direction of solving the problem. This may sound somewhat pollyannish, especially from a card-carrying member of the dismal science. But evidence from 2 or 3 of the more successful development cases indicates it may nevertheless be true.

PART TWO   Aid Instruments
and Allocation Criteria

Foreign Assistance as Capital Inflow
THOMAS C. SCHELLING

Thomas C. Schelling is Professor of Economics at Harvard University and associated with its Center for International Affairs. This excerpt is taken from his 1958 book entitled International Economics.

THE ESSENTIAL feature of most foreign assistance is the capital inflow that it finances—the transfer of resources from the country granting the aid to the country receiving it, through the import surplus of the latter. While the fiscal arrangements and administrative techniques for effecting the transfer of resources have varied from program to program, most of the arrangements amount to the same thing as far as the economics are concerned. This is not to say that the forms and techniques are unimportant; they may be very important in a political and administrative sense, and have much to do with the behavior of the recipient government and the relations between the granting and receiving governments. But while these differences in technique are important, it is perhaps even more important to recognize the fundamental economic process that lies behind the multiplicity of techniques.

Figures 1, 2, and 3 will illustrate this process and help to compare the results obtained with different techniques. As the diagrams make clear, there is a financial flow and a flow of goods involved. In fact there may be several flows, and it is worth while to identify the correspondence among the various flows. We can begin with a diagram that represents the method used in the

No Foreign Assistance

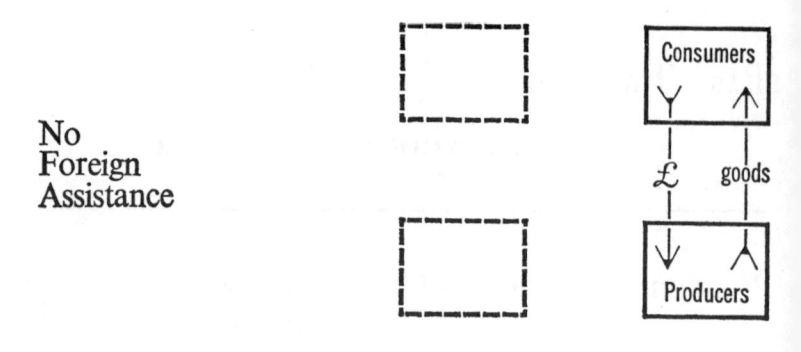

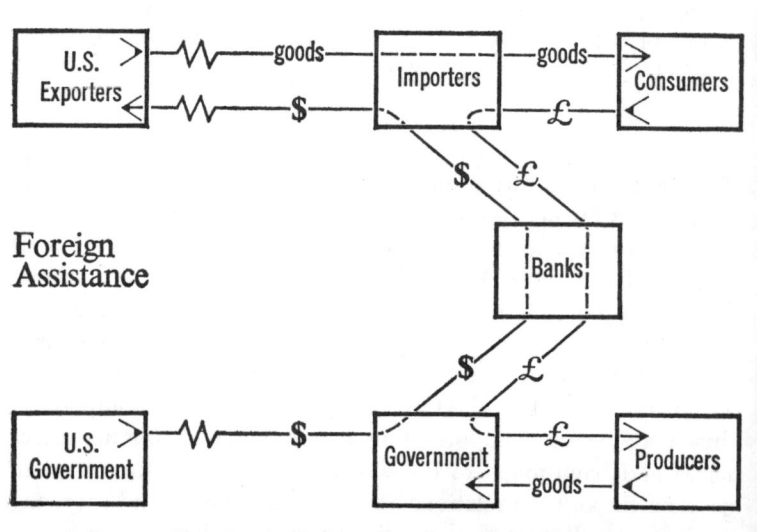

Foreign Assistance

FIGURE 1. *Aid in the Form of Dollars*

Marshall Plan and that has generally been used in connection with defense-support assistance. It can be modified to reflect other techniques.

Figure 1 is in two parts. The upper part—with no foreign aid—shows consumers in the receiving country purchasing domestically produced goods and services. Goods flow from producers to consumers, and there is a corresponding flow of money (denoted by the £ sign) from consumers to producers. The lower part of the diagram shows the foreign-aid process. The government receives a grant of foreign currency (denoted by the $ sign) from abroad; it exchanges the foreign currency with the banking system to obtain its own currency. It spends its own currency on goods and services, thereby absorbing part of what is produced domestically. Imports equivalent in value to what the government is now buying are being bought by consumers, whose total expenditure is thus unchanged. The consumers pay their own currency, of course, which the importers exchange for dollars through the banking system, in order to pay for the imports.

If we concentrate on the *goods* alone, imports come into the country and displace some domestic production that consumers have been buying, and the displaced production becomes available to the government. The total goods and services purchased in the country is increased by exactly the amount of the government's spending of local currency equivalent to the dollars it received.

There are two *money flows* to observe. One is the flow of dollars from the aid-granting government to the aid-receiving government, from the latter to the banking system (which could be the central bank, a foreign-exchange agency, or ordinary commercial banks, as far as the essentials of the process are concerned), from the banking system to the importers, and from the importers to the producers abroad. The other currency flow is from consumers to importers, from importers to the banking system, from the banking system to the government, and from the government to the producing sector of the economy.

If we now ask who in the economy possesses something as a result of the gift from abroad, the answer is the government; and what the government has as a result of the aid is whatever it bought with the local currency that it obtained for the dollars it received from abroad.

VARIANTS OF THE MODEL

This basic model could be varied in several ways. Suppose that the receiving government obtains physical goods instead of money from abroad. It can sell these goods on the local market and spend the proceeds on the particular goods and services that it needs. To show that process we need only to compress the government, the importers, and the banking system into a single block on the diagram, and label the block "government." The resulting diagram

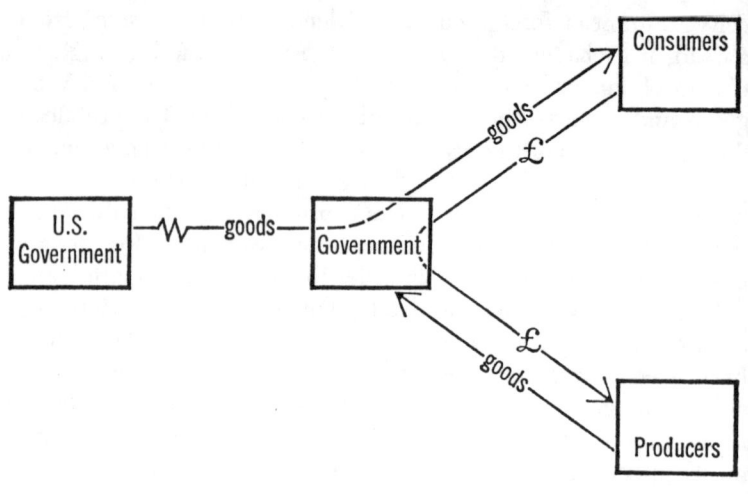

FIGURE 2. *Aid in the Form of Goods*

shows goods coming into the government and proceeding on to consumers in exchange for local currency, with the government spending the local currency on domestically produced goods and services, as in Figure 2.

"OFFSHORE PROCUREMENT"

Another variant is represented by the process that was called "offshore procurement" in connection with the military assistance program. While the military assistance programs have mainly provided countries with military equipment and supplies produced in the United States, such funds have also been used for procurement of equipment in the European countries themselves. If equipment is bought by the United States in Britain and given to the Italian government, the process is analogous to an American import from Britain coupled with a direct transfer of equipment to the Italian armed forces. But if the equipment is bought in Britain and given to the British government the two parts of the process—the import transaction and the aid transaction—combine to provide the process shown in Figure 3, which can be compared with Figure 1.

If we assume that the goods bought by the government in Figure 1 were military equipment, the end result of the two diagrams is identical. In each case the result for the government is posses-

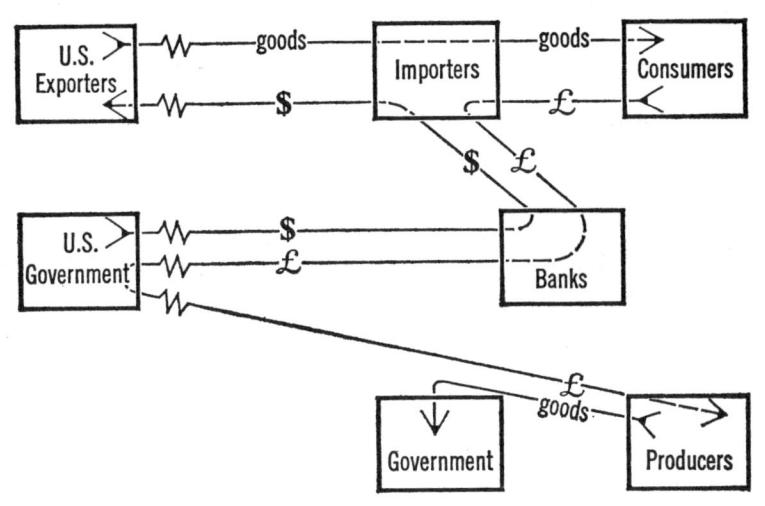

FIGURE 3. *Aid in the Form of "Offshore Procurement"*

sion of equipment that was paid for in the process. In each case domestic production is diverted from domestic consumers to the government's demand. In each case additional imports come into the country in an amount equivalent to the production that has been diverted to the government.

The administrative formalities for the two cases are very different. In one case the aid-giving government has bought equipment for the armed forces of a foreign country; in the other case it has financed its own export of raw materials and consumer goods to a foreign country. In one case the aid would have been classified as "military"; in the other case it might have been classified as "economic." But a comparison of the diagrams makes clear that insofar as the pure *economic logic* is concerned the difference is inconsequential.

The Role of External "Aid"

W. B. REDDAWAY

W. B. Reddaway is Director of the Department of Applied Economics at Cambridge, England. This statement, in the form of a letter written to a friend shortly after his arrival in India for a year's research, first appeared as Appendix D to his 1962 volume, The Development of the Indian Economy.

Dear C.,

In the rush at the end of our talk I was not as coherent as I should have been about the role which Aid might need to play if India has a Big Plan. This note is to try to make the *principles* clear, as I see them, without attempting any real quantitative assessment: the figures are probably of the right general size, but one can make the Aid figures change greatly by moving all the others in the appropriate direction, whilst *still* claiming that they are all 'of the right general size'.[1]

As I see it, there are two main roles which Aid plays: it adds to the amount of savings available for capital formation, and it helps with the balance of payments problem. Some people try to argue that these are two aspects of the same thing, but I disagree: what follows may make the point clearer than general reasoning would.

ADDITION TO SAVING

A big plan requires an average of 2,000 crores [2] per annum of net investment in India, and there are repayments due to other countries averaging (say) 100 crores per annum. To save 2,100 crores per annum *net* out of a national income averaging perhaps

1. In addition, I would like to emphasize that this note is written entirely on my own responsibility, and commits nobody else in any way.
2. [One crore rupees is equivalent to $2 million or £750,000. *Editor*]

15,000 would be a formidable task for a poor country; the most nearly comparable figures for the United Kingdom in 1958 are *net* saving of just over £2,000 million out of a national income of £18,235 million, so that India would have to save a rather higher proportion. Moreover, the United Kingdom proportion was considerably lower in earlier years—e.g. in 1948, it was only 6 per cent, and it did not reach 10 per cent until 1955.

The role of Aid here is to enable the investment to be done without so much saving (which to my mind would only come in the 'forced' form, through taxation or so-called deficit finance). Even 600 crores per annum (i.e. 500 'net new Aid' plus 100 to cover repayment on old debts) would leave the savings requirement at 10 per cent.

(A point which seems to me very important in this connection is best developed after looking at the Balance of Payments—see the final paragraph.)

BALANCE OF PAYMENTS

The basic difficulty here is, I think, greater than many simple presentations of it suggest.

A 10,000 crore Plan would require some 2,000 crores of imported machinery, etc., to go into the various projects—i.e. 400 crores per annum.

The rest of India's international payments (apart from Aid in any of its forms) might look like this in an average year of Plan III:

Receipts from exports (including net invisibles, which will be small as interest payments rise)	600–700
Imports of raw materials, and other 'essentials' (including some Defence stuff and food outside P.L. 480, but not machinery for the Plan)	600–700
Capital repayments	100

The whole account would be 'balanced' if Aid amounted to 500 crores per annum *plus* grain, etc., under P.L. 480 to cover any shortage. (The figures are, as I said, 'illustrative only', though they may be uncomfortably near the truth in their general effect.)

One 'technical' problem seems almost certain to arise, if Aid can only take the form of P.L. 480 or of loans for the imported plant needed for specific projects: it would be impossible for India to find the free foreign exchange to cover debt repayments, essential materials, etc., and plant for projects not in the Aid programme.

With the above figures there would indeed be a shortfall even if loans were obtained for the machinery needed for every single project in both public and private sectors—a condition which clearly could not be met with present procedures. There would be some mitigation of this if foreign companies develop Indian subsidiaries, since they will often buy rupees with foreign exchange to cover the Indian component of the expenditure; but it looks to me as if some additional means of providing India with general purchasing power will be needed, now that this cannot be secured by running down £ balances. Without this there seems no hope of escaping from the frustrations caused by a very tight control of imports, even of industrial materials and components.

A SMALLER PLAN?

This last point largely remains even if the Plan is made smaller, because the direct effect of reducing the Plan is to reduce the imports of plant, etc., for which loans are considered respectable. There are, however, some indirect gains to the balance of payments:

A. The reduced capital expenditure on construction work, etc., in India would mean lower employment and less wages to be spent; this in turn means less purchasing of food—with a saving on imports or a gain in exportable surplus—and of other goods which often require materials that have to be imported or could be exported.
B. There is a 'multiplier' effect, since employment (and profits, as well as wages) will be lower in other Indian industries when demand is reduced.
C. There *may* also be a gain in exports of manufactures (e.g. textiles) if the firms become keener to secure orders, even at cut prices, and the rise in money wages is moderated.

I doubt myself whether this would suffice (with any 'acceptable' Plan) to avert the need for some *generally available aid*—or at least for Aid which could be used to repay trade debts and refinance old loans. Apart from anything else, the imports which would be indirectly saved would consist largely of grain and other items coming under P.L. 480.

Naturally, a smaller Plan would reduce the total requirement of Aid, because it would reduce the Aid needed for imported plant, etc.—especially if the cut were concentrated on the industrial projects. The objection to that is of course that it reduces the chance of ever becoming 'viable'.

SOME GENERAL REFLECTIONS

Here are a few assorted reflections which have occurred to me:

1. *Can Aid for 'current' imports be justifiable?* I find the analogy with our own position under the Marshall Plan very helpful here. Our Aid was in effect used 'for capital purposes' even though we spent the dollars on food, cotton and even tobacco, rather than machinery: we did the construction work ourselves, and the Aid only financed a small part of it—and that indirectly. In the Indian case too the greater part of their Plan projects will be 'made in India'—all the construction and civil engineering, some part of the machinery, the installation work, etc. Similarly, even if there were 'net new Aid' of 2,500 crores, the saving would still be 75 per cent Indian. The doctrine of a 'correspondence' between external finance and the direct import component of capital projects has no support in economic theory at all: nor has it much historical support—the Argentine railway companies, the oil companies, the tea plantations, etc., have traditionally provided the *whole* finance for their projects from abroad; the foreign exchange which they converted into local currency to cover local expenditure has been available to the country for general purposes.

2. *Does Aid have to continue for ever?* Logically there is a strong case, on the savings approach, for saying *both* that India's need is for permanent capital (so that if individual loans are repaid they should be balanced by new ones) *and* that a continuing net inflow would be desirable for a long time to come. But as India's income per head rises, the case for further net Aid on these grounds gets weaker, and logically there could be net repayments.

It is the balance of payments problem which is disquieting. Even if Indian incomes rise to the point where the Indians can 'afford' to do all their further development out of their own savings, will they be able to sell enough abroad to buy essential imports?

Neither theory nor experience provides much reason for saying that a country will be permanently stuck with 'an insoluble balance of payments problem'—or one which is 'soluble' only by keeping the economy depressed. The Indian case now seems difficult largely because:

a. Exports are very small in relation to national income (only about 5 per cent) and seem very difficult to expand in traditional lines.
b. Raising the national income by (say) 5 per cent a year requires capital expenditure equal to perhaps 15 per cent of the national income, and these projects require a relatively high proportion of machinery which (at present) has to be imported; although the imported machinery amounts to only about 3 per cent of the national *income,* it is over 50 per cent of national *exports,* and so raises a very difficult problem for the balance of payments.
c. Raising the national income also raises the Indian demand for other imports (including food and raw materials), and for agricultural products in inelastic supply, such as hides, which have traditionally been exported.

For the payments to balance after (say) ten to fifteen years, even though development is still continuing, the most plausible assumptions are that:

i. Indian production of machinery (and of the steel to make it) will grow greatly, so that (*b*) ceases to be so much of a problem.
ii. Other import-savers will be developed (e.g. oil) as a powerful off-set to (*c*)—and (above all) food output will be increased to meet the higher demand.
iii. Some new exports will be developed, mainly of manufactures —e.g. steel and machinery to Asian countries—as capacity in particular lines exceeds Indian requirements.

In a sense one can be confident that things *will* develop along these lines: the questions are how smooth the process will be, how autarchic the pattern will be, and how long it will take to secure a balance. Lenders might plausibly add to the list 'Will there be default on debts as one ingredient in the balance?' There are plenty of historical precedents both ways!

3. '*More trade means less Aid*'. If, as I believe, the need for Aid on balance of payments grounds is greater than the need on savings grounds then the amount required could be reduced if Western countries were more prepared to admit Indian exports of

things which could easily be supplied—notably textiles.

Such a move would also directly raise Indian incomes and employment, and so ease the problem of providing savings for development. This is a particular example of a general point: *if* the balance of payments bottleneck is removed, whether by trade or Aid, inadequately used resources in India can 'safely' be brought into fuller employment by expanding demand, and the rise in the national income will lead to increased savings. There may of course be other bottlenecks which cannot be overcome by imports—e.g. in power or transport—and the process certainly cannot be continued 'indefinitely'; but that is too big a subject to explore here!

The Food Problem of Developing Countries
THORKIL KRISTENSEN FOR OECD

OECD, the Organization for Economic Cooperation and Development, of which most Western industrialized countries are members, carries on a substantial volume of information gathering, consultation, and research on aid to the developing world.

IT WAS IN 1954 that food aid started on a large scale with the passing by the United States Congress of the law that has become so well known under the designation P L 480. Under this legislation the American food aid program soon reached the dimensions it has maintained since, though there have been annual fluctuations. Australia, Canada and a few other countries have used deliveries of food in their aid programs and a multilateral "World Food Program" has been established by the United Nations and the FAO. However, the bulk of food aid has remained the United States' program.

Food aid, in common with other kinds of tied aid, serves a dual purpose: helping less developed countries and supporting exports that are desirable from the point of view of the donor country. It is in the nature of things that a transaction between two countries must in one way or other serve the interest of both, but of course tying of aid can lead to a deflection of trade that is not always desirable, and one cannot be sure that it serves the most urgent needs of the receiving country. On the other hand, tied aid is normally better than no aid and the main argument for a certain aid tying is that it permits the flow of aid to increase more than it would have otherwise.

In the case of food aid, there can be no doubt that it has increased the total flow of assistance rather considerably. In 1965 it represented 33 percent of the United States' gross aid disbursements and more than 20 percent of the total flow of aid from OECD/DAC countries.

A contribution of that size became possible mainly because the United States had accumulated large stocks of agricultural products primarily to support its own agriculture. In general it can be said that aid shipments of food have made the agricultural markets of western countries easier than they would otherwise have been. They have therefore served a purpose, both in the donor and the recipient countries.

Unavoidably there have been some drawbacks. The need to put more emphasis on agriculture in the development programs of the recipients has been somewhat diminished, and there have no doubt been cases where such deliveries from abroad have contributed to the maintenance of prices in the receiving countries that were lower than desirable. Agricultural prices in developing countries should not be too low, both because farm production needs a stimulus and because the farmers usually are the poorest part of the population.

It seems likely that these drawbacks are less important now than in the first years of food aid. This is so, both because the programs are administered with increasing understanding of how to avoid market disruptions and because the import needs of developing countries are rising. It is, therefore, easier now than ten or twelve years ago to be sure that the deliveries serve a real and important purpose in the receiving countries. This will be so even more in the next few years since import needs are likely to go on increasing. The fact that developing countries now are heightening their efforts to improve agriculture further reduces the risks that food aid could do harm as well as good.

In the donor countries and especially in the United States, the situation has changed in recent years.

The surplus stocks have been declining since 1961, and at present stocks are no longer in excess of the desirable working level. This means that food aid in the biggest donor country now has to come out of current production, to be paid for by the government, and the United States Government has, mainly for that very reason, permitted a substantial increase of the area under wheat and rice since 1966. A certain reduction was, however, decided for 1968.

This of course means that food aid represents much more of a real sacrifice for the main donor country than in the past. There could therefore be a risk that it would be drastically reduced. This would be very dangerous because it would entail a substantial reduction of the total aid flow, already too small. Therefore, and because it is recognized that food aid now meets a real need, efforts have been made in two different ways to make a continuation of such aid possible on a large scale.

Firstly, the United States, in order to reduce the balance of payments effects of food aid shipments, will now sell an increasing part of the food against dollars, though on long term credits. Up to now most of the sales were in the currency of the receiving country. The new arrangement will of course add to the debt service burden of the recipients. This should, by the way, encourage them not to ask for food aid unless there are good reasons for it, and this further reduces the risk of abuse of this form of aid.

Secondly, an agreement that was part of the Kennedy Round in the GATT will make other countries than the United States contribute more to the total burden of food aid. Under this agreement in the next three years 4.5 million tons of wheat a year will be made available as food aid by a number of countries, some of which are wheat importers themselves so that they will have to buy the wheat.

It remains to be seen how this arrangement will influence the total flow of aid. Will the countries who are now committed to give more food aid reduce other parts of their aid program or will the Kennedy Round food shipments be "additional" in the true sense of the word?

Whatever the answer to that question may be it must be remembered that the 4.5 million tons of wheat is a small quantity compared with the recent American food aid deliveries. In the years 1961-65 the United States alone provided under government financed programs on the average 13.65 million tons of wheat, 0.56 million tons of rice and 1.96 million tons of coarse grains annually, plus certain quantities of other food items. In fact, the United States had proposed a Kennedy Round agreement comprising 10 million tons of wheat but only 4.5 million were agreed upon.

There is therefore a serious risk of a drastic reduction of the total flow of food aid if the Kennedy Round arrangement is not supplemented by other programs. And if food aid is reduced there is no guarantee that it will be replaced by other forms of aid. Since there is a need for an increase in the total flow of aid this situation may well become dangerous if nothing is done to improve it. This is the background on which the considerations to follow should be seen.

The main question is whether food aid still represents a domain where interests in the donor and the recipient countries can be served at the same time. If this is so it should be possible to get more food aid from a number of countries without a corresponding reduction of other forms of aid, and this may be one of the easiest ways of obtaining an increase in total aid.

Food aid was of course particularly easy to give as long as it could be taken out of surplus stocks already accumulated. There are no longer such stocks available but *there is still surplus capacity*. In fact, large areas of farm land are still lying idle in the United States and in the developed countries in general production of a number of important food items tends to outrun demand. Since incomes in agriculture are still too low compared with other incomes in most developed countries, additional demand for farm products coming from the outside is highly desirable from the point of view of agriculture in these countries. Donor countries can therefore help to mitigate one of their own internal problems by supplying more food aid.

Recent studies within the OECD have shown that, on the assumption that policies are not radically changed, the developed countries combined are likely to see their production of *cereals* increase to an extent that will permit them to satisfy their own demand and at the same time increase their net exports to other parts of the world substantially. In fact, the surplus available for exports is likely to exceed the quantity that would be imported by the developing countries.

Only some of the developed countries are net exporters of cereals. On the other hand, various European countries, while being net importers of grains, have a surplus problem of milk production. The food aid deliveries to be added to the deliveries under the Kennedy Round agreement should normally come from countries that have a surplus of the products in question. In this way it will be relatively easy to get more aid without disturbing the economics of the donor countries unnecessarily. It will in fact help these countries to mitigate their internal agricultural problems.

If this principle is followed as a general rule, most of the additional food aid will of course come from the main grain exporting countries and—to a smaller extent—from countries that have a milk surplus problem. It so happens that there is a third group of products where developed countries that would be only modest participants in a cereals and milk powder program can make an important contribution.

Developing countries need large and increasing imports of *fertilizers*. Existing information indicates that a rather significant surplus capacity for the production of fertilizers is at hand in various developed countries where surpluses of grains or of milk products are modest or nonexistent. It would therefore be possible to obtain a more complete participation of developed countries if the additional aid effort also comprised fertilizers.

Also from the point of view of the recipients would such a combined *food and fertilizer aid* make good sense. More aid could be obtained in this way than through a pure food aid program. In fact, fertilizers are used in some aid programs; furthermore, there is a certain connection between the import needs for food, especially cereals, and for fertilizers. The more a developing country can increase its own agricultural production the less it needs its imports of grains, but to increase production it will need more fertilizers.

This means that while an offer of food aid alone can sometimes discourage efforts to develop agriculture, a combined offer of food and/or fertilizers can be formulated in such a way as to be an encouragement to do as much as possible in this field. It can be worked out as an integral part of a coherent aid policy where help to the improvement of agricultural production goes hand in hand with some aid in the form of food.

In the foregoing considerations emphasis is placed on cereals, milk products, and fertilizers because they are likely to be the most important elements in any food and food producing aid policy. It can, of course, be useful to include other food items and other inputs for agricultural production such as pesticides, certain implements, etc., in aid programs.

One must also be careful not to *institutionalize* food and fertilizer aid too much.

No one can say in advance how much will be needed each individual year or how the total contribution should be composed. One year more grains may be needed, another year more fertilizers, and so on. Great flexibility is therefore needed and it would not be desirable for donors to commit themselves to deliver large, predetermined quantities of wheat or other commodities for a certain period to an international institution.

In fact, it is important to stress that food aid should not be established as something *permanent* or even near-permanent. For some years to come, large amounts of such aid will no doubt be needed, probably no less than in recent years, but in the somewhat longer run it is preferable that the developing countries get their food imports more and more on a commercial basis. This means that their capital inflow increasingly should consist of untied aid and of private investment. For reasons mentioned in the foregoing section the prospects for such a development in the near future are not good but it is certainly something to aim at and to prepare.

Consequently, for some years to come—nobody knows for how many years—food aid will be an important component of total aid and it should be an integral part of coherent aid programs, but it should not become an institution with a permanent or semipermanent status. It would be enough to make an evaluation of the orders of magnitude of the desirable programs a few years ahead, but more detailed evaluations should be undertaken on a yearly basis.

There is one final consideration to make in connection with food aid. The partial failure of the monsoon in India in two consecutive years has shown how important it is to have a *World Food Reserve*. Until recently the surplus stocks in the United States have acted as such a reserve but they have now disappeared. A good harvest in most of the world can make stocks increase again but then one or two bad years may follow and the situation can become critical in a number of countries.

World stocks, especially of wheat, but probably also of rice, should therefore always be kept above a certain level. If they are reduced below that level in a bad year they should be restored, in principle, in the following year.

The reserve stock situation of the more important developed and developing countries should, therefore, be kept under review internationally to make sure that dangerous development is avoided.

Technical Assistance

GERALD M. MEIER AND ROBERT E. BALDWIN

Professor Gerald M. Meier teaches at Stanford University and Professor Robert E. Baldwin at the University of Wisconsin. In 1957 they collaborated in writing a book entitled Economic Development: Theory, History, Policy, *from which this selection is taken.*

TECHNICAL ASSISTANCE is an important area of international development policy. If foreign capital is actually to be incorporated into new patterns of activity, there must be educational investment in individuals as well as investment in plant and equipment. For, as Marshall said, "Ideas, whether those of art and science or those embodied in practical appliances, are the most 'real' of the gifts that each generation receives from its predecessors. The world's material wealth would quickly be replaced, if it were destroyed but the ideas by which it was made were retained. If, however, the ideas were lost, but not the material wealth, then that would dwindle and the world would go back to poverty." [1]

Beyond providing capital, the rich countries must also make available to the peoples of the poor countries the knowledge and technical experience which they have accumulated. The flow of capital during the nineteenth century was accompanied by parallel migrations of people and technology. Although the migration of labor is necessarily insignificant today, the transfer of technical knowledge can be highly important. To transfer technical knowledge and help overcome the shortage of skills and organizational abilities in the poor areas, several technical assistance programs are in operation. Some of these programs are organized bilaterally between countries, while others are internationally organized.

Direct attention to industrial projects has been only a minor part of the program. The major fields have been health, agricul-

---

1. Alfred Marshall, *Principles of Economics*, 8th edn., Macmillan and Co. Ltd., London, 1930, p. 780.

ture, and education. Assistance schemes have taken a wide variety of forms. Some involve lending American engineers, technicians, and other expert personnel to poor countries; others involve the offering of training facilities in the United States; and others consist of pilot projects to demonstrate more efficient means of production. . . .

Although experience with technical assistance programs is still limited, some questions can be raised regarding how to derive the maximum advantage from a continuing program of technical aid. A basic issue is whether the program should operate on a bilateral basis, such as in the United States program, or on a multilateral basis such as in the Colombo Plan and the United Nations program. So far the United States program has been the most important quantitatively: in terms of personnel, the United States program is about twice as extensive as the United Nations program; in terms of expenditures, it is approximately ten times as large. There are, however, certain advantages to having technical assistance administered under international auspices. First, it may be politically more acceptable since receiving countries do not wish to be tied too closely to the grantor nation and may prefer to receive help from a multilateral organization to which they belong. In many countries "the exploitation and abuses often associated with development in the past have left a legacy of distrust, which in some cases hampers the introduction of new techniques into the less advanced countries. . . . Their confidence and cooperation is likely to be given most freely to a program under international auspices, in the direction of which the underdeveloped countries can take as full a part as the economically advanced countries."[2] Second, the contribution of one country to the international agency may set an example for other countries, thereby stimulating the contributions of funds and making more available than would otherwise be forthcoming under bilateral programs. A third advantage of the multilateral approach is that it generates a spirit of mutuality and cooperation which allows experts to be drawn from many countries, regardless of their country of origin. Fourth, the international approach avoids the limitations of tied loans which make technical assistance conditional upon purchases from the grantor nation. Fifth, it is likely to provide greater continuity in aid in so far as the necessity of re-

2. United Nations, *Technical Assistance for Economic Development*, New York, May 1949, E/1327, *Add. I*, 12–13.

ceiving annual approval of a national legislature is avoided. Finally, the nature of many of the problems requires international action: transportation, communication, and health programs frequently transcend national borders.

Another important lesson from the experience of technical assistance programs is that the more advanced technologies of Western industrialized nations cannot be transplanted without considerable modification and adaptation to the particular economic, technical, and social needs of the poor countries. Extremely primitive conditions may rule out the use of modern machinery or modern methods. For example, in Haiti where, in the interior, the principle of the wheel is still unknown and where a plough has not been seen, technical aid might be better devoted simply to bringing the farmer from the hoe to the animal-drawn plough rather than from the hoe to the gasoline-driven tractor. Moreover, much of the technological research in industrialized countries is directed towards capital-using innovations, but in poor areas the relative factor supply commonly calls for labor-intensive technology. Modern technology which is capital-intensive also requires complementary supplies of skilled labor and managerial and technical skills which are scarce in the poor countries. Furthermore, the effective life of modern equipment is much shorter in poor countries than in industrialized countries because operation is less careful, standards of maintenance are lower, and repair facilities are inadequate. Modern technology also tends to be designed for large-scale production units, whereas the narrower market in poor countries dictates small-scale operations; this may require that the large-scale production process be broken down into smaller scale and simpler procedures which involve a reduction in the degree of mechanization.

These conditions do not mean that the poor country should utilize the technology of a bygone century and retrace the technological evolution of the West, but it does raise the question of whether technological research which would conform to the needs of poor countries should not be directed towards a technology that is somewhere between the outdated technology of a previous era and the most modern technology now used in the technologically advanced countries.[3] The full range of technological

3. Cf. Yale Brozen, "Invention, Innovation, and Imitation," *American Economic Review, Papers and Proceedings,* XLI, No. 2, 255–256 (May 1951); H. De Graff, "Some Problems Involved in Transferring Technology

alternatives and their possible modifications and combinations must be evaluated in terms of relative factor prices, and the particular socioeconomic conditions of the country concerned. If the technology of industrial countries is transferred to poor countries without suitable modification, the results may simply be repeated breakdowns in the equipment, waste of capital, a low coefficient of utilization, and high unit costs of production.

This problem of appropriate technology cannot be settled in any general manner: the exact technologies required for different uses in different countries have to be decided upon within the framework of technical conditions, economic relationships, and sociocultural characteristics peculiar to each country. By and large, however, it may be said that "the most suitable technologies are likely to be those which yield the maximum social return per unit of capital, reckoning labor at its social cost rather than market cost. In many instances this means that the answer probably lies in the direction of choosing the simplest of alternative techniques, the sturdiest of available capital equipment, the smallest type of plant consistent with technical efficiency, the technology that makes the best use of the most plentiful factors of production." [4]

To these broad conclusions might be added the following: (1) it is preferable to introduce techniques that require less time to learn than those that require a longer time; (2) techniques that reduce the gestation period of investment are more suitable to poor countries; (3) techniques that save raw materials or other scarce resources do not meet with so much resistance as those that save labor; (4) techniques that enable the poor countries to expand their stocks of factors of production, such as an increase in minerals or land or electricity, are generally most welcome in these countries.[5]

Above all, the major problem of technical aid is that of succeeding in getting the new knowledge and new techniques actually applied on an extensive scale in the receiving country. The gap

to Underdeveloped Areas," *Journal of Farm Economics*, XXXIII, No. 4, 697–704 (Nov. 1951); R. L. Meier, *Science and Economic Development*, John Wiley & Sons & The Technology Press, New York, 1956, Appendix.

4. United Nations, *Processes and Problems of Industrialization in Underdeveloped Countries*, New York, 1955, p. 48.

5. C. N. Vakil and P. R. Brahmanand, "Technical Knowledge and Managerial Capacity as Limiting Factors in Industrial Expansion in Underdeveloped Countries," in L. H. Dupriez (ed.), *Economic Progress*, Institut de recherches économiques et sociales, Louvain, 1955, pp. 280–281.

between the known techniques of the rich industrial country and the application of more advanced production techniques in the poor country must be reduced. In part this is a problem of recruiting additional personnel, improving the field organization, and establishing more demonstration projects. More significantly, it is a problem of incentives: without the incentive, the innovation may never be applied in practice. Relatively simple measures may help here: for example, the provision of low credit rates may be made conditional upon the acceptance of improved technical methods, and land reform may furnish a new security of tenure which will allow a former share tenant to have now an interest in land improvement. Moreover, much more progress may still be made in introducing techniques that, although more advanced than those that now exist, are nonetheless still in conformity with existing values and institutions in the poor country. Ultimately, however, changes in the value structure and character structure of the poor country's society will be necessary if technological progress is to occur extensively throughout the economy. As with all the requirements for accelerating development, technical aid is but one of the elements in the total problem. To achieve its full power as a catalyst, a technical assistance program must be accompanied by other complementary changes in the rest of the poor country's society—extending from an improved educational and administrative structure through which the producers can learn the new technology to social and economic changes which will provide an inducement to adopt the new technology.

Loans, Grants, and the Tying of Aid

GORAN OHLIN

Goran Ohlin is Professor of Economics, Uppsala University, Sweden. He was previously a fellow at the OECD Development Center and worked with the Pearson Commission staff. This selection is taken from his book Foreign Aid Policies Reconsidered *published by the OECD in 1966.*

To A LARGE EXTENT, discussions about loans versus grants or about tied and untied aid have focused on the value of different kinds of aid to receiving countries. But different forms of aid also impose different burdens on donors. A tied loan, or a grant out of a surplus disposal program, means a smaller sacrifice than a straight grant of the same amount in convertible currency.

Rational aid policy must mean a search for forms of aid that achieve their effect at a minimum cost, or maximize their effect at given level of sacrifice. Such calculations may not be possible, but there is nevertheless reason to ask which principles are reflected in the forms of development assistance as currently practiced.

LOANS AND GRANTS

Although the bulk of the development assistance by OECD countries consists of grants and grantlike contributions, the role of lending has increased rapidly. In 1956, about 20 percent of the bilateral gross flow of assistance consisted of lending; in 1963, this share was over 35 percent and almost 50 percent of new commitments took this form. But the role of lending in the aid systems varies widely among donor countries. In France, and in smaller countries, whose aid consists mostly of technical assistance, it is fairly minor; in Italy, Japan, and Germany, on the other hand, it accounts for more than two-thirds of the total flow.

Loans are made on widely differing terms, and there is actually a whole scale of assistance of different hardness—from straight grants, and soft 40 or 50-year loans at token interest rates, to export credits for 5 years carrying interest rates of 7 percent or more. Grace periods and waivers of various kinds add to the gamut.

It is doubtful whether this variety of terms reflects any valid rationale. A number of different principles are usually evoked when the terms are set or explained, but none are compelling. In the first place, it is often held that the terms should be related to the purpose of the project for which the aid is intended. Grants are thus by some donors reserved for technical assistance, soft terms are taken to be appropriate for improvements like roads and harbours and other infrastructure projects which do not yield any direct revenue, and hard terms for projects of greater pecuniary profitability. There are many objections to this principle, among them that it is simply not appropriate to base economic planning on the assumption that each project should pay for itself, or that it should get the type of finance for which it can pay. Whatever the risks attaching to individual projects, they do not apply to government loans. The capital costs charged by the borrowing government against its own projects, or from private borrowers, if the funds are re-lent, need have no relationship with the rates charged by the lender, and this is occasionally recognized, as in the two-step lending procedure increasingly used by the United States and some other governments.

It is striking to what extent the practices of lenders and donors vary on this point. The United States has a rich spectrum of hard and soft types of aid, but ordinary, repayable loans tend to fall into either a soft category of development loans (AID loans), or a hard one (mostly Export-Import Bank). French development finance has been largely in the form of grants, whatever the uses, but the financial assistance outside the franc area is in the form of credits. The EEC Development Fund started its operations supplying only grants but has recently shifted into lending. German assistance, on the other hand, tends to take the form of loans of a wide range of interest rates and maturities. UK loans have had a rate of interest based on the government's borrowing rate plus a management charge; loans have been made softer by lengthening maturities and grace periods and by waivers of interest payments which left nominal rates intact while reducing the effective cost of borrowing; in June, 1965, it was announced that this practice would occasionally be extended to a waiver of all interest payments.

Secondly, terms are influenced by the relationship between the assisting and the receiving country. Grants are much more common to colonies and ex-colonies than to other countries. In 1962, for instance, bilateral assistance to former and/or present colonies of the donor contained only 22 percent net loans, other bilateral aid 42 percent. In part, this reflects the fact that, in the context of "special relationships," aid tends to be of a different character altogether; general program aid and budgetary support is given almost exclusively to ex-dependencies and in grant form. But, clearly, it is also a widespread view that capital assistance in the form of grants expresses a generosity and a confidence appropriate only where the links to the recipient are especially intimate.

According to a third set of arguments, loans are generally superior to grants as a form of foreign assistance as the obligation to repay is assumed to discourage waste and impose a salutary economic discipline on recipients. The implication is that governments of developing countries use funds irrationally, and that repayment obligations will achieve a more rational use of funds than the pressure of scarcity alone. But if governments are assumed to be irrational, then even though they may service their loans there is no presumption that they will use them particularly rationally.[1]

It is also asserted that loans are politically preferable in that they make the aid relationship reciprocal and businesslike and thus spare the sensibilities of recipients, while gifts humiliate and offend. Such arguments were especially common when soft Soviet loans were described as politically more effective than United States aid, which in the middle of the 1950s still contained only grants and relatively hard loans.

From a strictly economic and fairly abstract point of view, the issue may be seen as a matter of the relative productivity of capital. If capital can be more productively employed in the recipient economy than in the country supplying the aid, the transfer results in an overall gain for both economies combined, and this

---

1. *Cf.* Wilson E. Schmidt, "The Economics of Charity: Loans versus Grants", *Journal of Political Economy*, Vol. LXXII (August, 1964), p. 386.

gain is larger the greater the volume of the aid. The benefit to the recipient will consist of this gain plus the concession the donor may make by providing the funds at a lower rate of interest than the yield available to him in domestic uses of funds. This concession is the only burden to the donor: it is proportional both to the volume and to the margin of "softness" so that the burden will remain constant if the volume of lending is increased while interest rates are raised appropriately. It can then be shown rigorously that the objective of maximizing benefits with a given burden will be achieved by "hard"—but also very large—loans. If on the other hand capital is less productively employed in the recipient economy than by the donor, the two countries combined will suffer a loss by the transfer. The benefit to the recipient will then fall below the burden to the donor by the amount of this loss, which again will be proportional to the volume of the transfer. As the smallest volume compatible with a given burden arises from a straight grant, the conclusion is that in this case the benefits associated with a given "sacrifice" will be maximized by grant aid. According to this argument, aid should thus be supplied either in the form of hard loans or grants, depending upon the relative productivity of capital in the two economies involved, and there is no room on rational grounds for intermediate terms.[2]

To these considerations, the force of events has added an overriding one: the ability to service external debt. The terms of aid should on this view be determined, or at least tempered, by the debt servicing capacity of the individual recipient. The indebtedness of underdeveloped countries is said to be so large that softer terms of development assistance are necessary. Lenders supplying credit on soft terms find it offensive if others supply it on harder terms, thus "pre-empting" debt servicing ability, and the question of terms thus becomes one of joint interest to the donors.

---

2. This brief summary takes no account of the complications arising from repayment terms. When these are considered the conclusion, paradoxical at first, is that even when hard loans are indicated they are best given with very long maturity, in the limit as perpetual loans. In other words, repayment terms should be soft although interest should be hard. The explanation, in terms of the above argument, is that *if* the postulated differential between the marginal yields to capital persists, the consequences of the transfer are only accentuated by an extension of the time during which it applies.

"Debt servicing capacity" is in this context an ambiguous concept. It might well be argued that a country that qualifies for foreign assistance has no debt servicing capacity at all. Debt service competes with essential imports for foreign exchange earnings which are regarded as insufficient, and with investment needs for inadequate savings. When debt is serviced in such a situation, it is in recognition of the fact that fulfillment of obligations is a prerequisite for further assistance, but no one expects a country in this position to liquidate its external debt.

As long as assistance continues, donors as a group may thus be said to pay their own service charges. If a constant or growing resource gap in the underdeveloped countries is to be met by the net flow of development loans, the growing reflow will require gross lending to increase at a faster rate the harder the terms, and the ratio between gross lending and net inflow will soon become very large. The magnitudes involved may be illustrated by a simple example. If the net flow of resources to underdeveloped countries is to grow at 5 percent a year and this is to be met by loans at 5 percent or 2 percent, the gross lending and the debt burden will increase according to the following schedules [3]:

INTEREST RATE		5 percent		2 percent	
Year	NET FLOW	GROSS LENDING	INDEBTEDNESS	GROSS LENDING	INDEBTEDNESS
			In Billion Dollars		
0	1.00	1.00	0	1.00	0
5	1.28	2.24	6.4	1.77	4.1
10	1.65	3.80	16.5	2.85	10.0
15	2.12	6.90	31.8	4.32	18.3
20	2.72	10.90	54.4	6.32	30.0
25	3.49	16.60	87.5	8.97	45.6
30	4.49	24.70	134.9	12.61	67.6

If assistance loans are given only for distinct projects, repayment may well put a strain on the balance of payments and raise a demand for balance of payments support and consolidation credits to "roll over" the debt. Actual debt service crises arise

3. The debt burdens are independent of the maturities: the gross lending required is affected by them in the early years, and for these calculations it was assumed that both loans were amortized at 10 percent on outstanding debt each year, corresponding roughly to a 20-year maturity.

from unforeseen short term developments: a bunching of repayment obligations, a sudden drop in export earnings, a failure to restrain imports. A high debt service ratio will increase the risks of such crises if creditors are not willing to continue lending, but, as experience has shown, countries can manage their balance of payments with very high long term debt service ratios, and it would be impossible to specify a permissible maximum for debt service. The tolerable limits depend on policies of the lenders as much as on those of the borrowers.[4]

For donor countries as a whole, then, the question of the terms of aid is in the long run a choice between a large gross flow of loans with a substantial reflow, and a smaller flow of grants or softer aid, with the same net effect on the balance of payments. Although it may be said that, in fact, donors themselves pay the service charges on loans, the point is precisely that they usually do not do so directly. The gross flow of assistance, over which they tend to have some control, may be tied to specific types of projects and exports. The reflow of service charges will certainly reduce the import capacity of the borrowing country, but it will not necessarily reduce imports from the donor in question.

To individual countries, therefore, the problem does not appear in the same light as to donors as a whole. As long as it is accepted that underdeveloped countries will not become net capital exporters until much progress has been made toward more rapid growth and higher levels of living, there will be no repayment and reduction of overall external debt. But individual lenders may expect repayment and reconsider their aid policies, or shift their lending to other countries. Especially to the extent that development lending is used for export promotion, but also when it serves other purposes of the donor, loans may thus have great advantages over a policy that would devote to assistance only the smaller amounts corresponding to the "real burden," but in grant form.

External indebtedness of many underdeveloped countries has indeed grown rapidly in the course of the last decade. Thus, the "public debt" of India has risen from $310 million to $2,936 million between the end of 1955 and 1962, and that of Pakistan

4. *Cf.* Dragoslav Avramovic *et al., Economic Growth and External Debt* (Baltimore, 1964).

from $147 million to $829 million. An IBRD study of these problems estimates that the service on public debt for 74 countries, including most of the underdeveloped world, amounted to $2.9 billion in 1963, of which $2.2 billion was an amortization and 0.7 in interest. With a wider definition of external debt, including commercial arrears, the author concludes that debt service obligations of these countries are no less than $4 billion and could have well reached $5 billion [5] a year.

There is, of course, nothing surprising about the fact that indebtedness of the underdeveloped countries has risen sharply. With net lending at several billions a year, the world system of assistance is bound rapidly to produce a debt of colossal magnitude. This may in itself discourage further lending and slow down the volume of assistance. It also raises fundamental problems about the nature of assistance in the form of lending.

Banking is not commonly regarded as a charitable activity, no matter how useful its services. A repaid loan on commercial terms is not considered a loss, and such benefits as the borrower derives from it he also pays for. Development banking, like all forms of banking, serves to reduce risks by improving the organization of the capital market and thus improving the terms on which credit is available. When it is nevertheless financed by voluntary subscriptions in capital markets, it cannot very well be described as an activity involving a sacrifice. Its contribution is the improvement of terms, and it is not measured by the gross volume of lending.

Characteristically, official development loans of all kinds are extended "when no other sources of finance are available," and in a great number of instances they are extended on terms covering the cost of raising the capital—with the use of the superior credit worthiness of governments or respected banking institutions, such as the World Bank. If the ultimate lenders supply their funds voluntarily, the burden must be nil. The use of official credit to help developing countries is cheap in such circumstances.

If the borrowing country has access to no alternative lender, or if the terms are better than those offered elsewhere, the benefit may indeed be very great. In the case of hard loans at World

5. *Ibid.*

Bank rates, this assumption is no longer accurate. There may now be said to exist at least an imperfect market for development loans, which, especially when they serve export promotion purposes, are not hard to raise for sensible projects, and within the framework of the international aid system it is not correct to assume that developing countries lack alternative sources of finance.

Concessionary loans are indeed another matter, but even these are not gifts, and the "burden" of such loans on the donor economy must, as argued in the previous chapter, be assessed in terms of the magnitude of the concession.

From a banking point of view, there is no reason that productive and remunerative projects should not be financed by loans, provided that the flexibility of the receiving country in managing its resources is sufficient to enable it to transfer the service charges, or this necessity is alleviated by the steady growth of further loans. But in the perspective of development policy, lending inevitably raises serious problems. However they are estimated, the "requirements" of developing countries are considerable and will remain so for a long time. It is unlikely that very many countries will be able to, or even be allowed to, turn themselves into net capital exporters for a very long time. Some models of the development process assume that capital imports into underdeveloped countries on concessionary terms will stop within a reasonably short time if self-sustained growth has been achieved, and that accumulated development debts could then be repaid. However, by that time, the gap between rich countries and poor will be even more overwhelming than it is today, and it seems more than doubtful that the factors underlying foreign aid will have lost their urgency. It is sometimes assumed that finance on conventional terms and from private sources will become increasingly easy. But developing nations, saddled with enormous debts and fixed charges, will, by traditional standards, be miserable credit risks. Indeed, it is hard to believe that, even if continued official aid dwindles to a halt, the next phase would not be a moratorium on debts falling due.

A few years ago, Ragnar Nurkse, speaking about international grants-in-aid, said, "Interest payments, from poor to rich, are now, it seems, not only basically unwanted by the rich countries, but indeed are felt to be somehow contrary to the spirit of the age." Events have not proved him right. So far, it is principally in the help of rich countries that grants have been given precedence. Not only in war finance and lend-lease, but also and most spectacularly in the Marshall Plan, recourse was had to grants in order to avoid the later complications of the transfer of repayments to a nation which was wrongly suspected of being intrinsically a creditor country. For similar wisdom to prevail in the field of development finance, the readiness to shoulder a real burden must be considerably greater in donor countries than it is today.

The role of foreign investment in the past is sometimes cited as a precedent to current development assistance, but such a comparison suffers from a number of weaknesses. To begin with, although there is general agreement that the intangible contribution of foreign investment to the transfer of technology was of great importance, the quantitative role of foreign investment in capital formation seems to have been surprisingly small, except during very short bursts.[6] Even these sufficed to raise the share of debt servicing in the balances of payments of the borrowers to very considerable proportions, and almost every burst of investment produced its painful aftermath of crisis.

Above all, however, it should be stressed that the classical cases of overseas investment before World War I did not involve a sustained transfer of resources to the debtor countries but precisely the opposite. The reflow of investment income to creditor countries almost from the start matched or exceeded the flow of new net investment. This was notably true in Britain where, in Imlah's words, "foreign investments . . . were a little like a revolving fund, a large part of the income was reinvested in the further development of other lands."[7] Before 1870, the balance of interest and dividends reflects the balance on current account fairly closely, and in the remaining decades before 1913, investment income was vastly greater than capital exports. Interest on foreign investments then represented about 10 percent of British national income; 4 percent of national income was invested overseas in 1870–1913—a staggering ratio by some measures, but only

6. *Cf.* Kenneth Berrill, "Foreign Capital and Take-off", in W.W. Rostow (ed.) *The Economics of Take-off into Sustained Growth* (1963).

7. Albert H. Imlah, *Economic Elements in the Pax Britannica* (Cambridge, Mass., 1958), p. 60.

40 percent of the income from past foreign investment.[8] The evidence on French foreign investment is conjectural but such as it is it points to a rate of growth from the beginning of the 19th century distinctly below the probable rate of return.[9]

Needless to say, this picture conceals complex geographic shifts in the gross flow of capital and, from the point of view of the borrowers, the situation was sometimes different, as it had to be. Thus, during the sharp burst of foreign investment in Canada during the period 1900–1913, net imports of capital rose rapidly from rough equality with payments of investment income, and over the period as a whole, investment income paid was only slightly more than one-third of total capital imports.

Generally speaking, however, it remains true that in the heyday of foreign investment, flows of capital only rarely and intermittently grew at a rate sufficient to offset the flow of interest and dividends in the opposite direction.

Much 19th and early 20th century investment was directed to territories capable of developing their export sectors and foreign exchange earnings, so as to be able to meet repayment obligations without difficulty, and crises were due to speculative excess. But in those countries which failed to develop their exports, chronic strains tended to arise in the balance of payments.

Historically, the contribution of foreign investment to the propagation of growth, significant though it was, was not that of creating a large and sustained net inflow of foreign exchange. That, however, is what development assistance efforts in the financial field aim to achieve. Provided that lending increases sufficiently rapidly, it is, of course, theoretically feasible, but the implications are serious. If lending is to create a genuine increase in available resources, the debt must grow faster than the rate of interest on old debt. If this rate of interest is higher than the rate of growth of national income, debt must thus grow faster than national income, and service charges are likely to grow faster than export earnings and to absorb an increasing share of them.

In the traditional view of foreign investment, there is no rea-

8. A.K. Cairncross, *Home and Foreign Investment, 1870–1913* (Cambridge, 1953) Ch. 1.
9. Rondo E. Cameron, *France and the Economic Development of Europe, 1800–1914,* (Princeton, 1961), p. 79.

son in principle why foreign investment could not be serviced as long as the investment is profitable enough and as long as there is sufficient flexibility in the economy to generate the export surplus for repayment. But when the point of departure of the discussion is the premise that foreign resources on a large scale will be necessary over a long period of time to close the gap between the capital and/or foreign exchange required for growth and the domestic resources available, a number of caveats are in place. Unless loans are made on very long terms, they will have to be frequently converted or succeeded by renewed borrowing. As service charges come to claim a larger share of foreign exchange, it becomes difficult to meet them out of free, i.e., earned, exchange and a pressure to borrow to pay interest and to support the balance of payment arises. Consolidation credits and general balance of payments support already figure in many aid programs and may be expected to become more frequent in the future, but this development will lend new content to the issue of project vs. program aid.

AID TYING

While the resort to project aid is largely meant to influence the use of resources in recipient countries, the "tying" of aid is caused by concern with the donor country's economy. The two restraints do not necessarily go together, but about two-thirds of all bilateral aid to underdeveloped countries is actually "tied" in the sense that it either consists of aid in kind in the form of commodities—principally U.S. agricultural surpluses—or that it is to be spent in the donor country.

The objective of such practices may be to promote exports and employment, or to protect a weak balance of payments, but their actual effect is hard to assess. It is clear that often aid would have been spent in the donor country anyway, either by virtue of traditionally close commercial relations, or because it is extended for a project for which the donor country is specially equipped to furnish materials. When not superfluous, the tying may be ineffectual, as when the receiver uses tied funds for imports that would in any case have been made, thus freeing foreign exchange for other purposes.

Finally, it must be recalled that there is little point in comparing tied aid with untied aid if it is unlikely that the aid would have been provided at all, or to the same extent, unless it were tied to exports. This may well be the case if the donor country is troubled by its balance of payments, or suffers from unemployment and surplus capacity, or if the linking of aid to the donor's products seems innocuous and natural to public opinion or vital enough to exporters to become a political condition of support for an aid program.

That untied aid would, in principle, be preferable from the receivers' point of view is quite clear. The restriction of competition involved in tying may mean that equipment is bought at higher prices, or lower quality, especially when the aid is also linked to a specific project. This need not mean more than that the real value of the aid is overstated. What is more serious is that the tying of aid aggravates the evils of limiting it to the foreign exchange components of projects. When tied aid looms large in foreign exchange availability, there will be a tendency to distort development programs in favor of projects with a high and special import content, while vital projects involving mostly local expenditure are neglected. Or, if they are undertaken, they might give rise to an indirect import demand that cannot be met.

When tying is a deliberate means of promoting specific exports, developing certain markets, or employing surplus capacity, donor countries can hardly be expected to renounce its use entirely. Tied aid is better than no aid, and the assistance effort cannot suffer from taking into account the mutual convenience of the partners.

Yet many governments declare, as the British in the White Paper of 1963, that "although we tie part of our aid, we are prepared to take part in any genuine international move towards the untying of aid." [10] To proceed alone to untie aid is said to be impossible as long as other donors continue to tie theirs in ways that promote their exports and markets. There are good political reasons for such hesitation, and this is, as the Chairman of DAC has emphasized, an appropriate area for collective action by donor countries. But when, as is often the case, the reason given for tying is balance-of-payments difficulty—as in the tightening of the procurement regulations for AID loans since 1959—the situation is not so clear.

10. *Aid to Developing Countries*, p. 13.

If it is assumed that underdeveloped countries accumulate no foreign exchange reserves, then industrial countries should not in the aggregate suffer any balance-of-payments deterioration as the result of their financial assistance. Aid should take the form of a transfer of goods and services and there would be no drop in gold or foreign exchange reserves.[11] The impact of the aid policy of any one donor country on her own balance of payments will chiefly depend on what happens to that fraction of the aid which is not spent with the donor, but in another industrialized country.[12] These exports from third countries will induce further trade in ways determined by their import content and their effects on incomes and prices. What cannot be assumed is that, in the end, such third countries will necessarily spend their increased holdings of the original donor's currency. They may increase their reserve position, and, however that is done, it will be at the expense of the reserves of the original donor country.

There would be no reason to expect the trade flows induced by aid to leave balances-of-payments neutral, and the present international monetary system is admittedly deficient in mechanisms for speedy correction of balance-of-payments disequilibria. It is understandable, therefore, that it should be suggested that countries in balance-of-payments difficulties may legitimately tie their aid while other countries have no such excuse.[13]

American procurement restrictions actually only rule out the spending of assistance funds in other industrialized countries, and so at least do not hamper trade among underdeveloped countries. A system for tying funds actually appropriated for local expenditures has also been devised by the United States. But whether or not the tying of aid actually achieves the object of relieving the balance of payments will depend both on respending by third countries and on the repercussions on commercial trade. If the main result were a corresponding displacement of commercial exports, there would be no change either in

---

11. Even if it is assumed that aid leads to an expansion of output with a certain import content, or, if there is no spare capacity to inflation in donor countries that spills over into imports from the underdeveloped bloc, this will be offset by the spending of such export earnings.

12. The switching of resources into aid exports may, of course, raise imports of raw materials, but in this case it is not to be taken for granted that these will give rise to "respending" and be completely offset by exports.

13. Walter S. Salant *et al.*, *The U.S. Balance of Payments in 1958*, p. 188.

trade patterns or in the balance-of-payments of the donor. Actually, the possibilities of substitution are never perfect, and usually the displacement of commercial exports is probably offset by the increase in respending that results from tying, but the net effects are clearly smaller than often imagined. When aid is dispensed in areas with traditionally close links to the donor, as French aid in the franc zone, most of it will be spent in the donor country without formal tying procedures, and it is in the nature of project assistance that the same will often be the case when projects are prepared in close collaboration with technicians from donor countries. It also stands to reason that the gains from tying are likely to be the greatest where the donor's traditional share of the market has been small, and these are precisely the cases in which most countries tie their aid if they only tie part of it—thus the ex-colonial powers generally do not tie their aid to their ex-dependencies but do in lending to countries they have not formerly assisted. Aid from the Soviet bloc is tied but, in addition, the service charges on bloc loans may be said to be tied the other way by the commitment to accept local currency or stipulated export commodities in repayment. If balance-of-payments problems in donor countries justify the tying of aid, it might well be argued that the far more disturbing balance-of-payments problems of recipients would justify such bilateral measures to facilitate repayment.[14]

Proposals have also been made to "take development aid out of the balance-of-payments" by trying to ensure that third countries would eventually respend aid funds rather than add them to reserves.[15] No doubt such arrangements would remove one of the obstacles to increasing aid appropriations in donor countries. But the inconveniences attaching to aid tying are very hard to estimate and are clearly exaggerated when reference is made only to the proportion of aid funds subject to procurement restrictions, for the effect of these restrictions is far more marginal than it indicates. When it is further considered that tying often provides the vital impulse for assistance and may serve other purposes besides balance-of-payment protection, it may well be asked

14. V.N. Bandera, "Tied Loans and International Payments Problems," *Oxford Economic Papers*, Vol. XVII, July, 1965, pp. 299–308.
15. *E.g.*, the suggestions by Professor Kiyoshi Kojima. See *The Economist*, July 25, 1964, pp. 401–402.

whether the practice deserves the opprobrium it often receives. Here, as in all facets of assistance policy, it must be rational to attempt to minimize donor's inconvenience at given level of benefit. When objections to aid tying come from competing industrial countries which fear the disturbance of normal trade and feel excluded from the market created by aid funds, intricate issues may indeed arise, but the commercial interest of one country cannot constitute a valid objection to the generosity of another.

Foreign Aid—A Critique
ALBERT O. HIRSCHMAN AND RICHARD M. BIRD

Albert O. Hirschman is Professor of Economics at Harvard University, and a well-known trade and development expert who has interested himself especially in the problems of Latin America. Richard M. Bird teaches at the University of Toronto.

FOREIGN AID is as Janus-faced an institution as can be found. In a world of sovereign nations, rich and poor, it is an instrument of national policy which can be used by the rich to acquire influence and to increase their power. At the same time, foreign aid redistributes income from the rich to the poor and can thus serve to speed the latter's development.

While foreign aid might never have come into this world without its appeal to both national and transnational interests, it has also suffered from the resulting ambiguity about its "real" function. Unlike such pure power instruments as national military establishments, on the one hand, and overt redistribution mechanisms like the progressive income tax, on the other, foreign aid has never been firmly institutionalized. It has led a precarious existence, bolstered from time to time by cold war conflicts and then flagging again as immediate dangers passed, or the lack of a "domestic constituency" in the aid giving countries made itself more strongly felt, or certain unpleasant side effects of aid giving became apparent. Lately, signals of a new crisis in aid giving have multiplied in the United States, there is disaffection and disenchantment as well in Western Europe and perhaps in the Soviet Union, and foreign aid is none too popular even in the recipient countries.

Current practice in foreign aid dates from the new principles introduced by the Kennedy Administration in the early sixties. Essentially, this country's doctrine moved at that time to embrace what has since become known as the "program approach" to foreign aid.

FROM PROJECT TO PROGRAM AID

The "project approach" had predominated through the fifties. The World Bank had been enjoined by its very statutes to extend loans only on the basis of specific projects (in transportation, power, agriculture, and so forth). The first activity of the United States in the field of aid to underdeveloped countries was technical (Point Four) assistance, which had necessarily a project content and which evolved naturally into capital assistance with a similar content. Important departures from this practice occurred in countries on the periphery of the Soviet bloc. To a number of these countries the United States extended massive military as well as economic assistance, with the latter usually being justified in terms of short term import or budgetary requirements.

By 1960, criticism of the project approach was widespread. It was easy to show how development depended not on a few specific projects, but on an adequate overall investment effort, with respect to both aggregate size and composition, and how ill-designed fiscal, monetary, and foreign exchange policies could undercut the positive contribution of any individual project to economic growth. Economists further pointed out that the donor country was not really financing the project for which it was ostensibly granting funds, but rather the "marginal" project which the aid recipient would have just given up had he not been handed the additional resources for a project which he probably would have undertaken in any event. For these reasons, so it was argued, a look at the total spending pattern of the recipient country is essential if one wishes to have some assurance that the aid funds are put to productive use. Finally, it was pointed out that project aid necessarily implies a series of biases and perverse incentives: it encourages the aid recipient to prepare large capital projects, to exaggerate the foreign exchange portion of the total cost of these projects, and to favor public infrastructure projects, which are most easily financed through loans or grants extended from one government to another for project purposes.

While these criticisms of the project approach all contributed to a change in the climate of expert opinion, another important reason for going from project to program aid was the desire to increase the level of aid to some key countries and to provide a solid institutional basis for aid giving at this higher level. Program aid was conceived as aid given "in bulk" on the basis of a general understanding between donor and recipient about the latter's development program and principal economic policies. (Other terms frequently used in connection with program aid are, in ascending order of euphemization, "leverage," "incentive programming," "making sure of self-help.")

As a result of what was then thought to be the model case of India, the accent was at first primarily on achieving agreement on the recipient's development plan, its size, priorities, and the resulting "resources gap" to be filled by aid in its various forms. But in most developing countries, development plans are primarily statements of intention. Further, even in the rare country with a highly operational development plan, the fulfillment of the plan's objectives would depend crucially, among other things, on "appropriate" fiscal, monetary, and other economic policies. In Latin America, moreover, program aid under the Alliance for Progress was to be forthcoming not only in connection with a broad agreement on economic development objectives, but was to be premised also on advances in social development that depended on the enactment and implementation of reforms in land tenure, income taxation, educational opportunity, and the like.

THE TWO AID BARGAINS COMPARED

The general idea of moving from the project to the program approach consisted, therefore, in laying the groundwork for a substantial and steady flow of aid through a meeting of minds between donor and recipient on central economic programs and policies of the recipient country.

When the matter is put in this way, the formidable difficulties of the program approach begin to appear. No doubt, by moving the discussion between donor and recipient from where to build what kind of power station to fiscal, monetary, or agrarian reform policies, one is turning from peripheral to central issues of the recipient's decisions. But is that a good thing? We shall now argue that this move raises at least as many problems as it solves.

To facilitate the discussion, it is useful to attempt at this point a conceptual distinction between "pure" project and "pure" program aid. In the real world this distinction will of course be blurred, as these two archetypes of aid hardly ever appear in their pure forms. Hence it should be understood that our subsequent discussion does not cover every conceivable case of project or program aid, but tries to catch the essential difference between two diverse forms of aid giving. Moreover, we do not aim at extolling project aid, with whose problems and drawbacks we are familiar, but rather at bringing out, with project aid as a backdrop, the heretofore largely neglected political implications and side effects of program aid.

As a starting point for the discussion, we may imagine that aid is given in the form of a check drawn by the donor to the order of the recipient, without conditions or strings of any kind. This unconditional aid can then turn into conditional aid along two principal routes.

First, the donor can insist that the money be spent for certain specific purposes; the result is pure project aid as here defined. Second, the donor may require that the recipient country change some of its ways and policies as a condition for receiving the funds; this is our definition of pure program aid.

From the point of view of the recipient, there is a fundamental difference between the two bargains which may conceivably accompany the transfer of aid funds. Pure project aid forces the recipient country to substitute to some extent the donor's investment preferences for its own insofar as the use of the aid funds is concerned. As a result, the recipient country lands in a situation it senses as inferior to the one in which the same amount of aid would be available unconditionally. Nevertheless, the aid permits the country to achieve a position in which it is unequivocally better off than without aid, in the sense that more funds are forthcoming for some purposes while, generally speaking, investments that the country would have made in the absence of aid will not be curtailed. Thus, the conditions attached to pure project aid are not likely to arouse strong hostility in the recipient country and do not require the policymakers to sacrifice any important objective which they would have been able to pursue in the absence of aid.

The situation changes significantly in the case of the bargain characteristic of pure program aid. The commitment a country undertakes in connection with this sort of aid is typically of the following kinds: to increase investment and decrease consumption, to increase the share of the private sector and decrease that of the public sector; to devalue the currency and thereby alter *relative* price relationships within the country; to throttle inflation and therefore strike a blow at the particular interest group whose turn it is to benefit from the next inflationary appropriation, credit expansion, or rise in prices or wages. There are others. In all these instances, compliance with the conditions attending program aid makes one group within the recipient country worse and another better off than before. The bargain preceding the granting of program aid also implies that the aid receiving government will alter its previous policy mix in such a way as to sacrifice in some measure objective A (say, a larger public sector) to objective B (say, growth).

Economists who have discussed the concept of community welfare have long been divided into two groups: those who deny, and those who affirm, that meaningful statements can be made about increases or decreases in collective welfare when, as a result of economic change, one group gains at the expense of another. There is no need for us to enter into this discussion, except to note that its protracted and stubborn nature testifies to the fundamental difference between the two situations that we have just described. With pure project aid, the recipient government can achieve all of its pre-aid objectives (plus some additional aid financed ones) and no group in the country need be any worse off. With the type of conditional program aid discussed here, the objectives of public policies will be reshuffled and some domestic group is likely to be hurt. Even though the total resources available to the country are increased through the aid, the hurt group cannot be directly compensated, at least in the short run, for its loss, by the very terms of the aid agreement.

We should mention here one particularly important way in which project aid shades off in the real world into program aid. When the project donor spends its funds on, say, a certain kind of power station, it will often have views, and will attempt to have them prevail, on such matters as accounting practices, power rates, administrative autonomy, and perhaps even public versus private ownership of the utility. Project aid may then also involve policy changes that would hurt some groups or individuals. Even in this case, however, an important difference between project and program aid remains. Program aid is usually given in connection with changes in *central* economic policies of the recipient, whereas the policy changes the donor is liable to insist on in connection with project aid are germane to the construction and operation of the project and are therefore likely to be concerned with matters that are at some remove from the central policy concerns around which the more important group conflicts rage.

THE PROGRAM AID BARGAIN FURTHER CONSIDERED

It will, of course, be argued that whatever sacrifice is entailed in the policy changes required by the program aid bargain is more than fully compensated by the other side, namely the aid package itself. The fact that aid is accepted on these terms could be considered as evidence that there is nothing to worry about. After all, the recipient government could have refused aid (as Burma did in general, and Brazil and Colombia at one time or another, in connection with assistance from the International Monetary Fund) if it felt that the conditions were too harsh. But this application of the notion of revealed preference misses several points. In the first place, we were intent on showing the difference between two forms of conditional aid-giving and on pointing out that the cost of obtaining aid is of a different nature in the two cases. In the second, it is a gross oversimplification to treat a government entering the program type of bargain on foreign aid like a consumer buying himself a bag of apples. Since aid, in this case, has as its counterpart a shift in national objectives and in the short term fortunes of different social groups, the bargain will be considered a bad one by the circles that value highly the objective that has been sacrificed and by those groups whose interests have been hurt. Hence, the very bargain that gives rise to program aid can and will be attacked directly by these circles and groups as being damaging to the national interest as they define it. Pure project aid is ordinarily immune to this kind of destabilizing side effect. Precisely for that reason, those who attack it will often resort to alleging that it is *impure* and carries some unavowed and excessive cost in terms of general economic or political policy commitments. In other words, to be effective, an attack on project aid will attempt to prove that it is *really* the program type of aid.

The difference between a country or a country's government adopting certain changes in its central economic policies as a *quid pro quo* for aid and a consumer disbursing cash for a pound of apples goes deeper still. The program aid bargain is effective only if the government is genuinely convinced of the positive value of the policies it has adopted in conjunction with the aid—if there has been, that is, a genuine meeting of minds between donor and recipient about the economic policy measures conducive to development. It is as if the consumer were not only made to hand over the cash, but were asked to positively enjoy this act instead of sensing it as a cost. Moreover, the commitment of the recipient government is ordinarily not just to a single policy action, but to a *policy* that requires implementation through a practically infinite *series* of actions. A more correct comparison of the program aid bargain would therefore be to the decision of a person who joins the monastic orders; he does not usually consider his vows of poverty and chastity as a payment for the promise of eternal afterlife, but as something to be valued and perhaps enjoyed directly and independently of that promise.

One matter is already becoming clear: for the commitments entered into in the course of program aid negotiations to be faithfully adhered to, the recipient government ought to be so convinced of the correctness of the policies to which it commits itself that it would have followed these policies even without aid. Paradoxically, therefore, program aid is fully effective only when it does not achieve anything—when, that is, no *quid pro quo* (in the sense of a policy that would not have been undertaken in the absence of aid) is exacted as the price of aid. (It is ironic that, at least when it is effective, program aid is vulnerable to the very charge that has long been levelled—wrongly, we think—against project aid: namely, that one can never be sure that the project thus financed would not have been undertaken even in the absence of aid.)

In these situations, the donor would set himself the task of *rewarding* virtue (or rather, what he considers as such) where virtue appears of its own accord.

This is indeed a modest and manageable task, but it is also one that does not usually satisfy the donors. Precisely because the institutional basis and public opinion support of aid are so precarious in the donor country, the proponents and dispensers of aid have quite naturally felt compelled to make extraordinary claims for what aid can accomplish. The most persistent of these claims has been that aid acts as a "catalyst." This term is meant to convey that aid makes the difference between stagnation (or perhaps deterioration) and vigorous economic growth of the recipient country, or between the recipient being hostile and being friendly to the donor country. To these traditional and exaggerated claims for aid, a new variant has been added by the program approach, namely, that aid, properly conditioned, makes the difference between the recipient following the "wrong" and adopting the "right" economic policies.

In this fashion, then, aid is not seen in the role of rewarding virtue, but in the role, infinitely more difficult, of bringing virtue into the world. Now the fact that aid is known to be available *if* certain policies are followed will sometimes serve to strengthen a domestic group genuinely and independently convinced of the correctness of these policies and it is therefore not inconceivable that aid will on occasion help this group to come to power. This is the ideal case in which program aid acts first as a catalyst and then achieves so complete a meeting of minds and so full a sharing of values and objectives between donor and recipient that from then on they will march hand in hand toward a better future.

We have on purpose drawn a caricature, for it is our conviction that this picture of program aid as a catalyst for virtuous policies belongs to the realm of rhapsodic fantasy. At best, situations in which aid helps virtue to triumph in this fashion are the exception rather than the rule. The normal case is far more prosaic: the knowledge that aid is available if certain policies are adopted serves to make these policies more attractive and less costly than they would otherwise be. These policies will therefore often be adopted by aid-hungry governments in spite of continuing doubts of the policy makers themselves, resistance from some quarters within the government, onslaught against the "deal" from the opposition, and general distaste for the whole procedure.

Naturally, doubts and reservations are not voiced at the moment of the aid compact; hence the delusion on the part of the donor that there has been a full meeting of minds. But soon after virtue has been "bought" through aid under these conditions, the reservations and resistances will find some expression—for example, through half-hearted implementation or sabotage of the policies agreed on—and relations between donor and recipient will promptly deteriorate as a result.

PROBLEMS ENCOUNTERED IN BUYING VIRTUE THROUGH AID

It may be argued that once a government has unequivocally committed itself to certain acts as a condition of receiving aid, there is a good chance it will convince itself that these acts are truly in the national interest, even though previously it may not have thought so. Psychologists have developed the theory of "cognitive dissonance" to analyze individual behavior in similar situations. The theory teaches that if a person engages in "discrepant behavior"—in acts, that is, which cannot be reconciled to what he considers his beliefs and values—he will attempt to reduce the resulting dissonance by changing his values in such a way that harmony is restored.

However, the theory also stresses another point that is crucial here: if the discrepant behavior *is induced by either carrot or stick*, there will be far less consequential value change than if the discrepant behavior occurs in some accidental, absent-minded, or experimental fashion. If the behavior is rewarded (as it is, in our case, by the granting of aid), dissonance hardly arises, because, in accounting for his behavior to himself, the actor has a ready explanation and excuse for the fact that he did something contrary to his principles, opinions, or preferences. (For the same reason, declarations of support for a cause against which one has previously fought are unlikely to change a subject's prior beliefs when such declarations are exacted under torture.) Therefore, the very act of rewarding policy changes through aid undermines the determination with which these changes will be carried out and makes backsliding and sabotage more likely.

These considerations explain why certain types of policy commitments on the part of aid receiving countries are more workable—and therefore have turned out to be more popular with the donors than others. The more workable and more popular commitments are precisely those that are highly visible, verifiable, measurable and, at their best, irreversible. One thinks of a revision of the customs tariff, of the imposition of credit restrictions in order to curb inflation, or, most typically perhaps, of a devaluation. In the latter case, there would seem to be little possibility of backsliding or of second thoughts. Yet, while devaluation cannot be retracted, its intended effects can usually be frustrated by subsequent monetary, fiscal, and wage-price policies. Hence, even in the case of devaluation, a government which harbors a feeling that it has been pushed into an unwise policy can often administer an "I-told-you-so" lesson to the donor just by not carrying out certain complementary policies after the devaluation.

In the case of other economic or social policies that sometimes have stood in the center of aid negotiations, the continued psychological resistance of the aid recipients to such policies after a formal compact has been sealed can manifest itself more directly and easily. Whether the aid negotiations were concerned with enlarging the private sector of the economy or with establishing the basis for a land reform, the commitments a government has undertaken in these areas can be rendered inoperative through bureaucratic harassment or through lack of administrative energy, respectively. The old Spanish colonial adage *se acata pero no se cumple* (one obeys but one does not comply) will thus be widely practiced once again, and properly so. A country which permits its key economic policies to be determined by this type of international negotiation finds itself in fact in a semicolonial situation and is likely to adopt all the time-honored methods of stealthy and indirect resistance appropriate to that situation.

THE HIDDEN COSTS OF PROGRAM AID

The resistance of the recipient country to some of the policy commitments it has underwritten in the course of the aid negotiations is not the whole story. The general unhappiness about having had its arm twisted can find other outlets than backsliding on these same commitments.

In a simple model of international relations we may assume that, for the sake of independence, self-respect, and defense against accusations of being a satellite, the government of B, a poor country, is determined to maintain a certain *average distance* from country A, a great power and a potential donor. Country B measures this distance along two dimensions, the extent to which it adopts economic policies suggested by A and the extent to which it takes A's position in the leading issues of international politics. Under these conditions, a success on the part of the great power in having B "do the right thing" in economic policy will result in a strong urge on the part of B to compensate for this move in the direction of A by a move in the opposite direction in international politics. Only in this fashion can the desired average distance be maintained. That this model of international behavior is not completely unrealistic, in spite of its simplicity, can be shown by recalling a few episodes of the recent past: the attempt of the Quandros government in Brazil to move in the direction of a strongly neutralist posture in international relations after having adopted economic policies long advocated by the United States and the International Monetary Fund; to some extent, Pakistan's *rapprochement* with China; and, lately, a number of "surprising" foreign policy positions taken by the present Indian government just after it had finally been so "reasonable" in its decisions on domestic economic policy.

In this manner, a "successful" program aid negotiation in the course of which the recipient agrees to a variety of economic policies suggested by the donor may well have hidden, though considerable, costs; first, a direct cost to the donor in terms of the loss of certain diplomatic and foreign policy supports he thought doubly secure because of the aid extended; second, a serious loss of public support for the aid program in the donor country, as a result of what will be felt as ingratitude, hostility, and "irresponsible antics" on the part of the recipient. In this indirect fashion, the attempt at maximizing the productivity of aid by exercising "leverage" involves the risk of drying up the flow of aid at its very source.

OTHER FRICTIONS CREATED BY THE PROGRAM APPROACH

Our case can be further bolstered by important differences between project and program aid related to the diplomacy of the aid process. Consider first the donor's claim to have his advice taken seriously on the ground that he contributes substantial resources. This claim is strong in the case of projects, where the donor's contribution often amounts to one-half or more of the total cost of the project. It is much weaker in the case of program aid, for here the donor's contribution is measured against the recipient country's national product or, at best, its total investment or imports. In such comparisons, the aid effort is almost always likely to look disproportionately small in relation to the important changes in national economic policies that are being sought.

Next, we may examine the donor country's implied claim that its own judgment is superior to that of the recipient. In the case of projects financed by the donor, the justification and credibility of the claim is usually quite strong. The donor country is likely to know more about the construction of highways and power stations than the recipient, simply because it is economically more advanced and has specialized knowledge in the areas in which it stands ready to finance projects. When it comes to appropriate economic policies to foster growth along with price stability and an acceptable distribution of income, the claim of the donor country to superiority is far more questionable. Frequently the donor country itself is far from having fully solved these very problems. Even if it has done better at them than the aid recipient, the applicability of its experience to the wholly different economic, social, historical, and political circumstances of another country must be much in doubt. The claim to superior knowledge is therefore fairly credible and innocuous in the case of project aid. It is not credible in the case of program aid—indeed, it is profoundly irritating.

The diplomacy of aid is even more directly involved in our final point. It is in the nature of the aid relationship that comparatively low level officials of the donor country are paired off in aid negotiations with high level officials of the recipient countries. This irksome difference in levels is far less pronounced in the case of project aid than program aid. In discussing the layout and specifications of a highway, an engineer of an aid mission or of the World Bank may perhaps exchange arguments at one point with the director of the highway agency of the aid receiving country. But the matters discussed in conjunction with program aid relate, as we have seen, to central economic policies and issues. Given the centralization of decision making and the thinness of the elite in the typical aid receiving country, these matters can ordinarily be decided only at the very top of the political structure, by the President and his Minister of Finance. And who are their counterparts around the negotiating table? At best, the director of the local aid mission and, usually, various mission staff members. In this way, program aid recreates a typical colonial situation in which the rulers of the recipient country have to deal as equals with, and often feel that they have to take orders from, persons who, within their own country, are miles away from the seat of power. There is no need to expand on the resentment created by this situation.

Since, in our opinion, the program approach overreaches itself when it attempts grandiosely to bring virtue into the world, the explicit or implicit conditioning of aid on changes in policies of the recipient countries should be avoided. This does not mean that the donor cannot make his opinions and preferences known; but it does imply that elaborate arrangements should be made to divorce the exchange of opinions about suitable economic policies from the actual aid giving process. The educational virtues of such discussions will be strengthened rather than weakened as a result. Finally, the donor should resist the temptation to measure "performance" of the recipient at frequent intervals by narrow quantitative indicators, when by its very nature such performance can be assessed properly only over a relatively long period of time by a combination of quantitative information and qualitative judgment.

External Aid: For Plans or Projects?

HANS W. SINGER

Hans W. Singer of the Institute of Development Studies at Sussex University previously spent many years as Senior Economist at the United Nations in New York. This selection was taken from his article in the Economic Journal, *September 1965.*

EXTERNAL FINANCIAL AID to underdeveloped countries is given in diverse forms. Some of it is clearly linked with specific projects; some of it is given in general support of annual budgets or longer term plans without reference to specific projects; some of it is in a great variety of forms between these two categories. Such intermediate forms include specific projects within the framework of a development plan, earmarked aid to be drawn upon only for specific agreed projects, support for groups of projects rather than individual projects, aid for specific import requirements (food, spare parts) not linked to specific projects.

In discussing some issues arising from this wide variety of forms of aid and aid policies, a distinction has first to be made between the *ostensible* tying of project aid to specific projects and the projects which the aid *actually* finances. Provided that the country which receives aid has some additional money of its own (or receives additional aid from other sources), and provided that this additional money is not entirely absorbed in the project or projects selected by the aid donor and to which his aid is tied, the project *actually* financed by aid may be quite different from the one to which the aid is *ostensibly* tied. If the project to which the aid is ostensibly tied is a "high priority project" which would in any case have been part of the recipient's plan, and which he otherwise would have undertaken with his own money, then obviously the aid given enables the recipient to release his own money from Project A (which is now aid financed), continue with Projects B, C, and D, which he financed with his own money, and utilize his money now released from Project A in order to add a new Project E to his original development plan or expenditure schedule. This could mean that the donor of aid ties his aid to Project A, studies it minutely and satisfies himself that it is technically sound and economically right, while in reality—as distinct from appearance—his aid may go into Project E, which he may know nothing about, which he does not study and which may be neither technically sound nor economically right, nor generally the kind of thing that the aid donor would want to support. In effect, he has given plan aid without knowing it—like Molière's prose speaker.

This situation is basically unsatisfactory. There is an element of makebelieve in that the donors of aid, as well as the parliaments and citizens of donor countries, believe or pretend that they are doing one thing when in fact they are doing something quite different. Such self-delusion or deception does not strike one as a happy basis for the kind of international cooperation and solidarity which aid should represent and permit. There may be good reasons for this situation. To tie the aid to the "high-priority" Project A may be politically necessary in order to rally support for aid. It may provide the opportunity to render technical assistance in connection with the high priority Project A, and indeed to improve it or redesign it fundamentally; it may be more important for the development of the recipient country to do this in respect of the high priority Project A than in respect of the marginal Project E, even though the latter is the project which the aid really finances (in the sense that Project E is the project which would have to be eliminated if the aid did not exist). Project A may enable the aid donor to tie his aid to the supply of his own equipment for Project A. It may be that untied aid [1] would be unacceptable or economically impossible for the donor (because of balance-of-payment difficulties), while Project E (which he really finances) may not need the kind of equipment that he would like (or be able) to supply.

But it still remains true that if specific project aid is viewed not only from the point of view of expediency or popularity but also as a continuing relationship and a contribution to the long run development and ultimate "takeoff" of the assisted country, then it is myopic of the aid giver to limit his attention, analysis, and technical assistance to Project A. He should be equally interested

1. *I.e.*, not tied to the donor's own equipment and supplies (as distinct from aid not tied to specific projects).

in Projects B, C, D and E—perhaps especially E, since this is the real result of his aid. Even if there is no substitution of resources between Projects A and E, the efficiency of Project A would still depend on the soundness of the recipients' total investment program. If the aid must be tied for balance-of-payment reasons, it would still be better to seek agreements with other aid givers so that the receiving country would be able to buy in the cheapest market while the balances-of-payments of the individual donor countries would benefit more or less in proportion to the aid which they give. It would also be more rational to tie the aid to specific items of equipment (or the products of specific depressed areas in the aid giving country), while still permitting the recipients to use the tied supplies in whatever projects and fields these supplies are cheapest in relation to alternate sources.

So far, we have assumed that the aid financed Project A is truly a high priority project which the country would and should have carried out with its own money if the aid had not been forthcoming. It is possible to imagine the worse case where Project A is not a true high priority project at all but is put forward only because it is the kind of project which attracts aid from the donor.

Because of the rules of the aid game as at present played, the donor may be prevented from financing local supplies needed for the true priority project, or from financing general supplies of food or raw materials or spare parts, or from taking account of the indirect developmental balance-of-payments needs of the assisted country. Where the project to which the aid is tied has been tailored to meet the needs of the aid donor rather than those of the aided country, there is not even the consolation that the aided country's own money will be released for Project E, and that with good luck and good planning Project E will be exactly the project which, with more sensible rules of the aid game, would have been selected in the first place. The fact is that there may be no true release. On the contrary, Project A which has been put forward to attract aid, although not among the real top priorities of the country, will also tie down some of the recipient country's own resources, which would otherwise have gone into a real top priority project (still, for the present assuming good planning). More local cost financing within the framework of project aid would help to eliminate this distortion. The best that can be hoped for in this case is that the value of the aid (which could not have been obtained for any other project) will outweigh the negative effect of the diversion of the recipient country's own resources away from its real priority. This will, of course, often, probably normally, be the case (especially if the aid is on soft terms), so that the net contribution of the aid is positive. But it is hardly an ideal state of affairs, and certainly does not maximize the contribution of aid to development.

So far we have implicitly assumed that the aid giving country and the receiving country are in broad agreement about the priorities and top needs of the aid receiving country. If this assumption is not true, then of course the case for specific project aid is greatly strengthened. If the donor country believes that Project A is the top priority, but if Project A would not be included by the receiving country in its development plans, so that without aid only Projects B, C, D, . . . would be executed, then the situation is fundamentally changed. The fact that Project A (which is not included in the country's own priorities) will be carried out only because aid is available exclusively for it, but not for other projects, ceases to be a vice and becomes a virtue. This is the case at least in the judgment of the aid giving country which believes that Project A is better than the receiving country's own Projects B, C, D, . . . It is also objectively the case if the aid giving country's judgment of the receiving country's priorities and needs is better than that of the receiving country itself.

This last assumption is, of course, contrary to the polite assumption underlying international economic relations that each country is the best judge of its own needs (or indeed that each government of the day is the best judge of its own country's needs). The opposite assumption, that another aid giving country is a better judge of a receiving country's needs than that country or its government itself, will be rarely made explicit, but it will nevertheless sometimes guide the actions of the aid giving country. In fact, the aid receiving countries on occasion may recognize this by specifically asking advice from aid giving sources about their proper priorities. One way in which this can be done without violating the polite assumption about each country's being the best judge of its own needs is to ask such assistance from international organizations whose advice is not "foreign," but who nevertheless may either themselves dispense aid or whose judgments concerning priorities may stand a better chance of being accepted by aid giving countries than those of the aid receiving countries. Thus, where there is some disagreement about priorities, specific project aid may be the only way in which aid can be forthcoming at all. Moreover, in this case there would be little self-deception; the aid will *actually* make Project A possible, as well as being *ostensibly* tied to it. The assisted country will still go on with Projects B, C, D, . . . which would also have been carried out in the absence of aid (except to the extent that its own resources are tied down in the new aid assisted Project A).

A somewhat related case for aid tied to the specific Project A can be made where the receiving country does have a general plan and priorities acceptable to the aid donor but has not worked out its general ideas in terms of specific projects. In that case, the tying of aid to specific projects has the advantage of being a convenient way of helping or forcing the assisted country to translate its acceptable development strategy into concrete projects. The element of self-deception will also disappear in this case. For what happens in fact is that the receiving country will carry out its own plans according to its own priorities (accepted by the donor), while if general plan aid had been given the plan would not actually have been carried out through lack of concrete projects. This is therefore a somewhat paradoxical position where specific project aid is given in order to give effective general plan aid.

The element of illusion or deception inherent in the specific project approach can also be avoided if the donor country or agency picks the marginal project (Project E), which the receiving country is able to add to its plan as the result of the additional aid which it is getting, as the project to which to tie its aid. It does, of course, presuppose a certain degree of sophistication on the part of the donor of aid, to expect him to tie his aid to a "marginal" project, instead of insisting on identification with a "high priority project." Perhaps more important, however, this procedure also presupposes a high degree of sophistication in the planning process of the aid receiving country. In order to identify the marginal project, that country must draw up not one plan but two: one without aid and one predicated on aid. It is difficult enough to draw up one plan, let alone two (or perhaps even several, predicated on different amounts of external aid). The economy of scarce planning capacity is precisely one of the main advantages of plan aid known in advance to the receiving country.

This last point brings us up against the major difficulty of "identifying" aid with any project, whether priority or marginal. So far, we have mechanistically assumed that a plan consists of separate projects, A, B, C, D, E, . . . which can be ranked according to priority, and without "feedback" effects among each other. This view of planning will, however, rarely be accurate, except perhaps in the most primitive conditions. In fact, the whole point about planning is that the developmental impact of any good expenditure pattern *plus* policy package is maximized, if these expenditures and policies are properly related to each other and taken as a whole. Thus, Plan II (prepared on the assumption of some aid and hence larger) will differ from Plan I (prepared on the assumption of no aid and hence smaller) not just by the addition of one or two projects. Rather, if the planning process in the country is at all meaningful, Plan II will be quite different from Plan I. There will be projects in Plan II which are not in Plan I, but there will also be projects in Plan I which are not in Plan II. Moreover, Plan I and Plan II may contain identical projects, but these may well be carried out with a different technology, on a different scale and on a different time schedule in the larger (aided) Plan II compared with the smaller (unaided) Plan I. Thus, the identification of a "marginal project" for purposes of tying aid to it without illusion or deception does not only require a high degree of sophistication, but is really inherently impossible except in rare circumstances. Thus, in the final analysis aid *can* only be given on a "macro" basis, to result in additional output in terms of value, but not on a "micro" basis in terms of specific projects.

It will be remembered that so far we have assumed that the aid given to a country is only part of the total available resources and accordingly that the aided project or projects are not the only developmental activity carried out. Where this assumption is not valid, the problem discussed here can hardly be said to exist. Project A (top priority) and Project E (marginal) are identical, since there is only one single Project A. Thus the question of deception or illusion cannot arise. The aid is bound to be attached to "the" project. The only question which arises in certain circumstances is whether the Project A (aided), which *is* the development plan of the country, is imposed upon the receiving country by the donor by the threat that the aid will disappear if Project A is changed, or whether Project A has been previously selected by the receiving country and is then accepted by the donor. This alternative may look superficially similar to a choice between project aid and plan aid, but it has really little to do with it. The tying of aid in this case may be of legal, political, or administrative importance, but it certainly has no economic meaning, not even the dangers of illusion or deception.

We have mentioned before as a possible advantage of project aid, especially if a high priority project is selected for attaching the aid, that this may serve as a convenient handle for improving the project or rendering technical assistance. Against this must be set the danger that project aid may lead to delays in negotiation and thus in project implementation, and this would be a greater danger and more harmful if the aid is attached to the high priority Project A rather than the marginal Project E. Project aid may result in additional aid which would not otherwise be forthcoming at all, but this may be offset by the possibility that project discussions and frictions and differences of opinion concerning specific projects result in delays and pipeline accumulations, so that the actual flow of aid may in fact be smaller than it would have been with plan aid not tied to projects. Even an argument that project aid is good because it forces the receiving country to come up with concrete projects finds its counterpart in the argument that planning aid is good because it forces the receiving country to come up with sound plans and think about the necessary interrelation of its projects and its total development policies. However, a plan solely prepared to please aid donors would not be likely to rest on a solid foundation.

Plan aid seems to be more popular among the receiving countries than project aid. This would be expected to be considered as an advantage of plan aid, since it may spur the receiving country to greater efforts in order to get the aid, apart from smoothing relations between the aid giver and the receiver, which is presumably also an objective of aid. However, the recipient's preference for plan aid over project aid is sometimes considered to be an argument in favor of project aid, because it shows that plan aid is "soft" and requires less "discipline."

It may be said that aid tied to specific projects is an inducement to receiving countries to think of development in terms of concrete projects, i.e., specific types of net investment of physical capital. Development is, of course, much more than that, and in fact many expenditures classified as current or as consumption are much more developmental than expenditures classified as "projects" or capital expenditure. From this latter point of view, plan aid, and, even more, annual budget aid, is clearly profitable if the donor agrees with the recipient on developmental policies and priorities.

Development plans in some countries may be highly unstable, with frequent revisions or even abrupt changes with changes of government. On the other hand, important projects will, or should, figure in all these plans, however frequently revised or upset. Here project aid has an advantage over plan aid. One suspects that much of the preference of donors for project aid has its real, if unacknowledged, basis in some mistrust of the recipient's planning stability.

A difficult problem exists in the case of small aid giving countries, especially in relation to large receiving countries (aid by Luxembourg to India, for example). The paradox consists in the fact that the aid giver will not want to go to the trouble of examining specific projects to which the aid would be tied, since the cost and delays of the examination would be out of proportion to the aid available. On the other hand, aid tied to the plan would make the aid appear too insignificant. The answer will usually lie in pooling the contributions of small donors with contributions of larger donors, both through international organizations and through participation of small donors in aid consortia.

Our discussion has not resulted in any clear cut statement on the superiority of plan aid over project aid, or vice versa. That was not to be expected. The rather tangled relationships which have been discussed reflect the state of the whole business of aid which has grown haphazardly and in a rather wild and disorderly manner. At present there certainly seems room for both kinds of aid. There seems some justification for the economist's instinctive preference for plan aid, but this preference may have to wait for a tidier period in the aid business. There are some indications that such a tidier period is on the horizon. One feels that the scope for plan aid through aid consortia combined with technical planning and project assistance to developing countries, with some emphasis on multilateral assistance, may be on the increase in the next phase. This could result in greater effectiveness of aid than uncoordinated project aid.

Project versus Program Aid: From the Donor's Viewpoint[1]

ALAN CARLIN

Alan Carlin, Director of the Implementation Research Division, Office of Research and Monitoring, Environmental Protection Agency, has worked in the field of development and land resources. This selection is from his article in the Economic Journal, *March 1967.*

HANS W. SINGER HAS RECENTLY reopened one of the longest-standing controversies in the administration of foreign aid, the question of project versus program aid.[2] Unfortunately, his analysis is limited largely to the much discussed fungibility issue.[3] While this is an important issue, it is far less so than Singer's treatment implies. As will be brought out later, there are even some major aid recipients, such as India, where it is not a major problem. Singer's conclusion that there is something to be said for both types of aid has some merit, but is inadequately supported by the remainder of the paper. This is almost entirely concerned with pointing out some (but by no means all) of

---

1. Any views expressed in this paper are those of the author. They should not be interpreted as reflecting the views of the RAND Corporation, his employer at the time he wrote this paper, or the official opinion or policy of any of its governmental or private research sponsors, or of the U.S. Environmental Protection Agency, where he is now Director, Implementation Research Division, Office of Research and Monitoring.

Owing to the interaction that has occurred between a number of RAND staff members engaged in studying the allocation and administration of foreign assistance, it is difficult fully to separate individual viewpoints. I am particularly indebted, however, to Robert Slighton of RAND for permission to use a section of an earlier joint study and his helpful suggestions, and to William Johnson, Richard Nelson, and Charles Wolf, Jr., of RAND for their detailed comments. I am also indebted to Joel Bergsman of the University of California, Berkeley, contract staff in Brazil for his comments on an earlier version.

2. See preceding selection.

3. See, for example, Thomas C. Schelling, *International Economics* (Boston: Allyn and Bacon, 1958, especially pp. 441–57. Fungibility will be discussed in more detail below.

the problems with project aid. Little is said concerning the drawbacks of program aid. In brief, the project-program question is just much more complex than Singer suggests. Before attempting to bring out these added complexities, it is useful to make several initial distinctions that set the problem in a more meaningful context.

The most basic of these distinctions is between the interests of the aid donor and the recipient. Singer addresses the project-program question with an implied recipient country welfare function. This gives rise to the question of whether either the donor or the recipient government knows what is "best" for the recipient country. But, much more important, it ignores the fact that the form of external assistance is determined largely by the donor rather than the recipient. An attempt either to understand or to influence the choice between the two approaches can much more usefully examine the donor's point of view.[4] Perhaps the least interesting point of view is that of the recipient government, which will almost always prefer program aid because of the increased flexibility it confers.

Once it has been decided that the relevant viewpoint is that of the donor, a related distinction arises between the domestic political motivations of the donor for the two types of aid and his objective reasons for adopting them in terms of his national (or institutional) self-interest.[5] Here the interesting question from an economic standpoint is which approach would be more suitable if the donor's domestic political considerations were ignored.

Before examining the relative merits of the two alternatives, it is worthwhile to clear up another source of confusion on the subject—the definitions of the terms involved. Project aid can be defined as assistance with disbursement tied to capital invest-

4. Although this paper assumes that the donor's primary objective is to promote the recipient's economic development, many of its conclusions are applicable either directly or with minor changes to aid given for other objectives, such as to increase the recipient's military capability or to compensate him for foreign military installations on his soil.

5. One of the strongest reasons for the continued partial use of the project approach by the United States Agency for International Development is undoubtedly the strong support for this type of assistance in Congress. This support is to a considerable extent based on the identification of project aid with traditional banking activities. The project approach of the International Bank for Reconstruction and Development may also be partly motivated by the conservative image that it helps to create in financial circles.

ment in a separable productive activity. Program aid is assistance with disbursement tied to the recipient's expenditures on a wide variety of items justified in terms of the total needs and development plan of the country rather than any particular project. The important distinction is that project aid carries added restrictions on its use. Because aid has usually been project-tied where possible, program aid has become identified with aid not nominally used in investments in productive activities or, in other words, with that used for maintenance imports. Nevertheless, there is an important conceptual difference and sometimes a practical difference between program aid and aid used for maintenance imports. It is quite possible, for example, to supply free foreign exchange (such as would be likely to be used for maintenance imports) with project aid.[6]

It is often difficult to classify some capital assistance, particularly that given by the United States Agency for International Development (AID), as either project or program. Thus AID has given substantial assistance to meet the foreign exchange needs of the Indian Railways. Although most of this assistance is tied to foreign exchange expenditures for a number of different railway capital projects, AID has made little effort to document the returns from each particular project,[7] even though such loans are considered project loans to India. They are really program loans to the Indian Railways for capital projects of their choosing, and are justified on the basis of the overall performance and needs of the Railways. Another example of assistance in the grey area between project and program aid is aid to intermediate credit institutions.

With these definitions in hand, it is possible to reformulate the original question somewhat more precisely. The objective of this

---

6. The procedure is to tie the aid (assumed to be in the form of foreign exchange) to more than the foreign exchange costs of projects. Part of such local cost financing will, of course, serve only to cover the increased imports indirectly resulting from the local currency expenditures. But the remainder (if any) will amount to a net increase in the foreign exchange available for other purposes. This remainder is not entirely hypothetical, since the International Development Association has on occasion supplied a significant amount of free exchange in connection with some projects in India and perhaps elsewhere, while AID has done so in some Latin American countries.

7. This paragraph is based on Alan Carlin, "An Evaluation of U.S. Government Aid to India" (unpublished doctoral dissertation, Massachusetts Institute of Technology, 1964), pp. 47–137.

paper is to set out the more important considerations that a rational donor should take into account in deciding whether it is more advantageous to give aid as project or as program assistance. Since project assistance can be considered program aid with certain additional restrictions on its use, a convenient way of reviewing the arguments on each side is by looking at the additional benefits and costs of these added restrictions.

BENEFITS OF THE PROJECT APPROACH

The more important potential benefits [8] of the project approach are:

(1) direct control by the recipient over the selection of projects *in certain circumstances*

(2) greater opportunity of influencing, in both their design and implementation, those projects nominally financed by the aid donor

(3) increased ease of influencing the recipient's policies in those sectors of the recipient's economy for which project aid has been made available

(4) incentives for improving the quantity and quality of projects

(5) better opportunities for publicizing the donor's aid program

(6) increased access to information on sectors of the recipient's economy in which projects are financed

(7) if aid is also tied on a country-of-origin basis, a somewhat *less* adverse effect on the balance of payments of the donor nation.

Micro-influence · The first three benefits are related and involve the exercise of micro or project influence over the recipient. As many have pointed out, the fungibility problem greatly limits the effectiveness with which project controls can influence the recipient's allocation of resources. The fungibility problem

8. Throughout the paper the discussion of benefits will be in terms of potential benefits. Since donors vary greatly in the extent to which they actually achieve these benefits, it is best to discuss the optimum case and allow readers to apply their own discounting factors for the donor in which they are interested.

arises because the particular project with which the aid is identified may or may not represent the actual use of the added funds provided by the aid.[9] This problem has often been overemphasized by economists, however, since there is a variety of circumstances in which influence can be exercised over the allocation of resources despite it. One such case arises when the donor offers aid for a project that the recipient regards as sufficiently marginal so that he would not finance it out of his own resources if the aid were not made available. This means that if the donor can find what he considers worthwhile projects neglected by the recipient he can influence the recipient's allocation of resources. Despite Singer's doubts on the subject, a number of aid donors have been able to identify marginal projects when they have set out to do so. In the early 1960s, for example, the International Development Association attempted to locate a number of such projects in India, and chose projects in the areas of highway development, telephone service, irrigation, and drainage to receive credits.

In the extreme case, all of a donor's projects can be considered marginal, and he can effectively determine the recipient's allocation of investment resources provided through project support. This occurs when the recipient's free foreign exchange resources are already tied down to uses given relatively high priority by the recipient while not including any of the projects financed by the donor. If no foreign private or public investment body is willing to finance a given project, the country must usually abandon it. This situation occurs most commonly when the recipient country cannot meet all of its essential "maintenance imports" out of its own foreign exchange holdings or earnings. India provides a good illustration within recent years. Her debt repayments and imports of food, essential consumer goods, and raw materials needed to keep existing industrial capacity in production exceed her free foreign exchange. Failure to meet the more basic of these requirements would have worse political and economic repercussions than failure to expand capacity, so that it is

---

9. Thus, although expenditures for imports for a power plant may be reimbursed by the aid donor, the plant might well have been built even if total aid had been reduced by the amount reimbursed. The funds can then hardly be said to have financed the power plant at all, but rather the use of the funds that would have been sacrificed if the aid had not been extended.

probable that the latter would be sacrificed should India have to choose between the two. As a result, the use of project aid can substantially influence the allocation of India's developmental resources. As long as the sum of available free foreign exchange plus untied program aid is less than essential maintenance imports, no project requiring substantial amounts of foreign exchange will normally be undertaken without some public or private international financing.

India's efforts to find a donor for its seventh steel mill (fifth in the public sector) illustrate the point involved. Since she has been unable to find a donor, the project has been delayed for lack of foreign exchange. Current Indian thinking centers on one possible loophole in the donor's ability to influence India's resource allocation, namely, the possibility of financing the project through short term supplier's credits arranged by a consortium of foreign equipment suppliers with maximum reliance on domestically produced equipment. But given a determination by the aid donors to avoid such an end-run, which could ultimately be financed only through larger program loans, this loophole should not prove impossible to close.

Besides enabling the donor to exercise some influence over the recipient's allocation of resources, at least in some cases, the use of project aid also enables the donor to influence more easily the projects nominally financed, whether or not they happen to be the projects that the aid actually makes possible. If the donor's goal is the recipient's economic development, this influence will presumably be directed towards improving the economic viability of the projects. The influence can be exercised in a number of ways, particularly by insisting on higher standards of project preparation, by introducing technical aid as part of the project, by imposing various conditions on the execution of the project or, in the extreme case, by partial supervision of the project itself. Much more than capital is usually needed by less developed countries. In many cases, technical aid and other influences do more than improve the economics of a project; without them, the project may not be economically viable.

One striking example is provided by the contrast between the steel mills erected in India in the late 1950s with British and German assistance and that erected with Russian aid. The markedly superior performance of the Russian-built mill (Bhilai) in the years following its completion can be ascribed in considerable measure to the close and constant supervision and aid furnished by the Russians after the mill went into operation.[10] The British and Germans did not insist on such supervision because of Indian reluctance to accept it. Not until the mills they built deteriorated to such a point that they became national issues did the Indian Government and the foreign equipment suppliers agree to meaningful foreign participation in the direction of the mills.

Investment in physical capital is only one essential requisite of industrial growth; it is also necessary to develop various skills, particularly managerial skills, to use the capital efficiently once it is built. Capital projects are an effective way to provide this form of technical aid. Most LDCs are reluctant to admit that such aid is vital to the success of many projects. Project aid provides the donor with some leverage for insisting that it is accepted.

In addition to making possible the exercise of greater influence on the allocation of resources between projects and on individual projects, the project approach also opens up opportunities for exercising greater influence than would be possible with program aid on policies in sectors related to the projects nominally financed by the aid. This can often be done by arguing that changes in these policies are necessary for the success of the project. For example, in the case of a railroad project, the donor might be able to insist on changes in the railroad's rate structure, or in the case of a fertilizer plant, a change in fertilizer prices or distribution practices.

Unfortunately, much of this section on the benefits of micro-influence has had to be rather general because so few examples are available of its effective use. One of the major conclusions of an earlier study of the United States aid program to India was that little micro-influence has been exercised through project restrictions on capital aid.[11] Although AID and IBRD projects in India appear to be worse in this respect than the average in other countries, the difference does not appear to be very great, particularly with respect to influencing policies not directly re-

10. See William A. Johnson, *The Steel Industry of India* (Cambridge: Harvard University Press, 1966), pp. 178–9, 183.

11. See Alan Carlin, *op. cit.*, pp. 232–4 and 241–2. The study includes detailed analyses of United States aid to Indian irrigation and transport and the extent of micro-influence through it.

velopment prospects of the country and, therefore, the desirability of giving it aid in the first place.

With country of origin tying, as in the case of AID loans, the addition of project restrictions to aid generally results in a larger net increase in the donor's exports per dollar of his aid than in the case of program aid. This, in turn, will mean that project aid has a somewhat less adverse effect on the balance-of-payments of the aid giver per dollar. Although the recipient usually suggests that aid be nominally ascribed to projects where the largest percentage of imported goods would be purchased from the aid giver if the project were financed from free foreign exchange, it is likely that a somewhat lower percentage of the goods purchased under a project loan would have been purchased from the aid giver in any case compared with the purchases under a program loan. It is not usually possible to find projects that consist entirely of goods normally or most advantageously purchased from any one donor country. On the other hand, from a long list of maintenance imports, from apples to oil, it is fairly simple for the recipient to pick out those goods that would normally be purchased from the aid giver anyway.

It has often been alleged that the project approach is also less likely to lead to a "politically frozen" aid level. A program aid level maintained over several years can take on a political status that makes for inflexibility. In contrast, project aid is at least theoretically tied directly to the submission of eligible project proposals by the recipient government. Either slow submission of good proposals or slow utilization of funds already obligated will automatically result in lower assistance levels, besides signaling inadequate performance by the recipient country.

COSTS OF THE PROJECT APPROACH

The potential costs of project aid can be grouped into the following categories, roughly in the order of their importance:

(1) possibility of reduced leverage over aggregate policies of the host country

(2) introduction of incentives favoring the construction of new capacity rather than providing raw materials that would make it possible to use existing capacity better

(3) intergovernmental problems arising from the bureau-

cratic frictions created by detailed supervision of project formulation and execution

(4) increased costs of aid administration

(5) increased real cost (to the recipient nation) of borrowing.

These costs are likely to be present even where the technical expertise and administrative efficiency associated with project aid are beyond reproach. An additional set of costs emerge if there are administrative or analytical failures on the part of the aid giver. Since it is doubtful whether any organization can avoid all mistakes, costs in this second category ought also to be considered. In particular, these are likely to arise from delays in the recipient's capital projects as a result of review and supervision by the donor, as well as in categories (3) and (4) above.

Many of these costs also depend in magnitude on the assiduity with which the aid giver attempts to exercise influence over the recipient. There are no costs in terms of macro-bargaining opportunities forgone if no bargaining would be attempted anyway, and few costs if no attempt is made to exercise project influence. Costs arising from the frictions involved in project scrutinization will be unimportant if the review of project proposals and the monitoring to project implementation is largely permissive. Assuming away the problem of creating an effective control system, the most important potential cost of giving aid in the form of projects is the loss of bargaining power over aggregate economic and political policies of the borrower. The intergovernmental *cum* interbureaucratic frictions of effective project control are chiefly important because they result in an erosion of the host country's willingness (and ability) to agree to restrictions on its freedom of action implied by aggregate performance criteria.

To the extent that project aid reduces the potential leverage per dollar of aid over broader policies,[15] this is indeed an important consideration. Such a reduction might occur for two reasons. First, project aid may be worth less to the recipient government, especially if there is a squeeze on maintenance im-

---

15. If the donor's objective is the economic development of the recipient, the donor will often be most interested in affecting fiscal and monetary policies.

ports. Second, any attempt to exercise micro or project influence will tend further to decrease the attractiveness of the aid to the recipient, and hence the potential macro-leverage per dollar. It should be pointed out, however, that the use of macro-leverage on the LDCs has been something less than wholly successful to date. Despite increasing interest and efforts in this direction in the early 1960s, it has been used successfully only in a few cases in the last decade. The problems arise mainly because of the administrative difficulties in making the criteria meaningful and the political difficulties in making conditions effective.

It is assumed here that it is quite possible to exercise macro-influence with project aid, preferably by bargaining over groups of projects or project packages. It can therefore be argued that to some extent micro- and macro-influence exercised through project assistance are complements rather than substitutes for each other. In fact, a considerable portion of the benefits from project level influence can be obtained without the recipient's feeling that he has been asked to make a major concession that greatly decreases the value of the aid. To a considerable extent this influence is quite similar to technical aid—suggestions for relatively minor improvements in a project or its operation, or perhaps insistence on certain standards in project submission and preparation. In addition, attempts at micro-influence can be partly justified by the "normal" banking practice of attempting to ensure the credit-worthiness of a given project, and hence may not be considered as great an interference in the internal affairs of the recipient country as they might otherwise.

Project aid undoubtedly introduces a number of biases into country development. Perhaps most important, it favors building new capacity rather than making better use of existing capacity. Since project aid is often more readily available than program aid, there are built-in incentives for the potential recipient to accept additional project aid even if his resources could be better devoted to fuller utilization of present capacity. The result is likely to be overbuilding of infrastructure and expansion of the public sector. Once again, perhaps the best example is India. Because her free foreign exchange and nonproject aid receipts are less than her nonproject needs, there is considerable underutilization of industrial capacity. Yet she continues to accept project-tied aid to build new industrial capacity, some of it in the same industries which are now suffering from a shortage of maintenance imports.

Even if project influence is inherently more palatable than program influence, project assistance may also give rise to a number of interbureaucratic frictions, often of the most nonsubstantive, petty type. These sometimes arise in the case of AID because of a number of specific prohibitions written into foreign aid legislation by Congress.

The real cost of loans to the recipient may be increased by the project approach in the case of country-tied aid from individual countries for the same reason that the foreign exchange costs to the aid giver are reduced—the recipient is forced to buy some items for a given project from a country other than the lowest cost producer. If the objectives of the donor include a concern for the economic welfare of the recipient, this may represent a cost to the donor as well.

CONCLUSIONS

The general conclusion from this analysis, that there is something to be said on both sides, is much the same as Singer's. But unlike Singer's, it stresses that the particular objectives of the donor in giving aid, and to some extent the particular circumstances of the recipient, are likely to make it advisable to pursue a project approach in one case, a program approach in another, and some combination in still others. This paper has attempted to outline what some of the more important considerations are. Undoubtedly, the most important of these is whether the objectives of the donor can be best served by attempting to exercise influence on the macro- or the micro-level.

Although micro-influence can result from program aid and macro-influence from project aid (properly "packaged"), such influence is usually more effectively exercised by project and program aid, respectively. The primary question is the level on which influence can most usefully be focused; the choice of type of aid is generally a second-order issue that follows from the first.

If, for example, the donor's objective is the recipient's economic development, and the donor believes that it is by influencing project preparation and execution and related sectoral policies that he can most fruitfully use the limited leverage provided by his aid, then the project approach would be preferable. If, on the other hand, the donor believes that his objectives can best be served by concentrating his influence on broader, more aggregate issues, program aid offers some advantages. If some mixture is desired in the direction of donor influence, project aid can be "packaged," with emphasis on macro-bargaining over the packages.

There are other considerations in selecting one or the other aid instrument besides the relation of donor objectives to the optimum level of influence. Another, for example, is the competence of the donor in exercising influence through project aid. In general, there are several factors to be taken into account in each donor-recipient relationship, and it is a question of weighing one against the other. The significant aspect of this (and Singer's) conclusion is that it differs markedly from the prevailing view of many economists that program aid is to be preferred. All too often, this judgment is based solely on the fungibility argument, which is but one of several important considerations to be taken into account.

Economic Dualism—At Home and Abroad

GUSTAV RANIS

This selection by the editor of this volume appeared in Public Policy, Fall 1969.

AFTER WORLD WAR II citizens, academics, and officialdom in the rich countries, especially the United States, became increasingly concerned with the problems of modernization in the less developed world. This interest and concern gave rise, on the one hand, to a new branch of economics, i.e., development economics, and, on the other, to a new phenomenon in the "normal" relations among nations, i.e., the provision of foreign assistance from haves to have-nots. More recently, these same rich countries, again especially the U.S., have noted and begun to worry about the existence of substantial pockets of poverty within their own societies and to train the guns of analysis, and the expenditure of public funds and energies, on this problem.

Strange as it may seem, development economics, moving beyond its antecedents in conventional economic theory and only recently itself pronounced respectable, is now considerably ahead of the economics of (domestic) poverty—just as we know more today about the process of foreign aid, with all its shortcomings, than we do about how best to help solve the problems of the urban ghetto. All of this would be neither here nor there if the two problems had relatively little to do with each other. But this, in fact, is not the case. There exist pronounced real-world and conceptual similarities between the situation of the poor countries abroad trying to achieve self-sustaining growth with the help of the rich, and the largely black urban minority at home trying to join the rest of a prosperous society with the help of the federal exchequer.

Let us begin by briefly examining the nature of the two landscapes under discussion. The typical less developed country achieving independence after World War II shows the heritage of what might be called "colonial dualism," namely, small growing islands of commercial and export oriented activity within a sea of stagnant subsistence agriculture and the beginnings of a vigorous industrial sector. Before independence, the proceeds from these primary exports were mainly plowed back into these very enclaves with little spillover effect for the rest of the economy. After independence, the desire to match political with economic independence naturally led to the attempt to capture these proceeds and utilize them for national development by redirecting them toward an expansion of public overheads and the industrial sector. And, finally, since the middle of the 1960s, we have been witness to a growing realization that forced industrialization without the active participation of the large preponderantly agricultural sector is difficult, if not impossible, to achieve. Simultaneously, there has emerged an increasing understanding of how the dualistic developing society can best be jostled into vigorous growth with the help of resources and advice from abroad.

Ghetto America once again presents a clearly dualistic landscape, i.e., pronounced asymmetries in structural conditions and behavior between different sectors of the economy. Here, however, we have the preponderantly large sector moving vigorously forward while substantial islands of poverty lag far behind. The relationship between these two Americas cannot be called "colonial" in the same sense as before, unless we accept the emotional premises of the separatists; profit maximization by those who control the advanced sector does not necessarily dictate the neglect of ghetto investment, nor are the social and economic overheads created by the government exclusively aimed at facilitating the growth of the advanced sector. Welfare and other legislation is directed to effect more income redistribution through budgetary transfers. Societal objectives are much less dominated by the shortrun profit motives of a foreign dominated elite and more by the desire to keep the society from splintering by maintaining aggregate full employment growth and striking a judicious balance between growth and equity considerations.

But there are also striking similarities between the two types of dualism which must be noted: the vastness of the reservoir of unemployed and underemployed labor in one sector, sector A; the tendency for this reservoir to be constantly replenished, in the short run, by migration racing ahead of employment opportunities and, in the longer run, population growth; the tendency for the advanced sector, sector B, to employ relatively capital-intensive technology—in spite of the availability of abundant supplies of cheap labor from sector A; the absence of sufficient public sector action to provide sector A with adequate transportation, education, and health facilities and to reduce disparities between private and social returns by fiscal and monetary policy; finally, the absence of a truly national market for capital or other scarce resources permitting a more impersonal allocation of investment, determined by relative rates of return, within and between the sectors.

With respect to the impact of the outside world on the two-sector configurations of both the typical LDC and the ghetto, the similarities are again striking and tend to swamp the differences. In the one case, exports continue to be concentrated on a small number of raw material and mineral products supplemented by the movement of food and labor to sector B. In the second case, the ghetto offers mainly labor services. Aid to sector A from the outside, in the form of capital as well as technical assistance, has played more of a role in the developing economy, but only in recent years; this is because, until the early 1960s, government-to-government foreign assistance was typically negotiated with, and utilized in behalf of, the elitist urban elements concerned most of all with accelerating the growth of overheads and of the large scale industrial sector. Until then it all too often provided little more than incremental resources and expertise for the already favored and growing urban-industrial enclave, sector B. At home, aid to the ghetto—not by foreigners but by other segments of the rich society, for example OEO funds—are of relatively recent vintage and have not yet been channeled very effectively into the ghetto. In fact, how this task is to be best accomplished is one of the main points on which illumination is required.

In what direction, then, can this relatively stagnant dualistic landscape be changed in each case? We need, first of all, a clearer view of what constitutes an ideal (or at least improved) working of the dualistic system—without which it is difficult and costly to prescribe appropriate policy. Moreover, it is here that recent LDC experience, both in theory and practice, may provide useful insights for application to the problems of the domestic ghetto.

In the early 1960s, some LDCs began to realize that the customary syndrome of import controls and import substitution, overvalued exchange rates, and protection, operating either through direct government ownership or through a network of direct controls over the private sector, had placed an intolerable burden on inexperienced bureaucracies, frozen out of innovative participation most of the existing domestic entrepreneurial talent, and led to a highly inefficient hothouse type of development. Agriculture and exports in particular were not permitted to play their natural role as fuel for the development process. Planners were forced to note that overall LDC per capita income growth rates fell from 2.5 percent during 1950–55 to 1.8 percent in 1955–60, and to conclude that the dynamic changes expected from a strategy of forced draft, large scale industrialization would not be forthcoming while domestic (mainly agricultural) savings languished and unemployment and underemployment mounted. Increasingly, such LDCs as Taiwan, Pakistan, Ghana, Korea, and India began to realize that while the objective of breaking out of the previous colonial pattern was admirable, the tools employed were not adequate to the job.

The routine conclusion these countries have gradually come to is that the key to avoiding overall stagnation in the presence of sometimes quite impressive industrial enclave development is to draw the economically disenfranchised sectors—agriculture and medium and small scale industry—into more active participation through a greater reliance on indirect (rather than direct) controls, working through (rather than in place of) the market mechanism. This does not mean that objectives have changed even one iota, but it does mean that profit maximization working through the market is no longer necessarily associated with colonialism but is, in fact, accepted as a superior method of restructuring the economy away from colonialism.

This version of a better functioning LDC capable of throwing off its dualistic characteristics over time is built on the following major considerations as they emerge from an analysis of not only the contemporary "success" cases cited but also the classical example of historical (nineteenth-century) Japan:

1. The population engaged in sector A, i.e., agriculture and small scale industry, must be given access to essential inputs such as credit, foreign exchange, and raw materials—at a price—rather

than to have to take their chances with the direct allocation system of an urban bureaucracy oriented to large scale industry. In this way, not only is static efficiency enhanced, but also the forgotten "little man" is given a chance to put his entrepreneurial talents to the test and, in the process, to increase productivity radically in these neglected sectors.

2. There must be opportunities for the surpluses generated in agriculture as a consequence of productivity change to be channeled into industrial capital formation over time. This requires a strong government fiscal system—rare, especially in agriculture—and/or good opportunities for private saving through a network of financial intermediaries serving the particular tastes of large numbers of small savers, or opportunities for direct investment in relatively familiar and easily understood activities. Such "proximity" or "connectedness" between sectors A and B by rural subcontracting or other forms of decentralized industrialization in turn will have strong feedback effects on the incentive to replenish the sources of saving by productivity increases in agriculture.

3. The ideal role of government in this setting is, as we have already hinted, to concentrate on perfecting the environment for millions of private actions rather than either substituting for these actions or attempting to direct them in detail. This aim means creating the necessary infrastructure in transportation, communication, education, and health; working to perfect highly imperfect markets by reducing the gap between social and private profit-loss calculations; and working more and more through such generalized across-the-board fiscal and monetary policies as taxes, tariffs, and exchange rates, and less through direct controls over dispersed decision makers, a method which puts an intolerable burden—both qualitatively and quantitatively—on the best intentioned bureaucracy.

4. Foreign trade provides the system with additional, more efficient production possibilities. Industrial consumer goods incorporating the use of relatively abundant labor drawn out of agriculture gradually increase in importance relative to the still predominant traditional primary exports. While "easy" (i.e., efficient) import substitution possibilities are usually quickly exploited, the preferred pattern over time is toward increasing "export substitution" as domestic skills and ingenuity levels increase. Imports continue to be concentrated in the area of capital

goods and raw materials for the growing industrial sector and some (limited but needed) consumer goods.

5. Foreign aid as well as private investment flow from abroad, serve to alleviate the overall resources tightness, but more importantly, if properly employed, they can have a catalytic effect on domestic performance by removing specific physical or institutional bottlenecks and lowering real or psychological barriers to policy changes and structural reform.

If this process of continuous growth, with agriculture increasing its productivity and releasing capital and workers to fuel the industrialization process—and trade and aid playing their important facilitating roles—continues long enough and proceeds at a pace in excess of population growth, the reservoir of unemployed or underemployed people in sector A will ultimately dry up and the system as a whole graduate from its initial dualistic status.

This, in very rough outline, is the direction in which an LDC can move if it hopes to emerge from dualism and into a state of self-sustaining growth. Some have chosen this path and some are well on their way. But for us here the relevant question is: What lessons can be learned from that conceptual framework and that experience for solving the problems of dualism within a country like the U.S.?

Let us, for the ghetto as well, begin by briefly recalling its contemporary structure and relationships with the rest of the system. Then, taking the major dimensions previously cited one by one, let us reflect on the relevance of the dualistic model developed for other purposes in defining an idealized modification of that structure and in choosing among the policy instruments available for achieving such modification.

The typical urban ghetto is plagued by unemployment rates far in excess of the rest of the economy (more than 9 percent recently) while "subemployment" or underemployment is estimated at 23 percent of the labor force. State-by-state welfare differentials together with higher wages for those lucky enough to land a job induce a continuing flow of immigrants from the rural South which, together with high rates of fertility, lead to population growth far in excess of the outward flow into productive employment. The physical capital stock is old, public services grossly inadequate, and educational and skill levels extremely low. There is relatively little industry; employment is concentrated in services, repair shops, and the distributive trades. Exports to the rest of the system consist mainly of labor services, and imports consist of consumer goods. The import surplus is financed mainly by welfare payments.

As in the peasant agricultural sector abroad, ghetto dwellers do not customarily have access to such scarce resources as credit, licenses, and permits to do business. With the recognition of political independence (civil rights), the clamor here also has been for the achievement of economic independence. The efforts of government to date have been more or less exclusively focused on constructing some (if inadequate) infrastructure, mainly education, and ensuring a minimum institutional wage through welfare and other transfer payments into the ghetto. As in the case of the "unresponsive illiterate peasant"—which once dominated the development literature but has now been thoroughly exploded by empirical findings—there persists a general feeling that the black ghetto dweller is not yet ready to participate in the market and that what one should instead concentrate on is how to protect him from it. What can be done to modify that structure in the direction of a balanced self-feeding interaction between the two sectors which ultimately permits the eroding of the dualistic characteristics cited?

1. First of all, there seems little point in once again waiting five to ten years before acknowledging that illiteracy should not be confused with lack of responsiveness to opportunities when these are offered on an impersonal, objective basis. Given the same access to resources, the same entrepreneurial juices are likely to flow, opportunities to be seized, and well-recognized learning by doing processes to provide their own dynamics. This does not mean disregard for the importance of investments to permit the ghetto to "catch up," e.g., investments to improve the physical resources to perfect markets and information flows, and investments to improve the human resource base through education, as in the case of infant industry. There will clearly be substantial need for deploying the fiscal powers of government during the introductory period. But from the point of view of the ghetto dweller, the (temporary) subsidy component underlying the new opportunities offered may be less crucial than the guarantee of continued availability and competitive access.

If what is really meant by "black capitalism," rhetoric aside, is a chance for millions of ghetto dwellers to participate in a "fair game," we may, in fact, be moving towards a sensible restructuring. As productivity in the ghetto increases, one would expect the savings generated to be largely reinvested there, and to be reinforced by sharply increasing flows of private saving from the rest of the economy. This expansion of industry and services must, of course, be in efficient directions; there is little point in trying to create and expand uneconomic Gandhian small industry establishments which could never survive in competition with larger firms outside of the ghetto. But there usually are substantial opportunities for the expansion of a viable modernized medium scale and small scale industry catering to a differentiated local demand, often related to larger units through subcontracting arrangements if sufficient initiative and imagination are deployed. In this fashion, the reservoir of urban unemployed and underemployed could, over time, be dried up by the increasing labor demand from the resulting growth of medium scale and small scale industries and services.

2. Since this net flow of saving over time must be from the rest of the economy into the ghetto, the problem of "connectedness" between the two sectors assumes considerable importance here also. This dimension requires considerable attention to the establishment of a variety of specialized financial intermediaries serving the differentiated needs of individual and institutional investors and ensuring a more efficient allocation of credit. Entrepreneurs who have one foot in each sector and are currently devoting their energies mainly to commercial activities, e.g., white merchants in the ghetto, could, given a different environment permissive of a longer time range for their activities, be induced to adjust their short run maximizing behavior and shift into industry. The creation of branch banks, black banks, and other institutions to help create a broader and more efficient money market within the ghetto must be given equally high priority. Where economies of scale are sufficiently important to swamp the advantages of labor intensive medium scale industry and services, cooperatives can prove very helpful. In all this, the incentive to increase productivity at its base is likely to be directly and powerfully related to the availability of a well-differentiated, easily understandable set of saving instruments to suit a variety

of tastes. Both the volume of ghetto saving and the efficiency of its allocation, as well as the volume and quality of the inflows from outside, can be substantially enhanced in this fashion.

3. What kind of trade pattern should be encouraged as between the black ghetto and the rest of the economy? One would expect simple services to continue to be an important export (just as the primary raw materials continue to be important in the LDC case) but to be gradually replaced by more sophisticated services and simple manufactures as skill and ingenuity levels increase as a consequence of broader participation and learning-by-doing processes. This would include the establishment of ghetto branches and subcontracting units by the large firm on the outside.

4. The ideal role of government in this overall context is obviously a central issue. Once again we should be able to profit from hard-earned experience abroad; government must concentrate, in the first instance, on social and economic overhead construction, particularly in education, health, and transportation, to help begin to redress some of the historical backlog of unequal rates of physical and human capital investment. Secondly, it must concentrate on reducing market imperfections, i.e., "clearing the boards" and eliminating some of the worst inequalities of access to resources currently faced by inhabitants of the two sectors. This means not only the elimination of the more blatant manifestations of prejudice in the social and economic spheres, but the provision of basic information on markets and opportunities and the enforcement of legal safeguards for minorities, so that ghetto inhabitants can begin to compete with others on an even-handed basis. Government will, of course, have to continue to be involved in direct welfare activities. But as the painful experience of the LDCs over the past two decades has indicated, a prime rule the civil service must set for itself is the exercise of self-restraint in terms of its capacity to make millions of horizontal allocative decisions directly, rather than inserting itself by means of vertical indirect controls working through an improved market mechanism.

5. We thus recognize that perfecting imperfect markets is clearly not enough, in terms of the generally acknowledged national goal of bringing the ghetto into the mainstream of the economy's growth processes and, ultimately, eliminating its separate existence. Additional funds have to be made available

in one fashion or another, not only for the infrastructural purposes already mentioned, but also to induce and support, at least during the infant industry period, directly productive activities. And this realization brings us to the really topical question, i.e., how can federal funds ("foreign aid") be most effectively channeled into the nation's ghettos? The choice seems to be essentially threefold: direct action by federal agencies administering programs and disbursing the funds to local government and local bodies—basically the original OEO model; federal fund support for activities administered and controlled by local government and local bodies—essentially the model cities approach; federal funds made available through the instrumentality of private corporations—i.e., a contracting out to the private sector, with or without tax incentives, somewhat on the defense industry model. (Not considered here is a fourth and more global approach, the negative income tax.) These choices clearly do not represent airtight compartments, but merge or can be made to merge into each other; yet the above differentiation may be useful for analytical purposes.

Relevant LDC experience would lead one to conclude that variants of the second alternative are to be preferred in most instances. The first alternative demands both too much wisdom and administrative capacity at the federal level and not enough reliance on local participation and the enlistment of local resources and ingenuity. The third alternative, on the other hand, does not fully take into account possible divergences between the private and the social calculus and assumes that corporations under government contract are as adept at solving human problems as they are at inventing new hardware. (This is less true of the use of private banks as financial intermediaries.) The second alternative has the chance of combining overall controls and supervision at the federal level with maximum scope for ghetto initiative and participation. Since this part of the spectrum comes closer, I think, to meeting the problem of the ghetto, it warrants fuller examination—once again in the light of relevant LDC experience.

The foreign assistance tools which come to mind in this context are the so-called program and sector loans. These are instruments providing additional financial resources from abroad, based on and related to a prior agreement on the objectives to be pursued (either for the economy as a whole or for a specific major sector) and the policy changes required, as well as the proposed allocation of total resources, foreign and domestic, to the effort. It does not insist on "tagging" the outcome of any particular inflow component by identification with a particular project or activity result, but, recognizing the fungibility of resources, carries explicit or implicit performance commitments with respect to the recipient's behavior. The argument comes down essentially to the choice between bloc grants (program and sector loans) and direct grants (project loans) as the best way of getting the job done and inducing the proper local response (self-help action). The bloc grant would seem to be superior to the direct grant in which a specific additional activity is seen to "result" from the additional resource flow while other relevant priority activities could simultaneously be allowed to lag if the recipient decided to withdraw support from them. Bloc grants can be committed for a particular period and set of objectives, but disbursed in installments in relation to a pace of self-help performance previously agreed on. Unless the federal aid mechanism is much more efficient in determining just what all the essential bottleneck projects are and at handling all the minutiae of ensuring their effective installation, a more generalized set of understandings to ensure pursuit of the agreed on objectives and program is likely to work much better, especially in ensuring substantially more local participation, strengthening the hand of the "good guys" locally *vis-à-vis* entrenched interests—and yet reducing the number of friction laden contacts between the federal government and local government and community action groups.

Large private corporations, which are best suited to dealing with other fairly large private industrial units, cannot be expected to do the job by themselves. It is essential that resources be made available to small scale and medium scale ghetto entrepreneurs, actual as well as potential (i.e., not yet visible to the naked eye but ready for activation). Once the market environment for large corporations is improved, the possibility of subcontracting a number of operations to medium scale and small scale enterprises in the ghetto—black and white—can be explored. It is here that federal funds for technical advice, training, and market exploration can be used in an expanded version of the Small Business Administration model. Such funds may, of course, also be deployed through private firms, either in the form of tax incentives or as subsidies to overcome the uncertainty of achieving an adequate rate of return in the early years of operation. This aim could be realized by the reimbursement of firms' extra trainee costs (e.g., the JOBS program) or by tax concessions over limited periods. It is also clear, however, that, if new ghetto firms, usually small and initially low profit, are to be assisted, as opposed to ghetto operations for the large established corporation, subsidies are preferable to tax credits—with essentially the same result for the federal budget. The private sector outside the ghetto can thus be harnessed to a total federal package with overall program control—in the flexible manner described—at the federal level and with fullest possible involvement of local government and associated private action groups. The second and third alternatives are therefore not necessarily mutually exclusive, but can be merged creatively.

In this setting, bloc grants (program loans) can be related to performance conditions (self-help criteria) worked out in advance by all the parties concerned, but subject to mutual review over time to insure necessary flexibility. These conditions will differ with the particular local circumstances, but they must, in all cases, relate to the inducement of ghetto productivity increase and the channeling of resulting ghetto saving back into indigenous enterprises. Pumping more outside money in at the margin is clearly not enough; the problem is one of breaking down the enclave characteristic of the ghetto by improving the connectivity between the ghetto and the rest of the economy and enlisting the productive and creative energies of large numbers of individuals in the growth process. Outside resources can never do the job, no matter how intelligently applied, but they can play a crucial catalytic role. If there is full *ex ante* agreement by all parties on what needs to be done, in terms of policy change as well as institution construction, program guidance and performance conditions can be used effectively without drawing the charge of interference by a distant federal government. In the absence of such a framework, we are likely to witness the construction of a few big prestige projects which can be labeled black capitalism for as long as they survive, continuous (self-imposed) "low absorptive capacity," and no self-generating growth process based on the mass participation of the inhabitants of the ghetto.

Private Foreign Investment

LESTER B. PEARSON

This selection was taken from the Pearson Report, Partners in Development.

DIRECT CORPORATE INVESTMENT

THE FLOW OF PRIVATE RESOURCES from the industrialized to the less developed world is substantial and, following a decline in the early 1960s, has recently been growing at a rapid pace. The total flow in 1968 reached $5.8 billion, somewhat below the official flow in that year but double the private flow of a decade earlier.

Direct corporate investment is the largest single part of this private flow, but it is also the most politically sensitive. Even in developed countries, private foreign investment is an issue of great political concern. When the historical record is recalled, it is hardly surprising that citizens in some countries look upon the subsidiaries of foreign corporations as the harbingers of new foreign domination. But this view neglects to take into account the vast improvement which has taken place in the behavior and attitude of foreign companies, partly in response to host country pressures, partly as a consequence of increasing international interdependence and cooperation. As will be seen below, we feel that foreign investment has contributed greatly to the growth of developing countries and can do even more in the future, but we wish to make clear at the outset our appreciation of the political problems it can generate.

These political problems, and their effect on the investment climate, are undoubtedly an important reason that, despite all the measures taken to stimulate it, direct investment, except in a few countries, has long been the least dynamic element in the flow of private capital to developing countries. There are, of course, other fundamental reasons: the high intrinsic risks often associated with investment in these countries, restrictions on the outflow of capital from many of the industrialized countries, ignorance of investment opportunities, administrative inefficiencies, and, in the case of manufacturing investments, the severely limited markets of most developing countries. The result of all this was that while the flow of direct investment to the developing countries averaged $2.3 billion a year in 1957–58, it was still only $2.4 billion a decade later (1967–68). Much of this investment has been in extractive industries. Of the total cumulative direct investment in developing countries, estimated at about $30 billion in 1966, 40 percent was in the petroleum sector, and a further 9 percent in mining and smelting; only 27 percent was in manufacturing, and 24 percent in utilities and other services.

Political sensitivity also explains why much discussion of the

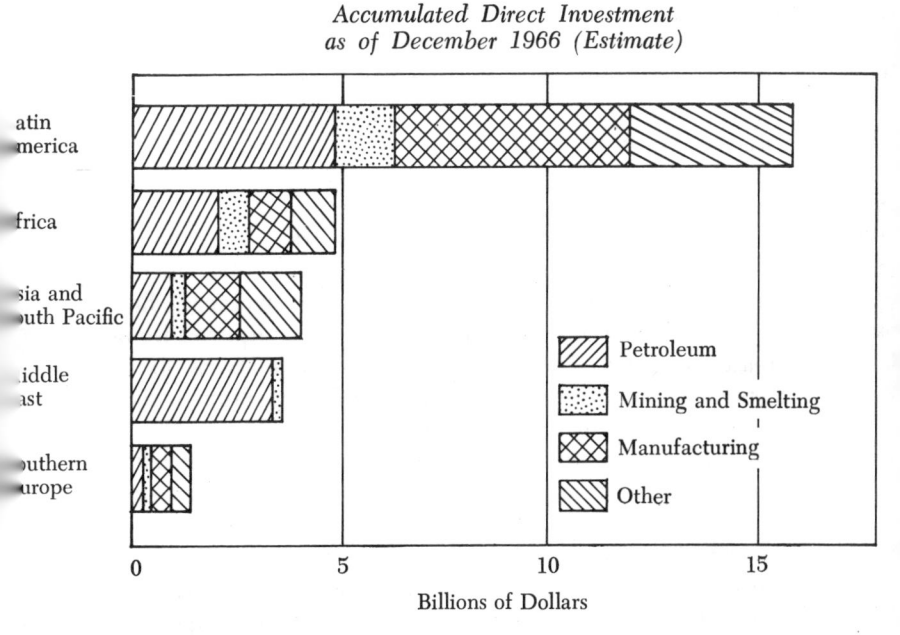

Accumulated Direct Investment as of December 1966 (Estimate)

economic impact of foreign investment has been couched in emotional language and has been clouded by many misunderstandings. Of the latter, perhaps the most common involves attempts to measure the balance-of-payments impact of foreign investment by comparing "new capital inflow" with the total profits of the accumulated foreign investment in the country. Such a comparison neglects to take into account the reinvestment of profits by foreign investors in the host country and fails to note the impact of foreign investment on export promotion and import saving. It does not make sense, for example, to evaluate the balance-of-payments effect of foreign investment in the oil producing countries of the Middle East by a simple comparison of capital inflows with profit remittances, neglecting oil exports. The correct way to look at the balance-of-payments effects of foreign investment is to ask what the balance-of-payments would have been like in its absence.

Once the question is posed in this fashion, emphasizing the need to take into account all direct and indirect effects, it becomes apparent that the key question is the productivity of foreign investments for the host economy as a whole. In most cases, its contribution goes beyond the taxes generated by foreign firms and payments to local labor and services. In particular, the contribution also includes the transfer of advanced technology into the host economy. In the absence of foreign investment, the acquisition of such know-how will typically be difficult and costly.

Furthermore, in many developing countries, the external economies radiating from foreign investments involve notable improvements in infrastructure and social overhead facilities. Foreign investors can also stimulate local enterprise through increased demand, demonstration effects, and access to foreign technology and business methods. And they often assist local supplying companies and train local personnel.

Failure to take all of these factors into account has led to another popular misunderstanding, that is, that direct investment is a particularly expensive form of capital. But unless it is assumed that profits derive from monopoly, or from distorted prices, high profits imply that such investment is particularly efficient. With free entry to the industry, high profits are a temporary phenomenon, calling attention to what society wants or can produce more cheaply than before. On the other hand, where monopoly profits are being earned, the proper remedy would be to reduce tariffs, take action against specific monopoly practices, renegotiate concession agreements, or initiate competitive enterprise rather than to restrict the inflow of foreign capital.

It is misleading to compare the "cost" of direct investment with that of fixed interest funds. Direct investment, it is sometimes noted, earns net profits of 10–12 percent on capital, whereas fixed interest capital costs only 7–9 percent. But to conclude from this that fixed interest capital is therefore generally to be preferred would be too simple a view. To be comparable, the costs of importing technical know-how, as well as training managers and entrepreneurs willing to assume risks, have to be taken into account. This usually involves a smaller additional cost where the foreign company has an equity interest than where the know-how is provided under a licensing arrangement or management contract. Amortization of the fixed interest debt is another major consideration. In terms of foreign exchange cost, there would, therefore, be a presumption in favor of direct equity investment even if low income countries had easy access to fixed interest funds, which of course they do not. It is also relevant that a significant fraction of the profit on direct investment is often reinvested, especially in the manufacturing sector. A recent survey by the Reserve Bank of India showed that subsidiaries of foreign companies remitted dividends equal to only 5–7 percent on equity in the early 1960s, probably little more than half the net profit earned in that period.

The comparison of the cost of direct investment with that of fixed interest funds must also take into account the greater flexibility involved in the servicing of the former. While interest and amortization payments on loans must be met regardless of whether or not projects built with those funds have successfully entered production, profit remittances only emerge *pari passu* with profitable domestic output. Equity capital, therefore, has a built-in grace period more favorable than bonds and loans. Furthermore, profit remittances flowing from equity investment add an element of flexibility not characteristic of debt servicing.

Another common misconception is that loan financing leads to less foreign control over host countries' economies than equity investment. Actually, fixed interest creditors are in a far stronger position with respect to national authorities than are foreign equity investors, who can often be influenced by fiscal, monetary, and other policies.

Foreign investment generally produces a net benefit for the host country, but there are instances where this is not the case.

For example, the level of tariffs, especially for manufactured goods, is often inappropriate. A protective tariff (or quantitative import control) involves the payment of a subsidy by the economy as a whole to producers in the industry protected. The usual justification for this, of course, is that the growth and development of the protected industry will eventually compensate for the present sacrifice. If a tariff can be justified on these grounds, there is a gain to the economy no matter what the ownership of the companies which invest in the protected industry, for by definition the protected industry eventually repays society for the initial subsidy. On the other hand, if an industry is unable to achieve such levels of efficiency, there is economic loss to the country and the loss is greater if the subsidy is initially paid to foreign shareholders.

Such inappropriate subsidies are often granted because of the desire of less developed countries to build new industries with advanced technology. As it is well known that most companies setting up facilities to serve a market in a developing country can be fairly sure of securing tariff protection, all companies who serve that market by imports fear that some competitor will begin local production and effectively exclude imports forthwith. The result often is a rush by each company to establish a small scale plant, importing most of its product and adding a minimal amount of domestic value (often only by packaging or assembly). For the foreign owned companies, the operation is likely to be quite profitable, but there have been cases where the host country has nevertheless sustained a net loss of real income through the excessive protection and fragmentation of the industry. It should be clear, however, that this results from the host country's misguided commercial policy and is not a cost of foreign investment per se.

While it is very difficult to ascertain the effect of foreign investment on the host country's balance-of-payments, an even more difficult question is what its growth pattern would have been in the absence of foreign investment. It is quite clear that foreign affiliated companies often have important advantages over domestic companies, such as better technical and managerial know-how, greater access to both product and factor markets, and more widely known brand names. Some have argued that precisely for this reason foreign investment, while benefiting domestic residents in the short run, may actually harm the host country in the longer run because of the stultifying effect which this competition has on local enterprise. In accordance with this view, foreign investment, even if it increases national income, will not necessarily promote the overriding objective of self-sustaining growth. When it is also considered that, in the long run, costs in local enterprise are likely to decline, this justification for restricting the inflow of foreign investment follows much the same line of argument as the traditional case for protecting industries in their infant stage.

But this reasoning does not add up to a case for general restrictions against direct foreign investment. Rather, it argues persuasively in favor of more and better policies in developing countries aimed at encouraging local entrepreneurs. Credit and fiscal policies of the host countries can, and should, be tailored not only to exercise proper control over foreign investors, but also to promote budding local entrepreneurship. This approach will involve a much lower cost to the economies of less developed countries than one which relies on discouragement of foreign investment. Foreign investment will benefit domestic incomes now, whereas the growth of infant domestic companies will produce equivalent benefit only after a lag. This lag is likely to be considerable, especially in technologically complex industries, and would involve economic loss.

In the absence of detailed empirical studies, it is difficult to pass a definitive verdict on the precise size of the contribution which foreign investment has made to development. But in our judgment, available facts do suggest that direct foreign investment has added substantially to the real national income of developing countries.[1] In so doing it has also enhanced their capacity to finance their future development. In the recent past, this has been especially true of investments in extractive industries, through the enormous tax revenues they have generated. In 1967, for example, foreign owned oil companies paid royalties and taxes to the main oil countries of the Middle East, Libya, and Venezuela totaling $4.7 billion, up from $2.8 billion in 1962

---

1. Professor Lewis and Sir Edward Boyle agree with this sentence but not with all the theoretical arguments adduced in the preceding paragraphs. They do not accept all the language that follows, but they agree with the recommendations at the end of the chapter.

and $2.0 billion in 1957. The governments of other countries exporting mineral products have benefited in a similar manner. The situation in this respect is now very different from that which prevailed earlier.

HOW TO INCREASE THE FLOW OF PRIVATE INVESTMENT

We have received the definite impression that most low income countries would welcome a larger flow of foreign investment, sharing our belief that such flows would contribute to their faster growth. How can that flow be stimulated?

There is probably little more that needs to be done to encourage the flow of foreign capital into extractive sectors. By its very nature, such investment will be attracted to ore bodies and oil deposits. Investment climate plays some part in this decision, but there is probably not more than a handful of countries in the world where that climate is bad enough to deter investment in a really attractive mineral project. What can be hoped for is perhaps that countries with rich natural resources will be able to use their resultant bargaining power to increase foreign investment in internationally competitive processing and/or fabricating facilities.

How can direct investment in other sectors be fostered? A first step is surely for developed countries to remove remaining restrictions on the flow of foreign investment to developing countries. However, these restrictions do not now appear to be a major obstacle to that flow. A more fundamental issue concerns the widening of the domestic markets in developing countries. However, in this chapter we confine our attention to four areas of action.

First, a start must be made on improving the general climate for all private investment, foreign and domestic.

Too few of these countries recognize the tremendous contribution which private enterprise can make to economic development, and in an environment unsympathetic to all private entrepreneurship it is hardly surprising that foreign investors sense danger. Changing this environment will require many specific actions. Measures to strengthen financial institutions and to encourage entrepreneurship are especially important, but their form must be tailored to the particular situation. As a general proposition, it is almost certainly true that improving the position of the private sector as a whole is the most important single step to improving the climate for foreign investment in developing countries. *We therefore recommend that developing countries take immediate steps, where consistent with legitimate national objectives, to identify and remove disincentives to domestic private investment.*

The poor image of developing countries in business circles is also the result of the cumbersome administrative procedures and inefficient decision making processes which companies often encounter when planning an investment in such a country. We recognize that many of these obstacles are often themselves a result of underdevelopment, but we also feel that many governments could even now streamline their procedures considerably. As an absolute minimum *we recommend that developing countries preserve the greatest possible stability in their laws and regulations affecting foreign investment.*

In some countries there is also a strong case for more balanced policies toward foreign investment. But if these are to emerge, there must be some defusing of the politically explosive forces which foreign investment can generate. One important way of doing this would seem to be to make more extensive use of the "joint venture" form. Exerting pressure on international corporations to share ownership in this way may involve certain real costs, but foreign investors would also be wise to realize the political cost that may be incurred by reluctance to accept local investors into partnership.

There are other ways of improving the relationship between governments and foreign companies and forestalling disruptive and costly conflicts between them. In particular, developing countries and international corporations alike could make specific provision, when initially negotiating the terms of investment agreements involving politically sensitive activities, such as mining and public utilities, for mutual reconsideration of those terms after a minimum period of years and for adequate compensation and freedom to repatriate such compensation if no accord can be reached at that time. This arrangement, already used by a few developing countries, has the advantage of recognizing the changes in relative bargaining power which are likely to take place over time, of reducing political tensions by giving the host government an agreed basis on which to change terms, and of increasing the likelihood that these terms will not be changed during the agreed period. It is preferable to most schemes of "planned nationalization" in that it provides an orderly procedure for re-examination of foreign holdings. Thus, it reduces the company's incentive to "milk" the operation and avoids prejudging whether it will be in the country's interests to assume ownership of a particular foreign owned property in the future. Present arrangements only too often compound uncertainty.

The attitudes of foreign investors to the aspirations of host countries, and their willingness to cooperate with development policies, are also crucial to harmonious relations. Foreign investors who in their home countries are subjected to a plethora of legislative and regulatory measures cannot expect to operate in conditions of nineteenth-century capitalism in the low income countries.

The governments of the richer countries, too, must be aware of their role in improving the investment climate. Interventions by the large industrial powers on behalf of their investors have a long history, the memory of which looms large in hostility toward private investment. Respect for the sovereignty of the host country is indispensable to the creation of mutual confidence. It is of course unrealistic to expect governments of capital exporting countries to remain passive when the property of their citizens is subject to discriminatory or confiscatory treatment by other countries, but intervention should take a form, whenever possible, which will not jeopardize long term relations. Specifically, we believe that developed countries should, as far as possible, keep separate aid policy and disputes concerning foreign investment.

Another suggestion relates to the problem of extraterritoriality, or the intrusion of the jurisdiction of one country into that of another. In the past, this issue has arisen primarily in connection with U.S. investments in other industrialized countries and with attempts to enforce U.S. antitrust law or U.S. policy with respect to trade with Communist countries. Recently, the problem has come to be of more general concern with the introduction of regulations designed to assist the U.S. balance-of-payments by requiring the foreign subsidiaries of American companies to repatriate specified proportions of their earnings. While we have not been able to study this question exhaustively, we believe that an appropriate solution might be the renunciation of the principle of extraterritoriality by all member states of the United Nations and, for the long term, the eventual creation of a system of international incorporation of companies doing business in more than one country.

A second major area where action is required concerns measures which promote investment by offsetting the poor investment climate and the disadvantages of the limited markets in developing countries. Some of these measures involve the governments of developed countries, which offer incentives such as tax advantages, guarantees against political and commercial risks, and special credit facilities to those investing in developing countries. The relative importance of each of these incentives differs from country to country, as does the appropriate improvement. However, taken together they certainly reinforce the favorable decisions of potential investors and should be strengthened whenever possible.

Large tax concessions, perhaps investment credits of 30–40 percent, would probably be required to increase substantially the flow of investment, but more modest steps may be highly useful with respect to some countries. For example, added incentive could result from lowering the fees now charged by governments or their affiliated agencies for investment guarantees. Consideration should also be given to the creation or strengthening of schemes which provide special credit facilities to firms which desire to invest in developing countries. None of these steps will transform the flow of investment unless accompanied by basic changes in the investment climate, but each is worth careful study by donor governments. *Therefore, we recommend that developed countries strengthen their investment incentive schemes, wherever possible.*

Tax concessions extended by developing countries are sometimes a useful way of temporarily shielding foreign companies from the full impact of an antiquated tax system, thereby providing governments with time to revise the basic structure. But only in a few cases do they seem to draw an investment opportunity to the attention of a foreign company, and they are generally reported to be of modest importance in the final investment decision. On the other hand, they restrict the growth of the host country's tax base, sometimes quite seriously. Accordingly, we would recommend that general tax concessions to attract foreign companies be used sparingly. In any event, developing countries should seek to stop the competition in tax concessions by international cooperation.

Tax concessions by developing countries raise the subject of "tax-sparing," that is, tax credits for international companies in their home countries to insure that tax concessions in host countries are not offset by increased taxation at home. The value of such provisions is not as obvious as it might seem. On the one hand, it is true that they may give slightly more weight to tax concessions which developing countries find worth trying. On the other hand, in the absence of tax-sparing, companies have an incentive to reinvest profits earned during the concession period and this may be a more valuable result. On balance, tax-sparing does not seem to be a policy which can be firmly prescribed, although it may be quite useful as an inducement to invest in lagging sectors or areas of developing countries.

We do, however, recommend that developing countries structure their tax system to encourage profit reinvestment by foreign companies. Profit reinvestment is a form of foreign capital which is more readily attracted by tax incentives than new capital, and positive incentives to reinvest are greatly to be preferred to penalties for remitting. The latter tend to be counterproductive by discouraging new capital inflow.

Third, at the international level, talks leading to the establishment of a multilateral investment insurance scheme should be pursued vigorously, as such a scheme could be quite helpful in mitigating the impact of an uncertain investment climate. In saying this, we do not dispute the value of the bilateral programs now operated by eight developed countries. Some of these, such as the extended risk scheme operated by the United States, are especially useful in permitting corporations to gear up their equity investments by tapping fixed interest funds from institutional investors in developed countries. But a soundly based multilateral system could: (a) permit insurance of investments made by companies based in countries not now operating bilateral systems, such as France and the United Kingdom; (b) permit insurance of multinational projects; (c) permit small bilateral insurance programs to reinsure large risks; and (d) involve both developed and developing countries in the insurance risks. It might even be appropriate eventually to link the scheme to the Convention on the Settlement of Investment Disputes, by providing for higher coverage and/or lower premiums for insuring investments in countries which accede to it, or to provide for recourse to equivalent regional arbitration facilities.

Serious consideration should also be given to concluding bilateral agreements on the treatment of foreign investors of the sort already concluded with some developing countries by the Federal Republic of Germany, Switzerland, and other donor nations. This might eventually lead to a network of such agreements which could be consolidated into a uniform multilateral agreement such as has been suggested by the Council of the OECD.

The fourth area in which action to stimulate the flow of private capital would be useful is that of project identification and investment promotion. Existing bilateral programs with this objective include the subsidization of investment surveys and the publicizing of known investment opportunities. These are useful programs, but they are often too small and imperfectly geared to the investor's needs (for example, the surveys subsidized are sometimes too general to be of real value in promotional work). They should also devote more attention to inducing small and medium sized investors to take up projects in developing countries, providing them, when necessary, with the required technical assistance. Programs of this kind are currently operated by the German Development Company and the Commonwealth Development Corporation.

Similar change should be encouraged with respect to the International Finance Corporation (IFC), which has in the past interpreted the clause in its Articles requiring it to finance only projects "where sufficient private capital is not available on reasonable terms" to mean that it should leave all project initiative to others. There are some signs that IFC and bilateral institutions of similar type are now beginning to appreciate the role they could play in actively identifying new investment opportunities and bringing together domestic and foreign partners to execute them. Certainly, *because of their links with the private sectors of both developed and developing countries, IFC, and organizations like it, are logical agents for project identification and investment promotion work, and we accordingly recommend that they become much more active in this field.*

GREATER BENEFITS FROM DIRECT INVESTMENT

Important as it is to increase the flow of direct investment, it is at least as important to consider how developing countries could use foreign investment to better advantage.

A first part of the answer is simply that they should pursue general economic policies which promote rather than impede economic development, regardless of whether foreign investment is involved or not. Especially important is policy on tariffs and import controls, the misuse of which often encourages investments which detract from rather than add to economic welfare. It is also important to design the tax system so as to offset distortions in factor prices which bias techniques of production against economically efficient labor intensive methods. Foreign owned companies, and companies employing engineers trained abroad, normally have a built-in tendency to prefer the capital intensive methods of production with which they are familiar. All too often, the tax incentives offered by developing countries actively foster this bias by extending particularly generous depreciation allowances. Company laws could often be improved so as to require a greater degree of financial disclosure both for domestic and foreign enterprise. This would reduce distrust, help to protect minority stockholders, and foster the development of a local capital market.

The encouragement of local entrepreneurs and assistance to the local capital market are not substitutes for, but complements to, foreign investment. Especially in the early stages of development, foreign investment tends to concentrate on a fairly narrow range of industries, and the vigor of local enterprise partially determines the extent of the linkages through which foreign investment may transmit benefits to the host company. Developed countries and multilateral institutions have played a useful role here by providing financial assistance to development finance companies. This type of aid should be extended in the future. The main responsibility for developing a local capital market must, of course, rest with the country concerned, but the evolution of viable capital markets should also be of interest to aid giving agencies. Assistance might take the form of advice on company law, rules for financial disclosure, proper accounting procedures, incentives to broaden the participation of private investors, and the underwriting of new share issues in developing countries. The IFC has done some useful work in this area but is in a position to do very much more.

Turning to policies specifically related to foreign investment, our principal suggestion is that developing countries use their bargaining position *vis-à-vis* foreign companies in order to secure advantages of first importance to sound development. Often, for instance, it seems unwise to expend all bargaining power upon the demand that foreign companies share ownership with local investors. The aversion of international companies to such shared ownership is often great, sometimes so great that the company simply refuses to invest if the claim is pressed. Such a reaction is most common in the technologically most advanced industries such as electronics and pharmaceuticals, and it is also very common in the auto industry. In other cases, the aversion can be overcome only by promises of cheap land and tax concessions.

We realize that there may be economic as well as political gains from urging foreign companies to share ownership. If ownership is widely spread, the growth of a capital market is fostered and the tendency to capital flight reduced. If it makes the foreign parent company regard the investment as more secure, the required rate of return from the investment may be lower. Some forms of local participation may provide training in entrepreneurship for local investors. But the domestic equity provided rarely secures control over important corporate decisions, and adds little or nothing to the developing country's capacity to influence company behavior by monetary, fiscal, and other policy measures. Local share participation may also lead the parent company to treat its affiliate in ways which are clearly not in the interest of the host country, for example, by limiting its access to technology or world markets.

Where there are alternative means to develop a capital market and check capital outflow, urging foreign companies to share ownership with domestic investors may thus involve real economic costs. It seems better, therefore, to press for things which give a greater assurance of gain, such as technical and managerial training of local personnel, assistance to local supplying industries, the establishment of a plant large enough to serve export markets, and limited tariff protection and tax concessions.

Nevertheless, we appreciate that a number of companies attach great value to domestic ownership of industry, and where this is the case *we recommend that their governments establish positive incentives for all companies, foreign and domestic, to share ownership with the public by sale of equity in suitable forms.* Such incentives will undoubtedly be ignored by some foreign companies, but others will respond to them. They will certainly deter investment less than more overt pressure, and have the advantage of making it clear that developing a local capital market and broadening the ownership of industry are important reasons for their existence.

What other controls on the magnitude or quality of direct investment are desirable from the host country's point of view? Some of the arguments for these restrictions are quite weak. It is sometimes suggested that foreign investment should be excluded from certain industries such as soft drinks, alcoholic beverages, and refrigerators. Clearly, what is required in such cases is a policy to discourage all companies, local and foreign, from investing in industries believed to be of marginal importance. The sales tax is a readily available instrument for this purpose.

Other arguments are sometimes more compelling. While it is not sensible to provide excessive tariff protection for any industry, political and social concerns may make it easier to prohibit foreign investment in a highly protected industry than to reduce tariffs. The latter would avoid the payment of an inappropriate subsidy to foreign investors, but might also expose a long established domestic industry to sudden and severe competition with imports. There may be similar grounds for restricting foreign investment where it would entail a substantial reduction in competition, or in "natural monopolies" where it almost inevitably leads to conflicts over rate fixing. Therefore, less developed countries can be expected to exercise selectivity in welcoming foreign investments.

We recognize the occasional need for a policy, already adopted by some countries, of placing limits on the freedom of foreign companies to borrow locally. This would not be warranted in a perfect capital market, or where domestic resources had few alternative uses. But where local companies find themselves at a substantial disadvantage in the capital market *vis-à-vis* foreign companies simply by virtue of the worldwide reputation of the latter, some countervailing interference with the market mechanism is desirable. Of course, some freedom to borrow locally is a condition for attracting foreign investment to some countries, especially when the exchange rate appears vulnerable, but there are evident disadvantages involved in allowing foreign companies to borrow locally many times their own equity contribution when pressure on domestic resources is great.[2]

To avoid excessive fragmentation of an industry where, because of the foreign affiliation of many of the companies, there is scant hope for future rationalization and mergers, developing countries should consider limiting the number of individual companies (though not their investment) in certain activities. The Latin American auto industry is the best known example of this problem, but there are others.

It is difficult to make comments of general applicability on this problem of negotiating with foreign companies. At the same time, it is an area where impartial advice is urgently needed. We accordingly believe that the international agencies should play a more active role in advising developing countries in their policies toward foreign investment.

In the past, such advice has been rare. IFC was long the only international organization active in the field of private foreign investment. The recent creation of the United Nations Industrial Development Organization (UNIDO) has changed the situation somewhat. The World Bank has tended to delegate much of its industrial work to the IFC. Often this has not worked out well because IFC has deliberately avoided involvement in government policy issues wherever possible. Its own investments require no host government guarantee and it normally behaves in very much the same manner as an ordinary commercial investment house, taking government policies as given. Moreover, IFC is not equipped to ascertain the economic implications of government policies. Many of the projects in which it has participated have certainly benefited the host country, but others have contributed only marginally, if at all, to economic development. In

---

2. This is especially true where, because of government controls on nominal interest rates and high rates of inflation, effective rates of interest are actually negative and imply a subsidy to the borrowing enterprise.

particular, they have often been in sectors subsidized by high effective tariff protection. In few cases are investments preceded by an analysis of their impact on the economy as a whole. In practice, profitability has been the principal investment criterion. This is clearly a necessary criterion for any agency which would stimulate the growth of the private sector, but it is not a sufficient criterion for an agency purporting to be concerned with economic development.

We hope that a reorientation of IFC policy is possible, for the sake of the economic impact of its own investment, and even more for that of the new investments that we believe it is well placed to promote. *However, we would also recommend that other international institutions, such as the World Bank and UNIDO, expand further their advisory role regarding industrial and foreign investment policies.* These activities could eventually be fully transferred to IFC if the proposed reorientation of IFC is successfully achieved.

BOND ISSUES AND OTHER PORTFOLIO INVESTMENT

Bond issues on international capital markets were once the main channel for foreign private investment. They are now much less important than direct investment, and even than export credits. Data compiled by the World Bank on a gross basis (that is, without allowance for amortization) indicate that in the five years from 1964–68, only three developing countries outside Europe—Israel, Mexico, and Argentina—were able to float bonds totaling more than $100 million on world capital markets.

Three main obstacles have prevented developing countries from raising a greater volume of funds. First, few borrowers in developing countries have established a record of creditworthiness. Second, legal restrictions in many developed countries limit the amounts which institutional investors can place in foreign securities. Third, several members of the Development Assistance Committee (DAC) limit foreign access to their capital markets for balance-of-payments reasons. Any one of these obstacles would be sufficient to explain the limited volume of resources raised by most developing countries in recent years, but in reality the factor most directly operative has been the poor credit rating of all but a handful of the developing countries.

What are the prospects? It seems that, as more of the middle income countries in the developing world establish creditworthiness records of their own, their ability to borrow on world markets will increase of itself. For this group, the restrictions of developed countries will be a serious barrier. *We therefore recommend the removal, in developed countries, of legal and other barriers to the purchase by institutional investors of bonds issued or guaranteed by governments of developing countries.*

In some developed countries, balance-of-payments difficulties have led to the imposition of specific restrictions against issues of this kind. We recognize the very great weight of balance-of-payments considerations, but we do not consider it acceptable that efforts to help developing countries should be the first casualty of the industrialized countries' failure to solve their international adjustment problems. *We therefore recommend the removal of balance-of-payments restrictions in developed countries presently inhibiting the bond issues of developing countries.*

For the foreseeable future, however, direct access to world capital markets will not be possible for most low income countries without some help. It has been suggested to us that one way of providing such help is for the governments of developed countries to guarantee bonds issued by those developing countries which, with some initial backing, will soon be able to raise capital on their account. In view of the distortions this procedure might create in the marketability of different bonds, the Commission is not prepared to endorse this idea, but suggests that greater efforts be made by governments and issue banks in capital exporting countries to develop ways and means to increase the number of developing countries and their government corporations which gain access to international securities markets.

For countries which are still far from being able to float their own bonds internationally, we believe that the best way to channel fixed interest funds at market prices to them is to expand the activities of multilateral development institutions such as the World Bank and the regional development banks. Given adequate market access by the governments of developed countries, such institutions should encounter little difficulty in increasing their borrowing.

There are, of course, many other types of private capital flow to developing countries which do not involve investor control over the borrowing entity. Commercial banks sometimes extend renewable credits to the governments of developing countries. Private corporations take small equity investments in licensees. Individuals in developed countries occasionally buy shares in companies in developing countries. The forms are many and the precise importance of each unknown. We ask only one question: What is the scope for stimulating the flow of equity capital from individual investors in the wealthy countries to companies in less developed economies?

At present this flow is almost certainly very small, comprising mostly investment in the shares of a handful of companies in more industrialized countries such as Mexico and Brazil. This is not hard to explain. Stock markets in developing countries, where they exist at all, are poorly developed. Since many of the major local industrial and commercial concerns are closely held by family groups, markets tend to be very thin, and any substantial transaction causes sharp movements in price. Second, potential investors are normally quite ignorant of investment opportunities in developing countries. Where they are aware of such opportunities they discount heavily for the unfamiliar environment. Third, most potential investors regard the exchange risk as high in all developing countries, even where such a view is unreasonable. For these reasons there is probably little to be gained from extending tax concessions to private individuals to induce them to invest in developing countries. The magnitude of such concessions would have to be very large indeed to move significant amounts of this type of capital.

We believe, however, that ways should be found, where possible, to stimulate the activities of organizations which could act as financial intermediaries for the equity capital of individual investors. There are a number of organizations which could perform this function. While they could by no means eliminate all the risks of investing in developing countries, they could, from the point of view of the individual investor, solve the problem of lack of market knowledge and reduce the exchange risk by providing an interest in a wide range of countries and sectors. These institutions already avoid the problem of inadequate stock market facilities by making their investments directly.

Among official institutions which could conceivably act as intermediaries for the funds of relatively small investors in developed countries are the IFC, the Commonwealth Development Corporation, and the German Development Company (DEG). Eventually, private bodies such as the ADELA group for Latin America and the recently formed Private Investment Company for Asia (PICA) may be able to play a similar role. Some of these bodies already sell participations in their investments to banks and other large scale investors in developed countries, but we believe it would be valuable if they were also to put together packages of their investments and sell shares in these units to individual investors. Such a scheme would both raise additional capital and acquaint a wider circle of investors with the possibility of profitable investment in developing countries; indeed, these institutions might eventually become intermediaries for a broader line of paper from developing countries.

EXPORT CREDITS

The net flow of private export credits from DAC members to low income countries has grown substantially in the past decade, from an average of $375 million in 1956–58 to $1,330 million annually in 1966–68. The gross flows have, of course, been substantially larger, and were estimated by the DAC at $3 billion in 1967. In addition, gross export credits from public institutions in DAC countries probably added almost another $1 billion to that total.

These credits have added significantly to the total external resources available to less developed countries, but are part of the normal trading relations between countries and have little if any concessional effect. The DAC estimated that private export credits made up almost 14 percent of the financial resources transferred to developing countries in 1968. As with other forms of private capital movement, the flow of export credits has been most unevenly distributed. Of the gross private and public credits of over five years' maturity which, in 1967, were extended from DAC members to developing countries, 42 percent went to countries with substantial oil revenues or per capita incomes above $500, and another 14 percent went to Liberia and Panama, most of it for the sale of ships to flag-of-convenience lines. However, such credits have been used extensively by many other countries too, and at present they are known to constitute more than a quarter of the total external debt outstanding for Argentina, Peru, Korea, Rwanda, Mauritania, Niger, Ivory Coast, Ghana, Chad, and Yugoslavia.

In recent years, the growing competition among capital goods exporters has tended to improve the terms of export credits. A number of developed countries blend finance from public and private sources to reduce the rate of interest below that which would be otherwise payable, and the importance of credits with maturities of more than five years has grown rapidly over the last decade. The Berne Union understanding that credits should not normally be extended for periods exceeding five years has effectively been abandoned by all major capital goods exporting countries, and maturities frequently exceed eight, and sometimes even ten years. Virtually the entire net flow of export credit to developing countries in 1967 involved credits with maturities of more than five years.

Export credits have a part to play in development, but their imprudent use revolves real dangers. First, export credits are usually an expensive form of external finance. This may be true even where the nominal rate of interest is low if this is offset by adjustments of the price of the equipment purchased. Cases were reported to the Commission involving price adjustments exceeding 100 percent of the world market prices. These are presumably rare, but smaller adjustments are understood to be common. Second, excessive use of export credits has created serious balance-of-payments problems for developing countries which have relied on such short term borrowing to finance long-term investments. Since the mid-1950s, an undue accumulation of short term suppliers' credits has been a major reason for the need to reschedule the debts of a number of countries, notably Argentina, Brazil, Chile, Ghana, Indonesia, and Turkey. This rescheduling will be more difficult in the future if export credits are imprudently used.

Why do the low income countries resort to this kind of finance? In some cases, monetary and fiscal policy have obviously been weak. Available savings are low, and there is strong pressure for finance for new investments in both the public and the private sectors. Especially when tariff and exchange rate policies distort the price structure, decision makers may be led to undertake investments which, though profitable in terms of local currency, have a marginal or negative return in terms of repayment capacity. Such investments would exacerbate balance-of-payments problems even if financed on concessional terms.

Countries with good fiscal performance have occasion to use export credits, although this sometimes reflects unavailability of adequate external fixed interest finance on softer terms. This is not merely a matter of the general insufficiency of aid finance. Export credits are frequently used to finance industrial projects in the public sector because, in general, neither international aid agencies nor the main bilateral aid donors are eager to finance industrial projects in that sector. Export credits are used as the next best alternative.

Sometimes developing countries are reluctant to submit projects to the scrutiny of international financial institutions even when they are of a type normally financed by these bodies. This hesitancy is sometimes due to the belief, regrettably justified, that these organizations often take an inordinately long time to reach an investment decision. More often, however, it is probably motivated by an awareness that the project at issue might not pass rigorous tests of economic desirability. More than one project rejected for financing by the World Bank Group on economic grounds has been promptly financed by an export credit. This is the most unfortunate aspect of export credit finance: it provides a temporarily painless way of financing projects conceived by overly optimistic civil servants, by politicians more concerned with immediate political advantage than with potential future economic problems, and by unscrupulous salesmen for the manufactures of capital equipment in developed countries.

The very enumeration of the factors which lead developing countries to accept export credits suggests the fundamental solutions to their excessive use: better economic policies, better project evaluation, and greater availability of concessional finance. But assuming it will take time to achieve these solutions, are there not second-best measures to improve the situation in the short run?

There are several ways open to developing countries to improve the terms on which export credits are available to them. They will often be better able to assess the real terms of a credit if they have an independent appraisal of the cost of the equipment. As a minimum, they should therefore, wherever possible, avoid the use of export credits where the only project feasibility study available is one prepared by the equipment supplier. A few countries have been partly successful in mitigating the effects of the tied nature of suppliers' credits by prescribing that borrowing enterprises present at least three suppliers' credit offers from three different countries before they can obtain guarantees, which are compulsory. One promising development is the recent growth in "buyers' credits," commercial loans directly extended to the capital equipment buyer, not the supplying company. Though in practice these have often been arranged for the purchaser by the supplying company, and so have no advantage over the conventional suppliers' credit, they offer scope for an enterprising buyer to see a number of competitive bids within the country supplying the credit. Similarly, the recent development of "joint financing" techniques for pooling export credits with resources from multi-lateral institutions combines these credits with all the advantages of international competitive bidding. The Commission endorses such arrangements and urges international institutions such as the World Bank to give suitable technical assistance to developing countries in appraising the terms of export credits offered to them.

Fundamentally, the task of preventing the excessive use of export credits for projects of low priority must be that of the individual developing country. Nevertheless, some restraint on the part of creditor governments is also indicated. They themselves have an immediate interest in avoiding excessive use of export credits, which is quite likely to lead to default or rescheduling of debt. We have considered a number of ways in which such restraint could be exercised. As things now stand, the problem is that suppliers of export credits are less concerned about the borrowing country's creditworthiness because of the facility of export credit insurance.

We recommend a strong "early warning system" based on the external debt reporting which is being evolved by the OECD and the World Bank. The World Bank should be charged with the responsibility of issuing definitive recommendations against further encouragement of export credits to countries which are in the danger zone from the standpoint of debt liabilities and interest burden. It should fix ceilings which should not be exceeded.

Export credits beyond these ceilings should, in the event of any debt rearrangement, enjoy significantly less favorable treatment than other claims.

PRIVATE CAPITAL: AN ALTERNATIVE TO AID?

There can be no doubt about the contribution which private capital can render to economic development. Indeed, dollar for dollar, it may be more effective than official aid both because it is more closely linked to the management and technology which industrial ventures require, and because those who risk their own money may be expected to be particularly interested in its efficient use.

In most industrialized countries, there are influential voices advocating that for these reasons private investment could and should replace official aid flows. In the present state of affairs, however, this is an illusion. To begin with, given the present limited access of developing countries to the capital markets of the world, private capital flows are simply not available to finance many of the investments which are a prime need in developing countries—schools, roads, hospitals, irrigation. Even through the mediation of the World Bank, such needs cannot be met on the basis of the capital that can, in the near future, be raised in capital markets. Second, the flow of private capital tends to be highly concentrated in countries with rich mineral resources and fairly high incomes. Many of the countries of Africa and Asia receive almost no private capital. It is precisely because private capital flows cannot meet the extraordinary demands posed by the imperatives of development that large government efforts have been called forth. Another basic consideration is that it is only through public aid that the developed countries assumed any burden on behalf of the weaker members of the international community.

It is fundamental to our strategy that the need for aid should eventually subside. Direct investment and access to capital markets would then increasingly meet the demand for development finance. But, for most developing countries, this is not possible in the short run. On the contrary, for many countries, official aid for investment in infrastructure is a prerequisite for private investment, and tends to stimulate it. Far from being alternatives, private investment and public aid can complement each other and it is to this end that immediate efforts should be made, both in bilateral and multilateral aid operations.

RECOMMENDATIONS

1. Developing countries should take immediate steps, where consistent with legitimate national objectives, to identify and remove disincentives to domestic private investment.

2. Developing countries should preserve the greatest possible stability in their laws and regulations affecting foreign investment.

3. Developed countries should strengthen their investment incentive schemes wherever possible.

4. Developing countries should structure their tax systems so as to encourage profit reinvestment by foreign companies.

5. Because the IFC and organizations like it have links with the private sectors of both developed and developing countries, they are logical agents for project identification and investment promotion work, and they should become much more active in this field.

6. Governments of developing countries which attach great value to domestic ownership of industry should establish positive incentives for all companies, foreign and domestic, to share ownership with the public by sale of equity in suitable forms.

7. International institutions, such as the World Bank and UNIDO, should expand further their advisory role regarding industrial and foreign investment policies.

8. Developed countries should remove legal and other barriers to the purchase by institutional investors of bonds issued or guaranteed by governments of developing countries.

9. Developed countries should remove balance-of-payments restrictions presently inhibiting the bond issues of developing countries in international capital markets.

10. In regard to the possible excessive use of export credits, a strong "early warning system" based on external debt reporting should be evolved by the OECD and the World Bank.

How to Divest in Latin America, and Why
ALBERT O. HIRSCHMAN

Albert O. Hirschman, Professor of Economics at Harvard University, has interested himself especially in the problems of Latin America. This article was originally written for the International Finance Section, Princeton University, and republished in A Bias for Hope: Essays on Development and Latin America, *Yale University Press, 1971.*

The President, in 1940, [recounted] that when he had visited Rio de Janeiro in 1936, President Getulio Vargas had told him that the bus lines in the capital were owned in Montreal and Toronto, and had asked: "What would the people of New York City do if the subways were all owned in Canada?" Roosevelt's reply had been: "Why, there would be a revolution." The President went on to say that he thought that, when foreign capital went into a Latin American country, the country should gain control of the utility or other business after the investment had been paid off in a period that might be set at twenty-five or thirty years. Thus, the country could look forward to gaining ultimate control of utilities and perhaps other foreign-financed corporations through having what Roosevelt called "an option on the equity."
—Bryce Wood

PRIVATE FOREIGN INVESTMENT—AN INCREASINGLY MIXED BLESSING

The positive contribution of foreign investment to an economy can be of various kinds. In the first place, it can supply one of several missing factors of production (capital, entrepreneurship, management, and so forth), factors, that is, which are simply and indisputably not to be found in the country receiving the investment. This is the situation often prevailing in the earliest stages of development of a poor country. More generally, foreign investment can make it possible for output to increase sharply, because it provides the recipient economy with a larger quantity of comparatively scarce (if not entirely missing) inputs.

Another contribution of foreign investment, conspicuous in relations among advanced industrial countries and inviting often a two-way flow, is of a rather different nature: it can have a teaching function and serve to improve the quality of the local factors of production. By on the spot example and through competitive pressures, foreign investment can act as a spur to the general efficiency of local enterprise. This effect is likely to be particularly important in economic sectors which are sheltered from the competition of merchandise imports from abroad. Such sectors (services, industries with strong locational advantages) appear to expand rapidly at advanced stages of economic development. If foreign investment is successful in enhancing the quality of local enterprise, then its inflow will be providentially self-limiting: once the local business community achieves greater efficiency, there will be fewer openings for the demonstration of superior foreign techniques, management, and know-how. But what if local businessmen, faced with overwhelming advantages of their foreign competitors, do not respond with adequate vigor and, instead, deteriorate further or sell out? This is, of course, the nub of recent European fears of the "American challenge." I cannot deal here with this problem, but the fact that it exists has interesting implications for the topic at hand.

If foreign investment can fail to improve and may even harm the quality of local factors of production, then the question arises whether it may also, under certain circumstances, lead to a decrease in the quantity of local inputs available to an economy. In other words, could the inflow of foreign investment stunt what might otherwise be vigorous local development of the so-called missing or scarce factors of production?

This question has been little discussed.[1] The reason for the neglect lies in the intellectual tradition which treats international investment under the rubric "export of capital." As long as one thinks in terms of this single factor of production being exported to a capital-poor country, it is natural to view it as highly complementary to various local factors—such as natural resources and labor—that are available in abundance and are only waiting to be combined with the "missing factor" to yield large additional out-

1. Important exceptions are the articles by J. Knapp, "Capital Exports and Growth," *Economic Journal* 67 (September 1957): 432–44, and by Felipe Pazos, "The Role of International Movements of Private Capital in Promoting Development," in John H. Adler, ed., *Capital Movements and Economic Development* (New York: St. Martin's Press, 1967).

puts. But, for a long time now, foreign investors have prided themselves on contributing "not just capital," but a whole bundle of other valuable inputs. In counterpart to these claims, however, the doubt might have arisen that some components of the bundle will no longer be purely complementary to local factors, but will be competitive with them and could cause them to wither or retard and even prevent their growth.

The possibility, and indeed likelihood, that international trade will lead to the shrinkage and/or disappearance of certain lines of local production as a result of cheaper imports has been at the root of international trade theory since Adam Smith and Ricardo. This effect of trade has been celebrated by free traders through such terms as "international specialization" and "efficient reallocation of resources." The opponents of free trade have often pointed out that for a variety of reasons it is imprudent and harmful for a country to become specialized along certain product lines in accordance with the dictates of comparative advantage. Whatever the merit of these critical arguments, they would certainly acquire overwhelming weight if the question arose as to whether a country should allow itself to become specialized not just along certain commodity lines, but along factor-of-production lines. Very few countries would ever consciously wish to specialize in unskilled labor, while foreigners with a comparative advantage in entrepreneurship, management, skilled labor, and capital took over these functions, replacing inferior "local talent." But this is precisely the direction in which events can move when international investment, proudly bringing in its bundle of factors, has unimpeded access to developing countries. In the fine paradoxical formulation of Felipe Pazos: "The main weakness of direct investment as a development agent is a consequence of the complete character of its contribution." [2]

The displacement of local factors and stunting of local abilities which can occur in the wake of international investment is sometimes absolute, as when local banks or businesses are bought out by foreign capital; this has in fact been happening recently with

2. Pazos, "International Movements of Private Capital," p. 196. A. K. Cairncross expresses the same thought in discussing the contribution of foreign owned branch plants and subsidiaries to economic development: "Their very power to break all the bottlenecks at once . . . can be, from the point of view of the host country, their most damning feature" (*Factors in Economic Development* [London: George Allen and Unwin, 1962], p. 181).

increasing frequency in Latin America. But the more common and perhaps more dangerous, because less noticeable, stunting effect is relative to what might have happened in the absence of the investment.

As already mentioned, foreign investment can be at its creative best by bringing in "missing" factors of production, complementary to those available locally, in the early stages of development of a poor country. The possibility that it will play a stunting role arises later on, when the poor country has begun to generate, to a large extent no doubt because of the prior injection of foreign investment, its own entrepreneurs, technicians, and savers and could now do even more along these lines if it were not for the institutional inertia that makes for a continued importing of so-called scarce factors of production which have become potentially dispensable. It is, of course, exceedingly difficult to judge at what point in time foreign investment changes in this fashion from a stimulant of development into a retarding influence, particularly since during the latter stage its contribution is still ostensibly positive—for example, the foreign capital that comes in is visible and measurable, in contrast to the domestic capital that might have been generated in its stead. One can never be certain, moreover, that restrictions against foreign investment will in fact call forth the local entrepreneurial, managerial, technological, and saving performances which are believed to be held back and waiting in the wings to take over from the foreign investors. Nevertheless, a considerable body of evidence, brought forth less by design than by accidents such as wars, depressions, nationalist expropriations, and international sanctions, suggests strongly that, after an initial period of development, the domestic supply of routinely imported factors of production is far more elastic than is ever suspected under business-as-usual conditions. If this is so, then the "climate for foreign investment" ought to turn from attractive at an early stage of development to much less inviting in some middle stretch—in which most of Latin America finds itself at present.

The preceding argument is the principal economic reason for anticipating increasing conflict between the goals of national development and the foreign investment community, even after the latter has thoroughly purged itself of the excesses that marred its early career. The argument is strengthened by related considerations pertaining to economic policy making, a "factor of production" not often taken into account by economists, but which nevertheless has an essential role to play. In the course of industrialization, resources for complementary investment in education and overhead capital must be generated through taxation, the opening up of new domestic and foreign markets must be made attractive, institutions hampering growth must be reformed, and powerful social groups that are antagonistic to development must be neutralized. The achievement of these tasks is considerably facilitated if the new industrialists are able to speak with a strong, influential, and even militant voice. But the emergence of such a voice is most unlikely if a large portion of the more dynamic new industries is in foreign hands. This is a somewhat novel reproach to foreign capital, which has normally been taken to task for being unduly interfering, wire-pulling, and domineering. Whatever the truth about these accusations in the past, the principal failing of the managers of today's foreign held branch plants and subsidiaries may well be the opposite. Given their position as "guests" in a "host country," their behavior is far too restrained and inhibited. The trouble with the foreign investor may well be not that he is so meddlesome, but that he is so mousy! It is the foreign investor's mousiness which deprives the policy makers of the guidance, pressures, and support they badly need to push through critically required development decisions and policies amid a welter of conflicting and antagonistic interests.

The situation is in fact even worse. Not only does policy making fail to be invigorated by the influence normally emanating from a strong, confident, and assertive group of industrialists; more directly, the presence of a strong foreign element in the dynamically expanding sectors of the economy is likely to have a debilitating and corroding effect on the rationality of official economic policy making for development. For, when newly arising investment opportunities are largely or predominantly seized upon by foreign firms, the national policy makers face in effect a dilemma: more development means at the same time less autonomy. In a situation in which many key points of the economy are occupied by foreigners while economic policy is made by nationals it is only too likely that these nationals will not excel in "rational" policy making for economic development; for, a good portion of the fruits of such rationality would accrue to nonnationals and would strengthen their position.[3] On the other hand, the role and importance of national economic policy making for development increases steadily as the array of available policy instruments widens, and as more group demands are articulated. Hence the scope for "irrationality" actually expands as development gains momentum. That its incidence increases as well could probably be demonstrated by a historical survey of tax, exchange rate, utility rate, and similar policies that were aimed directly or indirectly at "squeezing" or administering pin pricks to the foreigner, but managed, at the same time, to slow down economic growth.

The preceding pages have said next to nothing about the direct cost to the capital importing country of private international investment nor about the related question of the balance-of-payments drain such investment may occasion. While these matters have long been vigorously debated, with the critics charging exploitation and the defenders denying it, the outcome of the discussion seems highly inconclusive. Moreover, undue fascination with the dollars-and-cents aspects of international investment has led to the neglect of the topics here considered, which, I submit, raise issues of at least equal importance and suggest a simple conclusion: strictly from the point of view of development, private foreign investment is a mixed blessing, and the mixture is likely to become more noxious at the intermediate stage of development which characterizes much of present day Latin America.

Hence, if the broadly conceived national interest of the United States is served by the development of Latin America, then this interest enters into conflict with a continuing expansion and even with the maintenance of the present position of private investors from the United States. Purely political arguments lend strong support to this proposition. Internal disputes over the appropriate treatment of the foreign investor have gravely weakened, or helped to topple, some of the more progressive and democratic governments which have held power in recent years in such countries as Brazil, Chile, and Peru. Frictions between private investors from the United States and host governments

3. For some interesting remarks along these lines, see Hans O. Schmitt, "Foreign Capital and Social Conflict in Indonesia," *Economic Development and Cultural Change* 10 (April 1962): 284–93.

have an inevitable repercussion on United States-Latin America relations. In a number of cases such disputes have been responsible for a wholly disproportionate deterioration of bilateral relations. The continued presence and expansion of our private investment position and our insistence on a "favorable investment climate" decisively undermined, from the outset, the credibility of our Alliance for Progress proposals. Land reform and income redistribution through taxation are so obviously incompatible, in the short run, with the maintenance of a favorable investment climate for private capital that insistence on both could only be interpreted to signify that we did not really mean those fine phrases about achieving social justice through land and tax reform.

If these political arguments are added to those pertaining to economics and political economy, one thing becomes clear. A policy of selective liquidation and withdrawal of foreign private investment is in the best mutual interests of Latin America and the United States. Such a policy can be selective with respect to countries and to economic sectors and it ought to be combined with a policy of encouraging new capital outflows, also on a selective basis and with some safeguards.

THE "LOST ART" OF LIQUIDATING AND NATIONALIZING FOREIGN INVESTMENTS

Before the possible elements of such a policy are examined, it is worth noting that liquidation of foreign investment has frequently happened in the history of capital movements. But, as a result of convergent developments, such liquidation has strangely become a lost art. Worse, this art has not been properly recorded by economic historians. In part, this is so because economic historians, like both the advocates of foreign investment and its critics, have been far more interested in the tides of capital flow than in its occasional ebbs. Moreover, the tides have been more regular and easier to detect and measure.

Some of the "mechanisms" which in the past permitted partial liquidation of foreign investment have been the unintended side effects of such large scale, sporadic, and wholly unedifying events as wars and depressions. The two world wars led to a substantial decline in both the absolute and the relative importance of foreign investment in the national economies of Latin America. In the first place, with most Latin American countries joining the Allies, German investments, a not unimportant portion of the total (think of all those prosperous breweries!), were expropriated. Secondly, the British were forced in both world wars to liquidate a good portion of their security holdings, in order to pay for vitally needed food, materials, and munitions. Some of these securities were acquired by the citizens of the countries for which they had originally been issued. Thirdly, Latin American countries acquired large holdings of gold and foreign currencies during the wars, as they continued to export their primary products, but were unable to obtain industrial goods from the belligerents. These accumulated holdings made it possible for them to buy out some foreign investments in the immediate post-war period. The most conspicuous, but by no means the only, instance of this sort of operation was the purchase from their British shareholders of the Argentine railways by the Perón government in 1946. Finally, the wars led to a complete interruption of capital inflow. Since, at the same time, Latin America's industrial growth was strongly stimulated, the relative importance of activities controlled by foreign capital declined substantially.

The depressions which periodically afflicted the centers of capitalist development until the Second World War had similar results. Again, capital inflow would stop for a while during periods in which the Latin American economies frequently received growth impulses because, with foreign exchange receipts low, imports had to be throttled, giving domestic industrial production a fillip. Moreover, when overextended corporations based in the United States and Europe fell on hard times, a sound management reaction was frequently to retrench and consolidate. In the process, foreign branch plants and subsidiaries were sold off to local buyers, a process which has been well documented in the case of American investments in Canada during the depression of the thirties.[4] Sometimes, especially in the case of European firms, these transfers took the form of ownership and control passing into the hands of the parent company's local managers who, while of foreign origin, would eventually become integrated into the local economy. Finally, of course, there were cases of outright bankruptcy and forced liquidation.

The quantitative importance of these various factors remains

4. See H. Marshall, F. A. Southard Jr., and V. W. Taylor, *Canadian-American Industry* (New Haven: Yale University Press, 1936), pp. 252–62.

to be established. But, in the aggregate, they must have had a substantial limiting effect on the foreign investment position in Latin America during the first half of the twentieth century.

Actually, a less cruel mechanism permitting the nationalization of foreign investment was also at work before the "good old days" of portfolio investment had been eclipsed by direct investment. While those days were of course by no means wholly good, portfolio investment, which took primarily the form of fixed interest bond issues, did have several advantages for the capital importing country. Among these, the lower cost and the existence of a termination date have been mentioned most frequently. There is, however, one further property of portfolio investment which is of particular interest in the context of the present essay. This is the fact that nationalization of portfolio investment could take place at the option of the borrowing country and its citizens, who were free to purchase in the international capital markets securities that were originally issued and underwritten in London or Paris. I have collected (and hope eventually to publish) considerable evidence that these "repurchases" of securities by nationals of the borrowing countries took place on a large scale in such countries as the United States, Italy, Spain, Sweden, and Japan in the late nineteenth and early twentieth centuries. They also occurred in much poorer countries, such as Brazil, and were in general so widespread that the phenomenon is referred to in one source as "the well-known *Heimweh* [homesickness] of oversea issued securities." [5] As a result of this *Heimweh*, then, an increasing portion of maturing bond issues often came to be owned by the nationals of the borrowing country, so that payment at maturity did not occasion any balance-of-payments problem.

5. J. F. Normano, *Brazil: A Study of Economic Types* (Chapel Hill: University of North Carolina Press, 1935), p. 157. Note also the following concluding passage of a standard treatise on pre-World War I capital flows: "One and all looked forward to the time when foreign capital with the restraints it imposed would no longer be needed. Each country wanted to buy back its public securities, to redeem its railways from foreign ownership, to withdraw from foreign lenders all share in the making of national policy. Some countries advanced toward this goal, the United States, the British Dominions, Japan, and Italy, for example; some slid further and further away from it, as did China and Turkey. In short, borrowers wanted to nationalize the capital which was active in their domains, to assure themselves that this capital was subordinate to the national powers. It became clear that debts are not the kind of bond which can unite the world," Herbert Feis, *Europe: The World's Banker, 1870–1914* [New Haven: Yale University Press, 1930], pp. 466–67).

World Economic Adjustment

HARALD B. MALMGREN

Harald B. Malmgren is Deputy Special Representative for Trade Negotiations in the special White House Trade Office. As Assistant Special Representative in the same Office between 1964 and 1969, Mr. Malmgren participated actively in the Kennedy Round of trade negotiations. From 1969 to 1971, Mr. Malmgren was a Senior Fellow of the Overseas Development Council in Washington, D.C.

THE NEED TO EXPORT often appears long before a country can become competitive by world market standards. In the face of balance-of-payments difficulties, a heavy debt service problem, an abnormal exchange rate, the need to import capital equipment for basic development of home industry, and weak demand for the basic commodities they export, some countries find that in the absence of much greater aid something quite drastic must be done about diversifying and promoting exports. Even after a country starts to grow reasonably rapidly, there are significant trade requirements. Since import requirements rise as income grows, and sometimes rise even faster than the rate of income growth, export earnings must race ahead if a slowdown in growth is to be avoided. However, the poor countries rely heavily on exports of foodstuffs or basic commodities, which are relatively less sensitive to income changes in the developed countries, and they rely on exports of consumer staples like clothing when they export manufactures at all. Thus, high income growth in rich countries does not draw in imports from poor countries nearly as strongly as it stimulates trade among the rich themselves.

TECHNOLOGY AND INTERNATIONALIZATION
OF PRODUCTION

In pursuing industrialization and increased exportation, developing countries have often tended to follow the same technologies, the same ways of producing and distributing the product, the same reliance on heavy capital investment, as the developed countries. This emulation sometimes is the result of importing engineers from advanced countries whose knowledge is limited to the technology to which they are accustomed. At other times, the emulation is simply based on the assumption that if something works for Germany, it must also work for them. While this emulation may at first appear to be a sensible pattern of economic diversification and industrialization, it is in fact often wasteful. It may waste job opportunities, when labor is highly unemployed. It wastes capital, which is extremely scarce. Admittedly, emulation may be the only way in which some developing countries can acquire the technological capability to produce any manufactures at all, or to raise farm productivity. But wholesale emulation often pits the developing country producer against a more efficient counterpart in a developed country in world markets. Using the same techniques to produce the same product, the developing countries often find their own quality standards and labor productivity very low and thus find themselves to be uncompetitive.

Sometimes they can attain a competitive advantage in labor intensive manufactures. Earlier, we looked at the example of textiles, noting that some types of production, such as yarn spinning, were capital intensive, while other areas of production, such as apparel manufacture, were labor intensive. It was also pointed out that some types of production now carried on in one factory, such as television manufacture, could just as well be broken up into production of different components in different places, with assembly at one geographical point at the final stage only. More generally, the developing countries which are able to take on production of components of any type of product can capitalize on their relatively cheap and abundant labor. They can, in this way, practice emulation of individual processes, without duplicating the entire production and marketing approach utilized by the giant, highly integrated manufactures in developed countries.

This internationalization of production, which is taking place here and there for some products, is essentially a new pattern. It can take many forms. Swiss watchmakers, for example, send jewels to Mauritius for a precision drilling operation, to be returned to Switzerland for incorporation in watches. Rollei of

Germany announced in late 1970 its intention to open certain production facilities in Singapore, breaking decades of tradition in working from its German base exclusively. The process of distributing production operations around the world is perhaps going faster in electronics than in other product areas, insofar as the developing countries are concerned. In chemicals, this movement of components has been the underlying force within the multinational companies in the developed countries, but it is also moving into developing countries. In the case of Japan, with its pressing labor shortages, the process is much more full-blown. Many manufacturers are now actively diversifying their production bases to Taiwan, Korea, Singapore, and elsewhere to tap the vast labor reserve of Eastern Asia.

This is a positive development, because it leads to greater world efficiency in production, and because it offers to poor countries opportunities to break out of some of the constraints on development we have examined. However, this evolution of international production and investment worries certain labor unions, and in the United States it has become a major policy issue for them. Some labor unions are increasingly opposed to any incentives to move labor intensive production facilities from rich countries to developing countries. They seem particularly concerned by those cases in which production in a developing country is carried out under extremely poor labor conditions and extremely low wages. There is aversion to promoting what they call competition from "sweat shops." Beyond this, there is a fear that the movement of components and essential elements of production to other countries results in increased exports to the U.S. of products which would otherwise have been produced in the U.S. Thus job loss is feared. The concern is that there may be loss of new domestic investment expansion, loss of jobs from import displacement, and loss of jobs in export business which would have taken place in the absence of exports from other countries generated by American investment abroad. These questions are very real to the labor movement, and they have political consequences—especially when governments of rich countries are considering possible new policies to assist the trade of developing countries.

It should be added, however, that the fears of some parts of the labor movement are unnecessarily great in regard to this broad set of developments. Experience has so far shown that in the developed countries, employment of opportunities continue to rise as an economy continues to grow, and that the rate of overall economic growth is the dominant factor affecting employment opportunities, with trade playing only a marginal role.

The developing countries, in spite of their apparent advantage in labor costs, are extremely inefficient producers and marketers, and their exchange rates are unrealistic. Sometimes the argument is heard that labor conditions should be the same, or similar, in all countries. The equalization of labor wages and conditions around the world would not lead to greater equity; rather, it would lead to increased repression of the poor countries. Taking exchange rates into account, if manufacturing wages were as high in Calcutta as New York, there would be no exports of manufactures from Calcutta at all, but rather imports from New York. This would happen because of the higher productivity, quality, adaptability of product to changing consumer requirements, and other advantageous factors to be found in many of the developed countries. Moreover, in these high wage circumstances the rate of unemployment in labor surplus countries would soar, as investment was increasingly aimed at saving labor costs, and therefore minimizing the use of labor.

MULTINATIONAL BUSINESS ACTIVITY

The present trend towards internationalization of production, and with it the internationalization of marketing activities, confronts the developing countries with difficult policy options. In some developing countries, private investment from the developed countries is increasingly unwelcome. The fear of domination and exploitation is widespread. Politically, once a government in a developing country blames outside business interests for internal development weaknesses, it is difficult to turn around public sentiment when foreign investment is again desired. Nationalistic economic forces, once aroused, are difficult to turn back in the developing countries, just as they are difficult to reverse in the developed countries.

The experiences with mineral exploitation, such as of copper and oil, seem to underlie the sentiments expressed by many of these governments when they talk of the evils of foreign investment. Mineral exploitation is only one aspect of the rationalization of international production, however. It is also a problem which has solutions. For example, the Japanese utilize long term purchase contracts for minerals as a means of avoiding outright ownership of the production facilities, while at the same time ensuring a steady flow of raw materials for Japanese industrial use. These contracts, with a life of two decades or more, are guaranteed both by the exporting country and by the Japanese government. Under such an arrangement, buyers have a high degree of security with minimum capital investment and minimal problems with whatever local political reaction to foreign owned activities there may be.

This question of ownership, and the degree of local participation in management decisions, is at the heart of the controversy in some countries. With regard to production more generally, alternative methods of local participation can be more actively explored to meet these difficulties. For example, local participation in equity can be provided for as a normal working rule. Perhaps the host government fears outflow of local capital through equity ownership in the mother company, which is probably headquartered in a developed country. Companies can, as one answer to this, set up blocked equity accounts which provide shares in the subsidiaries which are not transferrable to equity in the multinational mother company.

Companies could more frequently scrutinize their production processes to see which activities can be contracted out to independent suppliers, maximizing the local independent entrepreneurial participation in new economic activities. In any factory which is not a continuous-flow system, there are many processes and intermediate products which can be carried out or produced independently. Some people may doubt the efficacy of doing this. Suffice it to say that the early stages of Japanese industrialization were based on extensive use of independent processes carried out in the cottage industries, with standards set and parts being assembled by the organizer-manager. Such conscious efforts to involve local financial participation, and to maximize local entrepreneurial activity, help allay suspicions of the motives of the international companies. Moreover, there should be at least as much willingness to diversify within the developing countries, where there is profitable activity, as there is willingness to do this in the developed country markets. A conglomerate at home should be willing to diversify its activities abroad. Often the government criticism in a poor country is leveled at the unwillingness of international companies to expand their operations into related production areas, or to use earnings from one investment for other types of employment generating activity. The tough laws in some developing countries are a reaction to this unwillingness on the part of the big companies of wealthy countries.

Viewed from the developing country's point of view, there is need for fundamental rethinking of government policies in many of the countries. Clearly, the flow of resources from rich to poor must be stepped up, and one means of doing so is to increase the flow of private investment. Moreover, international business investment usually brings with it technological know-how, an essential on the path to industrialization and diversification. There is much more to it than this, however. The developing countries need the marketing channels and stability of orders which international businesses provide. They need the identification of quality which is implicit in the names of large ventures. They need the current knowledge about the requirements of developed country marketing which only developed country organizations possess. *Quality and marketing are at least of equal importance to the prospects of developing countries as production efficiency.*

Thus, it is not sufficient to reach simplistic conclusions, as some economists do, that the path of the future must inevitably be one of expropriation, or advance agreements to divest after an initial period, or that management control must inevitably move in one direction or another. The issue is far more complex, considered from the viewpoint of promoting the interests of the poor countries. The developing countries will continue to need the international apparatus of at least some of the developed country companies, whether these companies are producers, or simply retailers reaching back into the developing countries for their inventories. The relationships must vary from one country to another, in relation to political sentiment, state of industrialization, rate of growth of the economy, and many other factors.

Simple answers may lead to more, rather than fewer, obstacles to economic progress. In the developing countries, more thought has to be given to the establishment of joint export organizations, marketing cooperatives, and the promotion of vertically integrated production and sales operations, so as to meet the challenges of the world market. This runs exactly counter to the tendency in rich countries to preach against monopolies, cartels, and any reduction in competition. For the poor countries, the competition comes from the world market, and they must build their economic entities up in ways which can compete with the organized world production and distributing system. The poor countries must also review their policies toward outside companies with an eye to developing more imaginative relationships between foreign investors and host governments. Overt indiscriminate hostility to all outsiders, and wholesale expropriation, amounts to throwing the baby out with the bath water. The poor country governments should be more sophisticated about what is in their own interest, and less caught up in generalized political rhetoric on this issue. The temptation of Ministers to blame foreign interests for domestic misfortunes must be resisted, because it is not in the interest of the poor countries themselves to fan this issue into flaming politics.

The international investors, particularly the big multinational companies, must on their side be willing to review the nature of their activities abroad and to be flexible on practices from one country to another. They should be continuously on the lookout for ways to increase local financial and entrepreneurial participation, especially through extensive use of licensing and subcontracting. They should diversify as willingly in Timbuctu as they would in Detroit, and complain less about being forced to take on activities beyond the scope of their initial investments. Many lessons can be learned from the nature of Japanese operations, especially in the area of mineral exploitation, which has been so politically explosive in the past.

This whole set of problems would be easier for both the rich and the poor parties involved if a major international effort were made to draw up international guidelines for the regulation of multinational activities and international investment. A list of do's and don'ts, in terms of broad principles, should be negotiated. Governments could commit themselves to such principles, so that their own laws, regulations, and administrative practices conformed to the multilaterally negotiated standards. Questions to be included would be tax sovereignty, antitrust sovereignty, price regulation, intracompany pricing, financial controls, fairness in rules on local participation, and so on. One way of dealing with all of this is to incorporate multinational companies in some international body, and put them under international supervision. The Pearson Commission Report of 1969 offers such a suggestion. This, however, fails to cope with many other types of international business investment, production, and selling activity. It is also asking a great deal of governments to pass supervision of major economic entities to a group of international civil servants.

The more modest approach of negotiating international guidelines for governments to live by would seem far more practicable. With some broad negotiated principles to refer to, governments in poor countries would be better protected from exploitation, and also better able to resist emotional domestic political pressures to do damage to foreign interests without regard to the real economic interest of the poor country itself. Under such a system, private enterprise in the developed countries would have a reasonable degree of certainty about the ground rules for investment in most developing countries, and thereby plan for longer term, more comprehensive programs of investment. Their willingness to diversify in poor countries in these circumstances would tend to be greater, just as it ought to be greater.

In conclusion, trade prospects of the poor countries in part depend on government policies toward international business. These policies are in need of review in the rich countries as well as in the poor, by companies as well as by governments. It is crucial that the poor countries be given a better deal in this area; but at the same time it should be a deal which leads ultimately to gain, not loss.

CONTINUOUS COMPETITIVE ADJUSTMENT

The United States today finds itself highly competitive in the export of agricultural products like soybeans and grains, in the export of new, innovative products, or in products which require sophisticated marketing. The production or marketing skill component in many American exports is high, and the relative capital intensity is probably a lesser factor for manufactures now than just a few years ago. Knowledge, highly effective management, and sophisticated marketing, together with highly efficient food production, constitute the cutting edge of the American competitive position. These advantages are likely to remain for some time yet, particularly in light of the broad and high level education system in the United States as compared with almost all countries, developed and developing alike. Even where knowledge is transferred internationally, it is usually transferred in a business context, requiring scientific labor input and production standards which cannot easily be duplicated by other countries on a large scale. Nevertheless, the developing countries, with their massive populations, must be encouraged and assisted to follow the paths broken by the United States and the other developed countries, perhaps taking their own methods of locomotion, but following nonetheless into the modern world economy.

Where they have an advantage that can be exploited, that advantage must be allowed to evolve into trade expansion. Since much of their advantage lies in labor intensity, and will perhaps be even more so in the future with the inevitable increase in their labor force, it must be assumed that labor intensive manufacture in the developed countries must be phased out or adjusted over the next two or three decades. Where skill counts heavily, this will be less of a problem. Where skill requirements are modest—as in much of the textile production—the manufacture of some of the basic consumer staples in developed countries inevitably involves trade repression of the poor countries. Rural adjustment and poverty programs in the rich countries which simply aim at employment of low skill workers in low skill production are doomed to failure in the long run. The value of such programs must lie in the training they provide, and in the inevitable upgrading of skills which will eventually allow further movement of the same labor to more complex tasks, or to different roles in the service sector, in a decade or two.

ADJUSTMENT ASSISTANCE

The problem for workers in the developed countries is really one of *adjusting*. They face the need to adjust to changing demands for different types of labor in different areas of the country. It is what historically economists have called the "frictional" problem of adjustment. Today, the frictions can be particularly painful in certain areas and certain skill classes of workers. Such adjustments are not solely or even mainly the consequence of imports, however. They are part of the process of changing labor requirements resulting from economic growth and technological progress in all developed countries. The solutions to frictional problems must in the main come from adequate management of the overall economy in the rich countries, with particular attention to the distribution of both income and demand.

However, specific adjustment assistance programs tailored to the impact of imports are desirable. Such programs can help to head off political pressures to restrict imports, pressures which can only harm the overall growth potential of any nation and add to structural and general inflationary pressures.

Most governments in the developed countries maintain general policies directed at increasing the mobility of labor, in the form of training programs, information services, unemployment compensation, partial payment of movement expenses, and incentives for creation of new employment opportunities. Selective relief from taxes or subsidies are often used to influence the rate of job expansion or contraction of specific industries.

The use of trade adjustment assistance is less widespread. The United States has a specific trade adjustment assistance program to provide relief where imports are found to have caused injury. The legal criteria of eligibility for such relief have proven in practice to be too strict, and until 1969 no relief had been granted, although provision for such relief was introduced into the trade legislation of 1962. The changes proposed by the Johnson and Nixon Administrations would ease the criteria significantly. If these programs were resorted to more frequently, there is a good chance that they would provide the answer to many of the problems of concern to American labor unions.

Other countries, such as Japan, have a long history of assisting industry with regard to research and technical assistance. In the United Kingdom, specific programs of major dimensions were undertaken to rationalize the textile industry. In addition, there are in force provisions to assist diversification of industry into areas of high unemployment in order to bring job opportunities into those areas. Building grants, grants and loans to assist new enterprises, and the erection of new production facilities, are among the measures available to encourage industrial development in the affected areas. Sweden has probably the most successful adjustment programs, but these are inextricably related to overall adjustment of the Swedish economy. There are many other specific examples.

In the United States, one of the major needs is to coordinate the various special assistance programs available for domestic adjustment, and bring them jointly to bear in those cases where trade is creating difficulties. It is patently unsound management to allow completely different programs to operate without some way of focusing their combined energies and powers. The Small Business Administration, the Economic Development Administration (for rural areas), and all the other paraphernalia of government programs for regional, sectoral, urban, and rural development and adjustment ought to be drawn upon when necessary in a comprehensive design for adjustment of labor opportunity whenever the adjustment problems appear severe. Finally, it would be wise to *require* businesses and workers benefiting from temporary measures of import protection to accept adjustment assistance relief and to participate in planned adjustment programs. In fact, it would help the public to assess these programs better if industries benefiting from such assistance be required to file with a government agency annual reports on their adjustment progress.

Much of American business can survive the adjustment problems. A good manager can usually see business trouble coming sufficiently far ahead to slowly phase out the troublesome parts of his business. Government should not be too heavily involved in supporting inefficient managers. It is labor which should be the focus of adjustment policies and programs. If governments in rich countries would pay more attention to labor adjustment needs, the fears of labor over internationalization of production would be sharply diminished. A way out of our present dilemma in domestic and international policy must be found, because in the long run it will not be possible to continue to repress the large majority of the world's population, keeping them in unemployment and poverty in order to benefit a relatively small number of workers in the developed countries. The labor unions themselves have always opposed inequity on that scale, internationally as well as domestically. They have always been opposed to massive unemployment in principle. Since massive global unemployment will be the inevitable result of unwillingness to adjust in the rich countries, labor unions should now, consistent with their own philosophy, join in the search for new means of global economic adjustment, and new policies of assistance to the poor countries.

SOME CONCLUDING COMMENTS

Total United States imports from developing countries amounted to $8.5 billion in 1968. Of this, manufactures represent only about one-eighth. Among these manufactures, about one-third are now in the sensitive manufactures of textiles, shoes, and leather products. The total duties collected on all imports from the poor countries into the United States, including agriculture and industry, are of the order of one-half billion dollars currently. Dropping these tariffs to zero would thus in the short run provide a resource flow of the same order of magnitude.

What does this mean in terms of policy? First of all, tariff preferences will initially have only a small effect. Once textiles and footwear are excepted, as proposed by the U.S. government, the current trade volume which might be covered by tariff preferences is small. If the reduction in duty allows a proportionate rise in sales or price of the exports of poor country manufactures, the increase in earnings for the developing countries as the result of tariff preferences granted by the U.S. would not be more than one-half to one billion dollars in the early years. The figures for Europe and Japan together might optimistically be the same. This is minor compared with present total exports from poor countries of about $45 million, and the total development assistance flow of $12 billion, in 1968.

The value of preferences in the longer run depends upon the extent to which new investment is stimulated in the developing countries to exploit the opportunities provided by tariff preferences. Will such expansion of investment and production activity then run up against import quotas, voluntary restrictions, and other impediments in the rich country markets? That is the real problem, for it is in the sensitive product areas where lies the real potential for growth in exports from the developing countries. And it is in these sensitive products where the obstacles to trade in manufactures are now growing.

Thus preferences can be only a beginning. They provide only partial relief. The rationalization and harmonization of quantitative import restrictions is far more important in trade terms, both measured by present flows and measured by potential trade expansion. Even this cannot be the end. There must be assistance by the rich related specifically to the needs of diversification of the exports of poor countries. At the same time, there must be a general housecleaning in the developing countries themselves in order to allow trade to flow in both directions, so that exports might grow at faster rates. This is especially important for the poor countries in the development of trade with each other.

To bring about the necessary improvement in trade, the developing countries have thus far put most of their energies into the promotion of general tariff preferences. They have, by being politically noisy in international meetings, brought out a sense of conscience among the governments of developed countries. But this pressure has not succeeded in bringing about truly generalized preferences, because Europe has insisted on retaining its special discriminatory arrangements with Mediterranean and African countries. Some of the developing countries will continue to be relatively disadvantaged. Others, like Taiwan and Korea, will likely get the lion's share of benefits of generalized preferences for manufactures, because they are already highly competitive.

Finally, the paramount global problem of broadening the base of participation in the world economy through industrialization, export promotion, and job creation in all countries must be recognized. Trade policies must allow export oriented job creation in the poor countries sufficient to allow a more rapid rate of foreign exchange earnings, which in turn allows more rapid growth of jobs in home economies. The assignment is massive, but it must be carried out. As the Pearson Commission said, trade is the "hard option" politically. But trade is the path to self-sufficiency. It represents nearly 80 percent of the total flow of foreign exchange from rich to poor countries. Rationalization of import policies in the rich countries, with a view to a major local economic readjustment, is an essential step. That step must be taken soon, or the economic plight of the poor countries will develop into political conflict with the developed countries and with each other, fighting over relative shares of world economic growth and world employment. In the end, jobs are also votes, and the jobless are the most likely source of revolution against systems which prevent them from participating in the benefits of the world economy. That is what the trade problem is coming to mean for world politics at the close of this millenium.

PART THREE The Economics of Foreign Assistance

Rationale for Development Assistance

ROBERT E. ASHER

Robert E. Asher is a Senior Fellow in the Foreign Policy Studies Program of the Brookings Institution. He has written many books and articles on foreign economic policy issues. This article was taken from his book Development Assistance in the Seventies: Alternatives for the U.S. *published in 1970 by Brookings.*

THE FUNDAMENTALLY CHANGED domestic and international environment means that virtually all the familiar geopolitical moorings of U.S. foreign policy have become unhitched. What for years seemed axiomatic now seems dubious, if not false. John F. Kennedy may be the last President who could, without creating a credibility gap, maintain that "we in this country . . . are—by destiny rather than choice—the watchmen on the walls of world freedom."[1]

The interventionist policy articulated in the Truman Doctrine in 1947 and widely supported within the United States for two decades thereafter found what appears to be its final fateful expression in Vietnam. At the deepest point of its involvement in the less developed world, the United States began to question most seriously the rationale for any real involvement. The arguments that for twenty years gave the greatest immediacy and urgency to the case for foreign aid—the communist threat, the essentiality of friends and allies, the need for continued access to vital raw materials, the economic benefits obtainable through

1. *Public Papers of the Presidents of the United States, John F. Kennedy . . . 1963*, remarks prepared for delivery at the Trade Mart in Dallas, Nov. 22, 1963 (1964), p. 894.

increased trade, and the political dividends to be reaped in terms of peace and democracy—have lost much of their force.

Communism now seems a less contagious disease than when, according to the domino theory, its presence on one side of a frontier was believed deadly also to the population on the other side of that frontier. Forward military bases have become less valuable to the United States. Military pacts that harness a mouse to an elephant do not add noticeably to the stability, strength, and security of the elephant. Nor is the proximity of the elephant always reassuring to the mouse; the willingness and capacity of outside powers to safeguard the security of their underdeveloped allies and exert a sustained, beneficent influence on their evolution are doubted. The exhaustion of domestic resources that would make the United States heavily dependent on distant sources of supply appears less imminent today, in the age of atomic energy, plastics, synthetic fibers, and other substitutes for internationally traded raw materials, than it did only yesterday. Mounting evidence of hunger, malnutrition, poverty, and widespread discontent within the United States has changed America's image of itself and raised fresh doubts about the propriety of mitigating poverty abroad when so much remains to be done at home.[2]

While some of the earlier arguments have lost force, others have gained adherents, with the result that a program of sorts—battered, barnacle-encrusted, and truncated—remains in being. Let us review then some of the argumentation that has been employed, concentrating primarily on the rationale most applicable to the world of the 1970s and bearing in mind the pluralism of contemporary society and the relevance of value systems in determining priorities.

In a pluralistic society, different people will support or oppose a policy at different times for different reasons or combinations of reasons. While the intensity with which views are held and the positions of the holders in the policy making process are germane, a broad measure of popular support is usually needed to sustain a policy. At the same time, agreement on the details of a rationale is not essential and is probably unobtainable. The legislator may feel obliged to look at foreign aid in traditional

2. I am indebted to my friend and former Brookings colleague, Robert H. Johnson, for much of the three foregoing paragraphs.

what's-in-it-for-us terms. On the other hand, the political, economic, and strategic considerations that seem extremely important to the legislator may be less persuasive than simple humanitarianism to the average citizen. He may favor helping the poor because they are hungry and needy but have considerable difficulty understanding that, in order to serve the national interest, helping them should help us as much as, if not more than, it helps them.

As John Pincus has said:

> The quest for a valid rationale for aid or concessions is ultimately insoluble when we limit our analysis to "objective" considerations, and forgo any resort to questions of values.... Ethical considerations, uncomfortable though they may be in a power-centered world, are underlying elements of North-South economic relations.... They are as real as any other factor in world politics, although more erratic in their influence on events. We cannot and should not rewrite economic analysis as a theory of social justice. But views of justice permeate and shape economic and political systems. Once the analysis is done, stubborn issues of equity remain.[3]

SECURITY AS A RATIONALE

During the 1950s, foreign aid was provided principally under the Mutual Security Act of 1951 as amended, and justified primarily as a national security measure needed to strengthen allies and to build up low income countries so that they would be less vulnerable to communist invasion or takeover. During the 1960s, the long term security argument remained a basic staple of the official rationale, but the definition of security changed with new perceptions of the nature of the East-West conflict, the U.S. role in world affairs, and the ambitions of the less developed countries for sophisticated weaponry, and with the accumulation of experience concerning the behavior of less developed countries. Security arguments will doubtless play a role also in the 1970s but will probably shade off still further from their strictly military connotations toward broadly political reasons.

Initially, economic aid was often the down payment on a military alliance with a less developed country. America wanted

---

3. John Pincus, *Trade, Aid and Development: The Rich and Poor Nations* (McGraw-Hill, 1967), pp. 13–14.

allies. The less developed country presumably wanted the protection and assistance of the United States, though not necessarily for the same reasons that the United States wanted it as an ally. Through its network of alliances, the United States did secure foreign bases in far off lands, which could be used as points of concentration for U.S. military forces and for intelligence gathering. It also secured some additional combat troops of other nationalities to fight in Korea and Vietnam.

The case for military bases in less developed countries, whatever strength it may once have had, is clearly less convincing in an age of intercontinental ballistic missiles, Polaris submarines, and spy satellites than it was before their invention. Although the United States may still want and need allies, its own military security can no longer be said to depend heavily on formal alliances with preindustrial societies.

A corollary security argument in the 1950s was the falling dominoes analogy. The Soviet threat was viewed by the United States as worldwide in scope but greatest to nations on the periphery of the Soviet empire and mainland China. Each weak country in the region, it was argued, must be aided economically and militarily, "because the fall of that country would make it easier for Communism to triumph somewhere else, and each country would be more costly for the West to defend." [4]

Others questioned whether, from the point of view of the military security of the West itself, the front line needed to be drawn at such a distant point and any breach thereof considered militarily so significant. "If the communizing of a half-dozen countries is of little importance to Western military defenses, then the military security arguments for opposing the fall of dominoes are unlikely to be impressive. On the other hand, the political arguments for bracing the dominoes may be persuasive and ultimately dominant." [5]

The potency of nationalism in less developed countries, the persistence of their quest for an independent niche in the world, and other well-known factors combined to discredit the falling dominoes argument. Although the dominoes are less of a pushover than was anticipated, it is not equally clear that there is no com-

---

4. Pincus, *Trade, Aid and Development,* p. 9.
5. *Ibid.*

munist threat or that the Soviet Union and mainland China have no interest in picking up bits of real estate at bargain prices.

Another series of security arguments (or political arguments) is based on the risk to the United States of being an island of prosperity in a tidal wave of misery. For a while, as Arnold Toynbee has said, the chief penalty may be the moral isolation that this type of prosperity brings. But engulfment is also a risk. In an age of instant communication, substantial disparities in income and status can be politically tolerable so long as those at the lower end of the spectrum have before them a reasonable prospect of improvement. If they can expect some alleviation of their own lot and more dramatic improvement in the next generation —so that their children will be better fed, better housed, better clad, and better educated than they—they may not become unduly excited about the level of living in the United States. But (according to one line of argument) if the hopes and dreams of people in poor countries appear doomed to frustration while people in rich countries grow steadily richer, the prospects for peace will be threatened.

If the dividing line between rich and poor countries is also a color line separating the white skinned minority from those of other hues, the threat will be increased. If it explodes, the poor will enter the fray with inferior equipment, more primitive technology, and fewer resources, but with little to lose except their lives. They may not win, but they might succeed in pulling the house down around their ears.

Since neither the more developed nor the less developed world is monolithic, Armageddon, in the opinion of most prophets, is unlikely to arrive in quite this way. Less developed countries, with different resource endowments, different leadership, and different aspirations, will not simultaneously reach the boiling point. When in a given area the peace is shattered, the violence is as likely to be directed against domestic leadership or neighboring countries as it is against the United States.

Not even the largest of the less developed countries now has the resources to threaten directly the security of the United States. Several of them, however, have the capacity to acquire significant nuclear capabilities before long. Some authorities, therefore, argue that the security interests of the United States require not only an effective nonproliferation treaty but also positive programs to prevent nations that might acquire nuclear capabilities from feeling beleaguered or alienated. Development assistance, sensitively administered, can serve this purpose.[6]

Well before nuclear weapons in the arsenals of less developed countries became a practical possibility, and before the term "alienation" was widely enough understood to be employed in general literature, a parallel argument for development assistance as a peaceproducing measure was advanced. Rather small scale local conflicts in the less developed world, it was said, could draw additional parties into the conflict. The struggle would escalate and might lead to general conflagration. Efforts to build national consensus around constructive programs for economic and social development were recommended as an important long run protection, though not a guarantee, against violence born of frustration with the slow pace of development, violence containing within it the seeds of a major war.[7]

Awareness of the risks of escalation, however, serves as a restraining influence at least on the major powers, particularly since they have also learned that not every square mile of underdeveloped territory that shifts its international allegiance is a damaging loss to the side from which it shifts. This decreases the possibility that local conflicts will trigger a global holocaust. The decreased possibility, in turn, weakens the case for development assistance on military security grounds and encourages a more critical look at the nature of the links between poverty and war, or absence of poverty and presence of peace.

Harking back to de Tocqueville's study of the French Revolution, Theodore Geiger reminds his readers that

> the likelihood of violent social upheavals is greatest not when exploitation and repression are greatest but when, following such a period, the condition of the subordinate groups begins to improve. The gains already achieved heighten the sense of frustration and impatience at the slowness and difficulty of further progress. At the same time, the reforms already conceded, voluntarily or perforce, by the ruling élite weaken its privileged position, political power, and self-confidence.[8]

He goes on to suggest that the circumstances in which a country will engage in aggression depend

6. Millikan, "The United States and Low-Income Countries," pp. 513–14.
7. Max F. Millikan, "Why Not Foreign Aid?" *Sun-Times* (Chicago), Dec. 23, 1964.
8. "Why Have a US Foreign Aid Effort?" p. 3.

not simply upon the extent of its economic progress but more importantly on the character of its institutions and values, particularly the motivations of its leadership groups, upon its internal problems and pressures, and upon the relationships and opportunities in the world political situation.

For these reasons, although a correlation does exist between economic growth and peaceful and constructive international behavior, it is low, tenuous and very long term. . . . Influence designed directly to affect the character of institutions and values is, by its nature, potentially much more important than [influence designed only to step up the rate of economic growth]. . . . For, what is decisive for the outcome of sociocultural change in Asia, Africa, and Latin America is not economic growth *per se* but the kinds of institutions, values, attitudes, and behavioral norms that evolve in those regions.[9]

Thus the case for development promotion, to the extent that it rests on security grounds, should take into consideration the capacity of the United States and other sources of aid to influence the character of institutions and values as well as their capacity to raise gross national product in low income areas. It need no longer be based heavily on the fear of imminent communist takeover in particular low income areas, the necessity of maintaining foreign bases, or the assumption that the outcome of a particular local dispute is in itself of transcendent importance to the United States. This change should make it easier to reconcile security considerations, which during the 1950s seemed overriding, with longer term economic, social, and political objectives.[10] Autocratic regimes, uninterested in a decent sharing of fruits of productivity increases, a functioning system of justice, and a voice for the voiceless in domestic decision making, need not be aided simply because they might otherwise leave the "free world" and fall forever into the hands of a monolithic enemy.

The security rationale for development assistance today would vary from country to country and, in an overall sense, would rest on the belief, the hope, and the faith that (1) the frustrations of poverty and the bitterness against the rich that such frustrations engender will ultimately be decreased rather than exacerbated by programs to reduce the poverty and the sense of injustice; (2) better living conditions—a growing stake

9. *Ibid.* See also Theodore Geiger, *The Conflicted Relationship* (McGraw-Hill, 1967), pp. 225–26.
10. Millikan, "The United States and Low-Income Countries," p. 515.

in the world as it is—together with new attitudes and institutions, will gradually decrease racial tensions and provide a less fertile breeding ground for demagogues; (3) poor countries will at least in some instances be diverted from the foreign adventures, irredentist pursuits, and international posturing that the absence of domestic achievements might stimulate; and (4) development, though it increases the overall capacities of low income countries, including their capacity to intervene elsewhere, improves their power to protect themselves against assault from abroad and subversion at home, and should also enhance their long term interest in machinery for the peaceful adjudication of international disputes.

ECONOMIC RATIONALE

The economic rationale for a U.S. commitment to the development of poor countries has been widely publicized. Basically, it is that development is good business. It widens the market for American exports. It provides new opportunities for productive private investments. It builds more promising, lower cost sources of supply for imports.

Poor countries make poor markets. Better markets will help the United States in two ways: directly, by buying more of its exports, and indirectly, by buying more in third countries which, in turn, may be able to take more American products. Insofar as imports are concerned, the United States can use a wide variety from many sources and would prefer the sources to be reasonably secure and stable. Poor countries tend to be unreliable sources for a very limited range of imports—typically one or two primary products that undergo sizable year-to-year fluctuations in price.

Numerous studies have been made to demonstrate that rich countries make better customers and better markets than poor ones. Unfortunately, one moral which can be drawn from this is that a given investment in expanding trade with countries that are already rich may pay off more rapidly and readily than the same sum invested in expanding trade with a country that is poor—and the investment in the first instance is more likely to be made voluntarily by nongovernmental sources.

Japan was not a rich country in 1950 and its foreign trade amounted to only $2 billion. By 1960, it was approaching $10 billion. By 1957, thanks to the spectacular growth of the Japanese economy (helped by $1.7 billion in American economic aid between 1945 and 1963), the level of Japanese foreign trade exceeded $20 billion, and Japan had become the largest overseas trading partner of the United States as well as the world's largest market for U.S. farm products.

In Taiwan, exports averaged about $110 million a year from 1951 to 1956, while annual imports were double this amount. The excess of imports over exports averaged $107 million a year, of which approximately 90 percent was covered by U.S. aid and less than 10 percent offset by private investment. After 1956, Taiwan's exports spurted.[11] By 1965, they exceeded $500 million, and by 1967, $750 million. Taiwan's principal trading partner was Japan, and the United States ranked second.

The story in Korea is similar: only $79 million earned from exports of goods and services as recently as 1957 and $117 million in 1960, but $290 million in 1965 and $643 million in 1967.

The argument that increased international trade will be both a corollary and a consequence of economic development is almost unassailable. It will be noted, however, that although the rise in exports of Taiwan and Korea (and consequently of their capacity to import) is dramatic and over a long enough time period will substantially exceed the amount of aid received, this is not yet the case.

In a broad sense, increased international trade serves the national interests of the trading nations. Most nations unquestionably want to step up their earnings from exports and, though more ambivalent about imports, will benefit from increased imports of things they do not or cannot produce at home as cheaply as they can buy in world markets. The huge U.S. market is far more important to the less developed countries, however, than their national markets, individually, are to the United States.

If a higher level of trade with the less developed countries serves the American national interest, it is not because of its income effects in the United States, but primarily because various political and social crises to which the United States cannot remain indifferent may be somewhat more easily resolved in the context of a broadly shared expansion of the world economy.

11. Neil H. Jacoby, *U.S. Aid to Taiwan: A Study of Foreign Aid, Self-Help, and Development* (Praeger, 1966), pp. 97–99 and 292.

Furthermore, the additional business and jobs resulting from a higher level of U.S. exports may be extremely important to particular groups of exporters, workers, and farmers. (On the other hand, increased imports by the United States, however much they may be appreciated by American consumers, will threaten or appear to threaten the jobs or sources of income of some domestic interests and will therefore not be universally welcomed.)

Finally, a higher level of production and trade in the low income world can enhance its interest in workable ground rules for the conduct of international trade and international financial transactions. Countries with weak, undiversified, inefficient economies make feeble, quixotic partners in the network of international institutions upon which, in this interdependent world, all nations, including the United States, rely increasingly.

With economic growth, less developed countries ought to become more responsible partners. The need to reconcile diverse domestic interests will make it harder for them to take extreme positions in international negotiations and they will have more to lose by disruptive tactics that jeopardize the flow of trade and investment.

According to Seymour Martin Lipset and others, more of the conditions favorable to democracy come into being as income increases and is more widely shared. A growing middle class "tempers conflict by rewarding moderate and democratic parties and penalizing extremist groups." An immense variety of organizations that serve as countervailing sources of power is spawned: labor unions, farm groups, chambers of commerce, trade associations, cooperatives, and professional societies.[12]

Samuel Huntington agrees that a large middle class, like widespread affluence, is a moderating force in politics, but believes that the creation of a middle class is often a highly destabilizing event.

Typically, the first middle class elements to appear on the social scene are intellectuals with traditional roots but modern values. They are then followed by the gradual proliferation of civil servants and army officers, teachers and lawyers, engineers and technicians, enterpreneurs and

---

12. Seymour Martin Lipset, *Political Man: The Social Bases of Politics* (Doubleday, 1960), pp. 66–67. See also Gabriel A. Almond and James S. Coleman (eds.), *The Politics of Developing Areas* (Princeton University Press, 1960), especially Coleman's concluding chapter.

managers. The first elements of the middle class to appear are the most revolutionary; as the middle class becomes larger, it becomes more conservative.[13]

Thus there is no guarantee that economic improvement in the low income countries will be accompanied by desirable social and political changes or, within a predictable time span, by economic benefits to the high income countries commensurate with the cost of development assistance. Furthermore, it is by no means certain that self-sustaining, self-governing, increasingly prosperous peoples will be prepared to live harmoniously with themselves, their neighbors, or the United States. It does seem more likely than that frustrated, insecure, starving populations will do so.

POLITICAL RATIONALE

The idea that development assistance should have an early and obvious political payoff in winning friends for the United States is discredited but not dead.[14] More frequently put forward in recent years as the political justification for stimulating growth in the low income world is the long range "world order" argument: the improved international climate that should prevail in an expanding world economy and the stronger institutional underpinning that growth can provide for the peaceful conduct of world affairs. In this view, development assistance becomes a tool—one of several—for fashioning an international environment less likely to be divisive, polarized, and in other ways uncongenial to the United States. An environment in which the United States can calmly cultivate its own garden without having to worry about soil conditions, horticultural practices, or crop yields elsewhere has obvious attractions but must be dismissed as a nostalgic dream. The world is too much with us.

Despite the power and persistence of nationalism, consciousness of the interdependence of nations and peoples is growing. Nevertheless, the institutional base for a better world order remains grossly inadequate.

13. Samuel P. Huntington, *Political Order in Changing Societies* (Yale University Press, 1968), p. 289.
14. See, for example, Bullock, *Staff Memorandum on What to Do About Foreign Aid,* or almost any year's Senate or House hearings on foreign aid legislation.

If we can give substance to the fundamental idea that we are joined [with the new countries] in a constitutional endeavor to create a world order in which all peoples can find their separate identities, it should be possible for us to achieve that degree of integrity in our relations which will make it possible to avoid hypocrisy and to disagree at times without malice. Acculturation need no longer appear as a process in which some people take on the ways of others, but instead as one in which everyone is seeking to change and develop in order to build a better world community.[15]

Why give substance to this idea? "It is one thing to be in good physical or financial condition within an orderly and prosperous community, but quite another thing to be privileged by the wealth of one's possessions in surroundings of misery, ill-health, lack of public order, and widespread resentment." [16]

Counterarguments take two forms.

1. World community is a utopian goal, beautiful in the mind's eyes, but as yet invisible even with a fairly powerful telescope. The role of development assistance in achieving it is tenuous at best. So long as we live in a world of sovereign states, the duty of the United States is to act in its own national interest, not in the interest of a nonexistent international community.

2. The world order argument is usually linked with the idea of peaceful change, but what is needed in most less developed lands is revolutionary change. Revolutions are inherently disorderly affairs.

For the harsh facts we have yet to acknowledge are these: (1) in many countries of the underdeveloped world only revolutionary activity will rescue the populace from its unending misery, and (2) the United States has consistently opposed the kinds of revolutionary action that might begin such a rescue operation. . . . What we call "economic development" is in truth little more than a holding action that has succeeded only in building up the dikes just enough to keep the mounting population from washing away everything, not a movement that has invested life with a new quality.[17]

15. Lucian W. Pye, "The Foreign Instrument: Search for Reality," in Roger Hilman and Robert C. Good (eds.), *Foreign Policy in the Sixties* (Johns Hopkins Press, 1965), p. 112.
16. Arnold Wolfers, *Discord and Collaboration: Essays on International Politics* (Johns Hopkins Press, 1961), p. 75.
17. Robert L. Heilbroner, "Making a Rational Foreign Policy Now," *Harper's Magazine* (September 1968), and *Congressional Record* (Sept. 18, 1968), pp. E8057–8060.

The counterarguments in turn engender retorts such as: The case for the violent overthrow of authority was also good when Marx and Engels made it in 1848. It was defused in most of what is now the developed world by a series of reforms, individually modest and often almost imperceptible, but cumulatively successful in transforming the lives of virtually the whole of society. Development assistance can expedite a similar evolutionary process in the less developed countries. A policy of investment in a more peaceful, better integrated world order as a long range goal, moreover, is not fundamentally inconsistent with revolutions *en route* to that goal in countries unable to reach nonviolent accommodations with the forces of history.

A more immediate political rationale for development assistance than its effectiveness in promoting a new world order is simply the high priority given to development by most of the less developed world. Development is said to be the wave of the future and riding it is smarter than resisting it, letting it wash by, or commanding it to stand still. Despite formidable barriers to modernization, perceptible headway—enough to prevent aspirations from getting too far ahead of achievements—is supremely important to almost every one of the less developed countries.

Not only the United States but every other major power and many minor ones too now provide economic aid to low income countries. Were it not for the prominent part the United States played in getting other high income Western nations into—or deeper into—the development business, the continuation of these nations' programs would create a presumption that an American effort would serve the interests of the United States. As things stand, however, it may not quite be cricket first to have been instrumental in getting others into the development business and then to claim that, because they are there, the United States must also be there. Yet so long as other rich countries remain contributors to overseas development, they strengthen the belief that high income countries have a political and moral obligation to help low income countries.

HUMANITARIAN CONSIDERATIONS

Closely related to the question of the type of world order the United States should seek among the divergent trends of recent years is the humanitarian argument for development assistance. Sometimes dismissed as soft headed and irrelevant; it remains durable and potent. It involves justice and decency and the moral basis for leadership among nations.

> The kind of inequality that exists between nations, the kind of grinding poverty that permeates so much of the world, are no longer tolerated within the borders of a modern, progressive nation-state. These torments are mitigated within a country like the United States, Great Britain, or Sweden by continuous transfers of wealth from the richer to the poorer citizens and from the richer areas to the poorer ones. Foreign aid is an extension of this process in a world that has become too small for fellow feeling between man and man to stop at political frontiers.[18]

> The rationale for attacking poverty is much the same at home and abroad, though better recognized domestically. The simple moral argument that the rich have an obligation to help the poor . . . is perhaps more compelling than it is fashionable to admit. And the connection between poverty and insecurity for the rich has been made frequently. While the urgency of attacking domestic poverty is easier for Americans to see—after all, *our* cities are burning—the argument on the international plane is still obvious enough. Basically, we must simply recognize that we are in the business of building a community, a sense of shared purpose and shared destiny, both at home and abroad. The central values of our civilization permit no less.[19]

In a similar vein, Barbara Ward has argued that "a sustained long term economic strategy on the part of the West would have more than economic consequences. It would begin to institutionalize human solidarity and human compassion and underpin a world order with some claim to be called humane."[20]

Participation in international development programs is believed by many to be a necessary way of strengthening the moral claim of the United States to a position of world leadership, counteracting the isolation that tends to be the social and moral price of tremendous wealth, and helping the United States to

---

18. "The Vienna Declaration on Cooperation for Development" (Vienna, Theodor Körner Foundation, July 1962; mimeographed), para. 2.
19. Blair, "The Dimension of Poverty," p. 683.
20. "A Strategy for the Wealthy West," *SAIS Review* (Summer 1965), p. 9.

live at peace with itself as well as with others. Given its traditions and ideals, the United States will find it hard to retain for itself the full fruits of its annual increases in output while the majority of mankind lives at the margin of subsistence.

The counterarguments are, in effect, that humanitarianism, admirable though it may be as a personal trait, has no permanent place in international relations, that compassion dwindles with distance, and that the less developed countries represent a bottomless pit into which the full resources of the United States could be poured with little visible effect other than the impoverishment of the United States. Roy Bullock says bluntly: "We should no longer endorse the position . . . that the developed countries have an obligation to share their resources with less fortunate nations." [21]

In its more elementary forms, the humanitarian appeal is simply a plea for the relief of suffering. A rationale based on the destitution of the recipients implies that aid is needed for consumption rather than investment. Only when it is conceded that relief is a palliative rather than a cure will the humanitarian appeal be transformed into an argument for the investments in agriculture, industry, and education that can help the receiving country overcome its poverty and move toward self-sustaining growth.

At this point, that fuzzy term "the national interest" comes sharply into focus. So long as the problem is the sheer saving of the present generation of humanity, whether resident in Mexico or Albania, the national interest can be equated with a larger "international interest" that rises above geography, politics, or ideology. But with economic growth comes the economic, military, and political power that cannot be ignored in a rational assessment of either the national interest or the international interest. Economic growth in Mexico is certainly of higher priority to the United States in the short run, and probably in the long run, than economic growth in Albania or any other nation seemingly dedicated to the destruction of the United States or of the values it cherishes.

Humanitarians, however, recognize the resource limitation which makes it useless to spread assistance too thinly, and recog-

21. *Staff Memorandum on What to Do About Foreign Aid*, p. 7.

nize also the obvious fact that no one feels equally well disposed toward the whole human race. Compassion moves in concentric circles. Empathy, the sense of community, and the compulsion to act are greatest for family and local community, strong for those living under the same flag, palpable for the inhabitants of nations that are not hostile, and feeble or nonexistent where hostile peoples are concerned. Such shadings in feeling are not inconsistent with a knowledge that the world is shrinking and that distinctions based on distance may blur with the passage of time.

Compassion, idealism, humanitarianism are more than personal traits. The collectivity of persons that constitutes a nation projects a national image which, as noted earlier in this chapter, is as "real" as any other factor in world politics. Though ideals are adopted for their own sake and not for their instrumental value, they can affect the distribution of world power. Throughout its history, the prestige and influence of the United States have depended on what the country stood for as well as on the strength of its economy and its military establishment. Its support for self-determination, for social justice, for political democracy, and for religious freedom has placed it in the mainstream of history and made it the lodestar of masses in the most faraway places.[22]

The national interest of the United States in a compatible and congenial world environment and its moral, humanitarian interest in the quality of life for the average man everywhere are said to come together in the growing American concern for the social and civic dimensions of the development process. The full potentials of human beings stand a better chance of realization in open societies in which all members have a voice in decision making and opportunity to advance without discrimination on account of caste, color, race, or creed. "Most Americans share with many people abroad a faith that in the long run this multi-

22. Power and prestige are far from synonymous. Prestige refers primarily to the attainment of a commanding position in men's minds and is a moral and intellectual achievement. Power implies some coercive authority and therefore depends more directly on armies, resources, technology, and the will to use them. As the exercise of power becomes more difficult and self-defeating, the maintenance of prestige and influence becomes more important. As Theodore Draper asked in *Encounter* in August 1968, "What is missing in the United States today? Is it power or influence?"

dimensional human development will greatly increase the prospects for a world environment of more open, more cooperative, and more liberated societies." [23]

THE WHOLE VERSUS THE PARTS

If on the home front one had to justify annually the whole concept of public investment in education, in agriculture, in social security, and in national defense, one would, I suspect, encounter grave difficulty in setting forth a fully convincing rationale. In matters of social policy, there appear to be no laws of physics; almost nothing is provable beyond doubt. Aid for less developed countries, examined *de novo* each year by the U.S. Congress, is a case in point.

Because so many of the propositions are not verifiable except over a long period of time, agreement or disagreement with the various rationales is in part a matter of personal preference and individual value judgments. One of my friends has accordingly suggested that I conclude this chapter by saying quite simply that I favor aid basically because it pleases me to see poor people making economic gains in countries that I do not fear. It does please me, but I would like to suggest a further conclusion or two.

Only a lunatic would contend that propositions which are not provably true are probably false and should be abandoned. There are sizable kernels of truth in the security argument for development assistance—that widespread poverty and frustration represent a threat to the peace; in the economic argument—that development produces jobs, markets, trade, investment opportunities, and material benefits for virtually all concerned; in the political argument—that a broadly shared expansion of the world economy will contribute to a better integrated political community with a greater stake in the peaceful resolution of conflict; and, above all, in the humanitarian argument—that aid is right and decent and that responsibility for the mitigation of poverty does not end at national boundaries.

Collectively, if not singly, these arguments may provide a more solid foundation for policy than the fact that it pleases me (and presumably others, too) to see poor people make economic gains.

23. Millikan, "The United States and Low-Income Countries," p. 519.

The moral imperative is, I think, clearer than the U.S. national interest calculated in traditional, short range terms. Fear, I suspect, has been overworked as a rationale.

While I much prefer the more positive approach, I am not repelled by the insurance salesman's argument that, though your house may never burn down, it is wise to take out fire insurance. The case for development assistance can be made analogously despite the impossibility of proving conclusively that outside aid is a *sine qua non* of development and that such development as may ensue will be worth the annual investment of 1 percent or some other fraction of the gross national product of the high income countries. In other words, the risks involved in forcing the less developed countries to remain mired in poverty or to rise entirely by their bootstraps are real and difficult to reconcile with the sense of international community and decency the United States should (and I believe does) seek to foster. At the same time, the costs of providing assistance in the volume that can be used effectively are demonstrably bearable.

Aid, to be sure, is not the only way to prove the reality of America's long term interest in the economic, social, and civic growth of the low income world. It is an appropriate technique if (1) the resources that can be transferred through foreign aid are needed and can be put to effective use; (2) they can be supplied without denying other higher priority claims on those same resources; (3) other techniques—for example, trade (with or without special concessions for low income countries), private investment, cultural exchanges, or modifications of immigration and emigration policies—will not suffice or have been rejected; and (4) the aid technique does more than ease the consciences of the rich and make them feel more virtuous. It should stimulate the adoption of sensible policies in the aid receiving nations and raise the level of available resources to a point more likely to provide a politically tolerable rate of development than would be provided in the absence of aid.

I believe these conditions are fulfilled often enough to justify the mounting of a sizable international development effort. Even the most convincing presentation of the general case for development assistance nevertheless begs the questions: How much? To whom? For how long? Suffice it to say here that the program should be big enough to have some noticeable impact on the problem with which it purports to deal and suffice it to reiterate that nothing here is intended to imply that all poor countries are equally deserving or that their development will inevitably have beneficial and stabilizing effects at home or abroad. Development can provide the context in which a number of difficult problems become less difficult: the growing pie permits larger slices for everyone. But development is not a universal solvent for the ills of the world; some problems will almost certainly become more acute if and when power is more evenly distributed. Moreover, revolutions, counterrevolutions, hostility to erstwhile friends, folly in economic policy, inhumanity in social policy, and irrational acts as yet undreamed of will occur.

Yet I associate myself with Ronald Steel's conclusion:

The object of foreign aid is . . . to help alleviate human misery by aiding those who show a capacity to aid themselves, and by doing so to help create an international order where compassion will be joined to self-interest and where the poor may seek to join the rich rather than exterminate them. For those of us privileged to live in societies affluent beyond the imagination of most of mankind, foreign aid is not simply charity, but . . . as Oliver Wendell Holmes once said of taxes, our investment in civilization.[24]

24. *Pax Americana*, p. 270.

Foreign Economic Aid: Means and Objectives
MILTON FRIEDMAN

Milton Friedman is Professor of Economics at the University of Chicago and is widely recognized as the leader of the "Chicago School" of economics. He has written extensively, especially in the monetary field. This article first appeared in the Summer,1958, issue of the Yale Review.

FOREIGN ECONOMIC AID is widely regarded as a weapon in the ideological war in which the United States is now involved. Its assigned role is to help win over to our side those uncommitted nations that are also underdeveloped and poor. According to this view, these nations are determined to develop economically. They will seek to do so, with or without our help. If we do not help them, they will turn to Russia. It is, therefore, in our own interest to help them to achieve their aims. And the way to help them is to make capital and technical assistance available largely free of charge, the cost to be borne by the United States and, we hope, those of its allies who are in a comparable stage of development.

This argument confuses two very different issues. One is the *objectives* toward which United States policy should be directed. The other is the *means* that are appropriate for the achievement of those objectives. I share fully the views of the proponents of foreign economic aid about objectives. It is clearly in our national interest that the underdeveloped nations choose the democratic rather than the totalitarian way of life. It is clearly in our national interest that they satisfy their aspirations for economic development as fully as possible in a democratic framework. And our national interest coincides with our humanitarian ideals: our fundamental objective is a world in which free men can peaceably use their capacities, abilities, and resources as effectively as possible to satisfy their aspirations. We cannot long hope to maintain a free island in a totalitarian world.

But this agreement about objectives does not settle the question of means. Is foreign economic aid as it has been administered, or as it is proposed that it should be administered, well adapted to secure these great objectives? This question is begged in most current discussion. Once the objectives are stated, it is generally simply taken for granted that foreign economic aid is an appropriate means, if not indeed the only appropriate means, to achieve these objectives. This conclusion seems to me fundamentally mistaken. Though foreign economic aid may win us some temporary allies, in the long run it will almost surely retard economic development and promote the triumph of Communism. It is playing into our enemies' hands, and should be abolished. Instead we should concentrate on promoting world-wide economic development through means that are consonant with the American tradition itself—strengthening of free market domestic economies in the less-developed nations, the removal of obstacles to private international trade, and the fostering of a climate favorable to private international investment.

To avoid confusion, it will be well to emphasize at the outset that this article is concerned solely with one particular category of United States expenditures on foreign aid—*economic aid*—and with one class of arguments for such expenditures—their value in promoting the economic development of other countries.

The case for military aid and defense support clearly rests on a very different range of considerations than the case for economic aid. Military aid and defense support are to be attacked or defended in terms of their contribution, first, to our effective military strength and, second, to the achievement of our direct political objectives. I can see no objection to them in principle; any criticism of them, or defense of their expansion, must rest on the severely practical grounds that, dollar for dollar, they yield less, or more, strength than alternative modes of expenditure. The one serious danger of confusion between these categories and economic aid is that the argument for economic aid which this article considers is sometimes used as a rationalization to permit straight military or political subsidies to be made under a different label. We shall be concerned with neither these types of expenditure nor this use of the argument for economic aid.

Economic aid proper raises much broader and certainly very different issues. These issues deserve far more public debate than they are getting. We are on the verge of committing ourselves to a policy which in my view can only have disastrous consequences for our country and our way of life. And we are doing so not after thoughtful and thorough consideration of the issues involved, but almost by inadvertence, by proceeding along what seems the line of least resistance.

Two questions must be answered in judging government economic aid. First, is it likely in fact to promote the economic development of the countries to whom aid is granted? Second, do its political effects in those countries promote democracy and freedom?

The second question, though not much discussed, is easy to answer and admits of little dispute. As it has so far been administered, our aid program has consisted predominantly of grants or loans or provision of personnel or material directly to the governments of recipient countries for specified projects regarded as contributing to economic development. It has thereby tended to strengthen the role of the government sector in general economic activity relative to the private sector. Yet democracy and freedom have never been either attained or maintained except in communities in which the bulk of economic activity is organized through private enterprise.

This problem has of course been recognized and partly explains why some grants or loans have been made to private enterprises in the recipient countries rather than directly to governments. Last year, John B. Hollister, on the occasion of his retirement as head of the International Cooperation Administration, proposed that a much enlarged fraction of total funds be channeled to private enterprises. This modification, which aroused strong opposition and is not likely to be carried far, would reduce the tendency of the aid program to strengthen the government sector. It would, however, not eliminate it. We are hardly likely to make funds available to enterprises in poor standing with their governments or for projects opposed by governments. The final result will therefore be much the same.

Many proponents of foreign aid recognize that its long-run political effects are adverse to freedom and democracy. To some extent, they plead special extenuating circumstances. For example, the group in power in a particular country may for the time being be in a shaky political position, yet its overthrow may mean the assumption of power by anti-democratic forces. And economic aid may help such a government over its temporary political crisis. Their main reply, however, is that economic progress is a prerequisite to freedom and democracy in underdeveloped countries, and that economic aid will contribute to this outcome and thereby on balance promote political freedom. This makes the crucial question, even for political effects, the first, namely, the economic effects of economic aid.

The belief that foreign aid effectively promotes economic development rests in turn on three basic propositions: first, that the key to economic development is the availability of capital; second, that underdeveloped countries are too poor to provide the capital for themselves; third, that centralized and comprehensive economic planning and control by government is an essential requisite for economic development.

All three propositions are at best misleading half-truths. Additional capital is certainly essential for development. And of course the more capital the better, *other things being the same*. But the way in which capital is provided will affect other things. The Pharaohs raised enormous sums of capital to build the Pyramids; this was capital formation on a grand scale; it certainly did not promote economic development in the fundamental sense of contributing to a self-sustaining growth in the standard of life of the Egyptian masses. Modern Egypt has under government auspices built a steel mill; this involves capital formation; but it is a drain on the economic resources of Egypt, not a contribution to economic strength, since the cost of making steel in Egypt is very much greater than the cost of buying it elsewhere; it is simply a modern equivalent of the Pyramids except that maintenance expenses are higher. Such modern monuments are by no means the exception; they are almost certain to be the rule when funds are made available directly or indirectly to governments that are inevitably under pressure to produce the symbols of modern industrialism. There is hardly an underdeveloped country that does not now waste its substance on the symbol of a government-owned or government-subsidized international airline. And there is hardly one that does not want its own steel mill as yet another potent symbol.

Some monuments are inevitable in the course of economic development and may indeed be politically desirable as tangible and dramatic signs of change. If the appetite for monuments were at once so intense as to make them the first claim on a country's resources and yet so limited and satiable that their extent was independent of the resources available, monument-building might be a costly fact of life but would have little relevance to foreign economic aid. Unfortunately, this is hardly the case. The appetite grows by what it feeds on. The availability of resources at little or no cost to the country in question inevitably stimulates monument-building. Thus while foreign aid grants may in the first instance add to the capital available to a country, they also lead to a notable increase in the amount of capital devoted to economically wasteful projects.

Cannot, it will be asked, these problems be solved by our exercising control over the use of the capital we make available to governments? And would they not be avoided even more directly if we adopted the proposal to make funds available directly to private enterprises? Aside from the political problems raised by any attempt at close control of even the funds we give, the answer is no. In the first place, there is a purely technical difficulty. Our grants are only part of the total capital available to a country and of the funds available to the government. It will do no good to control the use of the one part while exercising no control over the other; the effect would simply be to alter the bookkeeping—whatever we regarded as appropriate projects would be treated as financed with our funds, and the monuments would be built with local funds. Effective control would thus require us to control the whole of the capital investment of the country, a result that is hardly feasible on political grounds. But even if it were, the problem would by no means be solved. We would simply be substituting one central planning group for another. This leads to the third proposition: that central planning by government is essential to economic development.

Before turning to this issue, it will be well to consider the assertion that the underdeveloped countries are too poor to save and provide capital for themselves. Here, too, the alleged fact is most dubious. Currently developed countries were once underdeveloped. Whence came their capital? The key problem is not one of possibility but of incentive and of proper use. For generations, India was a "sink" for the precious metals, as the writers on money always put it. There was much saving, but it took the unproductive form of accumulation of specie. In Africa, natives on the very margin of subsistence have, given a market demand for their produce, extended greatly the area under cultivation, an activity involving the formation of capital, though seldom entering into recorded figures on savings. Domestic capital can be supplemented by foreign capital if the conditions are right—which means if property is secure against both private and public seizure. Many low-income countries cannot of course attract foreign capital; in most of these, in fact, locally owned capital is invested abroad, and for the same reason—because there is not an environment favorable to private property and free enterprise. And in this respect, too, government-to-government grants are likely to be adverse to economic development. They strengthen the government sector at the expense of the private sector, and reduce the pressure on the government to maintain an environment favorable to private enterprise. We may and do seek to counteract this effect by using our grants to get "concessions" from the government favorable to private enterprise. But this is seldom anything like a complete offset—the change in the objective power of the government sector is likely ultimately to outweigh by far the imposed restraint on how for the time being it uses that power. The final result of our grants is therefore likely to be a reduction in the amount of capital available from other sources both internally and from the outside.

In short, if any generalization is valid, it is that the availability of capital while an important problem is a subsidiary one—if other conditions for economic development are ripe, capital will be readily available; if they are not, capital made available is very likely to be wasted.

Let us turn now to the proposition that economic development requires centralized governmental control and planning, that it requires a coördinated "development program." This proposition, too, contains an element of truth. Government certainly has an important role to play in the process of development. It must provide a stable legal framework; it must provide law and order, security to person and property. Beyond this, it has an important role in promoting certain basic services, such as elementary education, roads, and a monetary system; it can make an important contribution by extension activities which help to spread knowledge of new and improved techniques. And numerous other activities of the same sort come to mind.

But none of these activities calls for a centralized program for economic development or detailed control of investment. And such a centralized program is likely to be a hindrance, not a help. Economic development is a process of changing old ways of doing things, of venturing into the unknown. It requires a maximum of flexibility, of possibility for experimentation. No one can predict in advance what will turn out to be the most effective use of a nation's productive resources. Yet the essence of a centralized program of economic development is that it introduces rigidity and inflexibility. It involves a central decision about what activities to undertake, and the use of central force and authority to enforce conformity with that decision.

It may well be that in many underdeveloped countries, existing or potential government officials are as competent both to judge what lines of activity will be profitable and to run particular plants as existing or potential private businessmen. There is yet a crucial advantage in letting private business do as much as possible. Private individuals risk their own funds and thus have a much stronger incentive to choose wisely and well. They can be more numerous and they have much detailed information about specific situations that cannot possibly be available to governmental officials. Even more important, however wisely the decisions are made, there are bound to be mistakes. Progress requires that these be recognized, that unsuccessful ventures be abandoned. There is at least some chance that unsuccessful private ventures will be allowed to fail. There is almost none that public ones will be—unless the failure is as flagrant as the British ground nuts venture. The mistake will simply be concealed by subsidy or tariff protection or prohibition of competition. If anything is clear from widespread experience with governmental economic activity, it is that a governmental venture, once established, is seldom abandoned. And surely it is almost as clear that governmental officials are less experimental, less flexible, less adaptive, than private individuals risking their own funds.

What is required in the underdeveloped countries is the release of the energies of millions of able, active, and vigorous people who have been chained by ignorance, custom, and tradition. Such people exist in every underdeveloped country. If it seems otherwise, it is because we tend to seek them in our own image in "big business" on the Western model rather than in the villages and on the farms and in the shops and bazaars that line the streets of the crowded cities of many a poor country. These people require only a favorable environment to transform the face of their countries. Instead there is real danger that the inherited set of cultural and social restraints will simply be replaced by an equally far-reaching imposed set of political and economic controls, that one strait jacket will be substituted for another. What is required is rather an atmosphere of freedom, of maximum opportunity for individuals to experiment, and of incentive for them to do so in an environment in which there are objective tests of success and failure —in short, a vigorous, free capitalistic market.

Thus central control would be a poor way to promote economic development even if the central authorities chose individual projects as wisely as private individuals and with the same end in view. In fact, as we have already seen, the government is almost sure to promote other ends—the national and personal prestige that can be attained through monument-building—so that the case against centralized control is even stronger.

The issues we have been discussing are strikingly illustrated in a report submitted in December, 1956 by the M.I.T. Center for International Studies to the Special Senate Committee to study the Foreign Aid Program. The report studies the problem of how to judge whether a country should be given additional aid. The answer is that the criterion should be whether the country is making an "additional national effort" toward economic development. Two, and only two, "rules of thumb" are given for deciding whether this is the case: "one index that national effort is being mobilized for development is the launching of measures to capture a good fraction of increases in income for the purpose of further investment"; another "measure of national effort . . . is the degree to which a country's leaders have worked out an overall development program."

Here are two of the basic propositions we started with. And the striking thing is that by these tests, the United States would never have qualified as a country making an "additional national effort" toward economic development! We have never had explicit "measures to capture a good fraction of increases in income for the purpose of further investment." Nor have our "leaders" ever "worked out an overall development program." And what is true of the United States is true of every other free nation that has achieved economic development. The only possible exceptions are the economic programs worked out after the Second World War by Britain and some other European countries, and these were largely abandoned because they were failures.

The only countries that satisfy the tests suggested by the M.I.T. report are the Communist countries—these all have measures "to capture a good fraction of increases in income for the purpose of further investment" and all have an "overall development program." And none of these has in fact achieved economic development in the sense of a self-sustaining rise in the standard of living of the ordinary man. In the satellite countries, the standard of living of the ordinary man has quite clearly fallen. Even in Russia, the ordinary man is by no means clearly better off now than before the Communists took over, and, indeed, may be worse off even in terms solely of material comforts. While education and health services have clearly improved, food, shelter, and clothing have all apparently deteriorated for the masses. The achievements of which Russia justifiably boasts are to be found elsewhere: in its heavy industries, its military output, and its space satellites—achievements that from the point of view of the consumer classify strictly as monument building.

It thus seems clear that a free market without central planning has, at least to date, been not only the most effective route to economic development but the *only* effective route to a rising standard of life for the masses of the people. And it is eminently clear that it has been the only route consistent with political freedom and democracy. Yet the M.I.T. report and most other writings on the subject simply take the opposite for granted, without even noting that in doing so they are going against the whole of the evidence to date, and without offering a shred of evidence of their own. This is modern mythology with a vengeance.

What is involved here is no less than another phase of the ideological war in which we are engaged. A central premise of the Communist ideology is that the state must exercise comprehensive control and direction over the economic activities of its citizens; a central premise of Western liberalism is that free men operating in a free market can promote their own objectives without the necessity for an all-powerful state.

Foreign economic aid implicitly accepts this premise of the Communist ideology; yet it is intended as a weapon against Communism. Many who favor it as applied abroad would be horrified at the idea of applying its principles at home. If they accept it, it is because they do not understand what it implies or because they take the word of the "experts" that it is the "only" way to win friends abroad. They, and the experts, are in the state of the man who discovered that he had been speaking prose all his life. Loyal Americans that they are, they have unthinkingly accepted a basic premise of the Communist ideology without recognizing it for what it is and in the face of the available evidence. This is a measure of the success of Marxist thought, which is most dangerous precisely when its products lose their labels.

Despite the intentions of foreign economic aid, its major effect, insofar as it has any effect at all, will be too speed the Communization of the underdeveloped world. It may, for a time, keep some of these countries nominally on our side. But neutral or even hostile democracies are less of a threat to the preservation of a free world than ostensibly friendly totalitarian countries.

An effective program to promote a free and prosperous world must be based on our own ideology, not on the ideology we are fighting. What policy would be consistent with our ideology?

The aim should be to promote free markets throughout the world and maximum reliance by all countries on free enterprise in an environment favorable to competition and to individual initiative. We cannot do this by telling other governments what to do or by bribing them to go against their own natures any more than we can force men to be free. What we can do is to set an example and to help establish an international climate favorable to economic and political freedom; we can make it easier for other countries to take the path of freedom if they wish to.

The most important area in which we can do this is foreign trade. Here, in particular, our policies belie our professions. We profess to believe in free competition and free markets, yet we have erected barriers to "protect" domestic producers from competition; we profess to believe in minimal government interference with economic activity, yet our government imposes quotas on imports and dumps exports abroad because of a policy of government support of farm prices. True, we have also reduced tariffs and barriers to trade in many areas, and these actions, ably supplemented by the unintended effects of inflation, have reduced our trade restrictions to their lowest level in many decades. Yet those that remain, as well as the fresh restrictions that have been imposed, particularly on agricultural products, have, I believe, done far more harm to our foreign relations than any good we have done even temporarily by our economic aid. The rest of the world regards us as hypocrites, and they are at least partly right.

Entirely aside from the problem of foreign relations, these policies do us direct economic harm. They prevent us from using our resources as effectively as we might both at home and abroad; they hurt us as well as the rest of the world. A free trader like myself would like to see them abolished for this reason alone— in order to enable us to have a higher standard of living. But this is only part of the case for free trade, and, in the present context, the lesser part.

A major factor pushing underdeveloped countries in the direction of central planning and of autarchy is their lack of confidence in a market for their products. Suppose, they argue, we do follow the route of free enterprise and free trade, concentrate on producing those things we can produce most cheaply, and count on getting the goods we want to consume through international trade. Is not success likely simply to produce increases in import barriers by the United States and other countries so that we find ourselves all dressed up with a fine export industry and nowhere to go? And, under present circumstances, can one say with any confidence that they are wrong? Ask the Swiss watchmakers and English bicycle producers.

It is not often recognized how widespread are the implications of the restrictions on trade and, in particular, the uncertainty about them. We do not, it will be said, offer a market for the potential products of most underdeveloped countries so that our trade barriers do not affect them. But this is clearly wrong. It is a major virtue of free international trade that it is multilateral not bilateral. Were we to import more from, say, Western Europe, Western Europe would be able to import more from still other countries, and so on in endless chain, so that our own greater exports might go to very different countries than those from whom we purchased products.

Or to take yet another facet of the problem—the effect on foreign investment. In part, such investment is stimulated by trade barriers: if India will not permit the import of complete cars, an automobile company may set up an assembly plant. But this investment is wasted from the point of view of world productivity: it is used simply to do in one country what could be done more efficiently elsewhere. Productive foreign investment is hindered by trade barriers, both directly and indirectly. It is hindered directly, because trade barriers distort the incentives to investment and also make it more difficult for the investor to receive the return on his investment in the currency he wants—a country can earn foreign currency to pay him only by exports. It is hindered indirectly because business and trade relations among nations are a major channel for the spread of information about investment opportunities and the establishment of contacts that make them possible. Commissions of V.I.P.'s assigned the task of finding "investment opportunities" are a poor substitute for the day-to-day contact of numerous individuals engaged in earning their daily living by selling goods and rendering services in a foreign country.

Or again, look for the sources of American influence on foreign attitudes and cultures and where will one find them? Not in the literature disseminated by USIS, useful though that may be, but in the activities of International Harvester, Caterpillar Tractor, Singer Sewing Machine, Coca-Cola, Hollywood, and so on. Channels of trade are by all odds the most effective means of disseminating understanding and knowledge of the United States.

British maintenance of free trade—whatever its motives—was surely a major factor knitting the nineteenth-century world together and promoting the rapid and effective development of many then underdeveloped countries. And trade barriers, currency controls, and other economic restrictions are surely a major factor dividing the twentieth-century world and impeding the effective development of the currently underdeveloped countries.

Suppose we were to announce to the world that we committed ourselves to abolish all tariffs, quotas, and other restrictions on trade by a specified date—say, in five or ten years—and that thereafter we would maintain complete free trade. Can there be any doubt that the effects on our international position—both immediately through the announcement effects and ultimately through the long-run economic effects—would be vastly more favorable than those achievable by any conceivable program of foreign economic aid even if one assigns to that aid all the virtues claimed by its proponents? We would be playing from our strength. We would be offering an opportunity to free men to make effective use of their freedom rather than contributing chains to enslave men.

It would, of course, be better if such action were taken by many nations. But it would be a serious mistake for us to link our actions to those of others; the result would be to slow the movement toward free trade to the pace desired by the most recalcitrant member. Far better to move unilaterally. We would benefit economically and politically from a unilateral move, and we might have far more effect on other countries through example than over the conference table.

A movement toward free trade would affect adversely many particular individuals and concerns—those who have invested talent and capital in "protected" industries. But our mobility and adaptability are such that a gradual movement—over the course of, say, ten years—would give the affected individuals ample opportunity to adjust to the new circumstances with little if any loss. The new opportunities afforded by the expansion of world trade, and the more efficient use of our resources involved therein, would benefit many more than were harmed. After all, the transition to free trade over ten years would have far less of an impact than the technological changes that occur decade after decade and that we take in our stride.

As of the moment, we have a bear by the tail in our foreign economic policy—and unfortunately, it is not the Russian Bear. We get little if any political kudos for continuing economic aid—the recipient countries have come to take it for granted and even to regard it as their right. Yet for this very reason, the sudden cessation of aid would be regarded as an unfriendly and hostile act and would arouse great hostility toward the United States. Thus even if one accepts the arguments of the preceding sections, there remains the problem of how to achieve the transition from our present policy to the alternative.

The simplest and least undesirable way seems to me to be to make a final terminal grant to each recipient country. The grant should be fairly generous, say something like two to three times the annual grants we have been making to the country. It should be completely unrestricted and preferably made in the form of a dollar—or even better a Swiss franc—balance on which the recipient country can draw as it wishes. In this way, our own involvement in central planning by other countries could be terminated at once, and the government of the recipient country would attach the greatest value to the grant.

The cost of such a termination program would be sizeable in

the year of termination. But it would be a once-for-all cost rather than the steady and growing drain to which we appear to be on the verge of committing ourselves.

Foreign economic aid needs to be sharply distinguished from direct military aid and defense support even though it may be hard to classify any particular expenditure. Foreign economic aid consists of grants or loans from our government to other governments or to enterprises in other countries for specified projects regarded as contributing to economic development. It includes both technical assistance and grants or loans of money.

The objectives of foreign economic aid are commendable. The means are, however, inappropriate to the objectives. Foreign economic aid, far from contributing to rapid economic development along democratic lines, is likely to retard improvement in the well-being of the masses, to strengthen the government sector at the expense of the private sector, and to undermine democracy and freedom. The proponents of foreign aid have unwittingly accepted a basic premise of the Communist ideology that foreign aid is intended to combat. They have accepted the view that centralized and comprehensive economic planning and control by government is an essential requisite for economic development. This view is contradicted by our own experience and the experience of every other free country.

An effective program must be based on our own ideology, not on the ideology we are fighting. Such a program would call for eliminating the inconsistency between the free trade and free enterprise policies we preach and the protectionist and interventionist policies we at least partly practice. An effective and dramatic program would be to commit ourselves unilaterally to achieving complete free trade by a specified and not too distant date. This would do much to promote an environment and international climate favorable to the rapid development of the uncommitted world along free and democratic lines. It would be an act of truly enlightened self-interest.

Economic Aid Reconsidered

CHARLES WOLF, JR.

Charles Wolf, Jr. is an economist with the RAND Corporation. He is an expert on development problems in South and Southeast Asia and has written extensively in the area. This article originally appeared in the Summer 1961 issue of the Yale Review.

THREE YEARS ago, Professor Milton Friedman, of the University of Chicago, wrote a sharply critical article on the subject of foreign aid.[1] The article argued that "despite the intentions of foreign economic aid, its major effect, insofar as it has an effect at all, will be to speed the Communization of the underdeveloped world." Coming from an economist as deservedly distinguished as Professor Friedman, these are inflammatory words. They are accompanied by many others of a similar intensity. But there is a wide gap in the article between the vigor of its criticism and the rigor of its analysis. My main purpose in writing this paper is to suggest just how wide the gap is.

In the course of these comments, I will be less concerned with making a case *for* foreign economic aid than with dispelling some of the general arguments *against* it which the Friedman article advances. Beyond this, I hope to suggest what I think are reasonable objectives of economic aid—"reasonable" in the sense that there is a significant probability that aid programs can really contribute to them—and to suggest, as well, the distinct limitations of aid as a means of accomplishing other objectives.

Economic aid is, after all, just one instrument of foreign policy.

1. See preceding article.

Diplomacy, the positioning and composition of the armed forces, military aid, public information and cultural relations, commercial and trade policy are other foreign policy instruments. But this does not mean that *all* foreign policy instruments are applicable to *each* foreign policy objective. Some instruments are, in fact, quite inapplicable to particular objectives simply because there is no predictable relationship between the instruments and the particular objective. The point is obvious, but it is especially relevant to economic aid. Disenchantment with aid often arises from judging it by quite unrealistic objectives in the first place. People who start out from the premise that aid should do more than it realistically can be expected to do, frequently end up convinced that it can do very little, if anything, of value.

Basically, Friedman's criticisms are not ostensibly concerned with the question of objectives at all. He acknowledges at the outset that it is an appropriate objective of United States foreign policy that the less-developed countries "satisfy their aspirations for economic development as fully as possible in a democratic framework." If economic aid can make a contribution toward this end that is sufficient relative to its costs, it presumably would be justified for Friedman, as it would for me. The burden of Friedman's argument is not that the objective is unsuitable, but rather that economic aid is an ill-suited means for attaining the objective. And his verdict that aid is ill-suited rests on the emphatically negative answers he gives to two questions: (a) is government aid "likely to promote the economic development of the countries to whom it is granted?" and (b) will its "political effects in those countries promote democracy and freedom?"

The second question, he asserts, is "easy to answer and admits of little dispute." Friedman's own answer is based on the following propositions: (1) Aid is extended on a government-to-government basis, and hence tends "to strengthen the role of the government sector relative to the private sector"; (2) "Democracy and freedom have never been either attained or maintained except in communities in which the bulk of economic activity is organized through private enterprise"; and, therefore, (3) Aid reduces prospects of political evolution along democratic lines in underdeveloped countries.

I believe that Friedman's argument is incorrect on two counts. Its factual assertions are inaccurate; and the conclusion drawn wouldn't logically follow even if the factual assertions were assumed to be accurate.

First, on the facts. It is true that aid is extended on a government-to-government basis, but it is not true that economic aid tends to "strengthen the government sector relative to the private sector." Leaving aside for the moment the conceptual ambiguity of the quoted phrase, the facts are more complex, and less conclusive, than Friedman's assertion implies. Often the effect of aid has been to *reduce* the encroachment on the private sector. The point isn't whether government projects *receive* aid, but whether, in the *absence* of aid, the pinch would fall on public or private projects. Probably it would fall on both, but there are two reasons why pressure on the private sector would very likely be greater than on the public sector. The first reason is that the zeal of governments and peoples in many of the less-developed countries for the development of sectors in which private investment has traditionally been negligible would result in a strenuous effort to sustain public investment at the expense of the private sector, in the absence of aid. The *étatisme* which understandably worries Friedman would very likely be greatly increased in a country like India, if foreign economic aid were eliminated or sharply reduced, by drastic efforts to capture private savings for public investment projects. This is not to say that some efforts to increase private savings may not be warranted and desirable anyhow. There seems to be fairly widespread agreement, for example, among both Indian and American economists who have studied the problem, that additional taxation, even of a mildly regressive sort, would be both feasible and desirable as a way of increasing the resources available for economic development. But, in the absence of aid, measures to capture additional resources for public projects would very likely become so intense and authoritarian that pressure on the private sector would rapidly erode it.

The second reason is that, in the *absence* of aid from the United States, the underdeveloped countries would be very likely to receive increased aid from the Communist bloc. The fact that the Communist bloc would become the only major source of intergovernmental aid would be as important as the increased amount of Soviet aid. One could argue that, *given* substantial and efficient United States aid programs, additional Soviet bloc aid programs need not be feared and might even be welcomed by the United States, as well as by the recipient countries. But, in the absence of United States aid, the Soviet bloc could exploit the additional influence which its monopolistic position would provide. This influence would surely not be directed toward the growth of a vigorous private sector.

There are other ways in which United States aid to government projects helps the private sector. One way is by widening the market for private sector output as a result of the increased public-sector demand. Another is by increasing the supply of inputs which are complementary to private enterprise. Consider, for example, United States aid for projects like community development, or irrigation, or fertilizer distribution, or river valley development. These are, typically, government-to-government projects, but they generally have the effect of providing inputs which raise the productivity of privately-owned agricultural and industrial enterprise. Would their diminution more seriously weaken the private sector or the public sector? On balance, I would say the private sector. At the least, Friedman's general assertion to the contrary is quite untenable.

Next, consider his assertion that democracy depends on the bulk of economic activity being "organized through private enterprise." I can think of no historical example that obviously negates it, although the assertion does leave open how much comprises "the bulk" of economic activity. But granting this assertion, and even if it were true that aid tends to increase the relative size of the government sector, it does not logically follow that the effect of aid will be adverse to democracy and freedom.

It is a tricky business to estimate how much economic activity is "organized through private enterprise," to use Friedman's term. It can, for instance, be measured in terms of how much of the national product is *produced* by private enterprise and how much by government; or by how much of the final produce is *purchased* by private individuals or institutions, and how much by government; or by how much is *expended* by private income earners and how much by government. The second measure will yield a higher figure for the government sector than the first since, in all non-Communist countries, some of what is purchased by government is produced by the private sector. And the expenditure measure will show the highest share for the government sector, because part of government expenditures represents income transfers (like veterans' bonuses, unemployment benefits, interest on the public debt, etc.) which are not included in government purchases of goods and services.

If one is concerned loosely with the question of the extent of government "influence" or "intervention" in the economy, as Friedman is, the third measure is probably the best of the three simply because it is the largest. Considering the underdeveloped country with the best statistics, India, which is also one with a relatively active government sector, the proportion of central government expenditures in gross national product in 1958 and 1959 was 12.6 percent and 12.9 percent, respectively. In the United States by comparison, the corresponding share of federal government expenditures in the national product was 18.8 percent and 19.7 percent, respectively. If we add to federal government outlays those by state governments, the resulting share for the United States was 25.1 percent and 25.7 percent for 1958 and 1959. In India, the share of gross national product represented by central and state government expenditures was 18.1 percent and 18.5 percent for the two years. If the extent of government activity were instead to be measured by product or by purchases rather than expenditures, the figures would be smaller still. However one looks at it, the overwhelming "bulk" of economic activity in India, and to an even greater extent in most other underdeveloped countries, is "organized through private enterprise." The figures above could be doubled and the statement would still be valid.

The point is simply this: even if the effect of economic aid were to increase the relative size of the government sector in underdeveloped countries substantially (a premise which, as we have seen, is highly doubtful), it would still be true, over a wide range of such an increase, that the "bulk of economic activity" would remain "organized through private enterprise." For Friedman's reasoning to hold, we would have to accept the hypothesis that any *increase* in the relative share of the government sector somehow reduces the degree of freedom, or raises the probability that the government sector will eventually encompass the "bulk of economic activity," *even if the increase still leaves the government sector small relative to the economy as a whole.* This is a much stronger hypothesis than the one he explicitly advances. It is one thing to say that democracy requires the *bulk* of economic activity to be in private hands, and quite something else to say that democracy also requires that there be no *decrease* in the share of economic activity in private hands, or that any such decrease reduces the degree of, or prospects for, democracy. As far as I know, there is absolutely no empirical justification for the stronger hypothesis, and Friedman offers none. Some examples seem quite inconsistent with it. In West Germany and Italy, for instance, the private sector was relatively *smaller* in 1959 than it was in the early 1950's, and yet I doubt that Friedman would argue that democracy and freedom have been correspondingly weakened. International comparisons make the stronger hypothesis look still more absurd. The United Kingdom, with a relatively large government sector, would emerge as "less democratic" than West Germany or Italy or India; and the United States as less democratic than West Germany!

The common sense of the matter would appear to be that, in most underdeveloped countries, there is plenty of room for growth in the absolute and relative size of the government sector without compromising prospects for democracy and freedom. Moreover, if expansion in the government sector is itself a response to widespread popular aspirations for accelerated economic growth, the consequence is very likely to be a strengthening, rather than a weakening, of prospects for democratic political evolution in the underdeveloped countries.

To summarize what has been said: A good case can be made for the contention that, as a result of economic aid, the private sector in most underdeveloped countries is very likely to be absolutely and relatively larger than it otherwise would be. Moreover, even if the government sector were to grow relative to the private sector as a *consequence* of aid, rather than independently of aid, within fairly wide limits such growth would be quite consistent with a maintenance of the bulk of economic activity in private hands, simply because the government sector in underdeveloped countries is so small to start with. Finally, whether some growth in the government sector relative to the private sector strengthens or weakens prospects for democracy, is apt to depend on what political, economic, and social changes are accomplished by that growth, and on how responsive the government is to the will of the people—neither of which can be inferred simply from the growth of the government sector alone. Proponents of foreign economic aid should not claim more than this.

Whether or not economic aid results in an expansion in the relative size of the government sector, it remains legitimate to ask, as Friedman does, if such aid is "likely to promote the economic development of the countries to whom it is granted." Friedman again answers, "Emphatically, no," for three reasons: first, the developmental effect of adding to a recipient country's resources is more than offset by the stimulus provided by aid to wasteful use of both the aid and the country's own non-aid resources; second, if a developing country wanted to develop badly enough, it could extract sufficient savings from its own economy to meet its capital requirements without aid; and third, aid tends to sustain or strengthen government planning of economic development, and government planning is the surest way to stifle development. To save space, I have paraphrased his arguments, without, I hope, distorting them. But no matter how they are put, they should be recognized as statements of ideology and doctrine, not of factual or logical analysis.

Consider the first point. Friedman contends that economic aid conduces to wasteful "monument-building" because it makes resources available to underdeveloped countries "at little or no cost." But clearly there are appreciable "costs" attached to aid. I am not thinking here simply of the "hardness" or "softness" of interest and repayment terms, which in most cases I would argue are quite properly lenient, and perhaps should be more so. As long as one accepts the obviously valid assumption that the quantity of aid available is not unlimited, *there are always appreciable costs attached to aid.* Freshman economics tells us that the "real" cost of using any limited resource for a particular purpose is the returns that are foregone by not employing that resource in its best alternative use. From the standpoint of any recipient country, these "alternative" or "opportunity" costs are positive and large, even if the aid is an outright gift.

Moreover, recognition of the reality of "opportunity costs" does not require that the populations or governments of underdeveloped countries attain a high degree of economic literacy. All it requires is that one government ministry be able to recognize that the use of scarce aid resources to build a "monument" desired by another ministry means that much less available for investing in the productive projects desired by the first ministry. And it requires, further, that people outside the government be able to recognize that wasteful use of government resources—whether derived from foreign or domestic sources—means that much less available for meeting the compelling needs of the public itself. Neither of these minimal requirements is unrealistic. Typically, both are actively operative, and their joint effect is generally to conduce toward economic use of the aid that is provided to underdeveloped countries.

There is still another incentive toward efficient use. The relationship between aid-source and aid-recipient is a continuing one. To the extent that the recipient's anticipation of future aid depends on his efficient use of current resources, he will have a strong incentive to limit monuments and waste. As in the case of opportunity costs, the "future-flow" incentive can operate regardless of whether or what repayment terms are incorporated in government-to-government agreements.

In practice, of course, there are many slips and inefficiencies. Anyone familiar with United States or other international aid programs cannot ignore them, and should not defend them. But to say, as Friedman does, that aid is typically wasted because it is costless, is not only bad economics, from a theoretical point of view; it is also a wrong-headed characterization of the actual record of government aid programs.

His second point is based on the contention that external aid is really superfluous. The underdeveloped countries are not too poor to provide capital for their own development. After all, "currently developed countries were once underdeveloped," and they managed to eke out a surplus above subsistence requirements in order to provide capital for their development. The currently underdeveloped countries could do likewise, simply by offering sufficient incentives to domestic saving and to foreign investment. Their failure to do so results from a lack of will, rather than an absolute lack of resources. If they had the will, foreign aid would be superfluous. Moreover, Friedman contends, aid is even worse than superfluous, because it tends to "reduce the pressure on government to maintain an environment favorable to private enterprise." Consequently, he concludes, "the final result of our grants is therefore likely to be a reduction in the amount of capital available from other sources both internally and from the outside."

There is an eighteenth-century nostalgia to these arguments, but they deserve reply, both because of their source and because of the extent to which they diverge from currently accepted views. Consider, first, the analogy between currently underdeveloped countries, and the currently developed countries before they developed. From an economic viewpoint, probably the main imperfection in the analogy is that the relationship of income and natural resources on the one hand, to population on the other, is tighter in the currently underdeveloped countries. The physical hardship accompanying self-financing of development in the currently less-developed countries would thus be more acute than it was in the seventeenth and eighteenth centuries in Western Europe, or the nineteenth century in the United States. To some extent, this may be offset by the fact that the currently underdeveloped countries are "late-comers" and hence can draw on technological possibilities that were not available to the early arrivals. But the offset is probably only partial. The economic problems of the currently underdeveloped countries are just harder.

None of this touches the core of what is wrong with Friedman's analogy. The big differences are not economic, but psychological and political. The currently underdeveloped countries live in a world populated by countries which have already developed, and which display the fruits of their development in higher living standards and greater power. The effect of this demonstration is to heighten the aspirations of the currently underdeveloped countries, and to intensify their impatience for development. The acceptable time period for development is consequently much shorter than in the classical examples of development. Diffusion of suffrage in the underdeveloped countries means that governments which tolerate the pace or the inequalities of seventeenth- and eighteenth-century European development will probably not survive. The crucial political difference characterizing the present development context is the obvious one that the currently underdeveloped countries live in a world in which Communism is a tangibly real alternative route to economic development. Hence, the risk of delayed development is just much greater in the currently underdeveloped countries. In effect, Friedman's analogy is misleading because the urgency of development is greater and the available resources smaller in the currently underdeveloped countries than in the classical examples he has in mind.

But what of the argument that the net effect of foreign aid is to reduce the capital that is available by reducing "the pressure on [recipient] governments to maintain an environment favorable to private enterprise"? Implicit in this assertion is the view that in the *absence* of aid, the "environment" would be more favorable to private enterprise. This prognosis seems to me quite unsupported, and, for reasons I've already mentioned above, unsupportable. In general, the effect of foreign aid, as I have seen it operate in South and Southeast Asia, has been to make foreign exchange more readily available to private enterprise, to lower the cost and increase the supply of publicly-provided inputs to private enterprise, and probably to lower the taxes that otherwise would be levied on individual and corporate incomes. In this connection, it is notable that during the past ten years of India's foreign-aided development plans, private enterprise has been more buoyant and expansionist than ever before. I am not denying that private domestic and foreign enterprises have their troubles in underdeveloped countries, or that governmental bureaucracy accounts for much of these troubles through capricious allocations of foreign exchange and through discriminatory collection of taxes from honest firms. What I am suggesting is that, in the absence of aid, these troubles would probably be more acute. Pressures on private enterprise would intensify, not abate. It is, of course, almost as hard to substantiate this prognosis as Friedman's. But besides the Indian example, I would also note that in every underdeveloped country I am familiar with, private business organizations strongly support the need for and desirability of foreign aid. If their interests were adversely affected by aid, it is quite unlikely that they would do so.

Friedman's third reason for asserting that aid does not in fact promote development is that aid sustains and propitiates centralized government planning, and planning is inherently counterdevelopmental. Planning is counterdevelopmental because it tends to be rigid and inflexible while effective development requires experimentation and flexibility. These characteristics are more likely to be obtained under a system of private enterprise than under government planning, because private enterprise provides strong incentives toward careful choice and toward rapid correction of mistakes.

There is an element of truth in Friedman's argument. But the argument is overstated and incomplete. There are powerful reasons why the case for planning is much stronger than Friedman allows. Some of these reasons concern what economic jargon refers to as "external economies" and "decreasing costs." "External economies" relate to the social benefits produced by a particular activity which are not recoverable or appropriable by the project's owners or investors. The usual examples include education and training, public utilities like roads and river valley development, and public health. Since these benefits are "non-appropriable," they will obviously not enter into private investors' calculations of the profitability of alternative investment opportunities. The consequence will be underinvestment in external-economy-generating activities, and a need for compensating government investment to offset the deficiency. "Decreasing costs" relate to activities which result in lower costs as the scale of the activity increases. Often the scale required for realizing "decreasing costs" entails investment outlays far beyond what is accessible to private enterprise in the underdeveloped countries. And even if the investment requirements were met, "decreasing costs" would preclude the continued existence of many firms and competitive markets. Without going into the technical ramifications of either "external economies" or "decreasing costs," the relevant point is that both considerations will result in underinvestment in potentially high-priority activities under a regime of private enterprise. Government initiative to compensate for these deficiencies will be necessary if available resources, domestic as well as foreign, are to have maximum effect on economic growth.

These reasons for active government planning in the underdeveloped countries are supplemented by other strongly practical considerations. Imperfections and rigidities in the market mechanism are many and notorious in underdeveloped countries. Although improvements in the flow of information and the mobility of capital and labor are possible and desirable in the underdeveloped countries, these rigidities are deep-seated and durable. The real alternative to some government intervention in these countries is not a smoothly functioning free market, but a market pervaded by barriers and rigidities. The distortion in Friedman's argument arises from comparing an ideal model of a free market regimen with casual observation of the worst features of government planning. In the real world of the underdeveloped economies, private enterprise and the free market are neither as flexible or adaptive as Friedman suggests, nor is government planning as rigid and inefficient. Both the market and planning have their justifications and shortcomings. As Edward Mason has put it: "The really good arguments for planning lie in the obvious inadequacies of the market, and the really good arguments for the market rest on the deficiencies of planning."

My conclusions from these remarks are in direct contradiction to Friedman's answer to the question of whether aid is likely to promote economic development. There have been examples of "monument building," but, in general, aid has been productively used, and the institutional mechanisms for extending aid have tended to increase the productive use of non-aid resources as well. It is, moreover, definitely not true that aid leads to wasteful use because it is "costless." The existence of alternative uses for aid means that there are always appreciable costs attached to its use in any wasteful activity. Although the bulk of capital requirements for development must be internally generated, the effect of complete self-financing would very likely be to induce the internal authoritarianism which Friedman wishes to avoid, and encourage the erosion of private enterprise which he wishes to protect. Finally, there are both strong theoretical and practical reasons for expecting and encouraging some degree of government planning in underdeveloped countries. True, planning by government can be rigid and inflexible, as can planning by private enterprise. But, more important, government planning that is rigid and inflexible can be improved. Economic aid is probably a much more appropriate tool for improving the quality of planning than it is for affecting the quantity.

In his zeal to discredit foreign aid, Friedman criticizes two criteria that have often been mentioned by advocates of aid as tests of the eligibility of a recipient country for additional aid. The eligibility criteria he criticizes are, first, whether a recipient is taking "measures to capture a good fraction of increases in income for the purpose of further investment," and, second, the extent to which the recipient has "worked out an overall development program." His criticism takes the form of noting that the United States itself would not have been able to qualify for aid under these criteria during the period of its own initial development, that "the only countries that satisfy [these] tests . . . are the Communist countries," and that none of the Communist countries has in fact achieved a continuing "rise in the standard of living of the ordinary man."

Actually, I agree that the particular aid criteria he refers to are vulnerable to criticism. In fact, I have criticized them elsewhere at length for, among other reasons, giving absolutely no attention to the relative productivity or efficiency of resource use in recipient countries in determining aid allocations among them. But the particular criticisms advanced by Friedman seem to me either misleading or just factually wrong.

The assertion that the United States would not have qualified for assistance under these criteria is true, but pointless. The United States didn't receive intergovernmental aid, and the objectives which motivate aid to the currently underdeveloped countries were quite irrelevant to our development in the nineteenth century. True, Communist countries would qualify under these criteria (though of course they would be disqualified under the implicit additional criterion that the objective of aid is to increase the chances of survival and success of non-Communist political systems). But it is palpably *untrue* that "the *only* countries that would satisfy the tests are the Communist countries." Currently, India, Pakistan, Burma, among others, eminently satisfy the criteria; historically, Japan would have done so.

Moreover, we should be wary about falling into the trap of assuming that anything the Communist countries do or have done is necessarily something we should avoid, or encourage others to avoid. Even if the assumption is often warranted, it sometimes is not. If, for example, the Communists retain a consequential capability to wage war with conventional weapons, it doesn't follow that we should avoid doing likewise or encouraging non-Communist countries to do likewise. If the Communists have tried to plan their economic development and have adopted various measures to capture increases in income for further investment, it does not follow that we should discourage the underdeveloped countries from doing so.

Friedman's last point, that none of the Communist countries has achieved increased living standards, is just wrong. Discussions of foreign aid, or of the uses and misuses of development planning in underdeveloped countries, are not advanced by erroneously asserting, as he does, that planned development in Communist Russia has not raised living standards for the mass of the people.

So much by way of rebuttal. As I mentioned at the outset, I have been less concerned here with making a case for economic aid than with dispelling some of the erroneous arguments against it which Friedman's article presents. But in conclusion, let me add a brief comment on the objectives that seem to me reasonable to attribute to aid, and hence appropriate to apply in assessing its performance. Frequently, advocates of economic aid, and of increased appropriations, do themselves and their aim a disservice by claiming too much. The unrealistic hopes generated by such advocacy usually return to plague the advocate and weaken his case.

Before suggesting some "reasonable" objectives, it is important to be clear about the "unreasonable" ones. It is as important to recognize the effects that cannot (or should not) be sought by extending aid, as it is to recognize the effects that can. By "effects that cannot or should not be sought," I mean either that effects are not predictably related to aid, or, if they are, that they are in general likely to be accompanied by disadvantageous side-effects at least as great as the advantageous effects themselves. From this standpoint, I would include as generally "unreasonable" objectives of economic aid most short-term political returns, such as winning votes in the U.N., weakening or eliminating "neutralism," buying the loyalties and support of particular groups of individuals in the underdeveloped countries, creating and cementing meaningful international alliances, or preventing acceptance by underdeveloped countries of aid from the Soviet bloc. In some cases these objectives may be reasonable, but such cases require especially discerning judgment to be identified and should be treated as exceptions.

There are many other things aid cannot do. It cannot reliably affect decisions by recipients concerning the "mix" of public and private enterprise they prefer, except perhaps in the negative sense of reducing the resource pressures that would otherwise probably induce recipients to crack down more severely on the private sector. (Incidentally, though Friedman disclaims any divergence of views on objectives, and asserts that his criticisms are confined to means, I wonder whether he does not mislead himself. What he seems to be most concerned with is not whether aid can be used to stimulate development, but whether aid can be used to stimulate free enterprise in the short run.) Nor can aid be expected to bring economic benefits to the United States in the form of greater supplies of raw materials at given prices, larger export markets (other than those financed by aid itself), or "national treatment" of United States investors in their access to local investment opportunities. Finally, economic aid cannot be expected to protect recipients against external military threats, and may sometimes even result in increased efforts by hostile forces to disrupt by military means the economic progress that aid itself is furthering.

What remains for the "reasonable" objectives? Aid can provide resources *additional* to those a country raises from domestic or other foreign sources for its own development, and it can provide incentives toward efficient use of the entire package by tying aid increments to productivity. In so doing, it can help provide new opportunities and options to enlist the enthusiasm, energies, and loyalties of peoples and governments in the underdeveloped countries. In addition, aid provides a channel, a working relationship, through which the United States and other developed countries can "illuminate choices" that are open to the recipient countries—to borrow Eugene Black's term. The particular decisions reached by an underdeveloped country—whether they concern industrialization or agriculture, public welfare services or consumption, taxation or price policy—will often be second- or third-best decisions from the standpoint of economic growth alone. But the process of "illuminating choices," of weighing the costs and benefits of alternative actions, can exercise over time a pervasive influence on political as well as economic development. Through its effects on more rapid development, and on rational habits of thought, aid can provide a significant contribution toward enhancing prospects for the survival and vitality of free political systems in the underdeveloped countries. Even if these "reasonable" objectives don't by any means touch some of the main objectives of United States foreign policy, they nevertheless provide strong justification for the economic aid we are extending, and, I would suggest, for making a larger and more disciplined effort in the future.

Using Aid to Promote Long-Run Political Development

JOAN NELSON

Joan Nelson is presently associated with the Center for International Affairs at Harvard University. She is a political scientist, has worked in AID and has a special interest in problems of political development. This selection was taken from her book Aid, Influence and Foreign Policy *published by Macmillan in 1968.*

THE FOREIGN ASSISTANCE ACT of 1961 called for an "historic demonstration that economic growth and political democracy can go hand in hand. . . ." The function of the economic assistance program that the Act established was, in short, to promote political as well as economic development.

Yet political development has been declared "the missing dimension in American policy toward the developing nations."[1] Little aid activity is directly addressed to political development objectives. In the elaborate process of program planning, the actual and potential impact of assistance on political development receives virtually no attention.

The past two years have seen increasing criticism of the aid program on this score. The Foreign Assistance Act of 1966 added several provisions to the basic foreign aid legislation designed to spur increased political development efforts. Before examining proposals for more vigorous action, however, it is useful to consider what is meant by political development, the pattern of past Agency for International Development (AID) efforts, and the reasons for the relative neglect of political development.

POLITICAL DEVELOPMENT, DEMOCRATIC EVOLUTION,
AND ECONOMIC GROWTH

An adequate definition of political development has been the topic of innumerable scholarly conferences and articles for more

---

1. Speech by the Hon. Donald M. Fraser, U.S. Congress, reprinted in the *Congressional Record*, July 13, 1966, p. 14765.

than a decade. It is less difficult to identify major aspects of governmental and political development that the United States seeks to promote. These include:

1. Administrative competence: reasonably efficient and honest administration, capable of maintaining civil peace and carrying out service and developmental functions.

2. National integration: growing identification with the nation rather than with local, regional, ethnic, religious, or tribal loyalties.

3. More equitable distribution of wealth, income, services, and opportunity among classes, regions, and ethnic groups and between rural and urban areas.

4. Fundamental civil liberties: observance of due process, freedom from arbitrary arrest, freedom of association, occupation, and movement.

5. Provision for the orderly transfer of political power.

6. Development of democratic institutions, that is, those which promote broad participation in government decision making and popular review and sanction of government performance. This in turn requires provision for wide dissemination and exchange of information; tolerance of nonviolent expression of individual and group opinion, including freedom of dissent; encouragement of responsible and effective voluntary associations and interest groups; and often, though not always, decentralization of authority to local (and sometimes regional) government.

Political development is, then, a broader concept than democratic evolution. Not all aspects of political development are uniquely or even necessarily associated with democracy.

Administrative efficiency plainly is compatible with authoritarian and totalitarian regimes; indeed, such governments are often defended in the developing countries because they claim to be more efficient than democratic regimes. National integration has been achieved—and not achieved—under all three forms of government, although conflict is normally more rapidly suppressed and hidden under totalitarianism. All forms of government may act to increase equity, and all have also perpetuated old and created new inequities. Basic civil liberties can be preserved under authoritarian but not under totalitarian systems.

Broad participation in governmental decision making, including popular review and sanction of governmental authority, is the aspect of political development most closely associated with democratic evolution. Policy makers have long faced the dilemma of formulating the appropriate U.S. policy toward a regime that is efficient, concerned for equity and growth, and reasonably respectful of civil liberties, but has sharply curtailed democratic rights and institutions—for example, the early years of President Ayub Khan's regime in Pakistan, the military junta that took over Ecuador in 1963, or the Branco government in Brazil. The United States has usually supported such regimes, while indicating its concern over suppression of democratic processes.

American public and academic acceptance of this course is growing. A decade ago, both military regimes and one party systems were rejected on principle both by the interested public and by most political scientists. The public is now more tolerant of one party systems, although antipathy for military regimes seems little affected by such cases as Ayub's Pakistan and the progressive junta in Ecuador. Most scholars now clearly dissociate the broader concept of political development from the specific connotations of parliamentary democracy. Many argue that other aspects of political development are prerequisite to (though no guarantee of) later democratic evolution; therefore, these aspects must take priority over development of democratic institutions.

It would be convenient to assume that political development and economic growth support each other. Indeed, much of the rationale for development aid rests on the assumption that economic stagnation, in the context of rising expectations, population growth, and political agitation, is virtually a formula for instability and extremism. More positively, economic growth is expected in the long run to help unify disparate regions, relieve class tensions, and create groups with a progressive but moderate outlook, in particular an entrepreneurial middle class and a landed peasantry. Conversely, aspects of political development, such as self-help efforts and initiatives of voluntary associations and interest groups, are expected to accelerate economic growth.

Yet the relationship between economic and political development is not always a mutually beneficial one. Rapid economic growth displaces whole social classes and threatens vested interests, often generating political crises. The increased mobility associated with economic growth can heighten ethnic, religious, or regional tensions by throwing hostile groups into close contact and competition. For example, resentment between Eastern Ibos and Northern Hausa tribesmen in Nigeria exploded into bloody rioting and massacres in 1966. Traditional tribal enmity had been exacerbated by Ibo control of professional and technical positions and a good deal of business in the North.

Some aspects of political development are essential for economic growth; others are compatible with growth but not prerequisites; still others have an ambiguous impact. Civil peace and administrative competence plainly promote economic progress. A degree of national integration is also essential, because unchecked rivalries can bring political chaos and economic slowdown or collapse, as in the Congo in the years immediately after independence. Even where there is no threat of widespread violence or secession, ethnic or regional loyalties can interfere with economic growth by distorting resource allocation—for example, by influencing the location of a steel mill or a university, or by creating pressures leading to ethnic or regional quotas in the civil service or in scholarship awards.

The relationship between equity and economic growth is less clear-cut. In most developing countries, broadened services and opportunities including housing, health care, and primary education require heavy initial investment and high recurring costs. Such services contribute only indirectly and in the long run to accelerated economic growth. Other uses of the same funds could promote growth more rapidly and directly. And upon growth depends future capacity to provide employment, higher standards of services, and greater opportunities for the population as a whole. Similarly, whereas privileged groups can and should bear more of the tax burden, investment incentives must not be destroyed. Land reform often results in reduced agricultural production, at least initially. In these and other ways, measures to increase equity may conflict with the requirements of economic growth.

On the other hand, many steps to increase equity promptly and directly are compatible with or even essential to economic progress. Improvements in certain services, notably education and health, contribute not only to well-being but also to productivity. The prospect of a greater share in income or the possibility of owning one's own house normally stimulates initiative and effort. Moreover, many measures to increase equity require little or no increased expenditures, for instance, reduced discrimination between classes or ethnic groups in law enforcement. Some measures, such as stricter tax administration, may even increase revenues as well as equity.

Fundamental civil liberties are compatible with and conducive to economic growth. Controls on movement and occupation are usually costly to administer as well as demoralizing, while arbitrary arrest and lack of due process probably inhibit growth by stifling initiative. But progress in the Soviet Union and several of the East European nations demonstrates that restrictions on such liberties need not prevent growth.

The development of democratic institutions that promote broad participation in governmental decision making has a complex and ambiguous relationship to economic growth. Political participation is sometimes confused with widespread participation in developmental programs. Mobilizing an ever growing part of the population to take part in and support development programs is an intrinsic and essential aspect of effective economic growth. Economic participation may be stimulated by and channelled through a great variety of organizations, including village self-help associations, cooperatives, labor unions, and other voluntary associations, as well as through vigorous private enterprise. Americans tend to associate cooperatives, labor unions, and other voluntary organizations with democratic forms of government. However, authoritarian and totalitarian regimes also recognize the value of such institutions as a means of mobilizing participation in development programs. Indeed, one of the hallmarks of modern totalitarianism is a proliferation of associations of all kinds to this end—not, of course, as vehicles for independent political initiative and pressure.

Although widespread participation in development efforts clearly promotes economic growth, broadened participation in public policy formulation may or may not do so. At the local level, decentralized decision making has immense advantages of speed and relevance to local conditions. Moreover, an effective voice in local decisions may often stimulate local self-help efforts. Striking progress has been made in the past few years in East Pakistan, where local councils have been given clear responsibility for selecting, designing, executing, and evaluating local projects, along with funds and access to the technical advice required to do so successfully. But it is risky to conclude that increased authority at local levels will automatically promote progress. Local politicians are often both more venal and more traditional in their outlook than national political leaders. If local decision making is dominated by a traditional and conservative local elite or by irresponsible local politicians, increased local authority may impede both economic and political progress.

Active popular participation in and pressure on national decision making also may either promote or impede measures essential for long run growth. Where political postwar is tightly held by conservative vested interests, broadened political participation in choice of leaders and determination of policies at the national level is a necessary condition for progress. But policies designed to stimulate growth and increase welfare in the long run may call for belt tightening, deferred claims to increased equity, or temporary suppression of nationalist pride. Higher taxes, lower government subsidies for food or gasoline, postponement of the expansion of elementary schools in order to concentrate on improved quality of secondary education, deferment of massive low cost housing projects, measures to attract foreign private investment—all are predictably unpopular, yet often necessary. Argentina under Perón and since his ouster offers what may be the most striking illustration of irresponsible public pressure on and participation in national policy: a once booming and relatively highly developed economy has stagnated. Partly for this reason, many leaders in the developing countries regard democratic rights and processes as luxuries their countries cannot yet afford.

The aspects of political development that most Americans would view as central—increased equity and broadened participation in governmental decision making—thus turn out to be the aspects that relate somewhat ambiguously to economic growth. Other aspects of political development—administrative competence, national integration, and fundamental civil liberties—while more clearly compatible with or essential for economic progress—tend to appear less important to Americans. This may be because we take for granted a relatively high degree of efficiency, unity, and civil liberty, and fail to recognize that absence of these qualities may make a political system as inadequate as marked inequity or restricted participation.

THE PATTERN OF A.I.D. POLITICAL DEVELOPMENT EFFORTS

The pattern of U.S. political development efforts can be explained partly in terms of the relations between different aspects of political development and economic growth. A second major factor is the degree of host country sensitivity associated with each facet of political development. To pursue those aspects which clearly promote economic growth and are in principle acceptable to the developing countries themselves creates no conflict of objectives and little diplomatic risk for the United States. Other aspects of political development involve more complicated diplomatic and technical considerations.

Because administrative competence and ability to maintain civil peace are prerequisites for economic growth and the developing countries themselves are eager to develop such competence, AID provides public administration training and advisors in most of its country programs. Sometimes leverage has been used to press for key administrative reforms. Aid to increase administrative competence is noncontroversial, and the problems of morality and risk discussed later in this chapter do not really apply to it. However, efforts to improve administrative capacity may often have been too narrowly conceived. For example, only recently has AID begun a few experimental projects to give lawyers a broader grasp of development problems, so that they will use their immense influence in drafting and interpreting laws and regulations to promote growth.

AID programs have deliberately attacked the problem of national integration in a few countries where particular isolated and disaffected regions appear to post an immediate threat of extremism and insurgency—Northeast Thailand, Northeast Brazil, the Peruvian high plateau. Where the problem does not appear as pressing, there has been little deliberate effort to consider ways to promote integration. Transportation projects—for example, roads in Bolivia, and airfields, roads, and bridges in Ethiopia—probably contribute to political integration as well as to economic progress, but the long run political contribution of the projects has usually been a secondary and almost always a nonoperational consideration. That is, it has had no effect on the design of the project. Long before the bloody tribal clashes of 1966, it was clear that national integration is Nigeria's most fundamental problem. Although the U.S. aid program in Nigeria did include large scale educational and agricultural projects in the North to help to narrow the disparity between that region and the more advanced South, such efforts were a minor theme in the overall aid effort. This is not to suggest that AID or any external action could have prevented the eruption of tribal hostilities, but merely to comment on failure to consider adequately a problem of the greatest importance.

Partly because increased equity coincides with many aspects of economic growth, it is tempting to list many of AID's activities as contributing to that goal. Expanded education and health services in poorer urban neighborhoods and rural areas, low cost housing projects, potable water and sewerage projects all improve the services and facilities available to less privileged groups. Stricter tax collection, revised tax structure, and land reform play directly on the distribution of income and wealth. Technical and capital assistance for cooperatives, labor unions, and credit associations may increase the economic and political power of previously unorganized and ineffective groups.

However, AID, like the developing countries themselves, must constantly seek a balance between efforts to increase immediately the income, services, and opportunities of the least privileged, and measures which will best accelerate growth. For example, there have been ardent disputes within AID over whether to concentrate agricultural assistance in particular countries on more "modern" (cash, sometimes export) crops or types of farms or regions producing such crops, or alternatively to focus on the much larger group of "traditional" farmers who are more difficult to reach and more resistant to change, but whose needs are far greater.

AID has done little to foster civil liberties. This may reflect the dual judgment that intervention in this sphere is likely to be resented, and that improved observance of such liberties is not of first importance for economic growth. Police training in many countries does stress respect for civil liberties, although police made more efficient through U.S. training and equipment may be and have sometimes been used to support repressive regimes.

Improved legal education and better organization and availability of legal reference material may promote this aspect of political development, as well as help lawyers to contribute more effectively to economic growth and administrative efficacy. AID is currently assisting legal education in Tanzania, Ethiopia, Brazil, and Central America.

The United States makes a greater effort to contribute, directly or indirectly, to development of democratic institutions and to broader and more responsible public participation in governmental decision making. Most of the activities clearly addressed to this goal take the form of attempts to broaden the understanding and influence the attitudes of key groups. The most obvious examples are the labor leadership training programs conducted in Latin America through the AFL-CIO-sponsored American Institute for Free Labor Development, and similar programs in several countries in Africa and Asia. These combine training union leaders for effective union organization and operation—such as instruction in administration, accounting, and arbitration skills—with political indoctrination, which varies from country to country in intensity and approach. One reason for the large number of labor training programs is strong support from U.S. unions which, concerned over leftist influence in union movements abroad, have contributed their own funds and urged broader U.S. Government programs to combat such trends.[2]

Aside from the labor leadership programs, efforts to influence key groups' attitudes are rather scattered. Small groups of political leaders have been brought for observation tours of U.S. political institutions. For example, five high ranking Kenyan political leaders were brought to the United States in August and September 1964; they observed the Democratic National Convention, took a course on American Government at Syracuse University, and toured polling places in Vermont during primary elections.[3] Groups of young Central American leaders from various fields —teaching, labor, business, administration, and politics—are invited to a continuing series of seminars offered by Loyola University, which feature no-holds-barred discussions of problems of development, including political development. The League of

2. See series of articles in the *Washington Post* on "Labor's Cold Warrior," starting December 30, 1965.
3. *Free Press*, Burlington, Vermont, September 9, 1964.

Women Voters, with AID support, annually selects and trains a small number of Latin American women in techniques of organizing civic groups. In Colombia in summer 1965, the U.S. Ambassador and the AID Mission Director brought together 35 leading Colombians from business, government, education, and journalism to discuss problems of agricultural development and land reform at a three day retreat. Many training programs financed from military assistance often include formal or informal discussion of the appropriate role of the military in political affairs.

Some short term actions, such as withholding aid to demonstrate disapproval of a coup or helping to insure that elections are held in an orderly atmosphere, are expected not only to gain their immediate goals but also to contribute to long run respect for and faith in democratic processes. For example, the successful elections and transfer of power in Venezuela in 1963, to which AID assistance made a modest contribution, probably greatly strengthened Venezuelan confidence in democracy, and may have heartened democratic forces in other Latin American countries.

The promotion of cooperatives, credit unions, peasant federations, and a variety of other associations is a less direct way of strengthening democratic processes. The primary motive for assisting such groups usually is to encourage more active and effective participation in economic activity. Farmers' cooperatives make it possible to obtain credit, purchase equipment, and market crops on better terms than individual farmers could obtain. Credit unions mobilize middle class savings and investment. The U.S. National Farmers' Union, with AID financing, has selected and trained several hundred rural leaders from several Latin American countries. AID planners hope and expect that in addition to promoting economic growth, such organizations and individuals, by providing leadership and experience in making group decisions, will create capacity for responsible participation in broader public policy realms.

AID also provides extensive assistance for education. Most AID officials believe that better education for more of the population eventually will lead to broader and more responsible participation in public policy formulation. However, the education programs are designed primarily to serve economic and manpower requirements. The expected contribution to political development is a by-product. While AID provides extensive technical assistance and finances buildings and equipment for university departments directly related to economic growth—engineering, agriculture, veterinary medicine, education, economics, business administration, even home economics—little effort has been made to improve the quality of the noneconomic social sciences and law faculties. Yet both political science and law are recruiting grounds for politics and the civil service. Similarly, at the secondary level, AID has stressed mathematics and science as essential background for training in technical and engineering skills. Civics, history, and social science in general have had low priority.

AID planners might thus identify an impressive number and variety of specific activities as contributing to one or more political development objectives. The goals of increased administrative competence, greater equity, and broadened political participation in particular seem well addressed. Yet this impression is misleading. The effectiveness of aid efforts depends not only on the number and variety of projects addressed to a problem, but also on their coherence and relevance. In most of its fields of activity, AID does attempt (albeit inadequately) to assess the nature of the problem and to tailor the pattern of activities to individual country circumstances. But AID political development efforts rarely are based on such analysis, nor do they form coherent, planned programs. When political considerations are seriously analyzed, it is usually in terms of barriers to economic progress. With few exceptions, AID does not attempt to establish operational political development objectives and to devise an integrated strategy for achieving them. AID political development efforts therefore are collections of disparate activities, mostly selected and designed with economic and technical criteria in mind. If they form a pattern with respect to political development at all, it is largely by accident.

Nor does AID seek to anticipate the effect upon political evolution of programs undertaken for economic reasons. Yet such effects may be as or more important than the impact of explicit political development efforts. For example, the network of roads financed by U.S. aid in Turkey in the 1950s, though motivated by economic objectives, almost certainly has contributed powerfully to the political activation of Turkish villagers throughout the nation, and thereby to far reaching changes in politics and the party system.

U.S. aid programs to Latin America may have a more pronounced political development dimension than programs elsewhere. This is partly due to the political and social goals of the Alliance for Progress and partly because of a retrospective analysis of what went wrong in Cuba. The Charter of Punta del Este provides a multilateral framework for U.S. aid planning with each Latin American country and records a consensus on broad goals, including political development goals. This consensus has some effect even on those governments which are not enthusiastic about the values of the Charter. Experience in Cuba is widely held to be a lesson that economic growth is not enough.

In short, with the partial exception of Latin American programs, AID acts as if it believed that if it takes care of economic development, political development will take care of itself.

There are several reasons for this economic outlook. First, most AID officials (and many State Department officers) believe that efforts to affect political developments are diplomatically risky. Not only may such efforts jeopardize U.S. relations with the country, but may defeat their purpose by compromising the groups or institutions we seek to support. Moreover, political development efforts that backfire might undermine U.S. ability to encourage better economic policies.

Second, most AID officials are skeptical about the efficacy of deliberate efforts, direct or indirect, to shape political evolution. Political development is at least as complex as economic development, but theory about political development is embryonic. Despite the inadequacies of current theory regarding economic development, far more is known than on the political side. Data on political attitudes, values, and patterns of behavior, and how these are related to economic and social variables which AID activities might affect, are also extremely sparse.

Moreover, AID's potential influence in the realm of political development is limited. We have seen that influence and occasional leverage are tools for promoting economic growth as powerful as direct contributions of skills and capital. But governments are likely to be much less receptive to advice and pressure regarding national integration, the extent and nature of popular participation, the role of interest groups, and the like, than to foreigners' suggestions regarding import control systems or power rates. While even fairly narrow economic policies may have important political repercussions, they appear to be more technical and neutral, hence more appropriate subjects for external intervention. In view of inadequate theory and data and constraints on influence, many Administration officials conclude that they should concentrate their efforts on the task they feel better equipped to handle—economic growth.

A third reason for reluctance to become involved in political development efforts is probably doubt regarding the morality of deliberate efforts to influence another country's political evolution. Moreover, many foreign aid officials probably view with distaste direct or indirect involvement with politics or politicians. AID staff are primarily technicians, with a sprinkling of economists and programmers. Both the scope of their work and their professional temperament tend to limit their contacts to host country executive agencies. There is more than a touch of the technocratic outlook that politics is an unfortunate and perhaps even unnecessary hindrance to the constructive work of development.

These arguments carry some weight, but do not make a persuasive case against any and all deliberate attempts to promote political development. To argue that it is immoral to attempt to influence another country's political evolution is to set up a false dilemma. In any sizable and continuing program, the United States cannot choose *not* to exert political influence. Regardless of U.S. intent, the volume, content, and administration of U.S. aid will in some measure fortify or undermine the distribution of political power and affect the content of political pressures and the extent of political participation. Deliberate intervention, therefore, is not an alternative to no intervention; it is an alternative to inadvertent intervention, which may be adverse.

The traditional American antipathy to intervention is often linked to a different point: that to impose U.S. or Western European institutions and procedures on developing countries is neither feasible nor desirable. Those who advocate stronger political development efforts usually are well aware of the need to adapt Western forms and to develop essentially new institutions in response to different national circumstances and political cultures. They do not have in mind carbon copies of U.S. or British institutions. But as noted earlier, many political development advocates do emphasize certain aspects, particularly equity and broadened political participation, more than other aspects, including national integration, administrative capacity, and development of civil liberties. These priorities may be quite appropriate in some of the developing countries. In others basic administrative competence and capacity to maintain civil peace, or national integration, or some other aspect of political development may take priority. Any direct or indirect promotion of political development should be based on a far more careful assessment than the U.S. Government now attempts of individual countries' political development trends, prospects, and priorities.

Assuming such analysis were available, what are the chances that foreign aid could really influence political development? No one really knows what might be accomplished, because no serious effort has yet been made. It is clear that the two major impediments are our own ignorance and host country sensitivity. Our ignorance argues for a cautious and experimental approach, rather than for bold departures. Diplomatic prudence points in the same direction. Regarding risk, however, it should be noted that political development activities do not have to be identified as such. Moreover, not all aspects of political development are particularly sensitive in every country. When U.S. goals coincide with the host government's and the topic is not extremely touchy, fairly open consultation and cooperation may be possible. For example, there may be mutual interest in strengthening local government institutions or promoting regional integration. Finally, if an objective is important, it is probably worth some risk. The United States has been increasingly willing to intervene in delicate economic decisions, such as devaluation, when it believes there is a reasonable chance of influencing host government action.

Much of this growing interest in political development crystallized in a new section in the Foreign Assistance Act of 1966. The House Foreign Affairs Committee report on the 1966 bill stated:

There is a close relationship between popular participation in the process of development and the effectiveness of this process. . . . Failure to engage all of the available human resources in the task of development not only acts as a brake on economic growth but also does little to cure the basic causes of social and political instability which pose a constant threat to the gains being achieved on economic fronts.[4]

Therefore, the Committee proposed and the House and Senate subsequently approved a new Title IX for the Act, entitled "Uti-

4. 89th Congress, 2d session, House Report No. 1651, June 23, 1966.

lization of Democratic Institutions in Development." The Title reads:

> In carrying out the programs authorized . . . emphasis shall be placed on assuring maximum participation in the task of development on the part of the people of the developing countries, through the encouragement of democratic private and local governmental institutions.

What is needed is the introduction of a serious political development dimension as an integral part of the programming process. This does not mean giving special priority to political development objectives, or necessarily including in each program some activities designed primarily to influence political development. It does call for explicit consideration of political development objectives and comparison of their priority with that of other goals, in the context of individual country circumstances and the nature of U.S. interests in the country. A political development dimension to aid programming also requires a continuing assessment of the ways in which the aid program as a whole, including aspects designed primarily to promote economic growth, may be affecting the aided country's long run political evolution. At a minimum, such an assessment should reduce unanticipated adverse effects, and suggest ways to increase the political development by-products of primarily economic programs. Different country programs would vary in the extent to which they incorporated additional elements designed with political development objectives primarily in mind. The degree of emphasis on political development in individual programs would reflect the relative priority of political development goals, the extent to which they appear to conflict with or complement other goals such as rapid economic growth or short run stability, and the likelihood that U.S. efforts to promote political development can be effective. Relying on the indirect approach, rather than attempting to influence specifically political institutions and processes, will reduce immediate diplomatic risk but will not automatically guarantee that actions best designed to promote political development will coincide with optimal economic policy. Under some circumstances, long run political gains may be worth some retardation of economic growth or some degree of short run instability; in other cases economic growth or stability may be more important, or the possibility of effective U.S. action in the political development realm may be too remote to warrant detracting from other goals.

Just as we have had to learn that promoting self-sustaining growth in the less developed world is a much more complex and long run task than restoring war torn Europe, so we have had to learn that the connection between economic progress and democratic political trends is much more tenuous in Asia, Africa, and Latin America than in Western Europe. We have barely begun to explore the extent and ways in which economic assistance, along with other instruments of foreign policy, may be used to promote political development. As analysis gets under way and specific lines of action are proposed, the principles derived from experience in using aid to encourage better economic policies may prove a useful guide. The most successful attempts to encourage economic reforms were based on extensive and detailed analysis of the specific problems to be addressed, often conducted over a period of several years. The reforms were also preceded by full and open consultation with the host government. In some cases the final impetus to reform depended partly on U.S. willingness to risk some diplomatic strain and some sacrifice of other goals. Although U.S. efforts to promote political development are likely to be less direct, the same broad principles are relevant.

Similarly, the factors constraining aid's effectiveness in encouraging economic reform will also limit the impact of political development efforts—concern that pressure for reform may jeopardize other high priority U.S. objectives, inadequate understanding of the development process and the measures needed for particular kinds of progress, and political or administrative weakness on the part of the host government. In both the economic and political realms, the less secure and capable the regime, the poorer the prospects of adopting and implementing reforms. Those countries most in need of reform are least capable of responding to outside persuasion and support and are often the most sensitive and resistant to foreign influence. Aid cannot determine the course of a country's economic or political destiny. But in both realms, donors can stimulate fresh perspectives in countries open to suggestions and ideas, reinforce progressive forces, and reduce the internal costs and risks of reform. This is a marginal contribution, but it is often important and sometimes crucial.

The United States and Latin America

J. P. MORRAY

J. P. Morray is presently Professor of Sociology at the University of Chile. Previously he was a Visiting Professor of Law at the University of California at Berkeley. He is the author of From Yalta to Disarmament *and* The Second Revolution in Cuba. *This article was taken from* Latin America: Reform or Revolution?, *Fawcett, 1968.*

DESPITE demonstrated feelings of impatience, condescension, and exasperation on one side and feelings of humiliation, resentment, and indignation on the other, we have what is called the Alliance for Progress. Why? The answer requires us to examine briefly the state of affairs in Latin America and the nature of the Alliance.

Concrete analysis of one country will give us clues to what has been happening in all. Let us take the largest of the Latin American countries, Brazil, with a population of 80 million people and a territory roughly equal to that of the United States. Before approximately 1930 Brazil's economy had developed as a colonial appendix to that of the United States and Europe. Agricultural products, especially coffee, sugar, cacao, and cotton, were cultivated and harvested for export to the European and North American markets. Capital for these enterprises came mainly from the *fazendeiros*, Brazilian owners of great rural estates, and from absentee investors who were nationals of the purchasing countries. Heavy industry did not exist in Brazil, and even light industry was insignificant. Most manufactured goods had to be imported from abroad at high prices, another source of profits and additional capital accumulation for the metropolitan countries. Brazil hardly existed as a unified nation. It was a group of agricultural regions isolated from each other, some serving the needs of foreign buyers and investors, some producing with primitive techniques for local and regional consumption. Government was dominated by the *fazendeiros* and especially by the great coffee planters of São Paulo and Minas Gerais, who were closely affiliated with foreign capital. Both federal and state governments depended on loans from foreign banks and investors. Commerce in imports and exports, electric power, the telephone monopolies, railways, shipping, urban transport, insurance, and the larger banks were in the hands of foreigners. Brazil was integrated financially and economically into the world capitalist economy as a semicolony.[1]

The worldwide crisis of the European and United States economies in 1929 and the 1930s inflicted such prolonged hardships on the Brazilians that new initiatives were begun, both economic and political, to repair the damage and give Brazil a new independence. The coffee and sugar barons, principal Brazilian beneficiaries of the colonial system, were driven from power in the federal government by a liberal Revolution headed by Getulio Vargas. A "Liberal Alliance" led by landowners and ranchers of Río Grande del Sur as well as landowners and bourgeoisie of other less important states took over the direction of affairs. The petty bourgeoisie of the cities gave support. For the first time in Brazilian history the masses, including industrial workers in the cities and in some of the rural areas, began to take part in political life. Young officers took over the direction of the army and converted it into an instrument of revolution in support of the Liberal Alliance led by the national bourgeoisie. Economic policy of the new leadership accorded with its class interests. It was capitalist, protectionist, and antiimperialist.

In the decades since 1930, Brazilian society has developed within the context of this struggle of a renovating alliance led by the national bourgeoisie against the coffee-sugar plantation owners, traditional Brazilian allies of foreign capitalists. Population has grown rapidly, and this growth has been accompanied by a great migration of persons born in the rural areas to the mushrooming cities. By 1965, one-half the population lived in cities, compared with 20 percent in 1930. Some heavy industry has been created, and light industry has grown within a protected market. The industrial working class, which has grown into a force of 2.5 million persons concentrated in a few cities, is now a political factor of major weight, as are the other five million

1. See the essay by Luis V. Sommi, which appears as a prologue to Franklin de Oliveira, *Revolución y Contrarevolución en el Brasil* (Buenos Aires: Ediciones Iguazu, 1965). (Translation from Portuguese into Spanish by Luis V. Sommi.)

Brazilians who work for wages. This is a change of historic importance. The petty bourgeoisie of the cities has also increased greatly in numbers.

The rural population, despite the migration to the cities, has grown in absolute numbers from 25 million in 1930 to 42 million in 1965. The continuing supply of surplus labor in the countryside has retarded modernization in agriculture, since manpower is still cheaper than machinery. Conditions of poverty and privation in the rural areas are the principal determining factors in the migration to the cities. In the latter, unemployment and underemployment are high, and life in the slum areas wretched but nevertheless not so hopeless as life in the countryside. This lesser evil of escape to the cities has also served as a kind of protection to the archaic and stagnated system of land tenure, since it removes some of the most desperate from the struggle between landlord and landless *campesino*.

Throughout this period the national bourgeoisie has continued to lead the major political parties, who compete with each other to enlist the support of the petty bourgeoisie and wage workers. As a stimulus to the development, some of these leaders advocated a resort to state capitalism, with the government playing a leading role in accumulating capital for investment in basic industries through taxation and borrowing on government credit. Others favored reliance on private enterprise, assisted by government policies favoring the private investor. Economists argued the convenience of agrarian reform to capitalist development to widen the internal market for manufactured products. Almost all political leaders gave this at least verbal support; those with social democratic tendencies, such as João Goulart, actually tried to persuade Congress to enact an agrarian reform. But the leadership of the parties includes many landowners and ranchers who would be hurt by land redistribution. They are able to weaken worker support for the reform with predictions of food scarcities and higher prices in the cities. The issue became more urgent and ominous in 1958 with the appearance of armed peasant leagues in northeastern Brazil, led by the lawyer Francisco Julião. These spread south into Minas Gerais, stronghold of an oligarchy of great landowners, hitherto impregnable. A national congress of more than 1,000 peasant leaders in Belo Horizonte in 1961 showed the impressive political strength of the new movement. Agrarian reform had passed from the realm of abstract discussion by experts to become an important factor in the struggles of the Brazilian masses.[2]

The rise of social tensions in the countryside was matched by growing strife in the cities and widespread discontent with the slow pace of development in the industrial sector. Brazil's bourgeoisie blend of free enterprise and state capitalism has not been meeting the needs of a rapidly growing population with rising aspirations and consciousness of revolutionary examples in other countries. This generalized and deepening impatience among the poor Brazilian masses, added to the antagonism between the growing working class and the owners of industry, threatens to bring on a struggle for a social revolution that would liquidate the bourgeois order and establish a working class dictatorship committed to the building of socialism. This is the goal of many leaders of the powerful labor organization, Workers' General Command (CGT). The Communist Party thinks that this is premature and has advocated instead a longer period of capitalist development under the leadership of the nationalist and anti-imperialist bourgeoisie. But the Communist Party finds itself pressed forward by excited masses, who are constantly inflamed by non-Party Marxists, Fidelistas, Pekinistas, Trotskyists, and petty bourgeois radicals. The objective situation, a "hidden civil war," as Franklin de Oliveria calls it, in which poverty kills millions before they reach the age of thirty, cries out for drastic remedy, and any vanguard party that counsels caution and delay finds itself on the defensive.

The bourgeois directorate of the faltering state was and is divided on what to do to save the social order from the threatening storm. Juscelino Kubitshek, President from 1956 to 1960, arrived at the conclusion that Brazil had to have outside help if disaster was to be averted. His *Operation Pan America* proposals, in which United States aid was entreated, set the stage for the new and noisy entry of the United States Government into Latin America with the Alliance for Progress. The plight of the Brazilian bourgeoisie is repeated in the other Latin American countries. It is unable with its own resources and techniques to produce a rate of development satisfying to the awakened masses.

2. Ruy Mauro Marini, "Contradicciones y Conflictos en el Brasil Contemporáneo," *Arauco*, Santiago de Chile, October 1966, p. 20.

It cannot force this rate under capitalist relations without exacerbating its difficult contradiction with the working class. And to seek help from the wealthy capitalist countries means a loss of economic independence to imperialism. No wonder spokesmen for the national bourgeoisie of these countries are divided and vacillating. Some, like Victor Haya de la Torre in Peru, have concluded that imperialism is the best form of development in the underdeveloped countries. He proclaims that "imperialism is necessary for Latin America's development."[3] President José María Velasco Ibarra of Ecuador came to a similar conclusion for his country. "Ecuador has no native capital," he said. "Only foreign investments will bring in such capital, needed to develop the country."[4] President Frei in Chile, though he does not state his position so plainly, expresses a similar opinion through his policies. So did Rómulo Betancourt in Venezuela.

But other representatives of the national bourgeoisie resist this turning to an old enemy for a dangerous kind of help. In Brazil, Janio Quadros and João Goulart shrugged off United States aid and tried to strengthen the state sector in the Brazilian economy. They were willing to accept help from the socialist countries in the fight to strengthen independence from imperialist domination. But they encountered powerful opposition from their own class in Brazil, as well as from a United States Government embarked on a vigorous new offensive, which we are about to examine; and they were handicapped by their own vacillations. Goulart won a great popular victory in a plebiscite in 1963, but this only fed the flames of social conflict. During the following months he lost support among the bourgeoisie and the petty bourgeoisie as his ability to contain the radical masses of workers and peasants became more doubtful.

The overthrow of Goulart in 1964 by the high command of the Army and a section of Congress was carried out with United States support as a necessary clearing of the ground for implementing the Alliance for Progress. Washington quickly recognized the new regime and the United States Ambassador in Brazil, Lincoln Gordon, publicized his satisfaction with the change of direction and command. Evidently the "Alliance" is open only to certain kinds of leaders and aims to promote only

3. John Gerassi, *The Great Fear* (New York: Macmillan, 1963), p. 122.
4. *Ibid.*, p. 127.

certain kinds of "Progress." The Alliance is discriminating and selective; it is not indifferent to the contests for power inside each Latin American country, not even the contests between competing bourgeois factions. The era of the Good Neighbor, during which the United States Government formally renounced the practice of intervention, is dead. Why this is a necessary corollary to the Alliance becomes evident from its character and content.

Getting to the heart of the Alliance is made somewhat difficult by the fanfare of verbiage that announced its birth. Speeches of the Latin American delegates to the Conference at Bogotá, Colombia, in 1960, and at Punta del Este, Uruguay, in 1961, reflected the reformist position, more or less demagogic, of many of these leaders in their internal struggles with an oligarchy that had always enjoyed imperialist support. There was repeated insistence on the need for land reform, for social progress, for raising rapidly the income and standard of living of the needier sections of the population, for a more equitable distribution of national income, and for industrialization. Special emphasis was placed on the development of capital goods industries to liberate the Latin American countries from their colonialist dependence on export of a limited number of primary products and importation of capital goods from the United States and Western Europe. The United States consented to the inclusion of these goals in the Charters of verbal commitments prepared at the conferences. The Punta del Este Charter even speaks of "taking full advantage of both private and public sectors . . . in the development of capital goods industries." [5]

But the United States delegates insisted on the inclusion of other phrases as well, for example, a clause in the Punta del Este Charter that commits the signatories to the promotion "of conditions that will encourage the flow of foreign investments." [6] Though these brief words are inconspicuous in the Charter as a whole, they are, from the point of view of Washington, the main

5. The Charter of Punta del Este Establishing an Alliance for Progress Within the Framework of Operation Pan America, Title I, Paragraph 4 (August 17, 1961). The Charter as well as other important reference material are reprinted in *Regional and Other Documents Concerning United States Relations With Latin America,* compiled by the House Committee on Foreign Affairs (Washington: U.S. Government Printing Office, 1966).
6. *Ibid.* Title II, Chapter II, Paragraph 2 (f).

purpose of the Alliance. To this must be added, as we shall see in the implementation of the Alliance by Congress, another purpose nowhere explicitly stated: the promotion of United States exports to Latin America by means of loans to purchasers and insurance against credit risks. Many have thought the Alliance represents an undertaking by the United States to finance the economic development plans of independent Latin American countries. In truth, it represents something quite different—the use of United States public funds in the battle to reopen Latin America to United States investors.

The task of checking the development of independent economies and reintegrating Latin America into the international capitalist system has many facets. Some of these lend themselves to ambiguous interpretations. For example, the initial emphasis on public health projects, on the elimination of malaria and the provision of potable water, on the construction of schools and the reduction of illiteracy drew favorable attention. Such laudable projects were not unrelated to a veiled strategic purpose. They were felt to be indispensable to the generation of a measure of hope in the restive masses, to the immediate reduction of explosive social tensions in the years of the portentous Cuban Revolution, which Washington read as a warning of what might occur throughout Latin America. They were measures designed to buy time and to revive faith in the potential of the existing bourgeois social order to meet the problems of the hemisphere. It was not necessary to agree on the role of imperialism in future development in order to agree on the necessity for such emergency steps. Likewise, all could agree on the importance of promoting the development of such infrastructure projects as road and bridge building and electrification and improvement of ports, harbors, and docks. In the eyes of the national bourgeoisie these improvements facilitate the development of an independent economy. In the eyes of U.S. officials they also enhance the prospects of profitable investments for themselves. The specification of who is to benefit most from these infrastructure expenditures depends on whether the other conditions of security and confidence are created for the foreign investor.

These other conditions are all related to the possibility of receiving high profits and remitting them more or less freely to the United States. And it is in the disputes between Washington and

Latin America over the creation of these conditions that the true character of the Alliance begins to appear. One of these conditions is security against expropriation. The right of a poor country to expropriate does not exist if it is conditioned on an obligation to pay full compensation promptly. Congress is using the offer of Alliance funds to purchase a renunciation by the Latin American countries of an effective right to expropriate the property of United States citizens. The Foreign Assistance Act, which fixes the conditions on the expenditure of Congressional appropriations of aid funds, prohibits their use to benefit a state that fails to make "speedy compensation . . . in convertible foreign exchange . . . to the full value" of any property expropriated from United States citizens.[7] U.S. aid funds may not be used to make the compensation.[8] This 1963 amendment to the original act proved to be an effective weapon in the hands of the United States Ambassador in Brazil. When the governor of Rio Grande del Sur, Leonel Brizola, carried out an expropriation of properties belonging to a United States telephone company, he received the support of President Goulart. But this blow at U.S. private investment divided the Brazilian bourgeoisie and the Brazilian Army, because it raised the threat of an end to all aid—economic, social, and military—from the United States. Ambassador Gordon, by bringing this clause to the attention of Brazilian generals and politicians, contributed to the plotting that forged the 1964 coup. It was an argument that united the oligarchy and the free enterprise bourgeoisie against the more radical champions of development along state-capitalist lines. The latter were prepared to accept the loss of U.S. aid and to turn to the Soviet Union for credits. This would be accompanied by a change in foreign policy toward independence and neutrality in the cold war between the United States and the U.S.S.R. To foreclose such a line of development is one of the purposes of the Alliance.

The investment-guarantee program also indicates Washington's intentions concerning the hemisphere. It insures United States investors in Latin America against loss of their investment due to

7. The Foreign Assistance Act of 1961, as amended, Section 620 (e) (1), *Regional and Other Documents Concerning United States Relations with Latin America,* House Committee on Foreign Affairs (Washington: U.S. Government Printing Office, 1966), p. 143.

8. *Ibid.* Section 620 (g).

war, revolution, insurrection, or expropriation. It also insures them against the inability to convert their profits into United States dollars.[9] The political climate in Latin America has been changing over the past few decades in a direction unfavorable to U.S. economic and political domination. Many parties are openly hostile to it and others have become indifferent to the effects of their policies on the foreign investor. Inflation, exchange controls, discriminatory taxation, expropriations, and insurrections are some of the realities that investors see in Latin America, and they are naturally disheartened. The level of United States investment in Latin America has risen slowly compared to its rise in such safer regions as Canada and Western Europe.[10] The Cuban Revolution dealt another blow to the confidence of investors in Latin America.[11] It was a situation that no single investor or investor group could resolve with its own resources. Yet the reluctance of investors to go into Latin America threatened the U.S. with the loss of the whole area by default. The Latin American governments seemed unable to prevent it.

9. *Ibid.* Section 221 (b) (1), Department of State, *American Foreign Policy: Current Documents 1961* (Washington: U.S. Government Printing Office, 1965), p. 1273.

10. Between 1950 and 1960 the value of United States direct investments in the Latin American Republics doubled (from $4.4 billion to $8.4 billion). During the same period their value in Canada tripled (from $3.6 billion to $11.2 billion), and their value in Europe quadrupled (from $1.7 billion to $6.6 billion). U.S. Department of Commerce, *Balance of Payments: Statistical Supplement, Revised Edition* (Washington, U.S. Government Printing Office, 1963), Table 57, pp. 208–9. The lagging rate of private investment in Latin America was the subject of Hearings held by a Subcommittee of the Joint Economic Committee of Congress on January 14, 15, and 16, 1964. The Subcommittee opened its report on the Hearings with the following statement: "North Americans (and Western Europeans, as well) who live under and enjoy the benefits of a predominantly free-enterprise, private-investment market system of economic organization are increasingly concerned about the lagging rate of private investment in the Latin American development program. They are concerned also with the attitude of seeming indifference in many parts of Latin America itself to the potential contributions of the private sector. This local apathy is manifest in a concentration of energies on governmental development programs, the reported exodus of domestic capital, the flight from local currencies, and the persistent discouragements which private, and especially foreign private, capital seemingly must face." *Private Investment in Latin America,* a Report of the Subcommittee on Inter-American Economic Relationships of the Joint Economic Committee (Washington: U.S. Government Printing Office, 1964), p. 1.

11. This factor is analyzed in Leland L. Johnson, *The Course of U.S. Private Investment in Latin America Since the Rise of Castro* (Santa Monica, California, The Rand Corporation RM-4091-ISA, 1964).

But there was one government to which the investors could turn for help. Through the investment guarantee program the extraordinary risks in the area are shifted to the U.S. Government, and investors can discount them in weighing their decisions. Furthermore, the insured investor and the Latin American governments both know that the relationship between them is altered by the investment guarantee of the United States Government. The investor enjoys the engaged solicitude of a powerful champion in any dispute that arises with the local government. Like other insurers, the United States Government, after making good the losses of its aggrieved investors, takes over their claims against the Latin American governments. The United States increases the pressure on the host country by insisting in advance on a recognition of this "subrogation," or substitution of government for investor in case of loss through expropriation or inconvertibility.[12] When Congress was informed of the resistance of Latin American governments to this substitution, it added an amendment cutting off aid to any country that had not given its formal consent prior to December 31, 1966.[13] This was an effective threat, and investment guarantee agreements have now been signed by nearly all.[14] Having improved the climate to this extent, the investors are now asking that the coverage be broadened to include the risks of damage by rioting and demonstrations of the kind that destroyed Sears Roebuck stores in Caracas, Venezuela, and Cali, Colombia, and seriously damaged properties of Pan-American Airways, Braniff-International, and the Goodyear Tire and Rubber Company in Panama.[15]

Washington has other levers for use in the effort to accelerate the rate of private American investment. A major factor in the

12. "Since these guarantees involve commitments on the part of the capital-importing as well as the capital-exporting government, an important part of their function goes beyond that of mere indemnification. They are intended also to prevent or discourage changes in the legal conditions under which an enterprise must operate in the host, capital-importing country." *Private Investment in Latin America*, A Report of the Subcommittee on Inter-American Economic Relationships of the Joint Economic Committee (Washington, U.S. Governmental Printing Office, 1964), p. 15.
13. The Foreign Assistance Act of 1961, as amended, Section 620 (1).
14. *Regional and Other Documents Concerning United States Relations with Latin America* (1966), pp. 259–330.
15. Testimony of N. R. Danielian, President, International Economic Policy Association, in Hearings on *Foreign Assistance Act of 1966* before the House Committee on Foreign Affairs, March 16 to May 17, 1966 (Washington: U.S. Government Printing Office, 1966), p. 861.

investment climate is the ease of converting profits into dollars, and this is affected by the amount of foreign exchange a government commands. Hence, it is an important Alliance goal in the view of the United States Government to press the Latin Americans into measures that will permanently improve their ability to accumulate reserves of foreign exchange. Pressure is applied through the device of the "program loan." The loan is not credited all at once but in periodic increments; it will be suspended if the local government is not acting to improve its foreign exchange position as required.[16] The United States can also apply pressure in the same direction through the International Monetary Fund, which was created to promote the freer convertibility required by international capitalism.

In some countries, such as Chile, governments are advised to reduce food imports by raising the selling price to consumers. This is supposed to stimulate the local farmers into increasing production as imports are reduced step by step. In all countries the United States presses for changes that would help raise the level of exports. This involves essentially an effort to lower costs of production through fiscal, credit, and monetary policies that will increase unemployment and keep wages down. There are also efforts to persuade the Latin Americans to devalue their currencies on the ground that they can sell their products at lower prices in foreign markets with a net increase in foreign exchange earnings due to increased volume of sales. But one consequence of devaluing a currency is an increase in the cost of living, since the cost in local currency of imports increases. Therefore, U.S. policies for Latin America imply lower real wages for working people and higher living costs. These are bitter issues in the daily struggle between workers and employers. Development policies designed to secure foreign investment exacerbate social tensions.[17] This contradiction between the proclaimed goals of

16. *United States Foreign Aid in Action: A Case Study,* submitted by Senator Ernest Gruening to the Subcommittee on Foreign Aid Expenditures of the Senate Committee on Government Operations (June 28, 1966), p. 30.

17. Arthur Schlesinger, Jr., blamed these policies for the crisis in the Dominican Republic that led to United States intervention in 1965. He wrote in *A Thousand Days* (Boston: Houghton Mifflin Company, 1965; Fawcett Crest paperback, 1967): "Undeterred by past error, the International Monetary Fund in 1964–65 persuaded a complaisant government in the Dominican Republic to accept a fiscal program that reduced per capita income, increased unemployment, and led in the spring of 1965 to political convulsion and United States intervention," p. 174.

social progress and economic development is one of the principal reasons for the failure of the Alliance to achieve the results hoped for. It also explains why implementation of the Alliance has been accompanied by a decline in democratic liberties and a turn to dictatorship and repression in so many countries. Force is needed to create an appearance of the peace and stability important to investors. They must feel that the local authorities have the situation securely in hand.

Aid Relationship for the Seventies—
A Comment on the Report of the
Commission on International Development

I. G. PATEL

I. G. Patel, previously economic advisor to the Ministry of Finance, is currently Secretary of Finance, Government of India. This paper was presented at the Columbia University Conference on International Economic Development, February 1970, organized by Barbara Ward.

I. THE SETTING [1]

1. The Pearson Commission was born out of a sense of crisis and despair about development assistance. From its modest beginning in the early fifties, foreign aid had increased to substantial proportions by the middle of the Development Decade. For the poorer two-thirds of mankind, the decade and a half before the establishment of the Commission was a period of rapid awakening and sizable progress towards modernization and a sense of national identity and purpose. And yet, the concept of international cooperation for building stable and self-reliant societies began to lose its shine before it had gained any widespread currency. Among donors and recipients alike, there was frequent talk of a crisis of confidence and a feeling of disenchantment with foreign aid. It was against this background that a "grand-assize" of internationally eminent persons was summoned to "meet together, study the consequences of twenty years of development assistance, assess the results, clarify the errors and propose the policies which will work better in the future."

2. The approach of Mr. Pearson and his colleagues to this challenge is essentially to demonstrate that aid in fact has

---

1. The mood reflected here is that of the author in his personal capacity. While valuable comments from Messrs. S. Guhan, M. R. Shroff, C. S. Swaminathan, R. M. Honavar and A. T. Bambawale and Alaknanda Patel have been incorporated, the attempt has been essentially to capture a feeling which is neither necessarily shared nor even sustained.

worked and to prescribe more of the same for the future. With their gaze set firmly toward a better future, the eminent and well-intentioned Commissioners have said all that is desirable in regard to foreign aid. Their Report is a heartwarming document, particularly for the advocates of aid whose passion for perfection and sophistication in making recommendations finds a response in almost every page of the document.

3. But when the initial exhilaration of hearing what one wants to hear is over, one is assailed by doubts. Can it be that the social and political roots of the malaise go much deeper than mere disappointment with the achievements of foreign aid? Is there not a danger here of attempting to cure a mental sickness as if it were a simple case of malnutrition? More often than not, the way out of a psychological malady is to set some ambitions to rest, at least for a while, and to focus instead on a few points of healthy endeavour that the mind can more easily fasten itself to. Equally, it is all too easy to succumb to the romanticism of "crisis of confidence" or "disenchantment" or even to create one out of what may be no more than, say, the temporary juxtaposition of some rather abrasive but powerful personalities in the constellation of aid. The Commissioners, with their vast experience of human affairs, may well be wise in ignoring the seeming psychosis of aid as either transient or grossly exaggerated and in concentrating instead on what is ideally desirable for world development. But it is at least worth trying to be a little more explicit about the reasons for the sense of crisis in aid and inquiring if a somewhat different emphasis from that of the Commission's would not make for a better recipe in the immediate future.

II. THE ROOTS OF THE CRISIS

4. It would be futile to trace the origin of the crisis in aid to a single or simple source if only because the aid giving as well as the aid receiving countries present a wide diversity of attitudes. Indeed, it is the way these differing attitudes acted and reacted on each other that seems to have led to the escalation of estrangement; and the best way to disentangle the story would be to see how the different threads had pulled at each other.

5. Foreign aid appeared for the first time on the world stage in 1948 in the frank guise of an adjunct to the cold war. The sim-

plicity and directness of such an approach to foreign aid, combined with its success in achieving the limited but well-defined objective in Europe, naturally gave it a sanctity which justified wider application. There was at least a pleasing ring to the word "ally," a concreteness in the number of armed divisions created and a satisfaction of one's sense of tough realism in distinguishing between allies and those who refused to stand up and be counted.

6. But such a state of affairs was bound to create its own repercussions. Among the poorer countries, it took the shape of an assertion of nonalignment. Perhaps the more interesting reaction was among the aid giving countries themselves. A hard-headed and frankly political or military approach to aid was bound to stir the liberal conscience. It was some such stirring of the conscience that had prompted President Truman to try to balance the Marshall Plan with the announcement of the Point Four program and support to the Colombo Plan. But for the major part of the fifties, liberalism was in exile except in Canada, and it is not an accident that in the Colombo Plan, Canada was perhaps the only country which looked on aid primarily as a matter of promoting development. The role of other Commonwealth countries in the Colombo Plan was then marginal. France had embarked on its own course of winning friends and influencing people. The U.S. was caught between the cold war philosophy and the nagging of liberals. And the rest were busy rebuilding themselves. The World Bank did its quiet work. But no one thought of identifying it as aid at the time.

7. Into this situation came India's foreign exchange crisis at the beginning of its second Plan and provided a major point of departure in the history of foreign aid. The Pearson Commission rightly emphasizes that the creation of the Aid India Consortium in 1958 marks an important—and indeed the first—landmark in the evolution of a new attitude toward foreign aid. But its claim [2] that it also marked "the development of institutions for mutual cooperation, which now make aid unquestionably more effective than it was when it began" deserves a closer look, as does the precise nature of the change that took place in the attitude toward foreign aid.

---

2. "Partners in Development," p. 128.

8. Certainly, the size of India, its commitment to political democracy, and the value of its example to others prompted a response in many quarters when, after successfully implementing its first Plan, it found itself in a serious foreign exchange crisis. Apart from the creation of the Aid India Consortium, the establishment of the U.S. Development Loan Fund in the latter part of the Eisenhower administration and of the International Development Association were in large part a response to India's needs. For many influential scholars and politicians in the U.S., Canada, Britain, and elsewhere, India became the rallying point for a new concept of foreign aid—an essentially humanitarian transfer of resources from the rich to the poor to achieve internationally the same goals of economic opportunity for all which had become an accepted part of national objectives for many decades in all modern societies. And let it be said without any reservation that the response was unstinting and spontaneous at least in the initial stages (from 1958 to 1964). What was true of India was even more so for several other countries.

9. But the relatively liberal phase in foreign aid which began around 1958 was not free from at least a tinge of cold war politics, and it brought with it its own seeds of contradiction and conflict. A certain distinction between "allies" and "friends," between neighbors and others, between like minded people and the rest remained and colored the assessment of needs as well as performance. The lip service to democratic values wore thin. Across the simmering continents of Asia, Africa, and Latin America with their deep discontents and rising social and economic passions and expectations, revolutionary and even self-destructive situations were bound to arise from time to time, and they made it difficult to strike consistent attitudes or to project an image of steady and orderly growth all around.

10. The liberal brings to this inevitable untidiness of world events his sense of purpose which often shades off into his own peculiar brand of toughness. While it is certainly true that it is the strategy of mobilizing larger sums for development assistance, in the teeth of opposition, by exaggerating what it can achieve in the short run and by advancing theories of the big push or the takeoff which recoiled on itself to produce the sense of crisis, there is something more to it than that. Most liberals believed in the theories and were anxious to witness dramatic results during

their tenure. In large part, the disenchantment also was theirs and not of others whom they were trying to persuade to part with a little more of their money. Even those among them who are not altogether free from a certain amount of diffidence are mortally afraid of being considered soft and are prone to invent their own form of toughness with a determination to use their power with skill and discrimination. They may be in favor of spending more money. But they will insist on performance, they will judge and assess, they will use money as an instrument for bringing about desirable changes in policies abroad and for supporting "rightminded" groups in the struggle for local leadership.

11. But a recipe for international intervention or even involvement on an extensive scale cannot suit the realities of the second half of the twentieth century. It is not surprising that it should produce so soon an attitude of mutual distrust and recrimination about foreign aid itself. First and foremost, it is difficult for the donor countries themselves to live up to a truly developmental concept of aid. Consequently, they can carry little conviction of their own adherence to the performance criterion. As long as the distribution of aid is governed at least to an important extent by considerations of political, ideological, geographic, or historical affinity, and as long as nation-states feel compelled to compromise with principles in the midst of a rapidly shifting kaleidoscope of events, it is idle to claim that the distribution of aid is or can be related strictly to performance.

12. And in the absence of such a correlation, the recipient countries are all the more likely to resent an interventionist aid policy. Assessment of relative performance with a view to determining aid shares is also an invitation to the recipient countries to denigrate each other's progress and to provide ammunition to critics of aid for opposing aid to one or the other country. Behind the facade of unity at international gatherings, there has been of late a tug-of-war behind the scenes among the developing countries for preserving or augmenting their particular apportionment of available aid.

13. There is no doubt also that the new style in aid aroused serious resentment in the developing world. In many of the nonaligned countries, the acceptance of massive aid was not so much an act of conscious policy as something into which one stumbled in a moment of foreign exchange crisis, something about which

powerful political and intellectual groups had a reservation right from the outset. Suspicions that, at bottom, aid was an instrument of neocolonialism or the cold war in a new guise were easily nourished and fanned in the context of increasing evidence of intervention in matters of internal social and economic policies, of open patronizing of particular local leaders, of the gap between the professions and the performance of aid givers and, occasionally, of some outrageous lapses in diplomacy. In such an atmosphere, everything assumes a somewhat abnormal air; the involvement of some U.S. universities in Pentagon activities makes most University teachers from the U.S. suspect in the eyes of many local intellectuals, and the willingness of some countries to let research, intelligence, and aid management get somewhat mixed up gives foreign aid an altogether new and unpleasant odor. Nor is it impossible to point to instances where the assessment or advice of even international agencies has been either biased or wrong or inconsistent, thus lending support to the thesis that the insistence on satisfying particular criteria of performance is yet another guise for promoting ideological conformity around the world. Recrimination, mistrust and even open hostility were further encouraged by the internal power struggle in many developing countries—and sometimes by the open conflict between them. One would not get even a glimpse of the deep undercurrents of feeling set in motion by what is considered a new landmark in aid history by reading in the Report of the Commissioners the chapters on India and Pakistan which seek in the main to prove, with some justification, that the policy of intervention was not without its rewards. But silence on the hazards and the costs of such a policy cannot make for an effective salvage operation.

14. Among the donors, by the mid-sixties, the advocates of aid as an instrument of the cold war had little to enthuse them—the cold war had either abated in some part or considerably heated up in others, allies in many cases had turned fickle or frankly opportunistic or were drawn into a more neutral posture by the pressure of internal or external events. The liberals, however, were the ones who were deeply lost in disenchantment—bewildered by the reaction to their well-intentioned attempts to improve economic performance and disillusioned about the pace of progress that was possible both in the mobilization of aid and

in the adherence to purely economic objectives even among those who so badly needed better economic performance. The more liberal among them turned tougher still, bemoaning the "softness" of the developing societies to the point where they saw foreign aid as a crutch to perpetuate this "softness"—a sentiment not without its echo among the poorer countries themselves.

15. Meanwhile, the impact of the Vietnam war and the emergence of a new post-war generation to full manhood were creating an altogether new situation in the affluent one-third of the world. Somehow, President Kennedy's Peace Corps soon became *passé*, and we have yet to comprehend what the younger generation in the U.S. and Europe really think of issues like foreign aid. Having renounced any sense of identity with their own nations, they seem to find it difficult to identify themselves with other nations. To many of them, aid and the desire to shape the policy of others is only another example of the kind of unnecessary and annoying meddlesomeness of the middle-aged which produced Vietnam. The more militant among them perhaps salve their conscience against the charge of indifference to the plight of the poorer countries by identifying themselves with more militant causes at home or by averring that the solution to the poverty of Asia and Africa lies in any case in a revolutionary transformation of their basic social structure. The young being young, perhaps most of them even today would be happy, in spite of their indifference, to pay their tithe for the development of the poorer two-thirds of the world. But perhaps they would prefer to do so without the fanfare of organizations and reviews and assessments, and certainly without getting involved in having to mete out rewards or punishment. But whatever their present mood, it is quite clear that the destiny of foreign aid and much else besides is now passing into the hands of a generation which seeks to assert its discontinuity with the past without having charted so far its own course of continuity into the future.

16. The new era in foreign aid which began around 1958 had yet another guiding principle: that the responsibility for giving aid must be shared widely and equitably among the richer countries of the world. There was a desire to rope in more and more countries among the category of donors and to insist on greater harmony in aid terms and on a better sharing of the aid

burden. While in itself unexceptionable and indeed beneficial to the cause of aid, this process of proliferation and standardization or coordination of aid has brought its own problems. Attitudes are bound to differ among any group of donors and attempts to coax, cajole, or coerce some into doing something generate their own reactions. The attitude to aid on the part of some donors was frankly commercial—as an inevitable adjunct to export promotion in an era of tied aid and fierce competition in the supply of capital goods. This, together with the harder terms of the loans of some countries, made aid worth much less than its face value, and since, even then, aid was in reality a loan which had to be repaid, it was easy to sneer at it as nothing more than ordinary commercial credit. For those donors whose aims were frankly commercial, the growing burden of repayments on the part of the debtors and the demand to rephase this burden were a signal to cut their losses by limiting their new commitments. Comparisons about aid burden are also not easy to make in an era of tied aid. While interest rates and maturity periods can be compared, the cost of tied aid varies so that a country can still claim that if its interest rate is high, its prices are lower. At any rate, the diversification of the sources of aid and the emphasis on better sharing and harmony in aid terms contributed their own share to the air of controversy and despair that surrounded aid toward the middle of the Development Decade.

17. To sum up, the crisis in aid was and is an amalgam of many factors and not just a reaction to exaggerated claims made earlier or the result of any general lack of appreciation of what had already been achieved in the developing world with marginal but crucial external assistance. It had much to do with the hangover of the cold war which still persists. The strident style of performance oriented aid diplomacy which smacks of neocolonialism to many if not most thinking persons and leaders in the developing world did not help either. In a sense, aid in the nature of things is bound to be doubly cursed. But the curse was perhaps heightened by the combination of a number of things including the balance-of-payments difficulties of some of the rich, the divisions and dissensions among the poor, the sharpening of internal social and political tensions in many parts of the developing world, the revival of old or sparking of new political ambitions among some of the new donors, and above all, the frustrating horrors of Vietnam. Right now, an altogether new

variety of retreat from international responsibility seems to be overtaking the young from which some of the more influential of the older guard are also not immune.

18. How are we to put new life in the aid chapter at this stage? What are the errors most particularly to avoid? And where are we to look for a new motivation, a new style, and a better aid relationship? There is no doubt that with all the aid-weariness and the desire to get rid of aid as quickly as possible, and with all the hankering after revolutionary panaceas, the developing countries can benefit immensely from a net inflow of external resources on concessional terms for many decades to come. There is no doubt either that the richer countries can afford to respond, with profit, to all the suggestions of the Pearson Commission. But equally, aid, however desirable, will continue to generate tensions unless there is a dramatic change in the present relationship between donors and recipients.

III. THE COMMISSION'S APPROACH

19. The Commission's basic approach, as already indicated, is one of advancing on all desirable fronts. Their main recommendations, as they relate to the subject matter of this paper, may be paraphrased as follows:

(a) It is possible to set most, if not all, developing countries on the path of adequate and self-reliant growth before the end of the century. Inferentially at any rate, it is possible also to eliminate the need for aid if not over the next decade or so, then over the next three decades.

(b) A 6 percent rate of growth will enable a progressive reduction in the savings and payments gap, and such a rate of growth among the developing countries is feasible if the flow of external resources reaches the magnitude of 1 percent of the GNP of the wealthier countries by 1975 (and presumably is continued at that level thereafter at least for some years).

(c) Since the objective cannot be achieved by aid alone and requires hard and protracted effort on the part of the developing countries themselves, "increases in development aid should in the future be closely linked to the economic objectives and the development performance of the aid-receivers." [3] At the

---

3. *Op. cit.*, p. 17.

same time, aid givers should eschew political and strictly non-developmental objectives.

(d) Since performance is not a one way street, the developing countries are entitled to ask for assurance of definite and long term commitments of aid. The Commissioners recognize that "there are virtually no facilities for the monitoring of recipients of the aid commitments."[4] But they hope that the monitoring and assessment of performance (presumably of both donors and recipients) "is best done in a multilateral context in which donors and aid receivers jointly review the past and plan for the future."[5] Accordingly, the existing Consortium technique must be reviewed, extended, and improved upon. There is an expression of hope "that each (consultative) group will increasingly provide for explicit and formal review of *donor* aid policies and procedures"[6] and thus give "recipients an opportunity to monitor donors, and donors to monitor other donors."[7]

(e) On the day-to-day administration of aid, since cumbersome procedures "on both sides" often hamper the effective use of aid, "a meeting of major aid donors and recipients should be held in 1970 to identify major procedural obstacles and means to overcome them."[8]

(f) To create a better sense of "partnership in development," there should be "a substantial enlargement of the responsibilities of international organizations" and "a thorough review of their practices and policies." The share of multilateral aid should be raised from its present level of 10 percent of total official development assistance to a minimum of 20 percent by 1975. It is worth noting that the Commission's recommendations call for a substantial absolute increase in both bilateral and multilateral aid.

(g) "The President of the World Bank should, in the course of 1970, invite the heads of the appropriate organs of the U.N. and other multilateral agencies, as well as representatives of bilateral aid givers and of developing countries, to a confer-

4. *Op. cit.*, p. 228.
5. *Op. cit.*, p. 17.
6. *Op. cit.*, p. 130.
7. *Op. cit.*, p. 130.
8. *Op. cit.*, p. 19.

ence to consider the creation of machinery essential to the efficiency and coordination of the international aid system." [9]

20. In a sense, when so much that is central to the proposed aid relationship is delegated to reviews and consultations yet to be undertaken, it is perhaps premature to subject these recommendations to too severe a scrutiny. But the DAC review of procedures is hardly likely to be more than a routine meeting of a Working Party or a Group of Experts. It would be interesting to see what the World Bank really makes out of the proposed conference on aid coordination. Chances are that perhaps not much would happen except larger attendance at the many meetings of Consortia, Consultative Groups, and the like.[10] There is talk of a separate institution or agency to review aid and performance without any direct responsibility for providing or administering aid—separateness itself somehow guaranteeing greater objectivity and influence. If the establishment of such an agency were to lead to a corresponding retrenchment in the activities of the bilateral aid missions, the World Bank, and I.M.F. and the U.N. family, there would at least be some gain. But that is hardly likely, and even the developing countries may not wish to have just one court of appeal this side of Heaven.

21. Already, a certain improvement in the aid relationship if not in the general aid climate has been discernible over the past year or two. The real question is whether the Commission's formula of mutual monitoring in multilateral forums is likely to generate a better aid climate without reviving some of the resentment which led to its appointment. Unfortunately, the concept of a genuine partnership in development, of mutual "monitoring" of performance, somehow lacks credibility. There has never been, so far, any real sense of equality between donors and recipients even when they attend the same Consortium

9. *Op. cit.*, p. 22.
10. Coordination within the U.N. Development System can certainly be improved along the very sensible lines suggested by Sir Robert Jackson. Between the U.N. System and the Bank-Fund group also, there has been of late greater exchange of views. But the Pearson Commission has a far more ambitious view of aid coordination. The improved coordination machinery it hopes for has four different objectives: better coordination among trade, aid, private investment and monetary policies; standardized reviews of economic performance according to explicit criteria which all agencies can use; an assessment of aid needs in the light of performance; and balanced and impartial reviews of donor aid policies and programs.

meetings and sit around the same table in many other forums. For the recipient to be frank about the policies or attitudes of donors in a forum where aid is to be distributed is about as difficult as the proverbial passage of the camel through the eye of a needle. Criticism of donor policies, even when it comes from nonrecipients, is seldom answered in the manner in which recipients are obliged to answer the most far reaching criticism of their own policies. There are obviously two sets of rules: the donors have parliaments and public opinion which reign supreme so that a mere reference to them should silence all criticism, whereas the recipients should obviously be able to manipulate at will their parliaments and public opinion in the interest of appropriate development policies. Put simply, a mere equality of opportunity in engaging a dialogue cannot establish parity in decision making. Nor can the platonic world of knowledge as a sufficient basis for right conduct be easily summoned into existence. One has only to look at the constitution and functioning of the World Bank and the I.M.F. and, by contrast, the persistent refusal to provide any real resources to the U.N. and its agencies to see how even multilateral institutions have to remain in line with the hard realities of economic and political power. Even when they assess relative needs and performance, they must keep one eye on what is feasible, *i.e.*, palatable to the powers that be.

22. If the doctrine of mutuality in monitorship or genuine partnership in development is impracticable, the insistence on performance as a yardstick for aid lacks both practical conviction and moral appeal. True, aid resources are scarce and must be widely used. Waste can only recoil on the total effort. But performance—or its cruder counterpart of absorptive capacity which was once fashionable—puts relatively backward societies at a disadvantage. One has only to attend a conference where African countries are represented to see how deep is the resentment against the approach of giving more to those who have already demonstrated the beneficial use of aid. There is also something awkward about punishing ordinary people for the temporary aberrations of their leaders. Performance for a society can only be judged over the long pull, as no society can be free from upsets and stresses and strains from time to time. The task of building societies is more akin to the bringing up of children than to the disciplining of sinners so that a stop-go policy

of aid in response to temporary vicissitudes becomes as unfair as it is artificial. The Commissioners rather carefully relate only increases in aid to better performance. But if their intention was to emphasize that all poor countries should continue to receive a reasonable share in aid irrespective of the twist and turn of their fortunes and that only the focus of concentrated spurts in international effort should change from time to time in the light of available opportunities for reaping rapid and increasing returns, they fail to say so. And in matters of this kind, there is all the difference in the world whether one gives one nuance or the other.

23. Many other comments are possible on the Commission's approach to an appropriate aid relationship. Would it not have been wise, for example, to prescribe goals for the next decade only and leave out speculations about the end of aid? Can the issue of bilateral versus multilateral aid be resolved simply by asking more of both? If there is aid weariness and a need to multilateralize the aid relationship, should not the question at least be raised whether an increase in the proportion of multilateral aid in the total would be desirable even if it comes about at the expense of bilateral aid? If the problems of coordination are becoming important, is it not time to advise at least the smaller donors to contract or wind up their bilateral programs by making over their funds to multilateral agencies? No discussion of the aid relationship can be complete without a searching look at the growing aid bureaucracy with its own brand of specialization, vested interests, and tendency to propagate and perpetuate itself. Why is it that when we are dealing with complex and even violent convulsions in the social and political order around the developing world, the arbiters of their performance and prospects are almost invariably drawn from the ranks of the modern know-alls, economists and lawyers? Is experience gained in the richer countries or even in the poorer countries some decades ago such a sure guide as to justify its preponderance in the counsels of our world organizations? Do we really need a large and specialized cadre of career aid professionals or an increasing proportion of those who perform developmental tasks in their own countries to be temporarily seconded to international organizations?

24. There are no easy answers to these questions. But they are

a vital part of any development strategy or aid relationship. The Commission perhaps can be well content with laying down the broad outlines, reasserting the ideal approach and reminding us of the basic facts and magnitude. There is no alternative either to the main thrust of their argument, *viz*, focus on development as the central objective of aid and a growing sense of partnership in the realization of the objective. But before we take for granted success along the road charted by them it is better to remind ourselves about the intricacies and pitfalls. At any rate, it is worth asking if our next few steps should not be rather carefully and warily chosen till we see a little more of a propitious opening towards the admirable course charted by them.

IV. AN ALTERNATIVE FRAMEWORK

25. In a basic or long term sense there is, and indeed there can be, no alternative to the Commission's recommendations. It is obviously true that aid levels should increase, aid terms improve, greater regard be paid to purely developmental objectives, appropriate developmental policies encouraged, the machinery for coordination and evaluation strengthened, and a franker and freer dialogue initiated among donors and recipients alike. These are endeavours which must persist and which will inevitably hover between different degrees of success from time to time. But there is still a question of immediate priorities and emphasis, of nuance and style, a question as intangible as it is vital. Absolute assertions are hardly appropriate in such a complex and emotionally surcharged endeavour. But at least as a means to invite debate and discussion, two propositions are worth placing on the table:

(a) the whole debate and discussion about foreign aid needs to be conducted for some time in a low key and the giving and receiving of aid conducted in as quiet and routine a fashion as possible so as to avoid any more grating on each other's nerves; and
(b) among all the possible ways of improving the quality and quantity of aid, the one that deserves more attention is that of imparting a greater sense of continuity or automaticity in aid by exploring some altogether new ways of mobilizing and

distributing aid without too scrupulous a regard for theoretical perfection or too much involvement in each other's affairs.

26. The style that is most likely to suit the decade of the seventies is not one of intervention or even involvement but of duty done without too much fuss or subsequent direct bother. The enemy today in the richer countries is not so much disenchantment as indifference. The poorer countries themselves are in a mood to call it a day if aid gives the slightest suspicion of intervention. And it is doubtful if most of the voters in the affluent countries share the appetite for detailed reviews and judgments about distant countries the inner logic of whose development they neither comprehend nor wish really to comprehend. There is sufficient vitality in the developing countries themselves to demand real and rapid performance from their leaders, and the advice of others, whether accompanied by aid or not, is more likely to be accepted the more tentatively and unconditionally it is given. The donors also are more likely to improve the quality and quantity of their aid the less they are continually badgered about matching the performance of others or invited to underwrite concrete and specific goals for advancing world development or reducing inequality. A quiet style in aid would also mean a rough and ready approach to equality of sacrifice in aid and equity in aid distribution. Over time, such kinks tend to get ironed out and it is perhaps better for the time being to summon everyone to do their best and to let every developing country share in available aid in terms of some easily acceptable and identifiable objectives such as bringing up the level of education or health facilities or urban housing or irrigation use or electricity available. Trying to add up everything into tests of performance, growth rates, takeoff points or formulae for equity is perhaps less important than taking up some concrete and urgent problems which exist in almost all developing countries and tackling them as a concrete contribution from the international community. Financing total costs and not just imports, which this would imply, might provide a welcome departure from looking at aid as largely an instrument of export promotion. Linking aid to projects with a predominantly social rather than economic content might generate more warmth and a broader based appreciation of the benefits of aid. It might even provide a

better outlet for the restlessness of the young in the richer countries. When one builds houses and clears slums rather than sets up industries, the points of conflict on issues of economic policy are also minimized and the dialogue on overall performance gets automatically divorced from particular acts of assistance.

27. There are, of course, several corollaries to this subdued and basically "aid on long term trust" approach. It implies an encouragement to internationalization of aid, a curtailment of aid establishments to the minimum, perhaps a greater role financially for a number of specialized agencies rather than concentration of international effort in one or two aggressively development minded institutions.

28. What is the guarantee that such an approach will augment the flow of aid or at least prevent a decline? The blunt fact is that there is no such guarantee anyway, and all that one can do is to hope for the best. The poorer countries at any rate would be well advised to plan on the basis of rather modest levels of aid, treating each increase in the level of aid if it comes as something to be subsequently deployed rather than assumed in advance. That way lies less frustration and greater cordiality. And it is at least arguable that a quiet approach which does not pretend to answer anything more than the satisfaction of some urgent and universally acceptable wants is as likely to evoke a generous response from the rich as anything else.

29. Side by side, we can explore some new and imaginative avenues for imparting a greater degree of continuity and automaticity in aid flows, taking them out as far as possible from the annual wrangles of appropriations and even from the consultative groups and Consortia whose endeavours have increasingly acquired the status of nondecisions. The appeal would be on many fronts, each with a recognizable justification of its own. There is reason to believe that even the richer countries would be anxious to trade off the right (or is it the annoyance) of annual reviews of their own intentions and policies in favor of a longer term commitment if simultaneously they are released from the constant pressure to do more and better.

30. It would be idle to pretend that alternatives can be easily suggested which are both acceptable and adequate. But one has to make a choice of where and how one chooses to fight and what rewards one is prepared to treat as a bonus if they

happen to come. On our reasoning, for example, it would be more important to seek a five year commitment for the third IDA replenishment than to settle for a three year replenishment —once again out of fear of sacrificing a better opportunity in the future. Equally, it would be better to settle as best one can this question of IDA replenishment in time rather than to drag out negotiations and create a hiatus as was done on the last occasion. Clearly, those who wish to do better now or later could be invited to make voluntary contributions and, indeed, there could be a general invitation to everyone to make additional contributions by way of a transfer from their bilateral aid budgets.

31. The idea of a link with the creation of the Special Drawing Rights is another device which needs to be seriously pursued. There is considerable appeal for this suggestion all over the world and it is somehow easy to convince ordinary citizens that if they get something for nothing, they should be willing to share a part of it with less fortunate people. Is it really necessary to go beyond the simple logic that convinces simple people and create difficulties for every solution by a display of our technical virtuosity?

32. Another promising idea (which has been endorsed in a different context by the Commission) would be to urge a convention whereby all developed countries agree to put repayments of capital and interest in a separate fund which would be used to make fresh loans. This, in the long run, is likely to be much more effective than the present procedures for multilateral debt refinancing which create problems of their own, such as generating a lack of faith in the creditworthiness of the countries concerned and the feelings of unfairness engendered among donors by a sort of retrospective harmonization of past aid terms. Instead, an ordinary citizen or politician is more likely to heed the argument that even if he is not prepared to vote for more aid, he should not be in a hurry to claim his due from the poorer countries. The simple device of a separate funding of repayments to create a revolving fund for aid can go a long way in imparting greater stability and continuity to aid levels. It will also result in a more equitable burden sharing among donors.

33. Perhaps it is also time to consider raising resources for aid by indirect rather than direct taxation—or at least by specific cesses on both direct and indirect taxes for specific purposes. It is

at least possible that the world community might more readily accept a cess on cigarettes for enabling the WHO to improve the standards of health and hygiene around the world and to alleviate the meanness of urban conglomerations. A cess on liquor can perhaps be more appropriately assigned to improvement of education or nutrition. There is understandable concern that what the poor countries gain in aid is more than offset by deterioration in their terms of trade. World action to stabilize and improve the prices of primary commodities has been singularly tardy. Can it not be that the developing countries would gain more if a part of the high powered advocacy of aid were devoted to the stabilization and improvement of the terms of trade for primary products? In the field of a more liberal access to rich markets, can we not agree, for example, that a part of the protective duties levied by the rich against the products of the poor should be made over to some international agency for the benefit of diversification of the trade and economies of the developing countries directly affected? Acceptance of such ideas cannot be easy. But it is worth knocking at many doors, as there is no knowing when which one would open. The basic advantage of such specific endeavors is that they appeal to an ordinary man's sense of justice and fair play. The more general appeal to man's responsibility to man in a world which is getting more and more interlinked is getting somewhat stale. And in the present mood, the international community is more likely to respond to suggestions which embody at least a rough and ready approach of paying a price for particular acts of unfairness or indulgence or of sharing a particular good fortune for obviously worthwhile purposes.

34. In conclusion, perhaps it may as well be made clear that the focus of this comment on the Report of the Commission on International Development is on the question of an appropriate aid relationship for the seventies. It seeks to offer a few suggestions not as a substitute for the Commission's recommendations but as a supplement. The point of departure is essentially one of style and nuance; and there is no reason to think that the Commissioners were unaware of much that has been said here or that some of them at any rate may not endorse many things that have been advocated here. The Commission was addressing itself mainly to the Parliament and the public in the aid giving

countries, and it is natural to assume that the time for making a proposal is hardly the time to dilate on the difficulties of marriage or on the need to take a less romantic view of each other. But the occasion is more like the reunion of an estranged couple. A better course may well be to carry on quietly for some time and build around obvious things like the children and the garden. Meanwhile, it can do no harm to read the old letters again or even to turn the pages of the manual on ideal marriage one read with such avidity not so long ago.

Toward Public Confidence in Foreign Aid

EDWARD K. HAMILTON

Edward K. Hamilton is presently Deputy Mayor of the City of New York. He previously worked on the White House Staff and was Staff Director of the Commission on International Development. This paper was taken from World Affairs, *March 1970.*

IT IS A CONSTANT CHALLENGE to students of American politics to discern when the complex of policies grouped under the term "foreign aid" is in a critical phase.[1] The curious chemistry which has evolved between these issues and our political and administrative institutions produces as one of its by-products an atmosphere of uncertainty and even high drama in which the hero (or villain, depending on one's point of view) is perpetually suspended over the pit of extinction.

Beginning in 1963, and ignoring important changes in the substantive and geographic emphasis of the economic aid program, the net effect of the bloody annual legislative battles was to maintain expenditures for official development assistance (including food aid) at a reasonably steady $3.6 billion a year, regularizing an increment to the annual level of just under $1 billion which had been added during 1960–62.[2] The 30–40 percent of the total amount supplied in the form of surplus food encountered no substantial legislative trouble, and the much smaller percentage in the form of contributions to international agencies achieved notable increases despite some anxious mo-

---

1. This article is entirely concerned with economic aid, except where specifically noted, and all figures refer to economic aid alone. The views expressed are the author's and do not necessarily reflect those of The Brookings Institution.

2. Nonspecialists sometimes confuse *appropriations* (new funds voted by the Congress) with *expenditures* (the amounts, drawn from current and past appropriations, which are actually spent in a given year). In the case of foreign aid there is usually a lag of two or more years before a new trend in appropriations is reflected in expenditures and, as shown here, if appropriations fluctuate back and forth over a limited range the annual rate of expenditures may not vary much at all.

ments. The core of the struggle was the cluster of appropriations for bilateral loans, grants of technical assistance, and security related supporting assistance, all of which have since 1961 been administered by the Agency for International Development (AID). The basic issue has always been the right of these programs to grow with overseas needs, the domestic economy, and the federal budget.

Throughout the 1960s, each President—Eisenhower, Kennedy, Johnson and Nixon—proposed an increase in bilateral aid appropriations each year. President Eisenhower managed the only significant expansion in 1960 (the Fiscal Year 1961) when Congress raised these appropriations by $700 million to $2.63 billion, a peak which has never been reached again.[3] Even in the following year when President Kennedy won congressional approval of a new aid philosophy as well as new techniques and a new agency, his money proposals were badly mauled and appropriations actually fell by over $300 million. Although AID appropriations have shown much greater variation than expenditures, until FY 1968 all the ups and downs were within the $2–$2.6 billion range and were generally designed by the Congress to continue the program at the level of the previous year. The relative stability of annual AID expenditures, again ignoring important changes in program composition, suggests that this goal was achieved. Although foreign economic aid became an ever smaller part of a rapidly growing Gross National Product (GNP) and almost halved its percentage share in the federal budget, its absolute magnitude was held roughly constant for five years.

The events of the past two years are powerful evidence that the program and the philosophy it expresses are now truly fighting for their lives. The congressional stalemate was broken in 1967, to the detriment of the pro-aid forces, when the AID appropriation for the following Fiscal Year was cut below $2

3. U.S. aid appropriations are voted by Congress according to Fiscal Years, each of which is numbered by the calendar year in which it ends. (Thus the 1960 session of Congress passed on appropriations for FY 1961.) Confusion is confounded by the fact that world aid totals are kept (by the Development Assistance Committee of the OECD) according to calendar years. Thus when the discussion herein refers to total U.S. expenditures for all types of economic aid (AID, food, and contributions to international organizations), the figures are related to calendar years.

billion for the first time since 1960. The following year witnessed a further slash to about $1.4 billion, less than was appropriated in 1955 and about 40 percent of the sums appropriated at the height of the Marshall Plan in 1950 in a much less affluent economy using much more potent dollars. The advent in 1969 of a new President, who only slightly amended the outgoing administration's budget request for AID, served to halt the trend at least temporarily, but not to reverse it. President Nixon's request suffered a cut of about $800 million and produced appropriations only slightly in excess of the previous year. Even these amounts were clearly based on an understanding that the President would soon advance new proposals reflecting a thorough review of all aspects of foreign aid.[4]

A crisis in American aid is a crisis in world aid. Although the United States is below the average of other donor countries in the percentage of GNP devoted to aid, it is so wealthy that even that small share amounts to about half the total flow of noncommunist aid.[5] Trends in most other donor nations are in precisely the opposite direction from those here, in part because of the relatively rapid economic progress in developing countries, and in part as a result of incessant pressure from Washington to do more. This is not a universal trend; for example, there seems to be little enthusiasm for major increases in French aid. But France already devotes a larger share of GNP to official aid than does any other major donor country, and support for overseas development is clearly growing rapidly in the Federal Republic of Germany, in Japan, and to a lesser degree in the United Kingdom—or in three of the five countries which together supply more than 80 percent of all noncommunist development aid. In such smaller countries as the Netherlands, Sweden, Norway, Denmark, and recently Canada, the wave of support for these activities has achieved almost phenomenal proportions. It is possible but un-

4. Another by-product of the past two decades of aid deliberations has been an incessant craving for comprehensive review of ends and means. Blue-ribbon panel has followed blue-ribbon panel in an endless procession with little variation in the high quality of the assessors and even less in their conclusions. By one count, the Task Force recently established by President Nixon is the fourteenth such group since 1950, and this does not count private or international studies, some of which will be discussed later.

5. Slightly less than four-tenths of one percent of the United States Gross National Product was provided in official aid in 1968.

likely that these trends can long survive a reverse movement in the policies of the largest supplier of aid and the one country with a self-professed interest in the broad evolution of world politics. Thus, the crisis is further defined in the year-to-year statistics for 1968 when disbursements of aid from the other donor countries rose by $76 million while those of the United States fell by $280 million. All indications are that figures for 1969, which are not yet available, will deepen this contrast.

Worldwide concern about this disarray produced in 1969 what the Overseas Development Council has dubbed the "year of reappraisal" of development aid. It spawned at least four major international studies of the past and future of the effort,[6] and two large studies—one private and the other official—in the United States.[7] Three of the former and both of the latter had reported by the end of February 1970. It is too early as this article goes to press to analyze the findings of President Nixon's Task Force on International Development (the Peterson Task Force), but the conclusions and recommendations of the Pearson Commission, the Tinbergen Committee, the Jackson Report, and the Report of the U.S. Committee for Economic Development (made up of leading U.S. businessmen and educators), while not identical, are very much in the same direction. Together, they add up to a powerful and tightly reasoned plea for a new commitment to long term development support, much larger than any heretofore and divorced from the methods and procedures by which every country pursues narrow and immediate political advantage abroad. All the studies conclude that a great deal more aid can be effectively used in developing countries and

6. Two of these have addressed the global problem and two have been somewhat more specialized. The former have been conducted by the Commission on International Development, consisting of eight prominent international figures chaired by the Right Honorable Lester B. Pearson and sponsored by the World Bank; and the United Nations Development Planning Committee, made up of eighteen eminent development specialists chaired by Professor Jan Tinbergen. The latter two are the study of the capacity of the U.N. development system sponsored by UNDP and carried out by Sir Robert Jackson, and the study of development prospects in Latin America financed by the Inter-American Development Bank and led by Dr. Raul Prebisch.

7. The private U.S. study is that conducted by the Research and Policy Committee of the Committee for Economic Development, a group of 200 leading businessmen and educators. The official group is the 16-man Task Force on International Development appointed by President Nixon in 1969 and chaired by Rudolph A. Peterson of the Bank of America.

recommend that the long established target of 1 percent of the wealthy countries' GNP in transfers of public and private resources from rich to poor be met by 1975 at the latest. The Pearson and Tinbergen Reports go further to suggest that transfers of official aid should reach .7–.75 percent of GNP by the same year.[8] In more standard parlance, this would mean a total flow of resources from all wealthy countries somewhat less than double the $12.8 billion achieved in 1968, and a flow of official aid not quite three times as large as the $6.4 billion provided in that year. The corresponding increases for the United States would be somewhat more dramatic, since this country is now below the average in both categories.

Many staunch champions of development are prepared, however, to stipulate every fact, second every argument, and support every consistent recommendation in each document, but they still believe that the basic conundrum in this country—how to build public and congressional support—has not been addressed. This is not a criticism of these reports; it is obvious that an international group cannot focus on the internal politics of a single country. But it is incumbent on American analysts to focus directly on this problem and to relate it to whatever theoretical or programmatic proposals are espoused. The following analysis develops the thesis that public and congressional support for development aid is highly sensitive to the structures and criteria created to monitor and administer it. It proceeds from a description of the political universe, in which aid must compete for public funds, to a broad outline of the international and national structures necessary not only to improve its quality and effectiveness, but also to assure and expand its volume.

THE POLITICAL PLIGHT OF FOREIGN AID

Overseas development is a profoundly peripheral concern for most Americans and their representatives in Congress. Experience suggests that no more than 25 members of the House of Representatives and perhaps 20 Senators have deep knowledge of current aid objectives and programs, and that there are major

8. The Pearson Report recommended .7% while the Tinbergen Committee proposed .75%; the difference between the two is not very significant and both would require a near tripling of present official aid levels.

disagreements among the literati. The solid majority of opinionated respondents which in every public opinion poll endorses the general notion of foreign aid is of little or no use on the really hard choices concerned with how much aid, of which kinds, to which countries, allocated according to which criteria. Public support of the general concept largely reflects a simple and laudable humanitarianism overlaid with vague Cold War fears. Humanitarian concern is of little use in arguing specifics because it cannot be conclusively shown for most large developing countries that any of the aid levels thus far proposed, even if maintained for decades, would result in achievement of income levels regarded as "decent" by American standards.[9] Cold War concern is less and less effective because of the general easing of the fear of nuclear war, the growing sophistication of the body politic with respect to the relation between development and political stability, and the general loss of faith in the precepts of mutual and indivisible security. Both arguments have also been impaired by growing concern about conditions at home, which, sensibly or otherwise, tends to establish an additional bias against foreign expenditures. As a result, the majority in favor of aid shatters immediately when the question is reduced in generality, e.g., to whether a billion dollars more or less is needed in any particular year.

These symptoms betray inherent political disadvantages which must be recognized and addressed if the problem of public confidence is to be solved. First, it is clear that there are powerful disincentives to wider interest and expertise in overseas development in both country and Congress. The time and attention of opinion leaders is preoccupied with domestic difficulties on the one hand and foreign crises on the other. This is especially true of the elected officials, most of whom allocate their attention fairly strictly according to the direct interest of their constituents. The United States government is a $200 billion enterprise operating in countless fields, almost any of which offers a higher political return for time invested by a legislator than does foreign aid.

Second, the private interest groups, lobbies, and professional associations which might be expected to be powerful advocates

9. We should also keep in mind that standards of decency are functions of present income; the standard in America is very different now than in the 1940s, and can be expected to be greatly changed again by the year 2000.

of foreign aid are not. The churches are not overly strong lobbies at best in the United States and have never been at full strength behind foreign aid.[10] The churches have not been effective supporters, partly because they have not taken the initiative to become knowledgeable on the subject, partly because they are leery of the political heat surrounding it, and partly because they find it awkward to fight for appropriations of which about 20 percent are requested for security related aid to Vietnam and surrounding areas and another 15 percent for outright military aid.[11] Corporations and other groups with a direct economic self-interest in aid generally divide into those capable of political influence but without the inclination to use it in behalf of aid (as opposed to their many other legislative interests) and those usually small concerns which have the inclination but lack the capacity to influence. The foreign policy establishment, made up largely of very senior business people and academics interested in foreign affairs, has been a well-meaning but ineffectual constituency. Its central interests tend to be East-West and Atlantic relations, so that it has not, by and large, accumulated the development expertise necessary to weigh in heavily on operational questions. Also, it is not organized to do timely, coordinated work with the Congress on programmatic issues.

Finally, each of these problems is greatly aggravated by the nature of the legislative struggle over foreign aid: an all-out annual confrontation, incorporating everything from basic philosophy to operating details, in which the proponents must be mustered and induced to declare themselves at ten separate crisis points in the legislative process each year. Quite apart from its harmful effects on the administration of programs, which are considerable, this process exacts an intolerable price from the aid advocate. Even granting that the constituency weaknesses identified above can be overcome, it seems highly

10. It is interesting that the churches are very strong lobbies for development in some donor countries, notably the Netherlands and Canada. In the U.S., however, they have never been deeply involved with development despite periodic waves of concern about such dramatic symptoms as hunger or an epidemic of disease.

11. These are approximate percentages; the actual portion varies somewhat each year. The security-related aid is counted in international aid statistics; the military aid is not, and is not contained in any of the figures used in this discussion.

unlikely that they can be overcome several times each year. Skillful management combined with full Administration backing can occasionally produce reasonably powerful lobbies on questions of foreign affairs (e.g., the Trade Expansion Act) where the cause is fairly majestic and the rewards durable. It is not easy to imagine marshaling the same forces for an infinite series of annual bloodbaths regardless of the energy and commitment of the President and his lieutenants.

Foreign aid has survived despite these debits because of the depth of humanitarian concern in the electorate, the strong conviction of every post-war President that aid is necessary to United States foreign policy, and an uneasy coalition in the Congress which reflects these and other factors. This coalition has always been flighty and hard to hold together on money cutting amendments, but it now seems to be unravelling on fundamentals. Broadly speaking it is composed of three parts: (1) a few members of both Houses, usually relatively junior and to the left of center, who have a thorough understanding of aid policies and programs; (2) another small group, sometimes quite conservative in general posture, who still view economic aid as an effective short term tool in worldwide confrontation between East and West; and (3) a much larger group who do not and probably cannot be expected to know a great deal about the specifics of development, but who combine a benign concern for the world's poor with a rather vague conviction that a more balanced distribution of economic progress is necessary to world peace and the survival of civilized values. This last group, which is absolutely critical to any hope of reviving the aid effort and establishing its rights to grow, is much more sensitive to what might be termed the atmospherics surrounding an aid debate than to the detailed arguments advanced for and against specific proposals. Their votes are heavily, perhaps decisively, influenced by the domestic scene (racial conflict, budget, and balance-of-payments problems) and by broad, largely intuitive perceptions of foreign events. The present congressional crisis results from the growing indifference to development support among this large borderline group, as domestic conditions command ever growing concern and as foreign affairs are more and more dominated by frustration over Vietnam.

These tendencies have always been present (recall the concern about domestic unemployment and recession in 1961, despite which the President pushed through a new aid program), but they have normally been susceptible to neutralization and even reversal by committed pro-aid leadership. This leadership has now been decimated by the trauma of Vietnam. It was to be expected in any event that the passing of the simpler notions of worldwide ideological competition, coupled with increasing experience with the relation between development and stability, would send shock waves through the pro-aid community. But Vietnam has magnified the doubts created by these factors to the point that the entire context for thought about foreign policy is suffused with suspicion of all foreign involvements and entanglements, particularly in the less developed world and even more particularly where the United States stands alone among major powers in a bilateral and profoundly political relation with a beleaguered local government. A by-product of this suspicion is the usually mistaken conviction that aid policy and operations are completely controlled by the classic executors of foreign policy—the diplomatic service, the military, and the intelligence agencies—and, therefore, are not to be trusted because they are operated for the same "interventionist" ends. Sensing this frame of mind among normally internationalist congressional leaders, regardless of their positions on strategies to end the war, the large borderline group finds the atmospherics surrounding aid ranging from negative to hostile. They are not (yet) moved thereby to deny the President any aid program at all, but, to put it conservatively, they are also not moved to struggle against attempts by the perennial anti-aid forces to cut appropriations and to add restrictive conditions which devalue the aid provided.

Hope for better things in the future lies first in the strength of the long term social factors which tend to make internationalists of Americans. Humanitarian concern about poverty is still very much present and probably getting stronger. Growing international travel and perspective among congressmen and their constituents is making it more and more difficult to ignore the poor two-thirds of the world. And greater sophistication about the East-West conflict and the political uses of development probably, over time, will increase rather than decrease the propensity to favor large scale development aid. It seems clear, however, that these factors will express themselves in a new wave of political support only if the U.S. government both provides a credible prospect of an end to the Vietnam War and commits itself to building an international aid system which provides reasonable assurance that development aid will be circumscribed, internationalized, and made clearly contingent on local efforts.

If this analysis is correct, the following conclusions would seem appropriate:

1. It is probably not possible to build much greater public or congressional support for foreign aid as presently organized and administered.
2. It is difficult to imagine an effective constituency for aid in any event as long as the program is condemned to an annual shootout which extends to first principles. Multiyear authorizations and appropriations are crucial to effective support even if all other factors are favorable.
3. A constituency sufficient to establish a growing aid program with a long term mandate requires that the Executive Branch present and demonstrate reasonable progress toward an *internationally led* aid system which
    (a) assures that development support is carried on as a separate activity independent of day-to-day bilateral strivings for immediate political or ideological advantage;
    (b) demonstrates that the development efforts of aid recipients are objectively monitored and their performance made the main basis for further allocations of aid;
    (c) produces regular, authoritative, and comprehensive statements of development objectives and associated aid requirements which present politicians with choices they can understand, while also providing churches and other "nonpolitical" lobbies with a focus for their support;
    (d) affords channels and safeguards whereby the great bulk of U.S. aid is directed to development purposes and administered through international authorities and groupings which, by definition, could not indulge in a marked political preference for a particular recipient government;

(e) presents an institutional image of sufficient professionalism and coherence so that the average nonexpert congressman can justify voting multiyear appropriations to be expended largely according to the international community's estimates and certifications; and

(f) offers a U.S. administrative structure for aid which seeks to "multilateralize" our development aid as quickly as possible; that is, a structure aimed at a gradual shift from direct operations to management of the U.S. role in increasingly multilateral agencies and programming enterprises.

None of these changes can be completed quickly, and there will be considerable need for redefinition of some of today's slogans to add flexibility. For example, rapid progress toward ending bilateral aid, which now comprises about 90 percent of the official flow, entails broadening the definition of multilateral aid to include aid that is allocated and programmed through multilateral decision making processes as well as aid that flows through formal multilateral organizations. This means that the focus should be more upon the decision making process than upon the delivery mechanism if there is to be substantial multilateralization in a context of rising total flows. As argued below, the formal organizations must also be accompanied by country and regional level programming bodies which multilateralize the assessment and allocation decisions even where the delivery system remains bilateral.

Nevertheless, in the best of circumstances, the annual legislative battle will probably be with us at least for a while yet. The best the President can do is to declare his intent to start building the necessary bases for long term support and to prove he means it by sustaining the effort. Even this will not, of course, convert the committed foes of aid; there will probably never be a dependable majority larger than 60–40 favorable to any proposition beyond the very existence of an aid program. But a reasonably solid 60–40 might be sufficient if skillfully used. For those who agree upon the importance of the objective, it is certainly worth a hard try.

RUDIMENTS OF THE NECESSARY INTERNATIONAL STRUCTURE

The needs sketched above are by no means entirely met by the present array of international institutions and groupings, nor is it clear that political and bureaucratic inertia will permit change on the scale required. Moreover, some of the most vital changes would almost certainly cost multilateral aid some of the support it now enjoys. Nevertheless, on balance, the gains represented by a more effective multilateral aid community seem weightier than the actual or potential losses.

Traditionally, as noted above, "multilateral aid" connotes the resources directly administered by the formal international organizations engaged in development finance. The major actors are the World Bank group, comprised of the Bank and its two affiliates, the International Development Association (IDA) and the International Finance Corporation (IFC); the regional development banks for Latin America, Asia, and Africa; and the United Nations (the United Nations Development Program [UNDP] operating through the ten U.N. specialized agencies). The World Bank group and the regional banks have largely been concerned with the transfer of capital, although they are now gradually expanding their scope, while the U.N. system has been confined almost exclusively (and not entirely by choice) to technical assistance and preinvestment work. Together, these organizations are vehicles each year for about $700 million in concessional finance which falls within the internationally accepted definition of aid.

As this assortment of agencies has evolved, other forms of multilateralism have developed which are essentially multilateral forums for pledging and allocating bilateral aid. Typically, these have been groups consisting of the donors or potential donors to a single developing country meeting under the chairmanship of an international organization. If there is a general commitment that each member will pledge some volume of aid, the precise amount to be negotiated, the group has usually been called a "consortium," of which there are now three (for India, Pakistan, and Turkey). If the pledging commitment is not present, the group is referred to as a "consultative group," of which there are about a dozen at varying levels of vitality. There are also *ad hoc* groups which do not yet fit into either category and which, as in the case of Ghana and Indonesia, often begin as creditors' clubs gathered to consult about an obviously unworkable problem of foreign debt which just as obviously depends for solution on the general health and growth of the debtor economy. All of these groups, though differing greatly in institutional quality and regularity, attempt to assess development performance and to allocate aid; however, none of them has a permanent staff and none can therefore be said to represent the international community in the policy debate or to program aid in any detail.

Structural evolution in Latin America has taken a somewhat different tack, in keeping with the longer tradition of regional cooperation. There have been consultative groups for such countries as Colombia, but the prime object, in accord with the philosophy of the Alliance for Progress, has been to devise means of development assessment and prescription which involve both the United States and a representative group of Latin countries. This has given rise to the Inter-American Committee on the Alliance for Progress (known by its Spanish acronym CIAP) in which seven such countries join with the United States in continuing reviews of performance and need in each member country of the Organization of American States, the economic staff of which provides technical support. CIAP is comparable to the consortia in function, but includes important innovations in that it is concerned with an entire region rather than with a single country, it has a permanent staff, and it involves aid recipients in the review process for other recipients.

These instruments, formal and informal, which make up the international aid community, constitute a remarkable and unprecedented set of vehicles for collective thought and action, but much remains to be done to integrate them into a rational system of organizations capable of directing a global attack upon the most formidable human problem of our age. Often labor is not divided rationally or even consciously among agencies. Standards are not uniform and sometimes not consistent. Contact between the aid agencies and those concerned with trade and capital movements is often weak and infrequent; field missions are increasingly duplicative. And there are still important doctrinal impediments in several agencies against techniques and criteria which refer to the health of the whole developing economy rather than to the benefits of a particular project. Perhaps most interesting from a programmatic standpoint, the formal agencies are simply too small, at a total of 10 percent of the official flow, to exert real leadership in more than a handful of developing countries.

Yet these inadequacies have more than programmatic consequences; the problem of public support in the donor countries is also deeply involved. One important characteristic of the present constellation of agencies is that it is incoherent to the layman or even to the reasonably well-informed legislator. In practice, given the intellectual and practical problems of determining sensible development policy, it is perhaps surprising how much rigor the existing machinery does inject into the process, but the *political* effect of this in donor countries is lost because, even with the best of intentions, the nonprofessional cannot sort out the actors without a prohibitive investment of time. If he is an ordinary citizen, he cannot find a rallying point where he and likeminded folk can take a stand for development which does not tie him to a proposal concerned as much with immediate security as with long range development. If he is a politician, he looks in vain for a central point where he can determine what the problem is, what can be done about it in the coming year, and how the myriad multilateral and bilateral instruments are being orchestrated to that end.

The gaps in the present multilateral structure are most evident at the country level. Despite the progress reflected in the consortia and other such groups, a multilaterally controlled network of resident aid missions has not been developed which conducts systematic reviews of overall economic performance in recipient countries, engages in constant dialogue with local officials as they develop their own plans and programs, and incorporates capital, technical, and food aid as integrated parts of a rational whole. The World Bank does periodic economic reports on a growing number of developing countries, but they are conducted by short term visiting missions which sometimes lack the perspective that would result from immersion in local conditions and which cannot establish the personal and institutional relationships necessary for a voice in policy deliberations. The International Monetary Fund (IMF) conducts similar surveys in connection with its periodic consultations, but they are heavily concentrated on the conditions of the local currency and financial system. Neither review process gives recipients the feeling that they and their neighbors are equal participants in the drawing of conclusions and framing of recommendations. CIAP does offer recipients this participation but its reports do not descend to a level of detail which could serve as a basis for the actual programming of aid funds. Moreover, despite the presumed political advantage of multilateral agencies in persuading aid recipients to undertake policy reforms, most such agencies have been extremely chary of any appearance of involvement in the policy debate, preferring to restrict their roles to the narrower confines of individual projects. There are exceptions, such as the IMF's activist posture in several Latin American countries and the role of the World Bank in the Indian devaluation of 1966, but these remain the exception rather than the rule.

Indeed, the only working examples of this comprehensive and resident programming are under bilateral control. The United States has the only extensive network of resident field missions which meet many of the specifications suggested. Its coverage is by no means complete and its capacity varies with country, but it is far and away the most competent and ambitious system yet created. This has been of enormous advantage in rationalizing the U.S. decision making process. (Even if one argues that development criteria have often been overridden, it has still been of great value to know what is being sacrificed.) It has also been of great help to the birth and growth of the consortia. However, the political problems associated with large bilateral field missions are multiplying at a rate which suggests that in many developing countries they may not be viable instruments for the indefinite future. If it is an important object of future policy to get multilateral instruments into a leading role, while at the same time halting the increasing confusion and duplication of multilateral field staff, then one imperative would seem to be early creation and rapid evolution of an integrated multilateral field organization which can gradually assume many of the functions of which only the U.S. field organization is now capable. This means properly staffed consortia, consultative groups, CIAP-type organizations, or other such bodies for *every* developing country willing to join in such enterprises. This is much more than a matter of calling a meeting once or twice a year. It involves great technical difficulty and political delicacy. It requires deep technical expertise combined with a willingness to venture into the controversial business of setting criteria and monitoring performance, a willingness not entirely characteristic of today's multilateral institutions. And it entails the assembling of new resident staffs capable of eventually taking over functions which at first probably must be performed in many cases by the World Bank or another established institution.

It seems clear that the establishing of new monitoring and programming groups, as well as the strengthening of existing ones, requires a center of action and coordination which does not now exist. It must incorporate the principal external players in the development drama—the bilateral donors, the multilateral donors and policy managers, and a strong representative group of aid recipients—and it must seek to unite the strengths and compensate for the weaknesses of each without arousing the political and jurisdictional fears which would result if any single actor tried to assume the lead alone. The structure most likely to succeed would seem to be an International Development Council composed of the heads of the major international aid agencies (the World Bank group, the UNDP, and the three regional banks); the ministers in charge of bilateral programs (the five largest plus one elected by the smaller donors); the principal agencies concerned with international trade and capital movements (the IMF, the General Agreement on Tariffs and Trade [GATT], and the United Nations Conference on Trade and Development [UNCTAD]); and perhaps five senior elected representatives of the developing countries (one each from Latin America, Africa, the Middle East including Pakistan, South Asia, and East Asia). This group could have no more than advisory authority, but if a reasonable degree of agreement could be reached among its members, it would have the political and technical muscle in its constituent parts to address the following agenda:

1. Work out a country-by-country plan for a worldwide system of monitoring and programming missions involving both donors and recipients along with a competent mutilateral staff for analysis and reporting. (These entities could be of subregional or regional scope where acceptable to recipients.)
2. Gradually build the intracountry capacity necessary to staff

the new groups. Existing institutions would have to provide many of the people and most of the analysis at first, but the object should be to get local facilities in place and operation in the shortest possible time.
3. Develop criteria for allocating aid among countries and regions based upon economic performance.
4. Aggregate the country-level estimates into an authoritative annual world aid budget, or a set of alternative budgets, which give political decision makers a reasonably coherent notion of what the development professionals believe can be done in what countries over what period at what cost. This might also include a proposed burden sharing plan for the year showing the precise role for each donor in financing the package. (This would enable the U.S. President to relate his recommendations to Congress to the proposals of an objective international body which was pressing the developing countries to do their part with at least as much vigor as it was urging donor countries to meet their aid objectives.)
5. Encourage the multilateral agencies to bring some unity to their field systems, liberalize their technical prejudices, standardize their project appraisal methods, and take the other internal reforms necessary to make them more useful as stimulants and supporters of development.

The structure of membership on such a council would be critical to its chances of success. The members proposed above are meant to suggest one pattern which might meet the following six principles:

1. The council should be so structured that it is possible both to reassure the donors that they have a strong presumption of a voting majority and to reassure recipients that they have a reasonable chance of persuading a majority to their point of view.
2. Every member should be "responsible," (i.e., each should finance and operate development programs and/or be concerned with a relevant flow of nonaid resources). Nothing would so encourage the tendency to evolve into an ineffectual debating society as the presence of individuals or organizations without chips in the game.
3. Each international member should include both donors and

recipients. (This assumes that the African Development Bank will succeed in persuading donor countries to help finance its soft loan window.)
4. The United Nations agencies should be represented by one man, not by the heads of the ten specialized agencies which administer development programs.
5. Explicit provision should be made for membership of the Soviet Union and Mainland China when and if they wish to join.
6. The group must be as high-level as possible and be backed by a small and highly competent staff headed by a strong executive director who stands well with both donors and recipients.

It must not be forgotten that, although the most important advantages sought through creation of the council are profoundly political in nature, they depend in large part upon its ability to establish itself as a nonpartisan force for development. If the council can manage the latter it could be the key to durable national constituencies for aid in donor countries, because it could provide the authoritative focal point to which decision making laymen could look for advice, coordination, criticism, self-improvement of the development community, and explanation of the choices in sight. As such, it could become a powerful means of keeping development priorities, now often forgotten in the welter of immediate concerns, in the forefront of the decision making processes of both donors and recipients, while at the same time providing a standard around which adherents could rally for the legislative struggle.

OUTLINES OF THE CORRESPONDING U.S. STRUCTURE

The first implication of the foregoing is that the United States government should not be organized toward foreign aid in the 1970s in the way that it has been—and for good reason—in the 1960s. After a decade of great effort and accomplishment, U.S. policy should take into account that the world has reached the point where the politics of predominantly bilateral aid are untenable over the long term and where the multilateral community appears capable, if assiduously enlarged and improved, of taking on a much larger share of the task. Thus, the main thrust of the United States organizational pattern should look to the day when multilateral bodies will handle the great bulk of U.S. development aid and operate a system of full range, integrated field missions of the type now run by AID. To make clear this goal, and to achieve the proper dramatic effect in the Congress, the President may even want to consider setting and perhaps announcing a year by which it is his intention to see that all of this country's development aid will be programmed and/or administered under multilateral auspices.[12]

The United States aid agency which expresses this concept should be a much smaller organization than the present one, built around administration of the U.S. role in the management of formal multilateral organizations and informal groupings, while at the same time administering a declining supply of strictly bilateral capital assistance. Principally, this means:

1. Formalizing the *de facto* separation of military and economic aid, and shifting the management of the security related aid known as supporting assistance from the aid agency to the Department of State. (The Secretary of State should continue to have policy control of military assistance, but he should not exercise it, as he now does, through the economic aid agency.) The supporting assistance programs, which are now concentrated almost entirely in East Asia, could quite properly be run by State's Bureau of Economic Affairs in cooperation with relevant regional bureaus.
2. Shifting the center of responsibility for formulating policy and instructing U.S. representatives in international financial institutions from the Treasury Department to the new aid agency. The present arrangement is an indefensible anomaly which has been maintained, aside from bureaucratic reasons, because of the supposed advantage of a partially separate set of congressional committees for multilateral aid.[13] As the

---

12. President Nixon has already suggested movement in this direction by pledging that the United States will pay more attention to development priorities evolved in CIAP and other Latin American forums.

13. In the House of Representatives funds for international financial institutions (the World Bank group and the regional banks) are authorized by the Banking and Currency Committee rather than the Committee on Foreign Affairs. This separation is not made in the Senate and the actual appropria-

latter becomes larger, the anomaly will become more visible and the advantage even less advantageous.
3. Giving the new agency great weight with respect to food aid policy (which will be of declining but still considerable importance), trade policy toward developing countries (for which it probably should be given some formal responsibility), and the policies of the Export-Import Bank with respect to lending in developing countries.
4. Moving the new agency out of the State Department to an independent status reporting directly to the President. Whether it is in or out of the Executive Office of the President is less important than that it be headed by someone of sufficient stature and presidential confidence to be a formidable opponent for a Cabinet officer bent on harnessing aid policy to some short term cause.
5. Adopting a formal policy of transferring the country programming function (which must be performed if resources are to be distributed rationally) to improving multilateral facilities (CIAP, a much strengthened India consortium, etc.). As argued above, this does not mean abandonment of the country-programming process, but rather a change in its locus.
6. Establishing a separate entity, subject to influence but not complete control from the capital aid agency, to administer technical assistance programs, most of which should be operated—as much is now—by private and public contractors rather than directly by the central technical assistance authority itself. The latter should be headed by a public-private board of which the head of the capital agency is a strong member.

It is perfectly valid to point out that the last of these suggestions does not follow necessarily from the others nor from the logic of the foregoing arguments. Indeed, it is in conflict with some of the ideas espoused here, particularly the stress on integrated programming of all resources provided to developing countries. Nevertheless, the separation is regretfully recom-

---

tions for these purposes are made in the same bill which finances bilateral aid and which must survive a single committee and subcommittee for appropriations in each house. Food aid, of course, follows an entirely separate route through the committees concerned with agriculture.

mended despite this acknowledged disadvantage, and in the face of all the other powerful arguments which are marshaled in support of unitary aid administration, because the writer is persuaded that they are overridden by some of the less pleasant lessons of the past decade during which they have been on trial. The broadest of these lies in the fact that when the final balance is drawn it cannot be said that the technical assistance programs of the past decade have harnessed the best in our society to their terribly difficult and important objectives. To do so in the future will require fundamental changes in the attitudes and outlook of our domestic institutions themselves, particularly our corporations and universities. For example, it must become a routine matter to provide the people and the training necessary for overseas service as a natural and recognized element in a corporate or academic career. This will not occur unless and until these institutions have a sense of confidence and participation in the technical aid instrument which an integrated agency simply has not been able to provide. As a result we just have not done very well in many fields, particularly in industry and education, and the prospect is not bright as long as the institutions most necessary to success are as disaffected as they now seem to be.

The disaffection of the sources of technical assistance has meant sizable political losses as well as professional ones. Traditionally, technical assistance has been one of the elements of the aid program most popular in the Congress, but there has been a notable falling off of this support in recent years which has produced no groundswell of protest from the business or academic communities. Rightly or wrongly, most of these potential constituents for foreign aid are not prepared to renew their active support until they are offered an agency which is principally interested in technical assistance, and not, as they view it, preoccupied with capital aid and macroeconomic analysis. If one believes there is any weight at all to their case on the merits, the political factors argue strongly for meeting their desires.

Similarly, it is fair to say that with respect to most developing countries the theoretical advantages of integrated programs have not been much realized in practice. There are important exceptions but, by and large, United States technical assistance programs show more evidence of the drive to have a full array of sectoral divisions in each mission than of the need to relate the technical resources supplied to the flows and purposes of capital aid. With reasonably skillful management it should be possible to achieve many of the benefits of integrated programming even if control is divided in Washington. In the long run, the objective is to build programming mechanisms on the ground in less developed countries under multilateral auspices, so that the U.S. agency, like all other bilateral agencies, should increasingly be in the business of filling requests determined elsewhere (hopefully in relation to capital aid goals and needs). In the short run, the key to coherent programming is the maintenance of a single integrated field mission as long as the United States continues to have full range bilateral programs. This places a heavy load on the field mission director, for he must serve two masters while bearing the brunt of reconciling the capital and technical aid programs into a totality which makes sense in the light of the country's overall economic situation. Still, this is probably the level where this function can be most efficiently performed (as it is often performed now) and, together with the interlocking of directorates in Washington, should provide a workable nucleus for maintaining many of the virtues of the integrated approach while acquiring those of separation.

Taken as a whole, the new organization and the new people should be carefully indoctrinated that their primary job is to effect a gradual and orderly transition from a predominantly bilateral program to a predominantly multilateral one in the shortest possible time. Success should be defined and progress measured in these terms. As direct operations become less important, the U.S. role in multilateral activities should become more so. It is here that officers and employees should be encouraged to invest increasing time and energy. The President probably should not request much larger or longer term appropriations immediately, but he should make it quite clear that they are part of his plan and will be requested as soon as institutional reform is well under way. This judgment is partly a practical assessment of the possible while Vietnam is in full cry and inflation is a critical domestic problem, but it also stems from recognition that the new arrangements must be at least in sight before the Congress is likely to grant the program a substantial lease on life or an established right to grow. Nevertheless, the President should make no bones about his intention to request much more money over a much longer term in the years ahead. The first test case of the new policy should come with the replenishment of the International Development Association which must be negotiated during 1970 and presented to the Congress in 1971.

CONCLUSION

The thrust of this analysis is that the standard ways suggested for building public confidence in foreign aid won't work. Neither better public information, nor more assiduous attention to congressmen, nor changes in program emphasis, nor any of the other usual suggestions will make a decisive difference, whether taken alone or in combination. The conditions do not exist, nor are they likely to exist, in which the Executive Branch can mount a powerful lobbying effort every year in behalf of a program of the present design. The problem is to develop a program which inspires the confidence necessary to begin a cycle of longer term mandates. If renewal were less frequent and public confidence reasonably high, it is entirely possible that the necessary backing could be formed to reach and even exceed the goals established by the various domestic and international groups which have studied the needs and opportunities. Thus, the problem is not to sell the present system; it is to build one that is salable because it reflects the political realities of the 1970s.

Suggested Further Readings

Asher, Robert E., *Development Assistance in the Seventies* (Brookings, 1970).
Bauer, P. T. and Wood, J. B., "Foreign Aid—The Soft Option," Banca Nazionale del Lavoro, *Quarterly Review*, December 1961.
Berliner, J., *Soviet Economic Aid: the New Trade and Aid Policy in Underdeveloped Countries* (Praeger, 1958).
Brown, Lester R., *The Social Impact of the Green Revolution* (International Conciliation, January 1971).
CED, *Assisting Development in Low Income Countries: Priorities for U.S. Government Policy*, September 1969.
Chenery, H. and Strout, A., "Foreign Assistance and Economic Development," *American Economic Review*, September 1966.
Collado, E., "Economic Development Through Private Enterprise," *Foreign Affairs*, July 1963.
Davis, J., "Agricultural Surpluses and Foreign Aid," *American Economic Review Papers and Proceedings*, May 1959.
Effective Aid: Report of an International Conference Held Jointly by The Ditchley Foundation and the Overseas Development Institute, 3–6 June 1966. London: Overseas Development Institute, 1967.
Fei, J.C.H. and Ranis, G., "Foreign Assistance and Economic Development: Comment," *American Economic Review*, September 1968.
Galbraith, J. K., *A Decade of Disasters in Foreign Policy* (Progressive, February 1971).
———, "A Positive Approach to Economic Aid," *Foreign Affairs*, April 1961.
Higgins, B., *Economic Development: Principles, Problems and Policies* (Norton, 1959).
Higgins, B., *United Nations and U.S. Foreign Economic Policy* (Irwin, 1962).
Hirschman, A. O., "Second Thoughts on the 'Alliance for Progress'," *The Reporter*, May 25, 1962.
Hoffman, P. G., *One Hundred Countries, One and One Quarter Billion People*, Albert D. and Mary Lasker Foundation, 1960.
Johnson, Harry, *Economic Policies Toward Less Developed Countries* (Brookings, 1967).
———, "Planning and the Market in Economic Development," *Pakistan Economic Journal*, June 1958.
Kaldor, N., "Will Underdeveloped Countries Learn to Tax?" *Foreign Affairs*, January 1963.
Kristol, I., "The Ideology of Economic Aid," *Yale Review*, Summer 1957.
Kust, M. J., "Economic Development and Agricultural Surpluses," *Foreign Affairs*, October 1956.
Lederer, W., "Foreign Aid and the U.S. Balance of Payments," *Social Sciences*, October 1954.
Leibenstein, Harvey, *Economic Backwardness and Economic Growth* (John Wiley, 1957).
Lewis, W. A., *The Theory of Economic Growth* (Irwin, 1955).
Little, I. D., "The Strategy of Indian Development," *National Institute Economic Review*, May 1960.

SUGGESTED FURTHER READINGS

McClelland, David C., "The Impulse to Modernize," *Economic Development: Readings in Theory and Practice*, edited by T. Morgan and G. Betz (Wadsworth, 1970).

Mason, E. S., "Foreign Money We Can't Spend," *The Atlantic Monthly*, May 1960.

———, "Foreign Aid and Foreign Policy" (Harper & Row, 1964).

Meier, G., *International Trade and Development* (Harper & Row, 1963).

Millikan, M., "New and Old Criteria for Aid," *AID Digest*, January 1962.

———, "The United States and Low-Income Countries," in Kermit Gordon (ed.), *Agenda for the Nation* (Brookings, 1968).

Myint, H., "Economic Theory and Development Policy," excerpt from a paper, delivered as an inaugural lecture at the London School of Economics and Political Science, December 1, 1966.

———, "The Gains from International Trade and the Backward Countries," *Review of Economic Studies*, 1954–55.

Myrdal, G., *Asian Drama* (Pantheon, 1968).

NPA, *A New Conception of U.S. Foreign Aid*, March 1969.

Nelson, Joan, *Aid, Influence, and Foreign Policy* (Macmillan, 1968).

Nurkse, R., *Equilibrium and Growth in the World Economy* (Harvard, 1961).

Ohlin, G., *Foreign Aid Policies Reconsidered*, OECD, Development Centre, 1966.

OECD, *Development Assistance*, 1970 Review.

Opie, R. and Brown, W. A., *American Foreign Assistance* (Brookings Institution, 1953).

Papanek, G., "Framing a Development Program," *International Conciliation*, March 1960.

Pearson, Lester B., *Partners in Development* (Praeger, 1969).

President's Task Force on International Development (Rudolph A. Peterson, Chairman, September 24, 1969).

Ranis, G., "Another Look at Foreign Aid: The Challenge of Coexistence," *Challenge*, November 1961.

———, "Trade, Aid and What?" *Kyklos*, 1964.

———, "Why Foreign Aid?" *Ventures Magazine*, Fall 1968.

Research Center in Economic Development and Cultural Change, University of Chicago, *The Role of Foreign Aid in the Development of Other Countries*, Special Committee to Study the Foreign Aid Program, 85th Congress, 1st Session (United States Government Printing Office, 1957).

Rosenstein-Rodan, P. N., "International Aid for Underdeveloped Countries," *Review of Economics and Statistics*, May 1961.

Stycos, J. Mayonne, "Prospects for World Population Control," a paper presented at the Indian University Conference on World Population Problems, May 1967, and reprinted in *World Population: The View Ahead*.

Viner, J., *International Trade and Economic Development* (Free Press, 1952).

Wolf, C., Jr., *Foreign Aid: Theory and Practice in Southern Asia* (Princeton, 1960).

Wood, C. T., "Problems of Foreign Aid Viewed from the Inside," *American Economic Review, Papers and Proceedings*, May 1959.

Zinkin, Maurice, "The Requirements for Development," *Development for Free Asia* (London: Chatto & Windus Ltd., 1956).